D1605643

CISTERCIAN STUDIES SERIES: NUMBER ONE HUNDRED FIFTY-EIGHT

WHAT NUNS READ: BOOKS AND LIBRARIES IN MEDIEVAL ENGLISH NUNNERIES

by

David N. Bell

CISTERCIAN STUDIES SERIES: NUMBER ONE HUNDRED FIFTY-EIGHT

WHAT NUNS READ: BOOKS AND LIBRARIES IN MEDIEVAL ENGLISH NUNNERIES

by

David N. Bell

Cistercian Publications
Kalamazoo, Michigan — Spencer, Massachusetts
1995

© Copyright, Cistercian Publications, Inc. 1995

The work of Cistercian Publications is made possible in part
by support from Western Michigan University to
The Institute of Cistercian Studies

Library of Congress Cataloging-in-Publication Data

Bell, David N., 1943–
    What nuns read : books and libraries in medieval English
nunneries / by David N. Bell.
        p.   cm. — (Cistercian studies series ; no. 158
    Includes bibliographical references (p.) and index.
    ISBN 0-87907-558-9 (hc : acid-free)
        1. Nuns—England—Books and reading—History. 2. Eng-
land—Intellectual life—Medieval period, 1066–1485. 3. Monastic libraries—England—History. 4. Books—England—
History—400–1400. 5. Manuscripts, Medieval—England.
I. title. II. Series.
Z1039.N76B44   1995
028'.90882'0942–dc20   94-27837
                                                              CIP

ACKNOWLEDGEMENTS

I
T IS ALWAYS a pleasure to acknowledge the help that one
has received from other scholars, and even more of a pleasure
when that help has been offered so freely and munificently.
In some cases I asked far too many questions, but received only
courteous replies; and I am especially grateful to Dr Christopher
de Hamel of Sotheby's, to Dr Ian Doyle of Durham University
Library, to Dr Jayne Ringrose of Cambridge University Library,
and to Dr Richard Sharpe, Reader in Diplomatic in the University
of Oxford, for their patient assistance.

Others who provided invaluable help were Anna Lou
Ashby of the Pierpont Morgan Library, Melanie Barber of Lam-
beth Palace Library, Rudolph Ellenbogen of Columbia Univer-
sity Library, Christina Foyle of Beeleigh Abbey, Essex, John
Goldfinch of the British Library, Adrian James of the Society
of Antiquaries, Sjöfn Kristjánsdóttir of the National Library of
Iceland, Helmut Rohlfing of the Nierdersächsische Staats- und
Universitäts-bibliothek Göttingen, Kathleen L. Scott of East Lans-
ing, L. H. L. Stapper of the Katholieke Universiteit Nijmegen,
F. H. Stubbings of Emmanuel College, Cambridge, and Adrienne
Wallman of the Blackburn Museum and Art Galleries.

I must also take this opportunity to thank Elizabeth Stan-
ford, Patti Thistle, and the staff of Inter-Library Loans at the
Memorial University of Newfoundland. They have an amazing
and well-deserved reputation for tracking down the rarest and
most obscure volumes, and without their continual help, neither
this book, nor any of the others I have written, would have
been possible.

TABLE OF CONTENTS

PREFACE

THIS BOOK is divided into two parts, and the second part is the more important. One may find there a comprehensive list of all manuscripts and printed books which have been traced with certainty or high probability to English (and one Scottish) nunneries. The list includes all the books from women's houses which are recorded in Neil Ker's *Medieval Libraries of Great Britain* (London, 1964²) and Andrew Watson's *Supplement to the Second Edition* (London, 1987). A few additional manuscripts have been added to their records, and where this has been done, I have indicated the fact in the appropriate entry. After the identification of each volume there follows an account of its contents (with references to standard *repertoria*); and following that, transcripts of any inscriptions which relate the volume to a particular nun or nunnery. The works contained in non-liturgical volumes are all identified by number and letter; the contents of liturgical manuscripts are described more generally. I should add, perhaps, that my only concern has been with identifying the contents and the owners of the various volumes, and my descriptions are in no way intended to be substitutes for those one might expect to find in a detailed catalogue.

In addition to the surviving books, the reader will also find *Miscellaneous Records* of volumes which once were to be found at particular nunneries, but which are now either lost or unidentified. These records derive primarily from wills and inventories and I do not pretend that they are complete. I have certainly not read every medieval will, though I have read a good many, and there is no doubt that other scholars will be able to add other books to those which I have recorded.

At the end of the list of books are comprehensive indexes of all the works cited, whether in English, French, or Latin, and of all the names which appear in the ownership inscriptions. There are also indexes of *incipit*s and of manuscripts and printed books.

The first part of the study derives from the second. It contains three chapters in which I have summarized the material in

1

Part II and have drawn certain conclusions—sometimes tentative conclusions—which seemed to me to be of interest. Chapter 1 is concerned with the cost of books and the ways in which they were acquired; Chapter 2 presents a summary of the number and nature of the surviving volumes; and Chapter 3 is devoted to an investigation of what this material may tell us—or what it may imply—about the learning and literacy of later medieval nuns. What I have said in those chapters does not exhaust the information presented in Part II, but it does, perhaps, demonstrate that what has long been assumed about the books, libraries, learning, and literacy of women religious in the later Middle Ages may require a certain amount of emendation.

Finally, I should point out that the period of my investigation ranges from about the twelfth century to the first half of the sixteenth. The later the date, the more books there are that have survived and the more information there is with which to work. I have nothing to say on the period before the Norman Conquest, and the study of women's learning in Anglo-Saxon England is another matter entirely.

PART ONE

ABBREVIATIONS

(PART I)

Names of religious houses in upper-case letters followed either by a number or *MR* (e.g. SYON 1, LACOCK *MR* a) refer to the descriptions contained in Part II of this study.

Ker   N. R. Ker, *Medieval Libraries of Great Britain* (London, 1964²), with Supplement to the Second Edition by A. G. Watson (London, 1987).

Knowles/Hadcock   D. Knowles & R. N. Hadcock, *Medieval Religious Houses: England and Wales* (New York, 1972²).

LP   *Letters and Papers, Foreign and Domestic, of the Reign of Henry VIII*, ed. J. S. Brewer *et al.*, (London, 1862-1910).

MR   *Miscellaneous Records.*

Power   E. E. Power, *Medieval English Nunneries, c.1275 to 1535* (Cambridge,1922; rpt. New York, 1964, 1988).

VCH   Victoria County History.

Watson   A. G. Watson's supplement to Ker (q.v.).

CHAPTER 1:
INCOMES AND ACQUISITIONS

THERE IS no better way of gaining an appreciation of the nature of later medieval nunneries and of the problems which beset them than by reading Eileen Power's admirable account, *Medieval English Nunneries*.[1] True, it was published seventy years ago, but the wealth of scholarship it contains, its breadth of vision, and the acuity of the author's insights ensure its place as a fundamental study. Power could also write good English, a talent which, though common enough in her day, has now, for the most part, gone the way of the horse-drawn carriage and the unsplit infinitive. It is obvious that in the last seven decades a very great deal has been added to our knowledge of the period, but an impressive amount of Power's analysis remains valid; and if, with Norman Cantor, we may refer to her as 'a forerunner and role model in women's history,'[2] she was the harbinger of that flood of material, some extremely good and some extremely bad, which has flooded the market in recent years.

My concern in this present study is not to attempt a general and comprehensive reexamination of the position of women religious in the Middle Ages (I have neither the time nor the competence to do so), but to focus on one small area: what books were to be found in medieval English nunneries, and what use the nuns made of them.[3] And since books could be expensive, sometimes very expensive, it behooves us to make some introductory comments on the economic condition of the nunneries, the sources of their income, and their necessary expenditures.

One of the most important sources of revenue for any religious house, whether of men or of women, was bequests and donations, and it may readily be appreciated that these varied dramatically, both in size and in character, from nunnery to nunnery.[4] The most important bequests were those of land, properties, and rentals, and these were sometimes munificent. The lands of Syon, for example, were scattered over twelve

7

English counties from Lancashire in the north to Cornwall in the south.[5] Secondly, there were individual legacies of money or goods, some of them very considerable. Thirdly, there might be gifts from pilgrims (an important source of revenue at Syon[6]), or donations, rewarded by indulgences, for building or rebuilding conventual structures.[7] Fourthly, there was a wide variety of miscellaneous gifts and privileges ranging from the perquisites that came from the administration of justice,[8] to donations of ale and wine (which sometimes proved very difficult to claim[9]), rights to timber and firewood (thus ensuring a regular supply of fuel[10]), rights to hold fairs and markets, and (in the case of Shaftesbury) rights to wreck of the sea.[11] Fifthly, there were the spiritualities: important and lucrative gifts of advowson (the right to appoint a cleric to a particular benefice), prebends, chantries, and (most importantly) appropriation, by which an abbey or priory was given the right to 'appropriate' a particular church and, with the church, a proportion of all the tithes and other endowments which went with it.[12] The gift of advowson was very often followed by appropriation, and appropriation, which was obviously of great economic benefit, was gravely abused.

From the monastic lands came rents for pasturage and pannage; income from the lease of monastic mills, especially water-mills; revenue from arable farming, sheep farming, and the sale of wool;[13] and, at Barking and elsewhere, perquisites from hunting rights.[14]

From the conventual enclosure were received revenues from dowries and fees for profession,[15] income from charging for corrodies, and whatever could be gained by taking in boarders, either older women who would live in the nunnery as paying guests (and who sometimes caused problems[16]), or youngsters who would come there for the benefits of education and instruction in etiquette.[17] We should note, however, that not all of these sources of revenue met with approval, and some of them were specifically condemned. At Brewood Black Ladies, for example, the bishop forbade simoniacal payments by women who wished to join the community;[18] and the secularizing presence of boarders in the nunneries proved a continual problem.[19] Time and again the local bishops condemned the practice; time and again the nuns ignored them.[20]

It may seem from this brief summary that medieval nunneries should have been places of considerable wealth, rich manorial estates supported by a variety of revenues. That this was not the case is well known, and three points must be taken into consideration. Firstly, major gifts of land, rentals, tithes, and so on applied to only a few great houses, and those often of royal foundation; secondly, the gross value an estate, whether monastic or otherwise, cannot be equated with its disposable income (one need only think of one's mortgage); and thirdly, we have not yet considered the matter of conventual expenses and taxation.

The burdens laid upon the nunneries were considerable. There was food to be bought for both nuns and guests (a large proportion of the annual income was spent on hospitality); each of the nuns needed an annual allowance for clothing; the poor expected alms (which, in any case, was a monastic obligation); episcopal visitations could prove expensive;[21] nunnery buildings demanded continual repair, and if it were not the nunnery buildings, it was the houses of the tenants; the home farm required 'purchases of grain for seed, or the food of livestock, of a cow here, of a couple of oxen there, of whip-cord and horse-collars, traces and sack-cloth and bran for a sick horse';[22] and there was the ever-present outlay of wages for all the various lay functionaries, from stewards to stable-boys, which any well-run nunnery required. The steward at the Benedictine house of St Helen's, Bishopsgate, for example, was paid no less than £12 a year 'with 20s. for his livery, eatables and drinkable, two cartloads of fuel, 10 qrs. of charcoal, and the use of a chamber within the priory precinct.'[23] But St Helen's, as we shall see in a moment, was a fairly wealthy house.[24]

To this list might also be added the costs of litigation and legal fees. Economically speaking, medieval monasteries, whether male or female, were no more than large estates or landowning corporations with all the judicial rights and obligations which such status involved.[25] J. L. Kirby has spoken of 'the constant litigation in which, like all medieval property-owners, nuns needed to engage simply to defend their lands,'[26] and although the wealthier houses like Amesbury or Syon could afford to retain their own permanent legal staff,[27] many nunneries could not afford even to consult a lawyer and (like the nuns of

Chester) were forced to appeal to their bishop for help.[28] When we consider that a fifteenth-century lawsuit at Denney could last twenty years, cost £200, and result in damage estimated at more than £800,[29] we can sympathize with the nuns of Arden and the monks of Byland who, in 1189, agreed mutually that any disputes should be solved by friendly discussion, and *never* by going to court.[30] Such a happy solution, however, was unfortunately rare. From the end of the thirteenth century the legal profession was becoming increasingly professionalized, lawyers were beginning to claim a monopoly in all legal matters, and, in the later Middle Ages, expensive and professional legal services became the norm.[31] In 1230 the nuns of St Michael's, Stamford, were themselves able to deal quite competently with their legal difficulties and did not require professional assistance; a century later that would probably have proved impossible.[32]

The five richest houses were Syon, Shaftesbury, Amesbury, Barking, and Wilton. They represent the earliest and, in the case of Syon, the latest foundations in England, and there was a well-known saying that 'if the abbot of Glastonbury could marry the abbess of Shaftesbury their heir would hold more land than the king of England.'[33] At the next level were such houses as Dartford, Elstow, Godstow, Romsey, Wherwell, and the London nunneries (St Helen's, Clerkenwell, Holywell, and the Minories);[34] and then, at various levels below this, came a multitude of foundations whose net income ranged from the barely adequate to abject poverty. The Cumberland nunneries, close to the perilous Scottish border, had no money to speak of;[35] the Cistercian houses (with the exceptions of Tarrant Keynston, Catesby, and Stixwould) were proverbially poor;[36] and the nuns of more than one house were reduced to begging in the streets 'to the scandal of womankind and the discredit of religion.'[37] Of Benedictine houses assessed in about 1535, the net annual income of Arden was £12, of Brewood Black Ladies £11, of Nunburnholme £8, and of Lambley £5.[38] Among the Cistercians, the income of Ellerton was £15, Esholt £13, Sewardsley £12, and Fosse £7.[39] And there are many other examples.

We may gain a better picture of the situation if we take those nunneries whose annual income was assessed c. 1535 and recorded in the *Valor Ecclesiasticus* (there were 132 of them), and divide them into six economic groups.[40] Only Syon, Shaftesbury,

Amesbury, Barking, and Wilton—the Big Five—had an income greater than £500 p.a., and they account for just 4% of the total (only Syon and Shaftesbury had incomes of more than £1000 p.a.); nine houses[41] possessed incomes in the range £250-499; and the incomes of all the rest—118 of them—were distributed as shown in the following table:

Annual Income	No. of Nunneries	% of Total Number
Over £500	5	4
£250–499	9	7
£100–249	16	12
£50–99	33	25
£20–49	45	34
Less than £20	24	18

The trend is immediately obvious: the lower the income, the higher the percentage; and elementary arithmetic reveals immediately that more than three-quarters of nunneries had annual incomes of less than £100, and more than half of them less than £50.

To put these figures in perspective, let us consider the average wages of skilled and unskilled workers in the period under investigation.[42] Before the Black Death in 1348-49, an unskilled labourer might earn between 1d. and 1½d. a day (perhaps £2 a year) and a skilled worker about 3d. a day (£4.10.0 a year). After the Black Death and the drastic diminution in available labour, wages commonly rose by about 60% and in some cases doubled. Legal attempts to peg wages were not, in general, successful, and fines and imprisonment for contraventions proved ineffective.[43] An unskilled worker could now earn 3d. a day (the same wage as a skilled worker before the Black Death); and a skilled worker 5d. a day or about £7.10.0 p.a. Experienced master-masons might earn as much as 7d. a day or more than £10 a year.

We may therefore understand the difficulties of a small Benedictine nunnery like Lambley with an annual income of £5—hardly more than the annual earnings of a single unskilled labourer—with six nuns to support, taxes to pay, continual problems with dilapidation, and the day-to-day running expenses of a small estate.[44] Similar stories could be told of the Benedictines of Nunburnholme, the Cistercians of Fosse, and the Augustinians of Grimsby and Rothwell, all of whom had annual incomes of less than £10 and all of whom had to support a number of nuns ranging from four at Rothwell, with an annual income of £5 derived from a single appropriated rectory,[45] to nine at Grimsby, with £9 *per annum.*

Even the larger and wealthier houses had problems, for land and property cannot be considered disposable income, and rents are only useful if they can be collected successfully. At the end of the fourteenth century, the great abbey of Shaftesbury, despite its rich properties and royal foundation, had little in the way of liquid assets, and Richard II directed that certain short-cuts be taken in the election of a new abbess 'in pity for the poverty of the house.'[46] Similar stories can be told of Godstow, Nuneaton, and St Radegund's.[47]

It is true that pleas of poverty cannot always be trusted[48] (who ever admits that they have enough money?), and most hard-headed prelates were well aware of this. In 1321, for example, the appropriation of a church to the priory of Kington St Michael was considered by the Chapter of the Diocese of Wells to be nothing more than an example of 'feminine greed' (*aviditas feminea*).[49] But Kington was, in truth, a poor house,[50] and although we may agree with the comment of Sally Thompson that 'claims of financial difficulty, particularly when made in the context of taxation, have to be treated with caution,'[51] there can be little doubt that the majority of English nunneries existed in a state of chronic financial difficulty.[52] We may agree, too, with Sister Elspeth of the Community of All Saints that 'poverty and obscurity are indeed in no sense a reproach to a convent of nuns,'[53] but the principle of monastic poverty was not intended to be equated with gross privation.

In some cases these financial difficulties were the fault of incompetent administration, and might be the result of electing an abbess who was too young and inexperienced or too old and doddery. Matilda Botetourt, for example, was elected abbess of Polesworth in 1362 when she was not yet twenty,[54] whereas Alice de Beverley may have been over eighty when she was appointed prioress of Nunburnholme at the end of the thirteenth century.[55] Furthermore, although most nuns came from noble families or the county gentry,[56] and although many noble women were admirably competent in household and estate administration,[57] this was not always the case. Much therefore depended on the quality of the superior and her obedientiaries. In 1350, for instance, Malling had been so ruined by bad management and administrative inadequacy that the episcopal visitor was of the opinion that the situation would not be remedied until the Day of Judgement.[58] But the other side of the coin is represented by Elizabeth Cressener of Dartford, an immensely efficient and intelligent woman whose administrative and financial skills can only arouse our admiration.[59] Eileen Power's generalization that 'nuns were never very good business women'[60] cannot be applied to all, and more recent studies have indicated that, especially in the period between the Black Death and the Dissolution, numerous external factors—factors quite beyond the nuns' control—played a vital role in diminishing the assets of a great many English nunneries.[61] In any case, in a large number of women's houses the administration of temporalities was placed in the hands of a master, warden, steward, custodian, or bailiff (the terminology varied),[62] and incompetence has never been restricted to either of the sexes.

Enough, I think, has been said to show that the majority of English nunneries had little money to spare, and the devastation of the Black Death only exacerbated their problems. Naturally, the situation varied with different houses at different times, but since this is not a treatise on monastic economics, these are not details we need consider. The broad picture is clear enough. Let us now, therefore, turn our attention to the other matter we must discuss in these introductory remarks: the price of books. One example will serve to illustrate its importance. In 1487 Master William Hemming gave to Syon Abbey a missal valued at ten marks or £6.13.4.[63] This is an amount greater than the entire annual revenue of Lambley or Rothwell, and considerably more than the annual income of an unskilled worker of the period. We are obviously talking about a very expensive luxury. On the other hand, in 1448, twelve books owned by one Simon Beryngton, a scholar at Oxford, were valued at no more than four pence the lot.[64] The price of books, in other words, covered a very wide range, and we must now consider the matter in a little more detail.

Classic, though brief, articles dealing with the cost of books in the Middle Ages were published by Wilbur Schramm in 1933 and H. E. Bell in 1937.[65] Both concentrate on the period after

1300 (evidence from earlier centuries is very limited) and although neither study is any more than a sketch (we still await a comprehensive examination), they both provide a useful glimpse of just how much a book might cost. The problem, however, is that buying a book in the Middle Ages was much like buying a car today. It all depends on what you want and how much you have to spend. You can, if you wish, invest in a custom-built Rolls Royce or Cadillac (the literary equivalent is the magnificent bible produced in nine volumes in 1276 for the abbot of the Cistercian abbey of Croxden, a production which cost over £33[66]). If this be too extravagant, you can substitute instead a large and elegant Jaguar or Oldsmobile (a service-book at £5). Most people, however, are limited by their resources to a compact or sub-compact model (a copy of the *Regula pastoralis* of Gregory the Great written in a cursive hand on paper and costing two shillings); and some make do with bicycles (a poorly written second-hand unbound paper copy of a common text costing a few pennies). But let it be remembered that even a few pennies represents a day's wage, and my analogy of car-buying was not chosen at random. Until the advent of printing, books were always a luxury.

> With the exception of bibliophiliacs like Richard de Bury, who owned perhaps 1,500 volumes, eminent churchmen would rarely have owned more than a hundred books, and aristocratic owners, to judge from their inventories, many fewer. Sir John Paston, by chance one of the best known collectors of the fifteenth century, owned only about twenty books or so. In an examination of 7,568 wills of the fourteenth and fifteenth centuries, Margaret Deanesly found mention of only 338 books, which, whatever qualification is made of the value of the evidence, is a remarkably small number.[67]

During the fourteenth and fifteenth centuries, however, certain developments took place which considerably reduced the cost of books, whether written in Latin or the vernacular, and offered the prospective buyer a greater choice of materials and style. Some of these developments were closely linked with the rapid growth of the universities, the secularization of learning, and a dramatic increase in vernacular literacy among the laity, a matter we shall discuss in more detail in Chapter 3.

One of these developments was the evolution of cursive book-hands, combined (in Latin texts) with a multitude of abbreviations,[68] which together enabled a scribe to write much more swiftly than had hitherto been the case, and, incidentally, to fit much more text onto a single page. Cursive script for books (as distinct from its earlier use in documents) was well established by 1300,[69] and its rapid development from that time to the advent of printing has been well illustrated by C. E. Wright and M. B. Parkes.[70]

A second development was the introduction of the *pecia* system, in which a book was broken down into its constituent gatherings (a gathering normally comprised eight or twelve folios) and each gathering copied by a different scribe. A volume of ten gatherings might therefore be copied ten times faster than if only a single scribe were employed. The individual gatherings could then be made available to students and other interested parties, who would pay a certain amount to borrow them, and then copy—of have copied—what they needed in accordance with their requirements or their funds.[71]

At about the same time we also witness the burgeoning of the book-trade, both new and second-hand. The earliest reference to a medieval public book-dealer (we should actually call him a double-dealer) appears in a letter of Peter of Blois dating from about 1170,[72] and from the early thirteenth century booksellers were operating in Oxford, London, Paris, Bologna and most other large commercial or academic centres.[73] The importance of this for our purposes is its effect on the way in which the members of religious houses obtained their books. In earlier days, from the beginnings of monasticism to the early thirteenth century, the monastic *scriptoria* played a major role, but as the book-trade became better organized and more widespread, and as the price of books decreased, it seems that monks (and, presumably, nuns) did what most other people did, and bought their books as they needed them. This is not to say that monastic book-production ceased entirely. A. I. Doyle has demonstrated conclusively that it did not.[74] But there is no doubt that after about 1300 the copying of books in monasteries greatly decreased, and the commercial world intruded yet further into the busy silence of the cloister.

A fourth development which occurred at this time was what R. J. Lyall has called 'the paper revolution'.[75] Making parchment had always been a long, smelly, time-consuming, and costly process,[76] but by the thirteenth century techniques for making paper had made their way from China (via the Arabs) to Spain and Italy; and although its impact in the early days of its adoption must not be overestimated,[77] the substitution of paper for parchment certainly played a significant role in decreasing the price of books. By about 1330 there were paper-mills in France and by 1390 in Germany, and although the English were slow to take up the process (the earliest known paper-mill in England dates from 1495), they were happy to import the new material in large quantities from France and Italy.[78] Paper was always cheaper than parchment, and the differential became ever greater as the paper-trade developed and spread. In 1400 one could buy twenty-five sheets of linen paper for about the same price as a single skin,[79] and a single skin could cost anything from a penny to six pence, depending on its quality.[80] By the middle of the fifteenth century, however, the cost of paper had halved, and by the end of the century it had halved again.[81] In other words, by c. 1500 an average skin cost about the same as a hundred sheets of paper.

Some books, however, were bound to be expensive by their very nature. The obvious example is service-books, especially those produced for communal use. They were normally written on parchment, for even though medieval linen paper is remarkably durable, parchment lasts for ever; they were often produced in a larger format than those for private or personal devotion; illumination tended to be more elaborate (this is true for both communal and private service-books); and the scripts in which they were written were generally more labour-intensive than those in the non-liturgical volumes. We do not find here the swift and flowing cursive hands which appear so commonly elsewhere, and a *textura* script such as *textualis prescissa*, the best of Gothic book-hands, which demands not only beauty and balance, but requires that the bottom of each minim (the upright strokes of the letters) be cut off cleanly at precisely ninety degrees, takes a long time to write.[82] To produce a book like this takes time and money, and Bell is right when he says that these works, relative to their length, were 'easily the most expensive volumes in use during the Middle Ages.'[83] Bell distinguishes two classes of service-book: the more expensive and more elaborate would normally cost between £5 and £10 (Mr Hemming's missal was one of these); the cheaper cost between £2 to £4.[84] But even £2 was a large amount of money: six months wages for an unskilled worker.

As for the other types of book noted by Bell—bibles, text-books, and students' notes—it was up to individual customers to decide what they wanted. A complete copy of Lombard's *Sentences*, written in *textura* on parchment, would cost a great deal of money; a paper copy of a short and common work, written in a heavily-abbreviated cursive hand, might cost a shilling or two. In general, and excluding the extremes of luxury volumes like the Croxden Bible or students' notes of hardly any value, Bell suggests a range of prices for bibles of between £2 and £4, and for text-books of between 2s. and £2. Bibles with glosses would, of course, be more expensive,[85] and the cost of text-books would depend upon their length. A short work might cost between 2s. and 4s., whereas something the length of Augustine's *De civitate Dei* could require an outlay of between £1 and £2.[86] Second-hand copies would, of course, be priced accordingly,[87] but the purchase of any book represented a considerable outlay. 'Books were always a luxury in the Middle Ages,' writes M. B. Parkes, 'but the production of cheaper books meant that they could become a luxury for poorer people.'[88]

At this point, perhaps, the reader may object that our discussion has concentrated solely on the cost of books, and that purchase was not the only way by which a medieval monastery built up its collection. That is true. There were, in fact, three ways in which a house might acquire books: by purchase, by donation, or by finding suitable exemplars and having them copied in the monastic scriptorium. We cannot for the moment enter upon an examination of the third of these three ways—the copying of books—for that would involve a consideration of nuns' abilities in reading and writing, a matter we must defer to a later chapter, but we can say something about the question of donations.

In many men's houses, especially in large and famous houses like Christ Church or St Augustine's in Canterbury, donation of books played a major role.[89] The catalogue of the brothers' library at Syon, for example, lists 1421 volumes, and

Christopher de Hamel has observed that if we extract from this total all those books which are *not* specifically listed as gifts, we end up with no more than about 200 volumes.[90] In other words, of all the brothers' books at Syon, about 86% were given as donations. Whether this was also the case with the library of the Syon sisters, we do not know. No catalogue of their books has survived, and we have no idea of the size of their collection. The same is true of other celebrated nunneries such as Shaftesbury, Amesbury, Barking, and Dartford. It is certainly possible that they were the recipients of major donations, but in the absence of any catalogues or inventories, we really have very little idea of how their books were obtained. The record of the surviving volumes gives us no more than a fragmentary glimpse of the overall picture, and to extrapolate from such unsatisfactory evidence is as foolhardy as it is dangerous. As it is, I know of only three instances in which a nun or nunnery received a donation of more than three or four volumes, and the circumstances of the donations differed in all three cases.

The first case was the bequest of Eleanor, duchess of Gloucester, who, in 1399, willed a collection of seven books in French to her daughter Isabel, a nun of the London Minoresses.[91] Since the possession of personal property by nuns was forbidden (at least in theory[92]), the volumes may have found their way into the abbey library.

The second case relates to the peculiar circumstances of the nuns at St Mary de Pré, a Benedictine priory near St Albans. The priory had originally been a leper hospital, and during the period of transition from hospital to priory, the sisters found themselves without service-books and unable to perform the Offices. The matter was resolved by Thomas de la Mare, abbot of St Albans, who supplied the nuns with seven Ordinals and required them henceforth to keep the *Rule of St Benedict* and profess it in writing (*in scriptis*).[93]

The third and final case occurred at the end of the fourteenth or beginning of the fifteenth century when Peter, vicar of Swine, gave a collection of twelve books (perhaps his entire personal library) to the nuns of Swine.[94] We have no idea of the size of the book-collection at Swine (only two manuscripts have been traced to the house[95]), but it is quite possible that these twelve volumes represented a substantial addition. Whether the nuns could actually have read and used the volumes—they were all in Latin—is a matter we shall discuss in Chapter 3.

Apart from these three instances, almost all the other bequests recorded in Part II of this study mention only single volumes.[96] There are bequests of primers and other liturgical books,[97] psalters (including the interesting bequest to Hampole of Richard Rolle's own copy of his English Psalter),[98] a number of books in English—moral discourses,[99] theological works,[100] lives of Christ,[101] lives of saints,[102] and the *Revelations* of St Bridget[103]—two volumes in French,[104] and one book, possibly in Latin, belonging to the cycle of Charlemagne.[105] It is not an impressive list, and although I readily admit that I have not read every medieval will, published and unpublished, and although it is certain that other books will be added by other scholars, I very much doubt that they will change the overall picture. It is true that bequests to nunneries are not uncommon in medieval wills, but such bequests are almost entirely restricted to money and goods other than books; and when we come across wills that do mention books—and there are a considerable number of them— the books in question were not normally left to nunneries.[106] If they were, it was usually because a daughter of the house happened to be a nun.

On the other hand, if we consider the total number of surviving volumes recorded in Part II of this study, we find that about twenty-eight of them—between 17% and 18%—contain inscriptions indicating that they were received as gifts, and even 17% is far from negligible. For a small and poor nunnery which might have possessed only a minimal number of volumes, a single primer or psalter would have been a useful addition, and the importance of even small donations must not be underestimated. But under no circumstances can we take this figure of 17%, contrast it with the 86% from the brothers' library at Syon, and thereby conclude that women's houses received 69% fewer donations than those of men. As we saw earlier, in order to arrive at an accurate estimate of what proportion of a library might have been obtained through donations, we need a catalogue of the collection which records the names of the donors. Without that we are simply groping in the dark. It is true that we have no reason to believe that small and obscure nunneries would have been the recipients of major donations any more than would small and obscure monasteries, but Syon, Amesbury, Barking, and a number of others were far from being small and obscure. Unfortunately, no catalogue of their libraries has survived, and without that information we have little idea either of the size or of the sources of their collections.

There is no doubt, then, that by whatever means they were acquired, books were valuable commodities. Sometimes, indeed, a donor or testator might stipulate that a volume be sold and the money, not the book, be divided among more than one recipient. Such was the case in 1502, when Elizabeth Swinburne required her executors to sell her best primer and divide the proceeds equally between Nun Monkton and St Clement's, York.[107] Further evidence of their value may be seen in the size of the monetary rewards offered for the safe return of a lost volume—Jasper Fyloll was offering 3s. 4d., two weeks wages for an unskilled worker[108]—and in the frequency with which books were used as securities for loans.[109] This last practice (understandably) was particularly prevalent in the university centres, but it was by no means restricted to them. It seems to have been fairly common in monasteries (and as commonly condemned),[110] and two of the manuscripts described in Part II of this present study may have been laid down as pledges. This was certainly the case with a psalter from Littlemore, for an inscription on the back of the first folio tells us that the prioress gave it as a *cautio* for £2.[111] This, as we have seen, was a substantial amount of money. A fifteenth-century manuscript of the Northern Homily Cycle in English verse from Denney may also have been pledged as security, but in this case the circumstances are not so clear.[112]

More common are valuations of volumes from the time of the Dissolution, but these must be treated with caution. So, too, must valuations which appear in individual wills.[113] Just as in the modern second-hand book-trade, the sale-value of any volume depends on condition and demand. The cost of a popular book in deplorable condition must obviously reflect its defects, and a book which no one wants must be priced accordingly. So when we find a book and two cruets at Campsey being priced at 6d.,[114] or six parchment books from Castle Hedingham being valued at 2s.,[115] or books of 'lytell worth' at Flixton and Redlingfield,[116] or books of no value at all at Kilburn and Minster in Sheppey (where there was a whole press of them),[117] we are not seeing a true reflection of what it cost to produce them. The eyes of the king's commissioners were fixed on plate and jewels, on furnishings and lead, and although they took note of a gospel-book from the Benedictine nunnery of Higham, it was only because the volume in question was 'covered with silver and over gilte with stones of cristall.'[118] And when an avowed enemy of the commissioners such as Sir Edmund Bedingfield paid 6s. 8d. for an Antiphoner from Redlingfield,[119] it might well have been for sentimental reasons. Sir Edmund was a staunch supporter of the Old Religion, a benefactor of Redlingfield, and two of his daughters were nuns. Sir Edmund, however, represents the exception, not the rule. Who, after all, needed monastic office-books in a country without monasteries?

In the years following the Dissolution, in the time of John Aubrey's grandfather,

> manuscripts flew about like butterflies. All musick bookes, account bookes, copie bookes, &c. were covered with old manuscripts, as wee cover them now with blew paper or marbled paper; and the glovers at Malmesbury made great havock of them; and gloves were wrapt up no doubt in many good pieces of antiquity. Before the late warres a world of rare manuscripts perished hereabout; for within half a dozen miles of this place were the abbey of Malmesbury, where it may be presumed the library was as well furnished with choice copies as most libraries of England.[120]

And when, in 1647, Aubrey went to see the manuscripts which had been collected in an earlier day by Parson Stump, he found them 'lost and disperst. His sons were gunners and souldiers, and scoured their gunnes with them.'[121] *Sic transit gloria scriptorii.*

What may surprise us, therefore, is not how few medieval manuscripts have survived in England, but how many. On the other hand, of those that have survived, only about thirteen or fourteen per cent have been traced to specific religious houses.[122] A comparison of surviving library catalogues with surviving volumes is a depressing experience, and some of the greatest libraries have left hardly any traces of their former glory. An inventory of the Cistercian abbey of Meaux in Yorkshire drawn up in 1396 reveals a collection of about four hundred volumes; five have been traced to the house.[123] The magnificent library of the Austin Friars at York contained at least 646 books at the end of the fourteenth century, but only a remnant—ten volumes—remains.[124]

Our purpose here, however, lies not in bewailing what has been lost, but in examining what has survived; and of the volumes which have survived, our interest lies only in those that have been traced to English nunneries. Let us therefore begin our investigation by presenting some statistics and by summarizing the materials contained in the lists and indexes which comprise the second part of this study.

NOTES

1. E. E. Power, *Medieval English Nunneries, c. 1275 to 1535* (Cambridge, 1922; rpt. New York, 1964, 1988).
2. N. F. Cantor, *Inventing the Middle Ages: The Lives, Works, and Ideas of the Great Medievalists of the Twentieth Century* (New York, 1991), p. 388. Cantor calls her *Medieval English Nunneries* 'the most underrated major work in medieval history, at least in English' (p. 387). He is wrong, however, in saying that it has 'long been out of print' (*ibid.*).
3. I have restricted myself to England not by choice but by necessity. Of all the books and manuscripts listed in the second part of this study, only two—both from the Convent of St Catherine of Siena in Edinburgh (EDINBURGH 1 and 2)—are from beyond the borders of England. The use of 'England' and 'English', therefore, is not, in the strictest sense, entirely accurate, but the two volumes from Edinburgh in no way affect my conclusions.
4. For a very sound summary of the sources of income of English nunneries, see Power, pp. 96–117. My brief discussion here derives primarily from her work and from a reading of every account of every nunnery published in the volumes of the Victoria County History.
5. VCH *Middlesex*, vol. 1, p. 189, and Power, p. 98 (summarizing the *Valor Ecclesiasticus, temp. Henr. VIII. Auctoritate Regia Institutus.* [London, 1810–34], vol. 1, pp. 424–8).
6. Syon, as F. R. Johnston has pointed out, was 'widely known for the *Vincula* indulgence and other pardons obtainable by pilgrims. . . . An added attraction . . . was the special faculty of the brethren for blessing rosaries, granted in 1500 by Pope Alexander VI' (VCH *Middlesex*, vol. 1, p. 186). See further J. T. Rhodes, 'Syon Abbey

and its Religious Publications in the Sixteenth Century', *Journal of Ecclesiastical History* 44 (1993), pp. 12–13.

7. One example must suffice: between the years 1277 and 1389, the priory of St Radegund's, Cambridge, underwent a singular succession of disasters. The bell-tower collapsed, the buildings burned down twice, and after they had been rebuilt the second time, they were partly demolished by violent storms. On each occasion, appeals for funds for reconstruction were supported by indulgences (VCH *Cambridgeshire*, vol. 2, p. 218). Other examples are given by Power, pp. 174–6.

8. For details, see Power, pp. 103–5. 'In the eyes of the middle ages,' she observes, 'justice had one outstanding characteristic: it filled the pocket of whoever administered it' (p. 104).

9. As at Dartford: see VCH *Kent*, vol. 2, pp. 184, 187.

10. A good example is Buckland Minchin, where 'the importance of a supply of fuel was recognized in 1382, when the prior of the Hospital granted the sisters 15 acres at Buckland, where furze grew, for fuel' (VCH *Somerset*, vol. 2, p. 149).

11. See VCH *Dorset*, vol. 2, p. 74.

12. See Power, pp. 113–5. A similar economic advantage could be gained by persuading a bishop to grant parochial status to a conventual church: once again, it was not so much the souls of the parishioners which were at issue, but their tithes. For the example of Chatteris, see VCH *Cambridgeshire*, vol. 2, p. 220.

13. The wool-trade was of particular interest to Power, and in 1939 she delivered the Ford Lectures at Oxford on *The Wool Trade in English Medieval History* (Oxford, 1955). Since that date a number of further studies have appeared (those of Terrence Lloyd are especially important), but in none of them does wool production by English nunneries play any large part.

14. See Power, p. 105, and VCH *Essex*, vol. 2, p. 118. The abbesses of Syon and Dartford also had the right of 'free warren' (Power, p. 105; VCH *Kent*, vol. 2, p. 183).

15. Neither dowry nor profession fees were cheap. The amounts recorded by Power, pp. 16–20, range from £5 to £17.6.2 (John of Gaunt's payment of more than £50 to Barking in 1381 is quite extraordinary). To the cases noted by Power may be added that of Elizabeth Langriche. When she took the veil at Romsey in 1523, she was given a magnificent psalter (the Wilton Psalter), a silver goblet, and two spoons; and Master Raufe Lepton was obliged to deliver five pounds in money to 'John Raye, baylyff of Romsey' (ROMSEY 2). A dowry was not merely a matter of hard cash: the expenses *circa velacionem* of Joan Samborne at Lacock in 1395

included payments to the abbess and the convent, and costs for veils, linen and other cloth, a bed, a mattress, a coverlet, a tester, blankets, mantles, fur, a drinking bowl, a spoon, the profession fees proper, and other necessaries (see W. G. Clark-Maxwell, 'The Outfit for the Profession of an Austin Canoness at Lacock, Wilts. in the Year 1395, and other Memoranda', *Archaeological Journal* 69 [1912], pp. 117–24).

16. Witness the case of Lady Audley's dogs: whenever she came into church (wrote the prioress of Langley to the bishop), she was followed by twelve of them. They made a great uproar, hindered the nuns in their psalmody, and generally terrified them (Power, p. 412). Much of the material in Power's tenth chapter, 'The World in the Cloister' (pp. 394–435), is relevant here.

17. See Power, pp. 112–3, 568–81 (to Power's list can be added the three girls at Buckland Minchin in 1228 [VCH *Somerset*, vol. 2, p. 149]). According to John Aubrey, in the days before the Dissolution, 'there were not schooles for young ladies as now, but they were educated at religious houses' (J. Aubrey, ed. J. Britton, *The Natural History of Wiltshire* [London, 1847; rpt. Newton Abbot, 1969], p. 57). We shall have more to say on this matter in Chapter 3.

18. But, like the modern televangelists, he left the door open for 'free-will offerings': see VCH *Staffordshire*, vol. 3, p. 221. For other examples of episcopal prohibitions (which were not a success), see Power, pp. 21–4. The situation in the late twelfth and thirteenth centuries is discussed in S. Thompson, *Women Religious: The Founding of English Nunneries after the Norman Conquest* (Oxford, 1991), pp. 187–9.

19. See Power, pp. 408–19.

20. As Power, p. 417, observes, 'no episcopal injunction was more consistently disobeyed,' but obedience was not, perhaps, the dominant characteristic of later medieval nuns. Witness the failure of the bishops to impose the *Pro clausura monialium* statute of Pope Boniface VIII. 'This statute [says Sr Elspeth of the Community of All Saints] was intended to compel the English nuns of all orders to observe a stricter enclosure; but . . . it seems to have been quite ineffectual. The English Benedictine nuns and Austin Canonesses never had been strictly enclosed, and quietly ignored the new regulations, even though they came from the pope himself' (VCH *Buckinghamshire*, vol. 1, p. 358).

21. When Archbishop Warham made a visitation of Davington in 1511, the convent had to pay £1 for his board. The annual income of the priory at this time was about £40 (VCH *Kent*, vol. 2, p. 144).

22. Power, p. 127.

23. VCH *London*, vol. 1, p. 460.

24. The material in this paragraph is simply a summary of Power, pp. 117–30.
25. See VCH *Wiltshire*, vol. 3, p. 307. The reference is specifically to Lacock, but is true for all other houses.
26. VCH *Middlesex*, vol. 1, p. 170.
27. See *ibid.*, p. 185 and VCH *Wiltshire*, vol. 3, pp. 249, 253.
28. VCH *Chester*, vol. 3, p. 148.
29. VCH *Cambridgeshire*, vol. 2, p. 299.
30. VCH *Yorkshire*, vol. 3, pp. 112–3.
31. The process really began towards the end of the reign of Henry III, when 'the law tended to become a close profession' (W. S. Holdsworth, *A History of English Law* [London, 1936[4]], vol. 2, p. 229). The tendency became stronger during the reign of Edward I with the professionalization of pleaders and attorneys (*ibid.*, pp. 311–9); and finally, in the fourteenth and fifteenth centuries, 'the legal profession organized itself and obtained that monopoly of legal business which it still continues to enjoy' (*ibid.*, p. 484).
32. See VCH *Northamptonshire*, vol. 2, p. 98.
33. Quoted in T. Fuller, ed. J. S. Brewer, *The Church History of Britain* (Oxford, 1845), vol. 3, p. 332.
34. See n. 41 below.
35. See VCH *Cumberland*, vol. 2, pp. 189–94. Other nunneries on the Scottish border had similar problems, as also did some of those on the border with Wales.
36. See Knowles/Hadcock, p. 272 for the incomes of Cistercian nunneries c. 1535.
37. The quotation comes from a letter of the prioress of Whistones, a Cistercian house in Worcestershire, to the bishop-elect of Worcester (VCH *Worcestershire*, vol. 2, p. 155). As for Cookhill, the other Cistercian priory in Worcestershire, 'the poverty of the house . . . is indeed almost the chief feature of its known history' (*ibid.*, p. 157). Even when begging for alms was permitted by the bishop (as at Rothwell [see VCH *Northamptonshire*, vol. 2, p. 137]), it was always regarded with opprobrium. The Bridgettines required all their convents to be so endowed that begging was unnecessary, and it was never a question for the wealthy nuns of Syon (VCH *Middlesex*, vol. 1, p. 182). For further discussion, see Power, pp. 172–4.
38. See Knowles/Hadcock, pp. 253–4.
39. See *ibid.*, p. 272.
40. I am using the simplified figures in Knowles/Hadcock, pp. 202 (Bridgettines [Syon]), 253–5 (Benedictines), 270 (Cluniacs), 272 (Cistercians), 278 (Augustinians), 283 (Premonstratensians), 285 (Dominicans [Dartford]), and 286 (Franciscans). It need hardly be

added that this picture is incomplete, but this is not an economic history of English nunneries.

41. They are listed at n. 34 above.
42. The discussion in this paragraph is based primarily on S. A. C. Penn & C. Dyer, 'Wages and Earnings in Late Medieval England: Evidence from the Enforcement of the Labour Laws', *Economic History Review* 43 (1990), pp. 356–76. Additional material has been derived from E. F. Jacob, *The Fifteenth Century 1399–1485* (Oxford, 1961), pp. 380–5, who provides useful information on food prices. Those who wish further detail will find a wealth of information in the first four volumes of J. E. Thorold Rogers, *A History of Agriculture and Prices in England* (Oxford, 1866–1902; rpt. Liechtenstein, 1963). The effects of the Black Death (and subsequent plagues) on the medieval economy are carefully examined by J. M. W. Bean in 'Plague, Population and Economic Decline in England in the Later Middle Ages', *Economic History Review* Ser. 2, 15 (1962–3), pp. 423–37.
43. See, for example, S. L. Thrupp, *The Merchant Class of Medieval London [1300–1500]* (Ann Arbor, 1948; rpt. 1962), pp. 112–4.
44. See Knowles/Hadcock, p. 260.
45. Power, p. 98.
46. See VCH *Dorset*, vol. 2, p. 78.
47. See VCH *Oxfordshire*, vol. 2, p. 73 (Godstow), *Warwickshire*, vol. 2, pp. 67–8 (Nuneaton), *Cambridgeshire*, vol. 2, p. 218 (St Radegund's).
48. I suspect at least the nuns of Dartford, Clerkenwell, and Marham of exaggerating their situation (see VCH *Kent*, vol. 2, p. 184; *Middlesex*, vol. 1, p. 170; Thompson, *Women Religious*, p. 12).
49. See VCH *Wiltshire*, vol. 3, p. 260.
50. Its annual income c. 1535 was about £20 (Knowles/Hadcock, p. 254).
51. Thompson, *Women Religious*, p. 12.
52. See generally Power, pp. 161–236 (Chapter V 'Financial Difficulties').
53. VCH *Buckinghamshire*, vol. 1, p. 354. Sister Elspeth is referring specifically to Ivinghoe, a small house which made up in devotion what it lacked in funds.
54. VCH *Warwickshire*, vol. 2, p. 63. Since the minimum age for a Benedictine abbess at this time was twenty-one, she needed episcopal dispensation to hold the office.
55. See VCH *Yorkshire*, vol. 3, p. 118.
56. See Power, pp. 4–14, and Chapter 3 of this present study, n. 77.
57. Much information on this matter is provided by Jennifer C. Ward in her *English Noblewomen in the Later Middle Ages* (London/New York, 1992), especially chapters 2, 3 and 6.

58. VCH *Kent*, vol. 2, p. 147.
59. See *ibid.*, p. 187. The detailed *Rentale* drawn up under her administration in 1507–08 is listed in Part II of this study (DARTFORD 3). The reverse of the coin is represented by Margaret Sandford, prioress of St Leonard's, Brewood, in the first half of the sixteenth century, who seems to have been wholly ignorant of even the most basic principles of accounting (VCH *Shropshire*, vol. 2, p. 84).
60. Power, p. 228.
61. See, for example, Jackie Mountain's brief study of 'Nunnery Finances in the Early Fifteenth Century', *Monastic Studies II*, ed. J. Loades (Bangor, 1991), pp. 263–72. Her account, however, deals with only three nunneries (Catesby, Marrick, and Romsey), and much work remains to be done in this very interesting area.
62. See Power, pp. 228–36 (but her discussion of double houses is out of date and must be corrected by the excellent account in chapter 4 of Sally Thompson's *Women Religious*).
63. See SYON *MR* c.
64. H. E. Bell, 'The Price of Books in Medieval England', *The Library*, Ser. 4, 17 (1937), p. 331. But 'such abnormally low prices,' says the author, can hardly indicate anything but 'rudely written, unbound copies.' (*ibid.*)
65. W. L. Schramm, 'The Cost of Books in Chaucer's Time', *Modern Language Notes* 48 (1933), pp. 139–45; Bell, 'Price of Books' (n. 64), pp. 312–32. See also n. 106 below.
66. Bell, 'Price of Books', p. 329.
67. Derek Pearsall's introduction to *Book Production and Publishing in Britain 1375–1475*, ed. J. Griffiths & D. Pearsall (Cambridge, 1989), p. 7.
68. Very few abbreviations were used in vernacular texts. The most common are listed in L. C. Hector, *The Handwriting of English Documents* (London, 1958), p. 37, and C. E. Wright, *English Vernacular Hands from the Twelfth to the Fifteenth Centuries* (Oxford, 1960), p. xvii.
69. See M. B. Parkes, *English Cursive Book Hands 1250–1500* (Oxford, 1969; rpt. Berkeley/Los Angeles/London, 1980), pp. xiii–xvii, and M. P. Brown, *A Guide to Western Historical Scripts from Antiquity to 1600* (London, 1990), p. 98.
70. For Wright's study, see n. 68; for Parkes', n. 69. By the time English vernacular texts were being produced in any quantity, *Anglicana* cursive script was fully developed.
71. The precise details of the operation of the *pecia* system are still not fully understood, but we need not concern ourselves with its complexities here. For a brief account, see C. H. Talbot, 'The Universities and the Medieval Library', in *The English Library Before*

1700, ed. F. Wormald & C. E. Wright (London, 1958), pp. 67–70. For later and more detailed studies, see G. Pollard, 'The *pecia* system in the medieval universities', in *Medieval Scribes, Manuscripts and Libraries: Essays presented to N. R. Ker*, ed. M. B. Parkes & A. G. Watson (London, 1978), pp. 145–61, and the important collection of papers in *La production du livre universitaire au moyen âge: exemplar et pecia. Actes du symposium tenu au Collegio San Bonaventura de Grottaferrata en mai 1983*, ed. L. J. Bataillon *et al.* (Paris, 1988).

72. Peter of Blois, *Ep.* 71; *PL* 207: 219–21. The story of how Peter was cheated is summarized by Talbot in 'The Universities and the Medieval Library', p. 71.

73. Much information of this matter may be found in *Book Production and Publishing in Britain 1375–1475* (n. 67), *passim*. Pearsall provides a useful and accurate summary on pp. 3–7.

74. See A. I. Doyle, 'Book Production by the Monastic Orders in England (c. 1375–1530)', in *Medieval Book Production: Assessing the Evidence*, ed. L. L. Brownrigg (Los Altos Hills, 1990), pp. 1–19, and *idem*, 'Publication by Members of the Religious Orders', in *Book Production and Publishing in Britain 1375–1475*, pp. 109–23.

75. R. J. Lyall, 'Materials: The Paper Revolution', in *ibid.*, pp. 11–29.

76. The whole procedure is splendidly described and illustrated by Christopher de Hamel in his *Medieval Craftsmen: Scribes and Illuminators* (London, 1992), pp. 8–16. Other accounts are noted by Lyall, 'Paper Revolution', p. 26, n. 2.

77. One must note the cautionary comments of L. Febvre & H.-J. Martin, tr. D. Gerard, ed. G. Nowell-Smith & D. Wootton, *The Coming of the Book and the Impact of Printing* (London, 1976), pp. 17–18.

78. See Jean Irigoin's article in the *Dictionary of the Middle Ages* (New York, 1987), vol. 9, pp. 388–90, who also provides a useful bibliography.

79. Lyall, 'Paper Revolution', p. 11.

80. De Hamel, *Scribes and Illuminators*, p. 13.

81. Lyall, 'Paper Revolution', p. 11. See also M. C. Erler, 'Syon Abbey's Care for Books: Its Sacristan's Account Rolls 1506/7–1535/6', *Scriptorium* 39 (1985), p. 301.

82. For a description and illustration of this script, see Brown, *Guide to Western Historical Scripts* (n. 69), pp. 82–3, no. 28.

83. Bell, 'Price of Books', p. 328.

84. *Ibid.*

85. The price of a psalter could range from 3s. (unglossed) to 26s. 8d. if it were glossed (Schramm, 'Cost of Books', p. 142). But, as always, much depended on choice of materials and script. Luxurious

glossed volumes such as those described in Chapter 5 of C. F. R. de Hamel's *Glossed Books of the Bible and the Origins of the Paris Booktrade* (Cambridge, 1984) were beyond the resources of all but the richest collectors.

86. Bell, 'Price of Books', pp. 329–30.

87. On the second-hand book-trade, see A. I. Doyle & M. B. Parkes, 'The Production of Copies of the *Canterbury Tales* and the *Confessio Amantis* in the Early Fifteenth Century', in *Medieval Scribes, Manuscripts and Libraries: Essays Presented to N. R. Ker*, ed. M. B. Parkes & A. G. Watson (London, 1978), p. 197, n. 88; C. F. R. de Hamel, *Syon Abbey. The Library of the Bridgettine Nuns and Their Peregrinations After the Reformation* (Roxburghe Club, 1991), pp. 49–50, 61–2. In Part II of this study there are listed numerous volumes which contain inscriptions of later date—sometimes of much later date—than the manuscripts in which they appear. Examples are ANKERWYKE 1, BARKING 15 (which we know was bought second-hand), BRUISYARD 1, BUCKLAND MINCHIN 1, CAMPSEY 1, 3, and 5, CARROW 1 and 3, DERBY 1, HEYNINGS 1, LITTLEMORE 1, ROMSEY 1 and 2, SWINE B.1, TARRANT KEYNSTON 3, THETFORD 1, and WHERWELL 4. Some of these volumes were undoubtedly second-hand purchases.

88. M. B. Parkes, 'The Literacy of the Laity', in *idem, Scribes, Scripts and Readers: Studies in the Communication, Presentation and Dissemination of Medieval Texts* (London/Rio Grande, Ohio, 1991), p. 287. This important article was first published in *Literature and Western Civilization: The Medieval World*, ed. D. Daiches & A. K. Thorlby (London, 1973), pp. 555–77.

89. See, for example, D. Knowles, *The Religious Orders in England* (Cambridge, 1955), vol. 2, pp. 339–41.

90. De Hamel, *Syon Abbey* (n. 87), p. 80. The sixteenth-century catalogue of Syon was carefully edited almost a century ago by Mary Bateson, *Catalogue of the Library of Syon Monastery Isleworth* (Cambridge, 1898) (a new edition is being prepared by Drs I. A. Doyle and V. Gillespie), who also demonstrates that the catalogue is that of the brothers' library alone (*ibid.*, p. xiii–xv). The names of the donors are listed conveniently in *ibid.*, pp. xxiii–xxvii. There was a special office at Syon for the donors of books: see the *Martyrology of Syon*, B.L., Add. 22285, fols. 4rv and 17v *De exequiis pro benefactoribus librariarum* (for a transcript, see Bateson, p. xxviii–xxix, and J. Hogg, *Richard Whytford's The Pype or Tonne of the Lyfe of Perfection* [Salzburg Studies in English Literature, 89/1; Salzburg, 1979], vol. 1, pp. 35–6, n. 66).

91. LONDON (ALDGATE) *MR* a.

92. See the discussion in Power, pp. 322–40, but by the late fifteenth/ early sixteenth century it is doubtful whether this principle was much honoured. See, for example, de Hamel, *Syon Abbey*, pp. 74, 97, 125. One of the problems with the invauable lists prepared by Ker and Watson is that they record as belonging to institutions many volumes which, to all intents and purposes, really belonged to individuals.

93. See *Gesta Abbatum Monasterii Sancti Albani*, compiled by Thomas Walsingham, ed. H. T. Riley (RS 28/4 [vol. 2 of the *Gesta*]; London, 1867), vol. 2, p. 402: 'Ne vero moniales incircumspecta gauderent licentia, ordinavit ut omnes advenientes de caetero Regulam Sancti Benedicti profiterentur in scriptis' ('To prevent the nuns from enjoying an unheeding lawlessness, he commanded that from thenceforth everyone entering [the convent] should profess the Rule of Saint Benedict in writing'). The circumstances are explained in Part II of this study s.v. ST MARY DE PRÉ *MR*. See also Chapter 3, n. 73.

94. SWINE A.

95. SWINE B.1 and B.2.

96. Bequests of two books were made to Easebourne, London (St Helen's), and Nun Appleton, of three books to Heynings, and of four books to London (Aldgate).

97. Primers were bequeathed to ARDEN *MR* and EASEBOURNE *MR* b.1; *portiforia* to BURNHAM *MR*, HEYNINGS *MR*, and LONDON (ST HELEN'S *MR*); and a missal to HEYNINGS *MR*. The primer (*primarium*) contained the Office of the Virgin, usually supplemented by the Penitential Psalms, Gradual Psalms, a litany, and the Office of the Dead.

98. BROADHOLME *MR*; GREENFIELD *MR*; HAMPOLE *MR*; HEYNINGS *MR*; LACOCK *MR* a; LONDON (ST HELEN'S) *MR*; NEWCASTLE UPON TYNE *MR*; NUN MONKTON *MR* a.

99. Walter Hilton's *Mixed Life* (SYON *MR* b.2); *The Book of Vices and Virtues* (NUN MONKTON *MR* b); *The Chastising of God's Children* (EASEBOURNE *MR* b.2; ESHOLT *MR*); *The Doctrine of the Heart* (BRUISYARD *MR* a); *The Prick of Conscience* (ARTHINGTON *MR*; LONDON [ALDGATE] *MR* b.4).

100. A book in English *de Pater Noster* (NUN MONKTON *MR* d).

101. See NUN MONKTON *MR* c, SINNINGTHWAITE *MR*, and SYON *MR* b.1. At Sinningthwaite and Syon the volume in question was Nicholas Love's *Mirror of the Blessed Life of Christ*. The volume bequeathed to Nun Monkton may have been the same work.

102. The *Golden Legend* (BRUISYARD *MR* b) and a life of St Catherine (SWINE *MR*).

103. SWINE *MR* and SYON *MR* b.3.
104. An unnamed 'French book' (DENNEY *MR*) and the *Manuel de pechiez*, commonly (but doubtfully) attributed to William of Waddington (MALLING *MR*).
105. POLSLOE *MR*.
106. A comprehensive study of book bequests in medieval wills is not here my business. Useful and interesting summaries may be found in M. Deanesly, 'Vernacular Books in England in the Fourteenth and Fifteenth Centuries', *Modern Language Review* 15 (1920), pp. 348–58 (see also *idem, The Lollard Bible and Other Medieval Biblical Versions* [Cambridge, 1920; rpt. 1966], pp. 391–8); H. R. Plomer, 'Books Mentioned in Wills', *Transactions of the Bibliographical Society* 7 (1902–4), pp. 99–121; Thrupp, *Merchant Class of Medieval London* (n. 43), pp. 161–3; J. T. Rosenthal, 'Aristocratic Cultural Patronage and Book Bequests, 1350–1500', *Bulletin of the John Rylands Library* 64 (1981–82), pp. 522–48; J. B. Friedman, 'Books, Owners and Makers in Fifteenth-Century Yorkshire: The Evidence from Some Wills and Extant Manuscripts', in *Latin and Vernacular: Studies in Late-Medieval Texts and Manuscripts*, ed. A. J. Minnis (Cambridge, 1989), pp. 111–27 (Friedman's paper also contains information on book prices); and, above all, S. H. Cavanaugh, *A Study of Books Privately Owned in England: 1300–1450* (University of Pennsylvania, Ph.D. Diss., 1980; University Microfilms International).
107. NUN MONKTON *MR* e.
108. SYON A.10. In WHERWELL 1 the amount of the reward is unknown: the part of the leaf containing it has been trimmed off.
109. See Bell, 'Price of Books', pp. 325–6; Schramm, 'Cost of Books', p. 143. It is significant that at the university of Cambridge in 1480 only books written on parchment could be accepted as pledges. By this time, paper had become too cheap (Bell, p. 321).
110. Bell, 'Price of Books', p. 325.
111. LITTLEMORE 1.
112. DENNEY 1.
113. For a few examples, see Bell, 'Price of Books', pp. 330–1; Thrupp, *Merchant Class of Medieval London* (n. 43), pp. 161–3; Parkes, 'Literacy of the Laity', pp. 286–7.
114. CAMPSEY *MR*.
115. CASTLE HEDINGHAM *MR*.
116. FLIXTON *MR*; REDLINGFIELD *MR* b.
117. KILBURN *MR*; MINSTER IN SHEPPEY *MR*.
118. HIGHAM *MR*. In the priory church of Minster in Sheppey there were eight books with silver clasps, but they are not priced in the 1536 inventory (MINSTER IN SHEPPEY *MR*).

119. REDLINGFIELD *MR* a.
120. Aubrey, *Natural History of Wiltshire* (n. 17), p. 79.
121. *Ibid.*
122. This is my own estimate, but Dr Richard Sharpe agrees with me.
123. The catalogue has been edited by D. N. Bell in *idem, The Libraries of the Cistercians, Gilbertines and Premonstratensians* (Corpus of British Medieval Library Catalogues, 3; London, 1992), pp. 34–82, and the surviving manuscripts are listed in Ker, p. 130.
124. The catalogue has been edited by K. W. Humphreys in *idem, The Friars' Libraries* (Corpus of British Medieval Library Catalogues, 1; London, 1990), pp. 11–154, and the surviving manuscripts are listed in Ker, p. 218, and Watson, p. 71. The location of one of the ten surviving manuscripts is unknown.

CHAPTER 2:
MANUSCRIPTS AND BOOKS

T HERE WERE in England during the later middle ages (c. 1270–1536),' says Eileen Power, 'some 138 nunneries, excluding double houses of the Gilbertine order, which contained brothers as well as nuns.'[1] The figure she suggests needs to be increased slightly to about 144,[2] but for our purposes the difference is not significant. Manuscripts or printed books have survived from forty-six houses (just less than a third of the total), and there are miscellaneous records from nineteen more.[3] In sum, we have books or records of books from sixty-five houses, representing about forty-five percent of the total number.

One hundred and forty-four surviving manuscripts are listed in Part II of this study, together with seventeen printed books, ten of which are from Syon.[4] The number is not large, but we must beware of comparing it with the magnificent collections which have survived from some men's houses. The greatest accumulations of surviving manuscripts come not from small and isolated monasteries, but from major Benedictine houses which were also cathedrals, monastic or secular, or which were converted into cathedrals in 1540 and 1541.[5] Durham, Worcester, Salisbury, Exeter, Hereford, and Lincoln are obvious examples. Here we have a continuity in custodianship which was not the case in any nunnery. But if we compare the numbers of manuscripts which have been traced to English nunneries with those which have survived from the houses of the Cluniacs, Premonstratensians, Gilbertines, Trinitarian Friars, and Austin Friars, the comparison is much more favourable.[6] Even among the Cistercians, the largest number of manuscripts which has been traced to any one house are the forty-three from Fountains,[7] the richest Cistercian monastery in England, and that is fewer than have been traced to the sisters of Syon.

The dates of these 144 surviving volumes range from the ninth century[8] to the sixteenth, and we find that, as a general rule, the later the century, the more abundant are the extant witnesses. This, as we shall see in a moment, is not a matter of chance. If we exclude the printed books and list the manuscripts, according to date, in six groups, we arrive at the following table:

Group	Date	No. of MSS	% of Total No.
1	s.ix–xi	5	3.5
2	s.xii	12	8.3
3	s.xii/xiii–xiii	20	13.9
4	s.xiii/xiv–xiv	18	12.5
5	s.xiv/xv–xv	72	50.0
6	s.xv/xvi–xvi	17	11.8

What is immediately obvious is that almost half the manuscripts date from the fifteenth century, and if we combine together groups 5 and 6 and include with them the seventeen printed books, we find that no less than two-thirds of all surviving volumes date from after c. 1400. As we saw in Chapter 1, this is precisely the period which was marked by a general increase in vernacular literacy and a corresponding decrease in the cost of books. In the fifteenth century, says Derek Pearsall, 'there was an increase in the demand for, availability and ownership of books of all kinds,'[9] and Charles Kingsford once referred to the period as 'an age of libraries.'[10] That the majority of surviving volumes from English nunneries date from this time is more than mere coincidence—more books might be bought and more given as donations—but a full investigation of this matter must be left until our next chapter.

With regard to the content of the surviving volumes, slightly more than half (about 53%) are primarily liturgical, and these include bibles and biblical books (two in Latin, two in French, and two in English), breviaries, calendars, hours (*horae*), hymnals, mortuary rolls, obituaries, the Office of the Dead, ordinals, various *ordines*, private collections of prayers, processionals, and psalters.[11] A detailed list of *liturgica* and related material is provided in Index IV and there is no need to repeat that information here.

Of these liturgical volumes, by far the greatest number are psalters, of which there are almost forty—about 45% of the total[12]—and it is important to remember that a medieval psalter was normally much more than merely a collection of psalms. The contents would generally include a calendar, psalms, canticles,

Te Deum, Athanasian Creed, a litany or litanies, and (after about 1200) the Office of the Dead.[13] Later in the thirteenth century the Hours of the Virgin, other Hours, and the Psalter of the Virgin might also be included, and after about 1400 we find that many psalters have been so expanded that they no longer represent a single biblical book, but have been transformed into small libraries of devotional texts for either communal or private use. A good example is a fifteenth-century psalter from Godstow.[14] In addition to the usual material—psalms, canticles, litanies, and the Office of the Dead—it also contains the Hours of the Virgin, Hours of the Holy Spirit, Hours of the Trinity, the Fifteen Oes of St Bridget (a popular text associated with substantial pardons[15]), and a collection of hymns and prayers. The Vernon Psalter from Hampole is similar: it dates from the second half of the fourteenth century and includes a calendar, psalms, canticles, litany, the Office of the Dead, various hymns, the Hours of the Passion in French and Latin, the Short Office of the Cross, the Hours of the Virgin, and the Psalter of St Jerome.[16] By this time, however, it was more usual for the Hours to be separated from the psalter and to appear as a separate volume—the earliest known English example dates from the mid-thirteenth century[17]—and, as such, Books of Hours were more important to lay-people than to religious, and, among religious, to women rather than men.[18]

It might be suggested that the large proportion of psalters and liturgical volumes which have survived from English nunneries indicates that their book collections consisted primarily of liturgical works. Such a conclusion would be too hasty. Many psalters, like many Books of Hours, were objects of conspicuous consumption,[19] and some of those that have survived are quite magnificent.[20] It is true that fanaticism has never balked at the wanton destruction of beauty, but most people, fortunately, are not fanatics. And if there were adherents of the Old Religion who, after the Dissolution, wished, with all due discretion, to continue the practice of their faith, a psalter or breviary would be infinitely more use than a copy of Augustine's *City of God* or Lombard's *Sentences*. In short, there are sound reasons for the survival of substantial numbers of liturgical volumes, and we cannot assume that the proportion they occupy among surviving books is an accurate reflection of the wider situation.

Similar caution must be exercised when considering the liturgical manuscripts from Syon. Half the volumes which have been traced to the sisters may be categorized broadly as liturgical, and if we include similar manuscripts which belonged to the brothers, we have a total of some forty books. This is an extraordinarily large number, but it is not difficult to explain. Syon was the only Bridgettine house in England and its liturgy, particularly the sisters' liturgy, was unique and distinctive. If, therefore, we come across an English manuscript containing (for example) a Bridgettine litany, we can be reasonably certain that it must have come from Syon. Such confidence is manifestly impossible in the case of the other Orders, and the large number of liturgical books from Syon should be seen not as a reflection of the overall content of the sisters' library, but of the unique character of their Offices.[21]

Let us now turn to the contents of the non-liturgical volumes that have survived. These are to be found in three languages—Latin, French, and English—and comprehensive lists of all the works they contain are to be found in Indexes I–III. There are about sixteen volumes (23%) primarily in Latin, seven (10%) in French, and no fewer than forty-eight (67%) in English. We shall examine the reasons for this last disproportionate number in our next chapter.

The material in Latin is, for the most part, unexceptional. There are biblical books with and without glosses, two volumes of *vitae sanctorum*, and among the more common writers and works represented are standard texts of Ambrose, the *De consolatione philosophiae* of Boethius, the *Rule* of St Benedict (a bilingual version at Wintney[22]), the *Scintillarium* of Defensor of Ligugé, the *Diadema monachorum* of Smaragdus of Saint-Mihiel, Peter Comestor's *Historia scholastica*, the *Allegories* of Richard of Saint-Victor, three works of Honorius Augustodunensis, the *Conquest of Ireland* and *Topography of Ireland* by Gerald of Wales, John Beleth's *Summa de ecclesiasticis officiis*, and the *Dictionarius* of William Brito. There are also common pseudonymous works attributed to Augustine, Bernard of Clairvaux, and Hugh of Saint-Victor. Less common are the letters of Alan of Tewkesbury in a manuscript from Nuneaton,[23] and, at Syon, the chronicle of Martin of Troppau,[24] and collections of the Latin works of Richard Rolle and Thomas à Kempis.[25] But as we shall see in due course,

Syon was always something of an anomaly. Classical writers are represented by a single volume from Dartford containing the pseudonymous *Disticha Catonis* in Latin and English.[26]

The dates of these Latin volumes are not without interest, for whereas the majority of manuscripts listed in Part II date from the period after 1400, the reverse is true for manuscripts in Latin. Ten of them (about two-thirds) were written before the fifteenth century; one (the *Dictionarius* of William Brito[27]) is a borderline case; and the other five, which date from the fifteenth or sixteenth centuries, all come either from Syon or Dartford, both of which were well-known as centres of learning. The reasons for this chronological inversion must be left for discussion until our next chapter.

The surviving volumes in French range in date from the thirteenth to the sixteenth centuries and were to be found at Barking, Campsey, Derby, Flixton, Nuneaton, Shaftesbury, Syon, and Tarrant Keynston.[28] We may also presume that the books bequeathed by Eleanor, duchess of Gloucester, to her daughter Isabel would have found their way into the library of the London Minoresses.[29] The volumes include a bible, metrical versions of biblical books, lives of the fathers and lives of saints (the volume from Campsey was for reading at mealtimes[30]), the *Chasteau d'amour* of Robert Grosseteste, the *Bestiary* of Guillaume le Clerc, *Le livre de Sydrac*, Peter of Peckham's *Lumière as lais*, and (at Syon) a printed edition of a French translation of Boccaccio's *De la ruine des nobles hommes et femmes*. The large collection of theological and devotional material in French which appears in a volume from Barking also appears in other manuscripts,[31] and it may reflect more the interests of its pious donor, Elizabeth de Vere, Countess of Oxford, than the nuns to whom it was given.

As to surviving volumes in English, there are so many that a simple summary is hardly possible. We find translations of works by or attributed to Adam the Carthusian, Albert the Great, Aristotle, Augustine of Hippo, Benedict, Bernard of Clairvaux, Bridget of Sweden, Bonaventure, Catherine of Siena, Cato, Guigo II of La Chartreuse, Guillaume de Digulleville, James of Voragine, Jerome, Jordan of Saxony, Laurent d'Orléans, Macarius the Great, Peter of Blois, Richard of Saint-Victor, Heinrich Suso, Thomas à Kempis, and Vegetius. There are original works by John Capgrave, Geoffrey Chaucer, Walter Hilton, Thomas

Hoccleve, Peter Idley, Nicholas Love, John Lydgate, William of
Nassington, Richard Rolle, and Richard Whytford. And there is
a host of anonymous works, some well known, some less so,
which we will not list here since they are all recorded in the
appropriate index. We should note, however, that of all these
collections in English—and there are almost fifty of them—about
a third come from Syon. The reasons for this are clear. Firstly,
Syon was not founded until the fifteenth century, and by that
time a huge amount of literature in English was being produced
and distributed; secondly, more manuscripts have been traced
to Syon than to any of the other nunneries listed in Part II; and
thirdly, the Syon nuns seem to have had a particular interest in
English spiritual writings. This last point is something we shall
discuss further in Chapter 3.

Fifteen volumes—less than 10%—carry *ex libris* inscriptions. The majority of these are in Latin (those from Barking,
Buckland Minchin, Dartford, Denney, Heynings, Marrick, Nuneaton, and Romsey), but we also find examples in French (three
of the manuscripts from Campsey) and in English (Marrick, but
the volume in question also contains two inscriptions in Latin).

Many more of the surviving books—just over a third—
contain inscriptions which indicate either private ownership or
private use. Sometimes we find no more than the name of a nun,
sometimes only her surname,[32] sometimes less than that: her
initials or a monogram.[33] More often, however, there are longer
inscriptions in Latin, English, or French. The most common are
in Latin and take the standard form *Iste liber constat . . .*[34] Next in
popularity are English inscriptions of the type *This book belongs
(longeth/belongyth) to . . .*[35] The rarest are two in French, one in a
volume from Barking and one from Syon. The Barking manuscript was bought for the abbey by its abbess, Sybil de Felton,
from the estate of Philippa Coucy;[36] and the volume from Syon,
a printed book, bears the formula *Cest liure apertient à . . .* , but it
is significant that it also contains the same sentence in English.[37]

In about a dozen cases, however, the inscription specifies
that the nun named has the use of the book only *ad terminum
vitae,* and that after her decease the volume is to pass into the
keeping of the convent. Some of these inscription are in Latin;
some are in English.[38] None is in French. They seem to represent
a compromise between a natural, if sinful, desire for private

ownership and the specific prohibition of such ownership by all the monastic rules.[39]

About a quarter of the surviving manuscripts contain inscriptions indicating the source of the volume. Twenty-eight (17.5%) were gifts or bequests, often given to the house in exchange for prayers.[40] Three were bought for a particular nunnery, and in one case—a lovely Book of Hours from Shaftesbury— we are told the price: it cost 10s.,[41] more than a month's wages for an unskilled labourer at the time. In three other cases, we learn that the volume in question was specifically commissioned by a member of the house for the benefit of the nuns. Sister Emma Winter had an Office of the Dead made for Dartford;[42] Elizabeth Gibbs, abbess of Syon, arranged for William Darker to copy an English translation of the first three books of Thomas à Kempis's *Imitation of Christ*;[43] and, most interesting of all, in 1191–92 Cecily de Chanvill, abbess of Elstow, commissioned a volume of Latin theological works *in eruditionem et profectum conventus sui et ceterorum inspicientium* ('for the instruction and advancement of her convent, and of others who consult it').[44] We shall say more about this volume in our next chapter. As to the other surviving books—about three-quarters of the total—we have no record of their origins.

Before we proceed to an analysis of these statistics, we should perhaps say a word about the cartularies listed in the Appendix to Part II of this study. N. R. Ker and A. G. Watson include only one of these—that of Godstow—among the manuscripts which may be traced with certainty to English nunneries,[45] but there can be little doubt that most, if not all, of the other volumes recorded were kept at their respective houses. There would not have been much point in keeping them elsewhere. In an age in which litigation over land was commonplace, collections of charters, title-deeds, and other *evidentiae* were of major importance and, as we shall see a moment, the greatest care was taken in preserving them.

Cartularies—or cartulary-like materials—from thirty-five houses are listed in the Appendix, though not all have survived. This represents just less than a quarter (actually 24%) of the total number of English nunneries which, as we noted at the beginning of this chapter, was about 144. Such a percentage is considerably less than the comparable figure—about 40%—from men's houses,[46] but I do not think we need look too far to find the reason. The majority of nunneries were small and poor, and once their lands had been distributed to others at the Dissolution, there was little point in keeping collections of charters which were now out of date.[47] In any case, in the opinion of most males of the time, women were just not as important as men, and, with a few notable exceptions, women's houses were likewise considered of little consequence. I would suggest, therefore, that the scarcity of cartularies from English nunneries simply reflects the fact that one does not preserve what one does not value.

Of the thirty-five cartularies and related documents listed in the Appendix, most are in Latin. Three are entirely or partly in English (those from Bruisyard, Crabhouse, and Godstow), and two partly in French (those from Canonsleigh and Crabhouse). To assess the significance of this, however, would take us deep into the question of female literacy in the later Middle Ages, and that is a topic which must be left for discussion until our next chapter.

We must now turn from the presentation of statistics to their interpretation. What, if anything, do these numbers and percentages tell us about the size, content, and characteristics of libraries in English nunneries? The answer, unfortunately, is not a great deal, but the little that can be gleaned is not without interest. Let us consider first the size of the libraries.

The actual number of surviving books which, in England, can be traced with certainty or high probability to any particular house tells us virtually nothing about the size of its library.[48] We saw in Chapter I that the large collections which once were owned by the Cistercians of Meaux or the Austin Friars of York have almost entirely disappeared, and were it not for the fortunate—and fortuitous—survival of the library catalogues, we could never have guessed at the size, variety, and richness of their collections. Far more informative than the actual numbers of survivors are the press-marks which appear on certain volumes, for since the essential principles of library cataloguing differed little from house to house, the *distinctio* and *gradus* assigned to a particular book can often provide a useful indication of the overall size of the collection.

Press-marks, catalogues, and the provision of separate book-rooms seem to have developed concurrently, and although examples of all three can be found dating from the thirteenth century, they become far more common in the century following.[49] Most press-marks take the form of a letter and a number. The letter normally indicates the *distinctio* or book-case (which usually corresponds, albeit loosely, to a particular subject-area) and the number, or *gradus*, locates the book on a particular shelf within the *distinctio*.[50] At the Cistercian abbey of Rievaulx, for example, there were sixteen *distinctiones* ranging from A to Q (I/J being counted as one letter). *Distinctio* A comprised primarily legal works and contained four books; *distinctiones* B and C, with fourteen and thirteen books apiece, were devoted to the writings of Augustine; *distinctio* D, which housed eighteen volumes, contained works of Bernard of Clairvaux, Anselm of Canterbury, and Aelred of Rievaulx, and so on.[51]

Sometimes the system of cataloguing was a little more complex. From the Premonstratensian abbey of Titchfield, for instance, we have a long and detailed catalogue which begins with a description of the Titchfield book-room.[52] There were four book-cases (*columpna*), and each book-case had eight shelves. To each shelf was assigned a letter (A to H and K to Q), and the position of each book on the shelf was indicated by a letter (corresponding to the shelf) and a number (corresponding to its position). In the catalogue which follows, each individual volume is identified by three separate criteria: the *distinctio* (theology, canon law, civil law, medicine, grammar, etc.), the *gradus* (the shelf), and the *numerus* (the actual position of the volume on the shelf). Augustine's *De civitate Dei*, for example, is book number 11 on shelf D in the class *theologia*.[53] But although it is true that each monastery developed its own system, there was a remarkable consistency between them; and until one comes to the late catalogue of Syon, reading medieval library catalogues is like listening to a series of simple variations on the same basic theme.

Only three of the manuscripts listed in Part II of this study contain press-marks, but although the examples are few, they are nevertheless of considerable interest. One of the three is from Barking and the other two from Campsey. The Barking volume contains glossed copies of the Song of Songs and Lamentations and is marked B.3;[54] the volumes from Campsey are both psalters and are marked O.E.94 and D.D.141.[55]

B.3 from Barking need not surprise us. We know from the Barking *Ordinale*[56] that there was a book-cupboard (*armarium*) and a female librarian (*libraria*) at the abbey, and we know that, in accordance with the *Rule of St Benedict*,[57] there was an annual distribution of books. On Monday in the first week of Lent the librarian would spread a carpet (*tapetum*) on the floor of the Chapter House, and each nun would bring in the book she had been given the previous year. The librarian would then seat herself *in medio capituli* and slowly read a list of the book titles and the names of those to whom they had been allocated. On hearing her name, each nun would rise from her seat and place her book on the carpet. If she had read it all, she bowed to the crucifix and returned to her seat; if she had not, she prostrated herself before the abbess and said '*Mea culpa.*' She would then be given an appropriate penance. Following this, and beginning with the abbess, the librarian would make a new distribution of books for the coming year, giving shorter volumes to those whose duties were heavier and more time-consuming, and longer ones to those with less to do. No nun was permitted to leave the Chapter House until she had received her book.[58] The *Ordinale* then adds some notes, in both Latin and French, on how the books were to be treated, not only by the nuns, but also by the children who were boarding in the abbey:[59] they were not to leave them open in choir or cloister; they were not to scribble in them; they were not to cut out leaves; they were not to lose them or lend them to people outside the abbey; and they were to return them at the end of the year in as good a condition as they had received them at the beginning.[60]

The statutory number of nuns at Barking was thirty-seven, but there were times when this number may well have been exceeded. In the fifteenth century, however, the numbers seem to have declined and at the Dissolution there were about thirty.[61] In other words, if each nun was to receive a book, the *armarium* at Barking must have contained at least forty volumes, and the press-mark B.3 is in no way exceptional. The B might possibly have indicated *biblica*, as it did at Bury St Edmunds, but we do not know that, and we have no idea of how many *distinctiones* there were.[62]

The case of the Augustinian priory of Campsey is much more intriguing.[63] The house was moderately wealthy and probably housed about twenty nuns,[64] but no surviving document mentions a book-cupboard or book-room, and we have no record of a librarian. The two press-marks, however, are of great interest:

O.E.94 and D.D.141. Both are fifteenth century, and the psalters in which they appear may both have been acquired second-hand.[65] But if these press-marks represent the usual classification of *distinctio* and *gradus*, they imply that Campsey had a very large library. Just how large we do not know, but if there were at least 94 books in one *distinctio* and 141 in another, and if there were a plurality of *distinctiones*, the library at Campsey might have rivalled that at Christ Church, Canterbury!

Another glimpse—albeit fragmentary—of the size of a nunnery library is provided by an inventory of St Sexburga (or Minster) in Sheppey which was conducted just before the house was dissolved in 1536. The commissioners reported fifty-eight books in the church, seven in the vestry (together with 'dyvers other good bokes'), one in the parlour, and in the lady chapel 'an olde presse full of old boks of no valew'[66]—of no value, that is to say, to the King's commissioners.[67] We do not know how many books the 'olde presse' contained, but it could well have been more than fifty;[68] and we may therefore be certain that the priory of St Sexburga, which was never a wealthy house,[69] owned a minimum of sixty-six books, and quite possibly double that number. Nor can we be sure that those responsible for the inventory included every volume in the possession of the priory.[70] It seems to me, therefore, that there can be little doubt that in some nunneries the book collections were far more extensive than has hitherto been supposed, and such bald and uncompromising statements as 'convents seem to have owned hardly any books'[71] are better avoided.

It is to be regretted that we have no idea of the size of the sisters' library at Syon. That there was one is not in doubt. The *Martyrology of Syon* specifically mentions a *libraria sororum* and *libraria fratrum*;[72] a 1482 Ordinance for Syon refers to 'the kepers of the libraris of the Bretherne and [Sys]terne Sydes there';[73] and the *Additions for the Sisters* of Syon, preserved in B.L., Arundel 146, mentions both the library and 'sche that hath the kepyng of the bokes.'[74] We are told, too, that 'silence after some conuenience, is to be kepte in the lybrary, whyls any suster is there alone in recordyng of her redynge,'[75] and that the younger sisters should help the older and more frail 'in beryng of heuy bokes or of any other grete berdons.'[76] We also know that there must have been a library catalogue, for the *Additions* stipulate that at the time of his visitation, the bishop should enquire 'if ther be an inuentory or register of the bokes of the library.'[77] The catalogue, however, has not survived. That edited by Mary Bateson in 1898 is the catalogue of the brothers' library,[78] and it cannot be taken as a guide to what might have been in the collection of the sisters. Apart from the fact that more than 85% of the collection came to the brothers through donations (and donations are not normally replicated), by the early sixteenth century the tastes of the sisters and brothers had diverged, and different tastes were inevitably reflected in different acquisitions.[79]

The bishop was also to enquire how the books in the library 'and other bokes of study be kepte and repayred,'[80] and that the books of Syon were indeed repaired is clear both from the 1482 Ordinance mentioned above and from the sacristan's account rolls for the first three decades of the sixteenth century.[81] In the Ordinance, the abbess of Syon, Elizabeth Muston, enters into a contract with Thomas Raile, 'nowe keper of the Brethernes locutorie,'[82] that the said Thomas will repair whatever books are delivered to him by the keepers of the brothers' and sisters' library, 'we fyndyng allemaner of stoffe as bordes, couerynges, curreys, hookes or claspes, glewe, and flowre for paaste.'[83] Such attention did not come cheap. The costs stipulated in the Ordinance for 'byndynge' range from 2d. to 8d. per book, and that was in addition to Master Thomas's 'wonte wages of xiijs. iiijd. wyth meete, drynke, and clothynge.'[84] We may suppose, therefore, that the sisters at Syon had a library which was well kept, well catalogued, and well used, but we have no idea how many volumes it contained. The question of its contents is something we will leave for discussion until our next chapter.

Evidence for libraries in other houses is very limited. There was a librarian at Nunnaminster in 1501 (her name was Elia Pitte),[85] and although we may presume that she had a library to administer, we have no idea of its size or content. Five manuscripts have been traced to the house, but none bears any press-mark.

In c. 1432 Dean Kentwode made a visitation of the Benedictine nunnery of St Helen's, Bishopsgate, and was apparently dissatisfied with what he found. The nuns were hurrying through the services, their clothes were too worldly, they entertained too many guests, and the prioress owned too many dogs.[86]

Such complaints were common,[87] but among his subsequent injunctions, the dean required the prioress to show 'who had the custody of the missals, books, and ornaments, and how they were kept.'[88] But apart from that brief reference, nothing more is known of the books at Bishopsgate or of their keeper.

To the best of my knowledge, in fact, it is only at Barking, Syon, and Nunnaminster that we find specific reference to a librarian. This, however, is not of great consequence since we may assume that the books in most women's houses, like those in most men's houses, were the responsibility of the *precentrix* or chantress.[89] Nor is it surprising that specific references to a library are so rare. We saw in Chapter 1 that the majority of English nunneries were financially insecure, and those that owned large numbers of books were almost certainly the exception rather than the rule. For most houses, a single book-cupboard might have sufficed to house the collection, but although there are plenty of *armaria* still to be seen in the ruins of men's houses, the archaeological remains of the English nunneries are so fragmentary that, so far as I am aware, no trace of a book-cupboard has yet been found. Nor does any of the inventories of English nunneries drawn up at the time of the Dissolution mention a library.[90]

On the other hand, books do not take up a great deal of space, and if they were few in number, they might have been kept in a variety of places. A copy of the *Golden Legend* was to be found in the parlour at Minster in Sheppey,[91] and at Cheshunt there was a valuable psalter in the dorter.[92] In any case, a library need not have been called a library. In the houses of Cistercian monks, for example, books were regularly kept in the sacristy, and even when we find a true book-room off the cloister, it need not have been very large.[93] A single aumbry (*armarium*) at Cockersand, a Premonstratensian abbey in Lancashire, contained fifty-four books,[94] and for a small abbey or priory, whether of men or of women, fifty-four books would represent a fair-sized collection.

The fact, then, that specific mention of libraries and librarians is so rare says nothing about the numbers of books a nunnery might have possessed. On the other hand, given that so many of them were so poor, it might have been thought inappropriate for the nuns to be begging on the highways when funds could easily be raised by the sale or pawn of valuable volumes. We saw in Chapter 1 that books were commonly used as pledges and securities for loans, and reports of abbesses pawning or selling nunnery property are not uncommon in the records of episcopal visitations.[95]

Similarly, the value of the books might make them a target for thieves, and we know that early in the fifteenth century the Benedictine priory of Rowney, a small and poor nunnery, was attacked by robbers who carried off the plate and the books, and that as a consequence, the nuns were unable to perform the Offices.[96] Later in the same century, in 1473, the Scots raided the Cumberland nunnery of Armathwaite—also small and poor— stole its goods, relics, ornaments, books, and jewels, and either burnt or carried off its muniments.[97] It is also possible that the nuns themselves were not above temptation in this matter. When Archbishop Corbridge visited Keldholme, a small Cistercian nunnery in Yorkshire, in 1314, he found it necessary to stipulate that 'no nun or other person belonging to the house was to take away books, ornaments or other things belonging to the church, without the express consent of the prioress and the convent.'[98] Again, in 1404, Juliana Bromhall, prioress of Bromhall (a Benedictine house in Berkshire), was accused by her nuns of usurping her position, living an evil life for twenty years, and of appropriating 'to her own nefarious use chalices, books, jewels, and rents and property of the convent.'[99] Juliana resigned the next year. And in 1441, the prioress of Ankerwyke was reported to have 'given away and alienated' some of the ten beautiful psalters, once the property of the house. When questioned on the matter, she admitted that she had 'lent' three, though she maintained that she had done so with the consent of the convent.[100] We should note, however, that such alienation was in no way restricted to women's houses, and that the records of episcopal visitations reveal plenty of monks and abbots who were equally criminous.

Books might also be destroyed by natural disasters or accidents. The most serious, as well as the most common, of these was fire, and at one time or another Bromhall, Buckland Minchin, Castle Hedingham, Catesby, Crabhouse, Cheshunt, Malling, St Bartholomew's, St Leonard's, St Radegund's, Wilton, and Wykeham were all ravaged by fire.[101] Sometimes, as at Wykeham, it is specifically stated that all the books were lost;[102] sometimes, as at Ickleton and Cheshunt, we are told that the charters and muniments had been destroyed.[103] The loss of the charters, we might add, could be extremely serious, for with ever-increasing litigation and the professionalization of the law from the fourteenth century onwards,[104] a loss of documentary evidence could all too easily lead to loss of land. Monastic muniments, therefore, together with the common seal, were kept not in the library or book-cupboard, but in a chest with two or three locks, the different keys being guarded by different obedientiaries.[105] In some cases the chest was actually kept in the abbess's chamber,[106] and so rigorous was the security that in some nunneries, the chest was used as a safety-deposit box by seculars.[107] Such trust, however, might sometimes have been misplaced, for the chest at Ulverscroft, a men's Benedictine priory in Leicestershire, was so frail that a little child (*infantulus*) could have broken into it with no great force and carried off all that it contained.[108]

Books also wore out. The actual parchment on which they were written might have been extremely durable, but the ink could be rubbed off, the clasps which held the books closed might be broken, and the bindings of liturgical volumes were put under continual strain by their constant use in choir.[109] In 1526, for example, the *precentrix* of Campsey told the visitor that the office-books of the abbey needed repair,[110] and at Thetford in 1514 the visitor himself made the suggestion.[111] It was a fairly common problem in houses of both sexes. Occasionally, of course, books might be mutilated deliberately,[112] but this was a rare occurrence and of little significance when compared with the depredations of daily wear and tear.

We have already seen that a rich house like Syon could afford to hire someone on a permanent basis to repair its books, but this would have been manifestly impossible for the poorer houses. A document from 1414 records that the cost for 'mending one old mass book almost worn out; for parchment and new writing in divers parts and for the binding and new clasps, and a skin to cover the book' was no less than 11s. 2p.[113] Few nunneries could have afforded such prices, and episcopal visitors were aware of this. In 1459, for example, Bishop Gray declared an indulgence of forty days for anyone who contributed to the repair of the bell-tower, and the maintenance of books, vestments, and church ornaments at the Benedictine nunnery of St Radegund in Cambridge;[114] but how successful his appeal was, and how many of the books were repaired, is unknown.

It seems, then, that we must be cautious in interpreting the material presented in Part II of this study. We cannot legitimately compare the limited number of manuscripts listed there with the huge collections from the great English cathedrals, and we really have very little idea of just how large or how small were the libraries of the English nunneries. Some—Campsey, for example—may have been much larger than has hitherto been suspected; others, such as those from the poorest of the Cistercian houses, cannot have included more than a few essential volumes. Nor do we know how many books were lost by theft, alienation, fire, or flood; nor have we any idea of how many just wore out; nor do we know how many of these were replaced. A majority—some 53%—of the surviving books listed may be loosely described as liturgical, but we have already seen that this may not necessarily be an accurate reflection of the overall contents of the collections.

It is significant, however, that almost two-thirds of the surviving volumes date from the fifteenth and early sixteenth centuries, and that more than two-thirds of the non-liturgical volumes are written in English. As we saw in Chapter 1, the fifteenth century witnessed a dramatic decrease in the cost of books (though they still remained expensive) and an equally dramatic increase in vernacular literacy; and, as we suggested at the beginning of this chapter, it is most improbable that this is simply coincidence. It is now time to turn our full attention to these matters and examine the questions of the learning—or lack of it—possessed by the English nuns, the languages they used and understood, and the nature and extent of their interests and their reading.

NOTES

1. Power, p. 1.
2. A useful list (but with a different total) is given in R. Midmer, *English Mediaeval Monasteries 1066–1540: A Summary* (Athens, GA, 1979), pp. 357–8. Calculation of the total number is complicated by nunneries which were founded late or which foundered early. As a consequence, the numbers varied somewhat throughout the period.

3. The question of the cartularies listed in the Appendix to Part II will be considered later in this chapter.
4. The printed books at Syon are all in section A, numbers 3, 13, 14, 17, 20, 27, 31, 37, 42 (in part), and 43 (see further C. F. R. de Hamel, *Syon Abbey. The Library of the Bridgettine Nuns and Their Peregrinations After the Reformation* [Roxburghe Club, 1991], pp. 101–2). The others are to be found at Barking, Bruisyard, Campsey, Edinburgh, Ickleton (in part), Polsloe, and Stamford. The two volumes which are part manuscript and part printed book (ICKLETON 1 and SYON A.42) have each been counted twice, both as manuscript as a printed volume. The volumes belonging to William Pownsett, a former steward of Barking, were (I suspect) all printed books and some of them may once have formed part of the Barking library. Unfortunately, the list presents special problems and the reader is referred to BARKING (APPENDIX) for a discussion of the matter.
5. See Ker, pp. x–xv. The only notable exception is the Augustinian priory of Lanthony *iuxta Gloucestriam* (see Ker, pp. 108–12, and Watson, pp. 41–3).
6. *Ibid.*, p. xi.
7. *Ibid.*, pp. 88–89, and Watson, p. 37.
8. WINCHESTER 3 (The Book of Nunnaminster).
9. Derek Pearsall's introduction to *Book Production and Publishing in Britain 1375–1475*, ed. J. Griffiths & D. Pearsall (Cambridge, 1989), p. 7. H. S. Bennett, 'The Production and Dissemination of Vernacular Manuscripts in the Fifteenth Century, *The Library*, Ser. 5, 1 (1946–47), p. 172, speaks of that century as 'an age interested in literature'.
10. C. L. Kingsford, *Prejudice and Promise in Fifteenth Century England* (Oxford, 1925; rpt. London, 1962), p. 42.
11. There are obviously overlaps between some of these categories, especially between psalters and calendars, calendars and obituaries, psalters and *horae*, and psalters and the Office of the Dead. In those cases where a manuscript contains two quite separate items—a psalter and a hymnal, for example—I have counted both; otherwise, I have classified the volumes according to the principal work or overall impression.
12. The next most numerous group, the breviaries, are far behind with only nine examples or just over 10%.
13. See C. Wordsworth & H. Littlehales, *The Old Service-Books of the English Church* (London, 1904), pp. 108–13. The canticles are listed in *ibid.*, p. 109 (which should be supplemented by the account in the *Oxford Dictionary of the Christian Church*, ed. F. L. Cross [London,

1958], pp. 232–3), but medieval psalters do not always include them all.

14. GODSTOW 1.
15. See W. P. Cummings, *The Revelations of Saint Birgitta* (EETS/OS, 178; London, 1929), pp. xxxvii–xxxviii, and J. T. Rhodes, 'Syon Abbey and its Religious Publications in the Sixteenth Century', *Journal of Ecclesiastical History* 44 (1993), pp. 13–14. See also Index IV s.v. Fifteen Oes of St Bridget, listing examples from Barking, Godstow, London (Aldgate), Malling, Syon, and Tarrant Keynston.
16. HAMPOLE 1.
17. These are the De Brailes Hours (B.L., Add. 49999), which probably date from sometime between 1230 and 1260. We should note, however, that the library catalogue of Rievaulx, which dates from c. 1190–1200, also lists a separate *Horae de sancta Maria* (D. N. Bell, *The Libraries of the Cistercians, Gilbertines and Premonstratensians* [Corpus of British Medieval Library Catalogues, 3; London, 1992], p. 119 [Z19. 217c]).
18. 'What had started as an accretion to the Breviary,' writes John Harthan, 'became the favourite prayerbook of layfolk everywhere' (J. Harthan, *Books of Hours and Their Owners* [London, 1977], p. 13]). The best introduction to Books of Hours is now R. S. Wieck, *The Book of Hours in Medieval Art and Life* (London, 1988).
19. See Wieck, *The Book of Hours*, pp. 33–4, and S. G. Bell, 'Medieval Women Book Owners: Arbiters of Lay Piety and Ambassadors of Culture', in *Sisters and Workers in the Middle Ages*, ed. J. M. Bennett *et al.* (Chicago/London, 1989), pp. 146–8.
20. See, for example, CARROW 1, HAMPOLE 1, MARKYATE 1, SHAFTESBURY 4, 5, and 6, SYON A.18 and A.33, TARRANT KEYNSTON 3, WILTON 2, and BRUISYARD 1, with its beautiful embroidered binding. On nuns' embroidery, see Power, pp. 255–8.
21. See further de Hamel, *Syon Abbey* (n. 4), pp. 49–51, 126, 128.
22. WINTNEY 1.
23. NUNEATON 2.
24. SYON A.11.
25. SYON A.7 and A.17.
26. DARTFORD 8. There *may* have been printed editions of Virgil and Cicero at Barking, but this is not certain: see BARKING (APPENDIX) 1 for discussion.
27. LACOCK 1.
28. The reader is referred to Index II.
29. See LONDON (ALDGATE) MR a. For other bequests of books in French, see DENNEY MR and MALLING MR.
30. See CAMPSEY 5: 'Cest liuere <est> deviseie a la priorie de Kampseie de lire a mengier.'

31. Some are listed in the introductory comments to BARKING 13.
32. As in SYON A.16.
33. As in SYON A.21 and A.29.
34. There are eleven of these. Other Latin formulae are *Iste liber est . . .* and *Iste liber pertinet . . .*
35. Other English formulae are *Thys boke perteyneth to . . .* and *Thys boke ys myne*, followed by a name.
36. BARKING 15.
37. SYON A.31.
38. BARKING 14, BRUISYARD 1, CAMPSEY 2, DARTFORD 1 and 7, LACOCK *MR* a, LONDON (HOLYWELL) 1, LONDON (ALD-GATE) 1, 2, 5, and 6. The same condition is sometimes stated in bequests: see, for example, BROADHOLME *MR*. When Elizabeth Darcy left her *portiforium* and psalter to Heynings, she made sure they would not be removed by stipulating that they be chained in the church (HEYNINGS *MR*).
39. See further Chapter 1, n. 92.
40. Good examples are GORING 1, LONDON (HOLYWELL) 1, LON-DON (ALDGATE) 2 and 5, and SHAFTESBURY 3.
41. SHAFTESBURY 1.
42. DARTFORD 5.
43. SYON A.19. The Syon sisters, in fact, commissioned a number of books: see Chapter 3, nn. 137–145.
44. ELSTOW 1.
45. GODSTOW 2 (Ker, p. 93).
46. To achieve such a comparable figure we must omit cartularies from those men's houses which have no female equivalents: i.e., from chantries, houses of secular canons, cathedrals, dioceses, parishes, parish churches, collegiate churches, guilds, university colleges, the military orders, hospitals, and various friaries.
47. See further S. Thompson, *Women Religious: The Founding of English Nunneries after the Norman Conquest* (Oxford, 1991), pp. 7–15. Thompson may inadvertently give the impression that fewer cartularies survive than is actually the case, but it must be remembered that her study is concerned only with the twelfth and early thirteenth centuries.
48. See Ker, p. xi.
49. For a brief account, see F. Wormald, 'The Monastic Library', in *The English Library Before 1700*, ed. F. Wormald & C. E. Wright (London, 1958), pp. 22–6.
50. See Wormald, pp. 22–6; Ker, pp. xviii–xix; M. R. James, *The Ancient Libraries of Canterbury and Dover* (Cambridge, 1903), pp. xxxviii–xliv; and, for a useful general survey, K. Christ, revd. A. Kern, tr.

T. M. Otto, _The Handbook of Medieval Library History_ (Metuchen/ London, 1984), pp. 35–45.

51. See Bell, _Libraries_ (n. 17), p. 89.
52. The catalogue is edited in _ibid._, pp. 180–254. For the description of the book-room, see p. 183 (English translations may be found in H. M. Colvin, _The White Canons in England_ [Oxford, 1951], pp. 317–8; J. W. Clark, _The Care of Books_ [Cambridge, 1902²; rpt. London, 1975], pp. 77–9, and elsewhere).
53. Bell, _Libraries_ (n. 17), p. 196 (P6. 56).
54. BARKING 12.
55. CAMPSEY 1 and 3.
56. BARKING 14.
57. _Regula S. Benedicti_ 48.15–16 (SCh 182, p. 602): 'In quibus diebus quadragesimae accipiant omnes singulos codices de bibliotheca, quos per ordinem ex integro legant; qui codices in caput quadragesimae dandi sunt.'
58. For the Latin text, see J. B. L. Tolhurst, _The Ordinale and Customary of the Benedictine Nuns of Barking Abbey_ (Henry Bradshaw Society, 65–66; London, 1927–28), vol. 1, pp. 67–8. An earlier edition was published by P. Gambier, 'Lending Books in a Mediaeval Nunnery', _Bodleian Quarterly Record_ 5 (1927), pp. 188–90.
59. See Chapter 1, n. 17.
60. Tolhurst, p. 68; Gambier, p. 190.
61. See Knowles/Hadcock, p. 256, and VCH _Essex_, vol. 2, pp. 115–22.
62. For the _biblica_ at Bury, see Ker, p. xix. Whether any or all of the 29 volumes owned by William Pownsett had once formed part of the Barking library is uncertain: see BARKING (APPENDIX) for discussion.
63. We should note at the beginning of our discussion of Campsey that the Augustinian customs placed considerable emphasis on reading: see J. C. Dickinson, _The Origins of the Austin Canons and Their Introduction into England_ (London, 1950), pp. 186–7.
64. See Knowles/Hadcock, p. 279, and VCH _Suffolk_, vol. 2, pp. 112–5.
65. CAMPSEY 1 is s.xiii and CAMPSEY 3 is s.xiv. The two volumes have identical French _ex libris_ inscriptions, and there is no reason to suppose that the press-marks were added either before or after the books came into the possession of the nunnery.
66. See MINSTER IN SHEPPEY MR.
67. See Chapter 1, nn. 114–119. Eight of the books in the church at Minster are recorded as having silver clasps; the others were clearly of no interest.
68. See n. 94 below, referring to the contents of a single _armarium_ at Cockersand.

69. See VCH *Kent*, vol. 2, pp. 149–50. In the second half of the thirteenth century the house was in dire straits, but its fortunes seem to have recovered somewhat during the 1400's. The *Valor Ecclesiasticus* reports a net value of £129:7:10½ in 1535 (*ibid.*, p. 150), but at that time more than three-quarters of the English nunneries were worth less (see Chapter 1, p. 11).

70. It is unusual for such inventories, whether of men's or women's houses, to list any but the most valuable volumes, and if there were other books at Sheppey which the commissioners regarded as no more than out-of-date rubbish, they might not have bothered to record them.

71. M. D. Legge, *Anglo-Norman in the Cloisters: The Influence of the Orders upon Anglo-Norman Literature* (Edinburgh, 1950), p. 49 (citing Power, pp. 241–2). Cf. M. Deanesly, *The Lollard Bible and Other Medieval Biblical Versions* (Cambridge, 1920; rpt. 1966), p. 341.

72. B.L., Add. 22285, fol. 17v; M. Bateson, *Catalogue of the Library of Syon Monastery Isleworth* (Cambridge, 1898), p. xxviii.

73. R. J. Whitwell, 'An Ordinance for Syon Library, 1482', *English Historical Review* 25 (1910), p. 121.

74. J. Hogg, *The Rewyll of Seynt Sauioure, Vol. 4: The Syon Additions for the Sisters from the British Library Ms. Arundel 146* (Salzburger Studien zur Anglistik and Amerikanistik, 6/4; Salzburg, 1980), p. 1, line 15.

75. *Ibid.*, p. 72, lines 9–11.

76. *Ibid.*, p. 154, lines 6–7. See further A. M. Hutchison, 'Devotional Reading in the Monastery and in the Late Medieval Household', in *De Cella in Seculum: Religious and Secular Life and Devotion in Late Medieval England*, ed. M. G. Sargent (Cambridge, 1989), pp. 217–8. The important place occupied by reading at Syon is admirably illustrated in *The Myroure of oure Ladye*, ed. J. H. Blunt (EETS/ES, 19; London, 1873; rpt. New York, 1973), pp. 65–71. The author considers the spiritual value of reading, the selection of books, the attitude of the reader, the amount that should be read at one time, the effects that books can have, and how his own book— the *Myroure*—should be used. See further Hutchison, 'Devotional Reading', pp. 219–24.

77. *Additions for the Sisters* (n. 74), p. 42, lines 13–14.

78. See Chapter 1, n. 90.

79. See Chapter 3, n. 147.

80. *Additions for the Sisters*, p. 42, lines 14–15.

81. See M. C. Erler, 'Syon Abbey's Care for Books: Its Sacristan's Account Rolls 1506/7–1535/6', *Scriptorium* 39 (1985), pp. 293–307.

82. The locutory, says Mary Erler, 'could be either the grate through which conversation with visitors was allowed, or the parlor in which it took place' ('Syon Abbey's Care for Books', p. 295, n. 15).

83. Whitwell, 'Ordinance for Syon' (n. 73), pp. 122–3. For further discussion of this Ordinance, see Erler, 'Syon Abbey's Care for Books', *passim*, and de Hamel, *Syon Abbey* (n. 4), pp. 83–90.

84. Whitwell, 'Ordinance for Syon', pp. 122–3. A great deal of detailed information on the cost of repairs may be found in Erler's study cited at n. 81 above, especially p. 299.

85. VCH *Hampshire and the Isle of Wight*, vol. 2, p. 124; Power, p. 241.

86. VCH *London*, vol. 1, pp. 458–9.

87. See Power, pp. 291–314. It must be stressed, however, that such problems were just as common in men's houses.

88. VCH *London*, vol. 1, p. 459.

89. See Christ, *Handbook of Medieval Library History* (n. 50), pp. 26–8, and F. A. Gasquet, *English Monastic Life* (London, 1924[6]), pp. 58–65. The primary responsibility of the *precentor* or *precentrix* was the direction and conduct of all offices sung in choir, but since this included the care and correction of all the service books, it was not unreasonable to extend his or her duties to other books as well. There is a good description of the role of the chantress in the *Syon Additions for the Sisters*, ed. J. Hogg, pp. 147–150 (see especially p. 149, lines 19–24). See also de Hamel, *Syon Abbey* (n. 4), pp. 69–70.

90. It is important to remember that these inventories (see Power, p. 698, though that list is not complete) are usually very detailed.

91. MINSTER IN SHEPPEY *MR*.

92. CHESHUNT *MR*. The volume was valued at £3:6:8, a very considerable sum.

93. See Clark, *Care of Books* (n. 52), pp. 70–82. At Valle Crucis, at one time the richest Cistercian abbey in Wales (though its fortunes varied), there is a book-room built into the thickness of the west wall of the chapter house which measures 2.8m in length, 2.8m in height, and 0.75m in breadth. Not all this space could be used, however, for a doorway divides the room into two bays, each about 0.9m x 0.75m (I am indebted to Professor Geoffrey Leytham for providing me with the dimensions of the Valle Crucis book-room). On the other hand, it seems that not every Cistercian house possessed a library. When George Elsworthy, rector of Exford, left all his books to the abbey of Cleeve in 1532, he did so on condition that within one year after his death, the monks should make a *librarium* to house them (F. W. Weaver, *Wells Wills* [London, 1890], pp. 84–5). Lack of a library, however, could be disastrous: at Fotheringhay College in 1438, one of the monks complained that because the

library (*libraria*) had not yet been built, the books of the college were being destroyed by dust and worms (*per pulveres et vermes*) (*Visitations of Religious Houses in the Diocese of Lincoln, Vol. 2: Records of Visitations held by William Alnwick, A.D. 1436–1449, Part 1* ed. A. H. Thompson [Canterbury and York Society, 24; London, 1919; rpt. 1969], p. 98).

94. *The Chartulary of Cockersand Abbey of the Premonstratensian Order*, ed. W. Farrer (Chetham Society, N.S. 56; Manchester, 1905), vol. 3, pt. 1, p. 1172 (inventory of 1536).

95. See Power, pp. 83–8, to which might be added cases of alienation at Bungay (VCH *Suffolk*, vol. 2, p. 81), Shaftesbury (VCH *Dorset*, vol. 2, p. 78), and elsewhere. Even wealthy Syon had to stipulate that abbesses were not to alienate the goods of the house, and that if they did, they were to be deprived of their office (*Syon Additions for the Sisters*, ed. J. Hogg, p. 202, lines 18–24). See also nn. 98–100 below.

96. VCH *Hertfordshire*, vol. 4, p. 434.

97. VCH *Cumberland*, vol. 2, p. 191.

98. VCH *Yorkshire*, vol. 3, p. 168.

99. VCH *Berkshire*, vol. 2, p. 80. See also Power, p. 87.

100. See ANKERWYKE *MR* a.

101. See Power, pp. 171–2, supplemented by Thompson, *Women Religious*, pp. 11–12, n. 28. Thompson, p. 12, states that 'at Ickleton the records of the prioress were said to have been destroyed in the rebellion of 1381,' but her reference to VCH *Cambridgeshire*, vol. 6, p. 232 is incorrect. VCH *Cambridgeshire*, vol. 2, p. 224 (the correct citation) actually says that 'in the riots of 1381 James Hogg of Ickleton, and others, burnt all the prioress's court rolls and documents on Sunday, 16 June, apparently the only case in Cambridgeshire in which the property of a nunnery was destroyed.'

102. VCH *Yorkshire*, vol. 3, p. 183; Power, p. 172.

103. See n. 101 above (Ickleton), and VCH *Hertfordshire*, vol. 4, p. 426 (Cheshunt).

104. See Chapter 1, n. 31.

105. The chest at Nunnaminster, for example, had three locks, the keys being kept by the abbess, prioress, and sacrist (VCH *Hampshire and the Isle of Wight*, vol. 2, p. 124). That at Syon had two (see R. Dunning, 'The Muniments of Syon Abbey: Their Administration and Migration in the Fifteenth and Sixteenth Centuries', *Bulletin of the Institute of Historical Research* 37 [1964], p. 105). For other examples, see *Visitations of Religious Houses in the Diocese of Lincoln, Vol. 2, Part 1* (n. 93), p. 6 (Ankerwyke), VCH *Nottinghamshire*, vol. 2, p. 139 (Broadholme), and elsewhere.

106. See CHESHUNT *MR*.
107. Such was the case at Romsey: see VCH *Hampshire and the Isle of Wight*, vol. 2, p. 128.
108. *Visitations of Religious Houses in the Diocese of Lincoln, Vol. 3: Records of Visitations held by William Alnwick, A.D. 1436–1449, Part 2* ed. A. H. Thompson (Canterbury and York Society, 33; London, 1927; rpt. 1969), p. 388.
109. The variety of repairs required is admirably illustrated in Whitwell's 'Ordinance for Syon' (n. 73), pp. 121–3, and Erler's 'Syon Abbey's Care for Books' (n. 81), *passim*.
110. VCH *Suffolk*, vol. 2, p. 114.
111. VCH *Norfolk*, vol. 2, p. 355 = VCH *Suffolk*, vol. 2, p. 86 (Thetford appears in two counties).
112. At Greetham, for example, Robert Freeman cut out a folio from a manuscript (*Visitations in the Diocese of Lincoln 1517–1531, Vol. 1: Visitations of Rural Deaneries by William Atwater, Bishop of Lincoln, and his Commissaries, 1517–1520*, ed. A. H. Thompson [Lincoln Record Society, 33; Hereford, 1940 (for 1936)], p. 67), and at Blackbourton an unnamed *curatus* mutilated a *portiforium* in anger (*ibid.*, p. 133). I cannot recall an example from a women's house, but such mutilation was specifically prohibited at Barking (see n. 60) and at Syon (see the *Syon Additions for the Sisters*, ed. J. Hogg, p. 2, lines 16–17).
113. W. L. Schramm, 'The Cost of Books in Chaucer's Time', *Modern Language Notes* 48 (1933), p. 142.
114. VCH *Cambridgeshire*, vol. 2, p. 219.

CHAPTER 3:
LITERACY AND LEARNING

W
E WILL be concerned in this chapter with three languages: Latin, French, and English. Latin may be regarded as the constant, for whether written or spoken, it remained the language of the liturgy and of learning throughout the Middle Ages. French was the native language of the Norman aristocrats who settled in England after 1066, and English—Middle English—was the child of this Norman-French father and an Anglo-Saxon mother. Within a generation or two, most of the Norman aristocracy would have been bilingual, speaking French among themselves and English to their servants and social inferiors. French was also the literary language of the aristocratic laity, and it is now recognized that Anglo-Norman (or, more accurately, Anglo-French[1]) is a language all of its own, and not just bad Parisian.[2] In sum, if we may quote Sir William Holdsworth, 'in the thirteenth century learned clerks may have thought and spoken in Latin; ordinary persons of the upper classes thought and spoke in French, while the lower classes spoke in various dialects of English.'[3]

In the course of the following century, however, English was dramatically transformed from a language of servility to a literary language of great charm and versatility. This is the era of Chaucer, of Langland, of *Gawain and the Green Knight*, and of the great English mystics: Rolle, Hilton, Julian of Norwich, and the anonymous author of *The Cloud of Unknowing*. At this time, although French was still commonly used and understood, it was fighting a losing battle against the ever increasing popularity of the native tongue.

By the middle of the fifteenth century the battle had been lost, and French had been almost entirely superseded.[4] The process had actually begun two centuries earlier when, in 1258, Henry III issued his proclamation on the Provisions of Oxford in English, but, as may be expected, it took time for the new movement to gain ground. A century later, however, in 1362, a statute was enacted which stated that henceforth pleas in the law-courts should not be made in French, 'which is much unknown in the realm,' but 'shall be pleaded, shewed, defended, answered, debated, and judged' in English,[5] and English, by this time, had clearly become the dominant language. The earliest of the Paston letters to be written in English is dated 1424, some sixty years after the statute of 1362, and the last letter in French (apart from a legal document from Jersey) dates from 1426.[6]

As living languages, both French and English would normally have been learned by children as children learn any living language: they would have picked them up from their parents and their peers. But as French began to yield to English, such informal instruction became progressively more rare, and medieval children in England, like modern children in England, found themselves learning French as a foreign tongue.[7] This, of course, had always been the case with Latin.

The studies by Nicholas Orme have revealed to us in fascinating detail the number and nature of schools in medieval England,[8] but such schools were intended for the education of boys, not girls. They were, for the most part, run by clerks for clerks, and their primary purpose was to provide instruction in the reading and writing of Latin. Boys began with reading and singing liturgical texts; they progressed to the study of grammar; they then moved on to verse and prose composition and Latin conversation; and concluded their studies (if indeed they went that far, and provided the school-master were capable) by reading selections from Latin literature and learning the basic principles of literary criticism.[9] How successful they were depended, naturally, upon the qualifications of the teacher and their own enthusiasm, but for most of those who wished to further their careers by attending the universities of Oxford or Cambridge, the grammar schools were a necessary preparation.[10] Once at university, the student could gain the recognition he needed to enter the higher—and more profitable—ranks of the clergy or civil service. As Thomas Gaisford observed in a Good Friday sermon preached many centuries later, 'The advantages of a classical education are two-fold—it enables us to look down with contempt on those who have not shared its advantages, and also fits us for places of emolument not only in this world, but in that which is to come.'[11] *Plus ça change, plus c'est la même chose.*

The education of women was, in general, far more re-stricted.[12] Before the rise of the universities, girls and boys in noble households may have shared the attentions of a tutor or domestic chaplain, and the limits of such private education might have been determined only by the capacities of the students or the consent of their parents.[13] But once the universities had been established as a necessary route to high office (and we must remember that a boy would enter the Faculty of Arts at the age of fourteen or fifteen), it became far more difficult for women to gain any sort of higher education at all. The universities were, of course, barred to them, and few fathers would have been prepared to retain a private tutor to teach their daughters what—in the fathers' view—were useless accomplishments. It may be that in certain noble households domestic chaplains made greater contributions than has generally been supposed, but there can be little doubt that, whatever it may have done for men, the development of the universities had a unfortunate impact on the education of women.

Less than noble women had even fewer opportunities. A small number might have been able to join their male colleagues in one of the public grammar schools[14] and receive instruction from a school-master or, in rare cases, school-mistress;[15] but for the majority of women of the middle and upper-middle classes, their only schooling was that provided by the English nunneries.[16] Opportunities for women of the lower classes were effectively non-existent. We must now, therefore, turn our attention to the nunneries and examine the sort of schooling they might have provided; and since the achievements of students invariably reflect the qualifications of their teachers, we shall begin our investigation by inquiring into the learning and literacy of the nuns themselves. Once again we are concerned with three languages—Latin, French, and English—and once again we shall consider them in that order.

We must start by clarifying the term 'literacy', for there is obviously a world of difference between being able to read the words of a simple Latin prayer with no comprehension of what one is saying, and being able to read, understand, and enjoy a letter of Augustine of Hippo or Bernard of Clairvaux. There is also a major difference between being able to read and understand someone else's letter, and being able to compose and

write one's own.[17] When speaking of Latin literacy, therefore, it
is best to divide it into a number of levels. The first and simplest
level is the ability to read a text without understanding it (this
is not difficult in Latin and requires only a few minutes of instruction); the second level is to read and understand a common
liturgical text; the third level involves reading and understanding
non-liturgical texts or less common texts from the liturgy; and
the fourth level is the ability to compose and write a text of
one's own.

That some nuns (and monks) could read and sing, yet not
understand what they were reading and singing, is not in doubt.
Even at Syon, that house of learning, there were unlettered sisters, and the anonymous author of *The Mirror of Our Lady* directs
his first preface to them:

> Forasmoche as many of you, though ye can synge and rede,
> yet ye can not se what the meanynge therof ys: therefore to
> the onely worshyp and praysyng of oure lorde Iesu chryste
> and of hys moste mercyfull mother oure lady and to the
> gostly comforte and profyte of youre soules I haue drawen
> youre legende and all youre seruyce in to Englyshe, that ye
> shulde se by the vnderstondyng therof, how worthy and
> holy praysynge of oure gloryous Lady is contente therin,
> & the more deuoutely and knowyngly synge yt & rede yt
> and say yt to her worshyp.[18]

What the author of the *Mirror* did for the Bridgettine Breviary, Richard Whytford did for the Martyrology, for there were
those (he said) who 'rede the same martiloge in latyn, not vn-
derstandynge what they redde.'[19] If this were the case at Syon,
we may assume that it would also have been the case at many
other less learned houses; and when bishops enjoined that nuns
should not be admitted to the choir unless they could read and
sing,[20] we may suspect that some of them could do no more
than that.[21]

On the other hand, if one could read at all, continual expo-
sure to the offices of the church might well have provided a man
or woman with some basic Latin and a general idea of how the
language worked.[22] Medieval school-masters always used liturgical texts—especially the psalter or primer[23]—as basic school-
books for learning Latin,[24] and we have no reason to believe

that the majority of nuns in choir had no idea what they were singing. In other words, we have now arrived at the second level of literacy: the reading and understanding of common liturgical texts. But even if one did pick up a little Latin in this way, it need not have been correct. It is not difficult to learn that *Pater noster, qui es in caelis* means 'Our Father, which art in heaven,' but without further instruction one might reasonably assume that *Pater* means 'our' and *noster* means 'father'.

To understand that this is not the case, and that Latin fathers precede their pronouns while English fathers follow them, requires some appreciation—albeit minimal—of the rules of Latin syntax, and this leads us naturally to a consideration of the third level of literacy: the ability to read and understand a non-liturgical text or a less common text from the liturgy. Were there nuns who could do this? The answer is certainly yes, but their numbers are unknown, and much seems to have depended upon the century in which they lived and the nunnery in which they dwelt. There is no reason to suppose that the Latin volumes listed in Index III of this study were kept in the nunneries purely for decoration, and when the vicar of Swine donated a dozen books to the local convent, he presumably thought they would have been used.[25]

If, however, we look a little more closely at the provenances of the Latin manuscripts listed in Index III—excluding for the moment the Swine donation and the books belonging to William Pownsett, which might or might not have once formed part of the Barking library—the results are interesting. Seven of them come from Syon, four from Barking, and three from Dartford; and Syon, Barking, and Dartford were all aristocratic institutions with long traditions of learning. All the other houses to which non-liturgical books in Latin have been traced—Elstow, Heynings, Horton, Lacock, Nuneaton, Polsloe (probably), Romsey, Swine, Wherwell, Winchester, and Wintney—are represented by no more than single volumes. Let us therefore continue our enquiry by looking a little more closely at Syon, Barking, and Dartford.

It is possible, as A. Jefferies Collins has pointed out, that 'at Syon the curriculum of the novices may have included Latin lessons from the first',[26] and we know of a number of nuns at the house who seem to have had little difficulty in reading and

appreciating Latin theology. Joan Sewell, who was professed at
the abbey in 1500, owned a printed edition of Walter Hilton's
Ladder of Perfection,[27] and also, at some time, had in her possession two manuscripts of Latin works by Richard Rolle.[28] Dorothy
Coderington, a nun of Syon at the time of its suppression in 1539
and a member of the house during the Marian revival, owned,
annotated, and corrected a printed copy of *The Tree and Twelve
Fruits of the Holy Ghost*.[29] Clemence Tresham who, like Dorothy
Codrington, was also a nun at the abbey both before and after its
suppression, owned the manuscript which contains the unique
copy of John Cressener's *Sawter of Mercy* (a devotional work
which, despite its title, was composed in Latin)[30] and also a
copy of the 1523 Paris edition of the *opera omnia* of Thomas à
Kempis.[31] And Catherine Palmer, a remarkable young woman
who led her nuns out from Syon into the wilderness of Antwerp
and Dendermonde before being appointed abbess of the restored
community in 1557, wrote her name in a printed copy of Laurentius Surius's Latin translation of the sermons of Johann Tauler.[32]
The record is not unimpressive.

With regard to Barking, we have already discussed its
library and annual book-distribution, but we also have clear
evidence that, in the second half of the twelfth century, at least
one sister was fully capable of reading and understanding a Latin
text. Sometime between 1163 and 1169 an anonymous nun of the
abbey took Aelred of Rievaulx's *Life of St Edward the Confessor*
and turned it from Latin into Anglo-Norman verse.[33] The poem
which resulted is no masterpiece (the author's piety was greater
than her poetry), but for the moment we are less concerned with
the quality of her verse than with her aptitude for Latin. She
seems to have had no difficulty in understanding Aelred's text,
though where she learned the language in unknown. It might, of
course, have been through a private tutor (for a nun of Barking,
fluent in Anglo-Norman, could only have come from a noble
family); but we do not know that, and it is also—if not equally—
possible that she learned the language at Barking itself. To what
extent the study of the language was continued at Barking in later
centuries is a question to which we shall return as little later.

As for Dartford, it was the only priory of Dominican nuns
in England and seems to have lived up to the Dominican reputation. It was well known locally as a place of education and was

certainly offering instruction in Latin as late as the last decades of the fifteenth century. In 1481 a Sister Jane Fisher of Dartford was permitted to have a preceptor in grammar and Latin,[34] and the instruction she received was not provided for her alone: a number of pupils, both old and young, assembled in the common parlour and they included not only other nuns and novices, but also the daughters, and, it seems, the sons of the local gentry.[35]

The Latin volumes which have survived from Syon, Barking, and Dartford, however, do not exhaust the list, and although the other houses we have mentioned are represented by only single manuscripts, we must never forget that the number of surviving books from any particular house is, as N. R. Ker has said, usually a matter of chance.[36] The fact that one volume of Latin works survives from, say, Elstow, tells us nothing whatever about the size or content of its library. How many other books in Latin were to be found there is wholly unknown, but there is no reason to doubt either their existence or that they were used. The long Latin inscription in the Elstow manuscript tells us that Abbess Cecily de Chanvill commissioned the volume *in eruditionem et profectum conventus sui et ceterorum inspicientium* ('for the instruction and advancement of her convent, and of others who consult it'),[37] and if the book really were commissioned *in eruditionem conventus sui*, we may presume that there were those at Elstow who could have profited from its use. The same was probably true of the books donated to Swine, and we cannot assume that the other volumes from the other houses—Horton, Lacock, Nuneaton, and so on—simply lay on their shelves unremarked and unread.

More nuns than we suppose might have been able to construe a Latin text, and more nunneries than we suspect might have taught the language. This was certainly the case at Romsey and Wilton, for Queen Maud, the first wife of Henry I, received her early education there and was trained in 'letters' (*littera*) as well as *foemineum pectus*.[38] In later life she was one of the most learned women of her generation, corresponding in excellent Latin with popes and archbishops, and earning the esteem of Hildebert of Le Mans.[39] It is difficult to believe that Barking would not also have offered such training, and it is perfectly possible that many of those medieval women who were fluent in Latin—the sister of Aelred of Rievaulx,[40] for example, or the mother of Baldwin of Forde,[41] or Eve, the companion of Goscelin[42]—either acquired or improved their facility in the language in some nunnery. On the other hand, of course, it is also possible that they acquired or improved it by private tuition— Maud, after all, was of noble birth and Aelred's sister's father was a priest—but we must always remember that one possibility does not necessarily preclude another, and the existence of Latin theological texts in English nunneries cannot be written off simply as irrelevant coincidence.

Aelred's sister, however, together with Baldwin's mother, Goscelin's companion, Henry's wife, and the anonymous nun of Barking all belonged to the twelfth century, and by the close of the century following the situation had changed. The twelfth century, as Malcolm Parkes has pointed out, was 'the turning-point in the history of lay literacy',[43] but lay literacy was generally vernacular literacy; and as vernacular literacy increased in the course of the thirteenth and subsequent centuries, Latin literacy declined. Why bother learning a foreign language when there is enough to read in your own? Clerics, of course, had no choice in the matter, but since most of the literate laity preferred to be entertained in the vernacular rather than educated in Latin, the latter was a language they could happily do without. The decline in the learning of Latin occurred both inside and outside the cloister, and there can be no doubt that from the end of the thirteenth century, the number of lay religious, both male and female, who could read and understand a Latin text became an ever increasing minority.

Until about 1300, bishops could send their injunctions to nunneries couched in Latin, but from the end of the thirteenth century they found it necessary to include a version in French and, later, in English.[44] And although it must not be forgotten that men's monasteries of the same period could also boast large numbers of ignorant monks,[45] and that there, too, episcopal injunctions had to be read *in lingua vulgari et materna*,[46] it is clear that in men's houses there was no major difficulty in finding clerics who could deal with a Latin document. Had nuns been able to become clerics, of course, the situation in the nunneries would have been very different, but since they could not, there is little point in our indulging in opiate dreams.

We know, too, of numerous cases where ignorance of Latin on the part of nuns led to legal difficulties. The intention of the anonymous translator of the Godstow cartulary was to provide the nuns with an English version of their records and charters so that unscrupulous manipulators could not take advantage of them;[47] and in 1535, shortly before the Dissolution, the prioress of Harrold was tricked by Lord Mordaunt into affixing her seal to a Latin document of which she could not understand a single word.[48] Again, the problems were not restricted to women—at Langley, in 1440, neither the abbess nor her chaplain could understand the bishop's Latin mandate[49]—but they were certainly more pronounced.

On the other hand, the plea that the nuns were ignorant of Latin might occasionally have been no more than a convenient ploy. At Farewell in 1331, for example, the bishop sent his injunctions in French and specifically stated his reason for doing so: 'because the nuns had pleaded their difficulty in understanding Latin as their excuse for not fully obeying the decree after the previous visitation.'[50] Precisely the same thing happened at Elstow in 1421–22, save that the bishop used English and not French,[51] and once again it is well to remember that such convenient ignorance was not restricted to women. When Bishop Alnwick sent his injunctions to the Benedictine monks of Humberstone Abbey in July 1440, he not only commanded that they be read publicly in chapter four times a year, but that they be read in 'the language which is best understood, lest any one among you be able to pretend ignorance of them.'[52]

There is also clear evidence that in some nunneries the study and use of Latin was continued well into the fourteenth and fifteenth centuries, and, certainly at Syon and possibly at Barking, even later. In 1316 the abbess of Romsey apparently had no difficulty in reading muniment rolls;[53] three years later, at Polsloe and Canonsleigh, the bishop required any nun who wished to speak during periods of obligatory silence to use Latin (though they were not required to use it grammatically);[54] in 1395, the chambress at Laock wrote a note, in Latin and in the first person, setting out the expenses for the veiling of Joan Samborne, who was received as a canoness of the abbey in the same year;[55] at Dartford, as we have already mentioned, instruction in Latin continued until at least 1481, and the novices at Syon may have been having Latin lessons as late as the first decades of the sixteenth century.[56] Nor must we forget that the Romsey collection of *vitae sanctorum* was written in the early fourteenth century;[57] that the date of the Lacock copy of the *Dictionarius* of William Brito is fourteenth-fifteenth century;[58] that Swine received its donation of twelve Latin treatises c. 1400;[59] and that Thomas Reymound's copy of the *Liber gestorum Karoli, regis Franciae* was bequeathed to Polsoe in 1418.[60] It is also possible, though unfortunately far from certain, that the nuns of Barking were acquiring, and presumably using, printed books in Latin almost to the time of the abbey's dissolution. Unfortunately, the list in which the books are recorded is not easy to interpret and it is also possible that the twenty-nine volumes listed were the property of the steward of the abbey rather than the nuns.[61]

In short, although it is undoubtedly true that from the early fourteenth century onwards, most nuns (and probably most lay-monks) were unable to read and understand a non-liturgical text in Latin, I would contend that the minority who could may well have been greater than has hitherto been supposed.

The Latin note of the chambress of Lacock leads us to a consideration of the fourth and final level of Latin literacy: the ability to write and compose in the language. In the Middle Ages, writing was always considered a skill quite separate from reading,[62] and the tradition of the great Anglo-Saxon *scriptoria*[63] seems to have faded away with the coming of the Normans. Nor was there any parallel between the situation in Europe, where female scribes seem to have been common,[64] and England, where they seem to have been exceedingly rare. An early twelfth-century volume from Nunnaminster—a Latin manuscript containing the *Diadema monachorum* of Smaragdus and a collection of pseudo-Augustinian sermons—was written by an anonymous *scriptrix*,[65] but the evidence for scribal activities on the part of nuns in the centuries following is extremely limited.[66] Sir John Fox suggested that the scribe of William Giffard's Anglo-Norman *Apocalypse* (a work we shall consider a little later) was a member of the Shaftesbury community,[67] but the evidence is tenuous; and the only other cases I can cite are of nuns copying liturgical manuscripts for their own private use. In the fifteenth century, Matilda Hayle of Barking *may* have copied Wycliffite translations of the books of Tobit and Susanna, together with various prayers;[68] at the end of that century or the beginning of the next, Elizabeth Trotter of Ickleton *may* have copied her own collection of Latin *liturgica*;[69] and at about the same time, Margery Birkenhead of Chester *may* have made her own copy of the Chester Processional.[70] None of these cases, however, is incontrovertible. Clearer evidence comes from Syon, where we know that after the suppression of the house in 1539, some of the sisters (including, in all probability, Elizabeth Yate[71]) wrote their own breviaries, but we also know that they wrote them very badly.[72] A large number of nuns could obviously write their own names,[73] but copying an entire manuscript is a very different matter.

Simple scribing, however, is not here our concern. We are interested in Latin composition, and the evidence for English nuns composing treatises in Latin is even rarer than the evidence for their abilities in writing. At the very end of the eleventh century or the beginning of the twelfth, Muriel, a nun of Wilton, was described as a *versificatrix* and her poetry was clearly much esteemed, though none of it has survived.[74] But after Muriel there is no one. When we list the names of the women who, from the twelfth to the mid-sixteenth century, composed in Latin—Constantia, Teresa of Portugal, Mathilde of Morit, Marsilia of Saint-Amand, Héloise, Clare of Assisi, Herrad of Hohenberg, Elisabeth of Schönau, Ida of Bingen, Hildegard of Bingen, Gertrude of Helfta, Katharina von Gebersweiler, Anna von Munzingen, Elisabeth von Kirchberg, Umiltà of Faenza, Lorenza Strozzi, Luisa Sigea de Velasco, Lea Ráskai, and the women of the Italian Renaissance like Battista de Montefeltro, Cassandra Fedele, Costanza da Varano, Ippolita Sforza, Isotta Nogarola, Laura Cereta, and Veronica Gambara—they are all European: French, Germanic, Hungarian, Italian, or Spanish.[75] This is not to say that there were no English nuns writing in Latin—the problem of anonymity may be greater than has been supposed[76]—but we do not know of any. Both Joan Sewell and Dorothy Codrington may well have been capable of producing an original work in the language, but we have no evidence that they ever did. The case with French, however, is quite different.

We have already seen that French was the living language of the Norman aristocracy, and since most nunneries from the eleventh century to about the thirteenth were populated by women of the upper or noble classes,[77] it is only natural that they took their language with them. In some cases, such as the Minoresses of Waterbeach,[78] the Dominicans of Dartford,[79] and the Benedictines of Amesbury,[80] the first nuns were not only French-speaking, but actually came from France. Others would have been drawn from the daughters of aristocratic families who, before the loss of Normandy, used to be sent to France to perfect their language and their manners.[81]

It is understandable, therefore, that as Latin became ever more the prerogative of university-trained clerics, French should take over as the main medium for both written and spoken communication.[82] From the end of the thirteenth century, episcopal injunctions for nuns begin to be written in both Latin and French,[83] and even at Wilton, the erudite *alma mater* of Muriel and Maud, the Benedictine Rule had to be translated into French so that the nuns could understand it better.[84] *O tempora! O mores!*

In the bustling secular world outside the nunneries, French would soon be superseded by English;[85] but within the conservative atmosphere of the cloister—or at least of some cloisters—French was retained much longer.[86] It is true that in some circles, especially royal circles, French was still being learned long after it had lost the battle with English,[87] but by far the best example of its preservation is the extraordinary case of Lacock. When the abbey was visited in 1535, shortly before the Dissolution, John Ap Rice wrote to Thomas Cromwell informing him that 'the Ladies [of Lacock] have their rule, th'institutes of their religion and ceremonies of the same writen in the frenche tonge which they understand well and are very perfitt in the same, albeit that it varieth from the vulgare frenche that is nowe used, and is moche like the frenche that the common Lawe in writen in.'[88] In other words, the ladies of Lacock were conversing in a language which, in England, had been moribund for a hundred and fifty years. Mary Dominica Legge has suggested that French survived longest in the ports.[89] It did not: it survived longest in the nunneries.

A large amount of French literature circulated in England; some of it appears in the manuscripts listed in Part II of this study. Apart from biblical and liturgical material, we find lives of the fathers and lives of saints, the anonymous *Livre de Sydrac*, works by Robert Grosseteste, Guillaume le Clerc, and Peter d'Abernon of Peckham, and (at Syon) a printed edition of a French translation of Boccaccio's *De la ruine des nobles hommes et femmes*.[90] The work by Grosseteste is his *Chasteau d'amour*, an outline in verse of the creation, fall, and redemption, which (the author tells us) he has written in French (*romanz*) for those who have 'neither letters nor learning' (*ne lettreure ne clergie*).[91] The volume by Guillaume le Clerc is his *Bestaire divin*;[92] and the treatise from the pen of Peter of Peckham is his immensely popular *Lumière as lais*, a dull and dreadfully written catechetical work modelled on the *Elucidarius* of Honorius Augustodunensis and deeply influenced by the *Sentences* of Peter Lombard.[93]

Some of this Anglo-Norman literature was written specifically for particular nuns or particular nunneries; some of it, though we do not know how much, was written by nuns themselves. Nicholas Trevet's *Chronicle* was written for Mary, the daughter of Edward I. She had entered Amesbury at the not-so-precocious age of six[94] (it did her no good: she had no vocation and was an inveterate gambler), but the work was not completed until about 1334, two years after her death.[95] Adgar's *Gracial* is dedicated to a 'Dame Mahaut', or Lady Maud, who was probably an illegitimate daughter of Henry II who became abbess of Barking c. 1175;[96] William Giffard's rhymed *Apocalypse* was composed (in dreadful verse) for the nuns of Shaftesbury;[97] Adam of Exeter's *Exposiciun sur la Pater nostre* was almost certainly written at the request of an unknown abbess or prioress and then adapted for male religious;[98] and it is possible, though far from certain, that the masterly *Merure de Seinte Eglise* of St Edmund of Abingdon was composed for Ela, Countess of Salisbury, who founded the abbey of Lacock in 1229–30 and became its abbess in 1239.[99]

As for nuns who were actually authors of works in Anglo-Norman, we know of three, and their works are all preserved in the same manuscript: the collection of saint's lives from Campsey.[100] Two of them certainly came from Barking; the third from an unknown nunnery. Sometime in the second half of the twelfth century Clemence of Barking wrote a *Life of St Catherine of Alexandria*;[101] and between 1163 and 1169 another nun of the same abbey—she does not give her name—wrote the *Life of St Edward the Confessor* which we have already mentioned.[102] The *Life of St Catherine* is an attractive and, it seems, fairly radical adaptation of an earlier French version of one of the standard Latin lives of the saint;[103] the *Life of St Edward* is, as we have seen, a translation of the well-known *vita* by Aelred of Rievaulx.[104] The third author is Marie, who took Thomas of Ely's Latin *Life of St Etheldreda of Ely* (Thomas had based his work on Bede), and translated it into pedestrian French verse as the *Life of St Audrey*.[105] Marie probably composed the *Life* in the early thirteenth century, but where she did so is unknown. Ely, Canonsleigh, and Chatteris have all been suggested, but Ely and Canonsleigh are impossible, and Chatteris is no more than a guess.[106] The tentative suggestion by A. T. Baker that the life of St Osyth, which occurs in the same manuscript from Campsey, was also written by a woman cannot be sustained.[107] It was almost certainly composed by a canon of the abbey of St Osyth at Chich.[108]

It is, however, possible that more was written by women than we know. The anonymous nun who composed the life of St Edward the Confessor apologises at the beginning of the poem for her 'false French of England' (*faus franceis d'Angletere*),[109] but that is not the reason she conceals her identity.

> If any of you who have heard this romance wish to know where it was made and who took it from the Latin, you will know it only on condition that you ask the good God to look mercifully upon the one who, by his grace, composed it. This life was translated in the abbey of Barking. A hand-maid of sweet Jesus Christ did it for love of Saint Edward. But for the moment she does not want to say her name, for she is well aware that she is not yet worthy for it to be heard or read in a book in which she has written so very holy a name [as that of Saint Edward]. She begs, therefore, that all who hear or who will hear this romance of hers will not hold it in contempt because a woman has translated it. This is no reason to despise it, nor to condemn the good which is in it. She asks for mercy, and seeks pardon for having had the presumption (*presumtïun*) to translate this life.[110]

One is reminded of the comments of another Benedictine— the humbly brilliant Dame Laurentia McLachlan—writing some eight centuries after her anonymous consoeur:

St Benedict's daughters have a traditional love of study, though they like to keep quiet and hidden and leave the more public part to their brethren. . . . As children of the Church we are ready under obedience, to take an active, though anonymous part in her apostolate, and if work of this sort is required of us, the very best, in both matter and form, is expected from a Benedictine house.[111]

It is perfectly possible, therefore, that the desire for—or perhaps the imposition of—such anonymity has resulted in the names of many female authors being irretrievably lost, and the anonymous translator from Barking may have been but one of many whose fear of 'presumption' prevented them from leaving a record of their identity.[112]

By about the middle of the fourteenth century the language of the literate laity had changed from French to English. The earliest petition in English dates from 1344,[113] and the statute requiring English in the courts was issued in 1362;[114] but by this time bishops had been putting their injunctions in 'the mother tongue'[115] as well as in Latin for a number of years. This, as we have already seen, was necessary for both nuns and monks, not only because of a lack of Latin, but so that recalcitrant religious could not plead ignorance of what the bishop required.[116]

We have also seen that as English became ever more widely used in the fourteenth and fifteenth centuries, and as the numbers of lay people who could read it soared,[117] the demand for books escalated accordingly. As a consequence of this and other factors, the price of books began to fall; and although they were never cheap, they were a great deal cheaper than they ever had been before. The interest in and demand for books in the world outside the cloister seems to have been reflected inside the enclosure, for I do not think it is mere chance that two-thirds of all surviving books from English nunneries date from after about 1400, and that more than two-thirds of the non-liturgical volumes are in English.

The quantity of English material is astonishing, and although we presented a brief summary of its content in Chapter 2, it will do no harm to remind ourselves of its variety. Apart from Wycliffite translations of the scriptures, we find numerous

English versions of patristic and medieval treatises, and a number of important original works by such writers as Capgrave, Chaucer, Hilton, Hoccleve, Peter Idley, Nicholas Love, Lydgate, William of Nassington, Rolle, and Richard Whytford. We also find well-known anonymous works and translations such as the *Ancrene Rule, The Book of the Craft of Dying, The Chastising of God's Children, The Cleansing of Man's Soul, Contemplations of the Dread and Love of God, Cursor Mundi, The Tree and Twelve Fruits of the Holy Ghost, The Doctrine of the Heart, The Dream of the Pilgrimage of the Soul,* the *Golden Legend,* and a large number of other tracts, some common and some less common, which the reader will find listed in Index I.

An examination of this multitude of titles reveals two important points: firstly, that many of the texts listed were, for the time, new and up to date; and secondly, that a large number of them come from Syon. *The Cleansing of Man's Soul,* for example, was probably composed at the end of the fourteenth century,[118] and the copy owned by Sybil de Felton, abbess of Barking, bears the date 1401.[119] If the date is reliable,[120] the writer's ink was hardly dry before the abbess received her copy; but even if the date is untrustworthy, she must have come into possession of the book before her death in March 1419. Sybil de Felton also owned an early fifteenth-century copy of Nicholas Love's *Mirror of the Life of Christ.*[121] This is a free translation of the *Meditationes Vitae Christi* attributed (incorrectly) to St Bonaventure, and it was authorized for circulation by Archbishop Arundel in 1410 as a deliberate counter-move to Lollard attempts at publishing English translations of the gospels.[122] Since Sybil de Felton died in 1419, the copy she owned cannot have been written too many years after 1410. It seems to me, therefore, that Ian Doyle is quite correct in suggesting that the abbess and community of Barking 'were in the fore-front of the public for such English theology.'[123]

It was not only at Barking, however, that we find such interest. Walter Hilton's *Epistle on the Mixed Life,* the first English treatise to recommend that layfolk read the gospels for themselves (albeit in Latin),[124] was to be found at Dartford and the London Minoresses;[125] and copies of *Poor Caitiff,* a tedious but popular work sometimes (though mistakenly) attributed to a Lollard or even to Wycliffe himself,[126] are recorded at Dartford, the London Minoresses, and Shaftesbury.[127] Even at Thetford, a small and poor house, we find a Wycliffite translation of the New Testament;[128] and it is interesting to note that at a visitation in 1514, Dame Sara Frost, one of nine sisters at Thetford, said that she was afraid that the prioress was about to accept as nuns certain 'untaught persons' (*indoctas personas*),[129] but exactly what Dame Sara understood by *indocta* is not stated.

Perhaps the best example of such interest in contemporary theology is the case of Elizabeth Throckmorton, the last abbess of Denney.[130] One of the books she owned was the wholly orthodox *Speculum Vitae* of William of Nassington, written about 1375,[131] but the interests of the abbess were not confined to the standard and unexceptional spirituality of a previous age. It seems that she was a friend of Erasmus,[132] and when, in 1521–3, William Tyndale translated into English Erasmus's *Enchiridion militis christiani*,[133] Elizabeth, either from interest, friendship, or both, was eager to read it. When Tyndale, a year later, set out for Germany to undertake his great work of translating the scriptures, he sent a copy of the book to a London merchant, Humphrey Monmouth, who had earlier, for six months, employed Tyndale as his chaplain and provided him with room and board.[134] In 1526, however, Tyndale's scriptural translations were publicly condemned in England, and the opprobrium attached to these versions swiftly passed to his other works, including his translation of the *Enchiridion*. Whatever Tyndale wrote was, by definition, heretical. In 1528, therefore, Humphrey Monmouth found himself imprisoned in the Tower of London for holding Tyndale's opinions and distributing his books. He immediately wrote to Cardinal Wolsey petitioning for his release, and, among other matters, explained that he no longer had the *Enchiridion* because he had sent it to the abbess of Denney at her request. He had also spent more than £50 on the house. He himself, he wrote, was innocent of any wrong-doing, and knew nothing evil of Tyndale prior to 1526; but as soon as he *did* know that there were problems, he had burned all Tyndale's letters, treatises, sermons, and books. His imprisonment, therefore, was unjust, and since it had resulted in the total loss of his name and his credit, he begged Wolsey and the Council for forgiveness.[135] The implication of Monmouth's petition is that he sent the *Enchiridion* to the abbess shortly after he had received it, and certainly before the condemnation of Tyndale in 1526. We need not, therefore, suspect Elizabeth Throckmorton of being a proto-Protestant, but we may note with interest her desire to read what was, for the time, one of the most up-to-date and original works of Christian spirituality.

Works in English (including those mentioned in wills, inventories, and the like) are recorded from half the houses listed in Part II of this study, but nowhere is this interest in vernacular literature more evident than at Syon. Of the forty-eight volumes listed under Syon (section A), twenty-five may be categorized broadly as liturgical and twenty-three as theological. But of these twenty-three, seventeen, or more than three-quarters, are in English. Of the remaining six, five are in Latin and one is in French. Let us note, too, that of these seventeen volumes, eight are printed books: it seems that at Syon both the sisters and the brothers were eager to take advantage of the benefits of printing.[136]

The volumes in Latin we have already discussed; the single French example reflects the fact that by the time of the foundation of Syon in 1415 French was no longer a living language in England; the books in English include not only *The Chastising of God's Children* (two printed copies), *The Tree and Twelve Fruits of the Holy Ghost* (again, two printed copies), *Disce mori*, and works, both printed and in manuscript, by Walter Hilton, Nicholas Love, Peter Idley, John Lydgate, and Thomas à Kempis—but also a number of treatises specifically composed for the Syon nuns: the *Additions to the Rule of Saint Saviour*, *The Mirror of Our Lady*, *The Orchard of Syon*, and Richard Whytford's *Pipe or Tun of the Life of Perfection*. Nor do these exhaust the volumes prepared for the Syon sisters. Whytford also translated for them the *Martyrology* of Syon, the *Rule of St Augustine* with the commentary of Hugh of Saint-Victor, and (probably) *The Following of Christ*, an English version of the *Imitatio Christi* of Thomas à Kempis printed first in 1556.[137] He also composed his *Daily Exercise and Experience of Death* for one of the abbesses of Syon, Elizabeth Gibbs, who died in 1518.[138] Thomas Prestius, a brother of Syon who was pensioned in 1539 and died at Stanwell five years later, copied (and probably translated) an *Instruction of Novices*, an English version of the very popular *De Exterioris et Interioris Hominis Compositione* of David of Augsburg.[139] Thomas Betson, the librarian of the brothers' library, compiled *A Right Profitable Treatise*, containing much material from Jerome, Bernard of Clairvaux, and the *Ars moriendi* printed by Caxton c. 1491.[140] From the pen of William Bonde came the *Devout Treatise for Those That are Timorous and Fearful in Conscience*, a work which was certainly written at the request of a nun, though not, perhaps, one from Syon.[141] And from John Fewterer, the last Confessor-General, we have the *Mirror or Glass of Christ's Passion*, an important work, translated mainly from Ludolf of Saxony and Jordan of Quedlinburg, which Jan Rhodes describes as 'a *summa* of late medieval devotion to the Passion.'[142] We might also note that William Darker, a Carthusian of Sheen, copied a number of manuscripts in English, some of which were certainly for the use of the Syon sisters.[143] And while it is true that Syon was not the only nunnery to be the recipient of such volumes,[144] it certainly seems to have been the one that benefited most.[145]

The high proportion of vernacular books owned by the sisters of Syon stands in marked contrast to the number owned by the brothers. Of the 1421 titles listed in the catalogue of the brothers' library, all but thirty are in Latin. Of the thirty, twenty-six are in English (less than 2% of the total) and four in French.[146] But the brothers at Syon were a learned lot: many had behind them a university education (this is especially true of those who entered the abbey in the sixteenth century), and very few of them would have been deficient in their knowledge of Latin or of Latin theology. 'Their interests,' says Roger Lovatt, 'lay in a predominantly latinate spiritual literature, often written more recently and invariably the work of continental authors.'[147] The same cannot be said of the sisters, and there seems little doubt that Latin scholars such as Joan Sewell and Dorothy Codrington were in a minority. This, however, was not necessarily a disadvantage.

We have seen already that more than two-thirds of all the surviving non-liturgical volumes that have been traced to English nunneries are written in English, and that the majority of books and manuscripts date from the fifteenth century. It was precisely at this time that English achieved (as Vincent Gillespie puts it) a 'new-found respectability' in religious contexts,[148] and to a very large extent, English spirituality was transmitted in the English language.[149] But since it was the nuns, not just at Syon but elsewhere, who, by choice or necessity, seem to have evinced the greatest interest in this vernacular literature, it was the nuns, not the monks, who stood at the fore-front of English spirituality.

The fifteenth century was not, in general, a productive period for men's monasteries;[150] and even in those houses which, in the past, had been justly renowned for their scholarship, the impetus for learning had died away. The study of theology was now the prerogative of the universities. It is true that in some abbeys, towards the end of the century, there seems to have been a brief resurgence of scholarly activity,[151] but with the exception of the Carthusians (of whom more in a moment), the overall impression is one of torpidity and stagnation. We may perhaps see a reflection of this general lack of interest in the limited numbers of fifteenth- and sixteenth-century books acquired by the monasteries, for if we consult the lists in Ker and Watson's *Medieval Libraries of Great Britain*, total up all the volumes which survive from male monastic houses (there are about 5000 of them), and examine their dates, we find that only about 13% were written in the fifteenth or early sixteenth century.[152] We may contrast this with the 50% which survive from the nunneries.[153] And if, instead of considering all surviving manuscripts, we limit ourselves to those from houses with the most complete collections, the proportions are even lower. At Christ Church, Canterbury, the percentage of fifteenth and sixteenth century manuscripts (excluding printed books) is just over 12%; at Bury St Edmunds, 11%; at Durham, 9%; at St Augustine's, Canterbury, 6%; and at Worcester, little more than 5%.[154] The only exceptions to this dismal record seem to be the Carthusians, but it must be stressed that our knowledge of their libraries is incomplete, and that the greatest number of books traced to any of their houses are the thirty or so from the London Charterhouse. Nevertheless, it is surely significant that of ninety-four manuscripts and books traced to the Charterhouse, Mount Grace, Sheen, and Witham, almost 60% of the manuscripts date from the fifteenth and early sixteenth centuries, and if we include with these the printed books, the proportion increases to no less than 80%.

The interest of the nuns in fifteenth-century books and literature stands in marked contrast to the unimpressive record of their male counterparts, and if almost all the books were in English and if, from a latinate theological point of view, most of the nuns were unlearned, what of it? A nunnery was not intended to be a university, and if one thinks (says the author of *The Book of Privy Counselling*) that one can attain the experience of God by one's scholarship (*clergie*) or natural intelligence (*kyndely witte*), this is nothing but sheer presumption. Truly, he says, 'þe contrary is soþ in þinges contemplatyue. For only in hem ben alle corious skyles of clergie or of kyndely kunnyng fer put bak, þat God be þe principal.'[155] The subtleties of scholarship, both 'of clergie & of kynde', serve only to blind one,[156] and if a soul in contemplation 'had tonge & langage to sey as it feliþ, þan alle þe clerkes of Cristendome schuld wondre on þat wisdam. Ye! & in comparison of it, al here grete clergie schuld seme apeerte foly.'[157]

As a consequence, therefore, of what most men would have seen as their limitations, the spiritual and devotional life of the English nuns could have been richer, fuller, and, one might say, more up to date than that of their more numerous brethren, who, for the most part, were still mired in the consequences of a conservative and traditional education.

Our brief investigation of learning and literacy in this chapter has led, I believe, to a number of interesting conclusions. We have seen that the prime purpose of schools in the Middle Ages was to instruct young boys in Latin, and that the establishment of the universities as the usual path for those bent on a career in the church or the civil service had a detrimental effect on the education of women. We have also seen, however, that in some of the nunneries, especially in the twelfth and thirteenth centuries, there might have been better provision for education in Latin and Latin letters than has hitherto been supposed. This was certainly the case at such learned and aristocratic houses as Barking (where the tradition may have continued into the era of printing), Dartford, Romsey, and Wilton, but the evidence of the manuscripts indicates that it may well have been true for other, lesser establishments as well. And although there can be little doubt that from the fourteenth century onwards most nuns would not have been able to read and understand a non-liturgical text in Latin, the minority of those who could was, I think, greater than most people have suspected. Nun authors writing in Latin, however, are exceedingly rare. I know of none in England after the early twelfth century, and the great names so frequently cited—Héloise, Hildegard, Gertrude, Herrad of Hohenberg, Elisabeth of Schönau, and the others—are all European.

The same is not true of nuns writing in Anglo-Norman. In the twelfth and thirteenth centuries it was the normal language of communication in most women's houses, and, in certain nunneries (Lacock is the best example), it was retained as a spoken language far longer than in the world outside. We know of three nuns who composed original works—saint's lives—in Anglo-Norman, but the plea for anonymity on the part of the unknown translator of the *Life of St Edward the Confessor* may lead us to suspect that more women wrote more books than is indicated by this meagre list. We cannot prove this, and argument from silence is stupid, but it is certainly a real possibility; and it may be useful to remember that not only are many saint's lives anonymous, but also a considerable amount of religious literature in Middle English.

Materials in English dominate the surviving books and manuscripts listed in Part II of this study. They account for more than two-thirds of the works recorded, and there can be no doubt that this proportion reflects a strong preference on the part of women religious for texts in the vernacular. Even at Syon, which could boast scholars like Joan Sewell, it is works in English that predominate, but as we suggested earlier, this was no real disadvantage. Most English spirituality and much English theology was transmitted in the mother tongue, and there is clear evidence that some nuns had every intention of keeping abreast of the most recent developments. With the possible exception of the Carthusians, we cannot say the same for the monks. The catalogues of abuses and problems which are so easy to extract from records of episcopal visitations, and which people nowadays find so fascinating, represent only one part of the life of nunneries in the later Middle Ages, and it is generally healthier to pay more attention to the highest common factor than to the lowest common denominator.

It is also easy to imply, if not to state, that the situation in men's houses during this period was radically different: that nuns were dissolute and ignorant, whereas monks were learned and virtuous. This is quite untrue. The bishops and their representatives condemned abuses in monasteries and nunneries with equal fervour; and before one succumbs to the easy temptation of contrasting the large number of male monastic authors with the dearth of females, one should recall certain pertinent points. There were five times as many monasteries as there were nunneries, and many of the monasteries housed far larger numbers of religious. Most of them, however, produced no writers at all, and those that did generally did so in the twelfth and thirteenth centuries. Out of more than eighty Cistercian houses, for example, only two or three could be called centres of learning,[158] and although we know that Meaux had a large and splendid library,[159] no one seems to have made much use of it.[160] As for the rest of them, the appearance of an occasional isolated writer serves only to draw attention to what was, for the most part, a literary desert. To draw a comparison between a large monastery in the twelfth century and a small nunnery in the fifteenth gets us nowhere; but if we were to compare, say, the Cistercian nunnery of Catesby and the Cistercian monastery of Bruern in about 1400, I doubt that we would see much difference.

The matters we have considered in these three chapters have not exhausted what may be learned from the lists and records presented in Part II of this study; but enough, I think, has been said to demonstrate a need for greater caution in dealing with the questions of libraries, learning, and literacy among later medieval nuns. The old and well-worn adages—'Nuns libraries were always small', 'Only Anglo-Saxon nuns had any pretensions to learning', 'Nuns in the later Middle Ages could not read Latin', and so on—require some revision, and although it would obviously be just as silly to state the direct opposite—'Nuns libraries were always large', and so forth—it is possible (I would say probable) that what has been long been accepted as unquestioned and canonical may not be quite true. I am not, therefore, calling for radical revision with regard to the scholarly attainments of women religious in the later Middle Ages, but only arguing for a modicum of honest reassessment.

NOTES

1. See M. T. Clanchy, *From Memory to Written Record: England 1066–1307* (Oxford, 1993[2]), p. 213.
2. See M. D. Legge, 'Anglo-Norman as a Spoken Language', *Proceedings of the Battle Conference on Anglo-Norman Studies, II, 1979*, ed. R. A. Brown (Woodbridge, 1980), pp. 108–17 (text), 188–90 (notes).

3. W. S. Holdsworth, *A History of English Law* (London, 1936[4]), vol. 2, p. 479. See further the excellent account in Clanchy, pp. 197–223.

4. See K. Lambley, *The Teaching and Cultivation of the French Language in England During Tudor and Stuart Times* (Manchester/London, 1920), pp. 7–25; L. Kingsford, *Prejudice and Promise in Fifteenth Century England* (Oxford, 1925; rpt. London, 1962), pp. 24–25; and H. Suggett, 'The Use of French in England in the Later Middle Ages', *Transactions of the Royal Historical Society*, Ser. 4, 28 (1946), pp. 61–83. After it had ceased to be a living language, French was retained as a professional medium in the law-courts until the later fifteenth century (see Holdsworth, *History of English Law*, vol. 2, pp. 477–82). What happened in the nunneries is something we shall discuss in due course.

5. Holdsworth, *History of English Law*, vol. 2, pp. 477–8.

6. See Kingsford, *Prejudice and Promise*, p. 24. According to Nicholas Orme, 'merchants' letters are generally in French until the end of the fourteenth century and in English or French thereafter, depending on the country of the correspondent' (N. Orme, *English Schools in the Middle Ages* [London, 1973], p. 45).

7. The instructional materials are comprehensively described in the first two chapters of Lambley, *Teaching of the French Language in England*.

8. See Orme, *English Schools; idem, Education in the West of England 1066–1548* (Exeter, 1976); and Orme's collected papers in his *Education and Society in Medieval and Renaissance England* (London, 1989). For a convenient summary, see *Education in the West of England*, pp. 1–26.

9. See Orme, *English Schools*, pp. 59–115; *idem, Education in the West of England*, p. 2 (a brief summary).

10. Aristocratic households often provided private tutors, but such households were a minority. See generally N. Orme, 'The Education of the Courtier', in *Education and Society in Medieval and Renaissance England*, pp. 153–75, and *idem, From Childhood to Chivalry: The Education of the English Kings and Aristocracy 1066–1530* (London/New York, 1984), *passim*.

11. *Oxford Dictionary of Quotations* (London, 1941), p. 158 (s.v. Thomas Gaisford). This is not the only version of Gaisford's comment.

12. See Orme, *English Schools*, pp. 52–5; *idem, Childhood to Chivalry*, pp. 106–9, 156–63.

13. See especially Orme, 'Education of the Courtier', pp. 160–61.

14. See Orme, *English Schools*, pp. 54–5, and the earlier, but more intriguing, study by J. W. Adamson, 'The Extent of Literacy in England in the Fifteenth and Sixteenth Centuries: Notes and

Conjectures', *The Library*, Ser. 4, 10 (1930), pp. 163–93 (reprinted in *idem, The Illiterate Anglo–Saxon and Other Essays* [Cambridge, 1946], pp. 38–61). Adamson suggests that the numbers of girls at grammar schools may have been underestimated, and that 'the instruction . . . of girls of the middle and lower ranks, whose parents were not absolutely poor but whose condition did not afford more than a competence, constitutes the most baffling problem of our educational history' (p. 188).

15. Orme cites three examples (*English Schools*, pp. 54–55) and contrasts the far larger numbers in Europe 'where the education of women was taken more seriously' (*English Schools*, p. 55). To Orme's brief list must be added Alice Whytingstale, mistress of the school at the abbey of Romsey in 1502 (VCH *Hampshire and the Isle of Wight*, vol. 2, p. 130).

16. See Power, pp. 260–84, 568–81. Orme is correct is saying that 'the role of the monasteries in noble education was equalled, indeed exceeded, by that of the nunneries' (*Childhood to Chivalry*, p. 63), but, as I hope to show in this chapter, both he and Power underrate the level of education which might have been available (see Orme, *English Schools*, p. 54).

17. See generally Clanchy, *Memory to Written Record*, Part II (especially chapter 7). This is essential reading.

18. *The Myroure of oure Ladye*, ed. J. H. Blunt (EETS/ES, 19; London, 1873; rpt. New York, 1973), pp. 2–3. Cf. Power, p. 251.

19. *The Martiloge in Englysshe*, ed. F. Procter & E. S. Dewick (Henry Bradshaw Society, 3; London, 1891), p. 1. See also *ibid.*, pp. vi–vii. Some of the sisters at Syon did not possess even this minimal degree of literacy, and for those who could not read at all a special service was prescribed: see *The Rewyll of Seynt Sauioure, Vol. 4: The Syon Additions for the Sisters from the British Library Ms. Arundel 146*, ed. J. Hogg (*Salzburger Studien zur Anglistik und Amerikanistik*, 6/4; Salzburg, 1980), pp. 152–3 'Of the seruise of sustres vnlettred.' The service consisted of various numbers of *Pater noster*s, *Ave*s, and *Credo*s.

20. As at the Premonstratensian houses of Orford and Broadholme (VCH *Lincolnshire*, vol. 2, p. 209; *Nottinghamshire*, vol. 2, p. 139), the Augustinian abbey of Burnham (*Visitations in the Diocese of Lincoln 1517–1531, Vol. 2: Visitations of Rural Deaneries by John Longland, Bishop of Lincoln, . . . 1517–1531*, ed. A. H. Thompson [Lincoln Record Society, 35; Hereford, 1944 (for 1938)], pp. 89, 90), the Benedictine abbey of Elstow (VCH *Bedfordshire*, vol. 1, p. 356), and elsewhere. At Ankerwyke an *informatrix* ('instructress') was supposed to instruct (*informare*) the younger nuns in reading and

singing, and we may assume that the same was true for many or
most other houses (*Visitations of Religious Houses in the Diocese of
Lincoln, Vol. 2: Records of Visitations held by William Alnwick, Bishop
of Lincoln, A.D. 1436–1449, Part 1*, ed. A. H. Thompson [Canterbury
and York Society, 24; London, 1919; rpt. 1969], pp. 4, 5).

21. This is not to say that such minimal literacy was approved. At
    Newnham Priory, a house of male Augustinian canons in Bedford-
    shire, Bishop Alnwick encountered just the same problem and told
    the canons that 'reading without understanding is carelessness.'
    Some of them, he went on, were so unlettered—virtually witless
    indeed—that they could barely read, and even what they read they
    did not understand, and so were rendered useless and unfit for
    study and contemplation ('Item cum secundum vulgare legere et
    non intelligere est necgligere, ac nonnulli, vt nobis detectum est,
    dicti prioratus canonici adeo illitterati sunt et quasi ideote quod vix
    legunt, sed et quod legunt non intelligunt, et sic inutiles studio et
    contemplacione redduntur et inepti') (*Visitations of Religious Houses
    in the Diocese of Lincoln, Vol. 3: Records of Visitations held by William
    Alnwick, A.D. 1436–1449, Part 2*, ed. A. H. Thompson [Canterbury
    and York Society, 33; Oxford, 1927; rpt. London, 1969], pp. 237–
    8). Much so-called 'lay literacy' in Latin was probably similar
    (see Orme, *English Schools*, pp. 49–50, referring to laymen taking
    advantage of the Benefit of Clergy clause).

22. See Clanchy, *Memory to Written Record*, p. 189. Cf. R. S. Wieck, *The
    Book of Hours in Medieval Art and Life* (London, 1988), p. 40: 'It
    is difficult to say with any assurance how much Latin people like
    Ogier Bénigne and Marie Caillet knew. As they were neither priests
    nor scholars, they probably never studied Latin formally. Yet a
    lifetime of immersion in the Church's liturgy and sacraments gave
    them a practical education in Latin that most twentieth-century
    observers would find alien.' Learning English or French could have
    the same effect: 'Medieval children, when they learnt to read, learnt
    the alphabet in Latin; when they first practised recognising and
    pronouncing words, the texts were also in Latin, so that every
    literate child was a minimal reader and speaker of that language'
    (Orme, 'Education of the Courtier' [n. 10], p. 170).

23. For the contents of the primer, See Chapter 1, n. 97. Examples are
    listed in Part II of this study at ARDEN *MR*, EASEBOURNE *MR*
    b.1; NUN MONKTON *MR* e, and SYON B.4.

24. See Orme, *English Schools*, pp. 23, 62–3; *idem*, 'Education of the
    Courtier' (n. 10), p. 170; and especially S. G. Bell, 'Medieval Women
    Book Owners: Arbiters of Lay Piety and Ambassadors of Culture',
    in *Sisters and Workers in the Middle Ages*, ed. J. M. Bennett *et al.*
    (Chicago/London, 1989), pp. 149–51.

25. On the other hand (if I may be my own devil's advocate), they might have been intended for the chaplain to the nunnery, though in another donation (NUN APPLETON *MR*) that is specifically stated. Nor is there any guarantee that the chaplain himself would have been able to read them (cf. n. 49 below). Another possibility is that the books were sold. This might have been the fate of some of the less appropriate volumes from a donation made to the Cistercian abbey of Bordesley by Guy de Beauchamp, Earl of Warwick, in 1306: see D. N. Bell, *The Libraries of the Cistercians, Gilbertines and Premonstratensians* (Corpus of British Medieval Library Catalogues, 3; London, 1992), pp. 4–10.

26. *The Bridgettine Breviary of Syon Abbey*, ed. A. J. Collins (Henry Bradshaw Society, 96; Worcester, 1969 [for 1963]), p. xxxi.

27. SYON A.43. See *The Incendium Amoris of Richard Rolle of Hampole*, ed. M. Deanesly (Manchester, 1915; rpt. Folcroft, 1974), p. 82. Both the sisters and the brothers at Syon seem to have had a marked interest in the writers of the English mystical tradition: see P. Hodgson, 'The Orcherd of Syon and the English Mystical Tradition', in *Middle English Literature: British Academy Gollancz Lectures*, ed. J. A. Burrow (Oxford, 1989 [the lecture was actually delivered 1 July 1964]), pp. 71–91 *passim*, and C. F. R. de Hamel, *Syon Abbey. The Library of the Bridgettine Nuns and Their Peregrinations After the Reformation* (Roxburghe Club, 1991), p. 56.

28. SYON A.7 and A.21. See Deanesly, *Incendium Amoris*, pp. 78–83. Sister Joan compared the long and short texts of the *Incendium Amoris* and marked the differences in her own copy (see *ibid.*).

29. SYON A.3. See *A Deuout Treatyse Called the Tree & the XII. Frutes of the Holy Goost*, ed. J. J. Vaissier (Groningen, 1960), pp. xxxvi–xxxviii. 'Throughout the two treatises [which constitute *The Tree*] are scattered marginal notes, most of which were made by Dorothy Coderington. . . . The editor is inclined to believe that this lady of Syon used the two books side by side, correcting the present Ampleforth printed copy [= SYON A.3] from the manuscript now in the British Museum' (*ibid.*, pp. xxxvii–xxxviii).

30. SYON A.16.

31. SYON A.17.

32. See SYON A.13.

33. See n. 102 below.

34. We may compare the case of Elizabeth de la Pole who was staying at Bruisyard in 1417: a certain friar was brought into the nunnery to provide her with teaching, though what she was taught is not specified (Orme, *Childhood to Chivalry*, p. 158). Whether this was a rare or a common practice is unknown.

35. See VCH *Kent*, vol. 2, p. 187. The evidence for male children in the
    priory comes from *LP*, vol. 7, p. 256 (no. 667) (not 939: the citation in
    VCH *Kent*, vol. 2, p. 187, n. 108, has been stolen from Gasquet, and
    both are incorrect). This is a letter, written in 1534, from Elizabeth
    George to her son, Friar John George, who is, she fears, 'of the new
    fashion, that is to say, a heretic. Never none of your kindred were
    so named, and it grieves me to hear that you are the first. I heard
    also of the letters you sent to the nuns of Detford (Dartford), and
    another to your 'bener.' I am sorry for it, but you are not, or you
    would be ashamed to write to such discreet persons, especially to
    those who have had to bring you up. . . . You can do nothing so
    privily but it is known in Detforde and to your 'bener."
36. Ker, p. xi.
37. ELSTOW 1, and Chapter 2, n. 44.
38. William of Malmesbury, *De Gestis Regum Anglorum*, ed. W. Stubbs
    (Rolls Series, 90/2; London, 1889), vol. 2, p. 493: 'A teneris an-
    nis inter sanctimoniales apud Wiltoniam et Rumesium educata,
    litteris quoque foemineum pectus exercuit.' *Foemineum pectus* may
    be translated as 'what it means to be a [medieval] woman.'
39. See the *Dictionary of National Biography*, vol. 13, pp. 52–3.
40. Aelred wrote his *De institutione inclusarum*, in Latin, for his sister;
    and although it has been suggested that this sister may be no more
    than a literary fiction, there is no sound reason to think so.
41. The case of Baldwin's mother is interesting. We know that she
    could read Latin (though she had problems with her eyesight)
    because when Roger of Forde sent a copy of the visions of Elizabeth
    of Schönau to Baldwin, his former teacher and now abbot of Forde,
    he suggested that Baldwin have one of his monks make a copy
    in 'more legible letters' (*legibiliori littera*) so that his mother, who
    had by now retired to a nunnery, could read it: 'Salutate, obsecro,
    dilectam mihi in Christo sanctimonialem matrem vestram, quam et
    frequenter consolari et meminisse debetis, quia pro vobis erumpnas
    et gemitus parturientis sustinuit. Ad cuius etiam consolationem et
    earum cum quibus habitat sororum dilectionem vestram peterem,
    si auderem, ut hunc libellum ab aliquo monachorum vestrorum
    legibiliori littera conscribi iuberet' (R. J. Dean, 'Elizabeth, Abbess
    of Schönau, and Roger of Ford', *Modern Philology* 41 [1944], p.
    213, n. 18). According to Gervase of Canterbury, however, Baldwin
    came of humble (*infimus*) stock (*The Historical Works of Gervase of
    Canterbury, Vol. 2: The Minor Works*, ed. W. Stubbs [Rolls Series,
    73/2; London, 1880], vol. 2, p. 400), and if we accept this, it
    would imply a wider knowledge of Latin among women than
    has been suspected. Christopher Holdsworth, however, sees the

matter differently: 'The normal view would be that the ability to read Latin was not widely spread in the twelfth century, and was especially rare among women, so I take Baldwin's lowly origins with a pinch of salt, believing that the Canterbury monk who told us of them was not too well informed, or alternatively that he wished to denigrate a man with whom his community had had a notorious row' (C. J. Holdsworth, *'Another Stage . . . A Different World': Ideas and People Around Exeter in the Twelfth Century* [Exeter, 1979], p. 12). For my own part, I am not sure that 'the normal view' is correct. I think it quite possible that there were a number of twelfth-century nunneries which offered sound instruction in Latin, and that more women might have taken advantage of it than 'the normal view' would have us believe. Baldwin's mother could have been one of them.

42. See A. Wilmart, 'Ève et Goscelin', *Revue Bénédictine* 46 (1934), pp. 414–38, and 50 (1938), pp. 42–83. Eve had been educated at Wilton.
43. M. B. Parkes, 'The Literacy of the Laity', in *idem, Scribes, Scripts and Readers: Studies in the Communication, Presentation and Dissemination of Medieval Texts* (London, 1991), p. 276. (This article was first published in *Literature and Western Civilization: The Medieval World*, ed. D. Daiches & A. K. Thorlby [London, 1973], pp. 555–77).
44. Power, p. 247. We shall see numerous examples in the course of this chapter.
45. See, for example, the texts translated in G. G. Coulton, *Life in the Middle Ages* (New York/Cambridge, 1935 [four vols. in one]), vol. 2, pp. 39–47, 86–7 (a fourteenth-century bishop with little Latin), vol. 4, pp. 280–1 (a fourteenth-century abbot with the same problem). Cf. n. 21 above. According to Margaret Deanesly, *The Lollard Bible and Other Medieval Biblical Versions* (Cambridge, 1920; rpt. 1966), p. 172, 'it might be said with tolerable certainty that there is no period in the history of English monasticism, between the Conquest and the Reformation, when the monks of even the best managed monastery numbered none but those who could read Latin freely and easily.'
46. See, for example, *Visitations of Religious Houses in the Diocese of Lincoln, Vol. 1: Injunctions and Other Documents from the Registers of Richard Flemyng and William Gray, Bishops of Lincoln, A.D. 1420–1436*, ed. A. H. Thompson (Canterbury and York Society, 17; London, 1915; rpt. 1969), pp. 10 (Bourne), 74 (Huntingdon), 80 (Kyme), 96 (St Frideswide's), 120 (Thornton), 126 (Wellow), and very many others. There are also numerous complaints about a lack of instructors *in grammatica*. At Newnham, for example, the prior stated that because there was no such instructor, the canons were virtually

mere laymen (*quasi mere laici*) and because of this, paid no attention to their books (*Visitations of Religious Houses in the Diocese of Lincoln, Vol. 3, Part 2* [n. 21], p. 232).

47. The translation dates from the second half of the fifteenth century (it was probably begun c. 1468) and was prepared (says the translator) because the nuns needed 'bettyr knowlyge of her munymentys', and greater facility in providing information to their 'seruauntys, rent gedurarys, and receyuowrs, in the absent of her lernyd councell' (*The English Register of Godstow Nunnery, near Oxford*, ed. A. Clark [EETS/OS, 129; London, 1911], p. 25).

48. See VCH *Bedfordshire*, vol. 1, p. 389.

49. See *Visitations of Religious Houses in the Diocese of Lincoln, Vol. 2, Part 1* (n. 20), p. 174: on being asked whether she could present a certificate stating that she had fulfilled the bishop's mandate, the prioress *dicit quod non, eo quod non intellexit illud* [i.e. the mandate], *nec eciam capellanus suus cui illud exhibuit.* See also S. L. Thrupp, *The Merchant Class of Medieval London [1300–1500]* (Ann Arbor, 1948; rpt. 1962), p. 158.

50. VCH *Staffordshire*, vol. 3, p. 224.

51. *Visitations of Religious Houses in the Diocese of Lincoln, Vol. 1* (n. 46), p. 52: the bishop commanded that his injunctions be read *in lingua vulgari et materna* eight times a year before the whole convent gathered together in the Chapter House, *ne monialis aliqua vel conuersa pretendere valeat ignoranciam de eisdem* ('so that no nun or lay-sister may be able to pretend ignorance of them').

52. *Visitations of Religious Houses in the Diocese of Lincoln, Vol. 2, Part 1* (n. 20), p. 147: . . . *ne quis vestrum eorum ignoranciam pretendere valeat, illa lingua que melius intelligi [possit] legi faciatis.* It seems to have been a common and convenient excuse.

53. See VCH *Hampshire and the Isle of Wight*, vol. 2, p. 128.

54. See Power, p. 248, and Orme, *English Schools*, p. 53. Whether this was to improve the nuns' Latin vocabulary or to cut down on conversation is a moot point, but similar injunctions applied to men's houses. In 1432 the monks at St Neot's were required to converse briefly, quietly, and in either Latin or French (*Visitations of Religious Houses in the Diocese of Lincoln, Vol. 1* [n. 46], p. 110).

55. The Latin text and an English translation may be found in W. G. Clark-Maxwell, 'The Outfit for the Profession of an Austin Canoness at Lacock, Wilts. in the Year 1395, and Other Memoranda', *Archaeological Journal* 69 (1912), pp. 117–24. It may perhaps be objected that writing up a list of expenses does not require much Latin. That is true, but what is remarkable is that it was written in Latin at all. One might have expected the chambress to jot it down in English.

56. See nn. 35 and 26 above.
57. ROMSEY 1. But the *ex libris* inscription is fifteenth century: see further n. 60 below.
58. LACOCK 1.
59. SWINE A (Donation).
60. POLSLOE MR. We should note, too, that in some cases, a nunnery acquired a Latin volume at a much later date than the volume was actually written. HEYNINGS 1 is a s.xii manuscript with a s.xv *ex libris*; ROMSEY 1 is a early s.xiv manuscript which also has a s.xv *ex libris*; and SWINE B.1 certainly came to the house some time after it was written in s.xii/xiii. These discrepancies may indicate that the volumes in question were donated to the nunneries as gifts (though nowhere is that stated); they may result from *ex libris* inscriptions being added at a later date to volumes which had long been in the possession of a particular house (a practice which can be parallelled elsewhere); or they may indicate that as late as the fifteenth century certain nuns or nunneries still had an interest in acquiring books in Latin (see further n. 61 below).
61. See BARKING (APPENDIX). My own view of the matter is that at least some of the books belonged to the abbey, but that it is impossible to tell which or how many.
62. Adamson, 'Extent of Literacy in England' (n. 14), p. 21; R. Hirsch, *Printing, Selling and Reading* (Wiesbaden, 1967), p. 127, n. 4; Clanchy, *Memory to Written Record*, pp. 125–6, 193–4, 268–70, 278–9.
63. See the works cited in M. B. Parkes, 'A Fragment of an Early-Tenth-Century Anglo-Saxon Manuscript and Its Significance', in *idem, Scribes, Scripts and Readers* (n. 43), p. 177, n. 13. (This article was first published in *Anglo-Saxon England* 12 [1983], pp. 129–40).
64. See K. Christ, revd. A. Kern, tr. T. M. Otto, *The Handbook of Medieval Library History* (Metuchen/London, 1984), pp. 261–2. In 1469, as part of a reform at Ebstorf, the prioress had all the existing choir books destroyed, and over a period of three years the nuns produced 'their own, more lavish, set of liturgical volumes, including codices *literis aureis et pictatis'* (J. F. Hamburger, 'Art, Enclosure and the *Cura Monialium*: Prolegomena in the Guise of a Postscript', *Gesta* 31 [1992], p. 121). We hear of nothing comparable in England.
65. WINCHESTER 4. At the end of the manuscript the copyist has written: *Salua et incolomis maneat per secula scriptrix* ('May the *scriptrix* remain forever safe and unharmed'). In some cases, however, it seems that the term *scriptrix* may refer to the rubricator rather than the scribe: see P. Saenger, *A Catalogue of the Pre-1500 Western Manuscript Books at the Newberry Library* (Chicago/London, 1989), pp. 118–9 (MS 64).

66. A. I. Doyle, 'Book Production by the Monastic Orders in England (c. 1375–1530)', in *Medieval Book Production: Assessing the Evidence*, ed. L. L. Brownrigg (Los Altos Hills, 1990), p. 15: 'I know of no certain evidence, in books signed or ascribed, of production by women religious in England at the period under discussion, in contrast with the Low Countries and Germany.'

67. J. C. Fox, 'An Anglo-Norman Apocalypse from Shaftesbury Abbey', *Modern Language Review* 8 (1913), p. 347. The manuscript is SHAFTESBURY *MR* b in Part II of this study.

68. BARKING 5.

69. ICKLETON 1. See also VCH *Cambridgeshire*, vol. 2, p. 225.

70. CHESTER 1.

71. SYON A.42.

72. See Collins, *The Bridgettine Breviary* (n. 26), pp. vii–viii, n. 4; de Hamel, *Syon Abbey* (n. 27), p. 128. It is possible that the first Syon scribe whom we can identify by name was a woman: Anna Kaarlsdottir (see *ibid.*, pp. 56–7).

73. As we can see from the ownership inscriptions recorded in Part II of this study. In the early 1350s, when the abbot of St Albans, Thomas de la Mare, required the nuns of St Mary de Pré to profess the *Rule* of St Benedict *in scriptis* (see Chapter 1, n. 93), the signing of their names would have been the most that was required of them.

74. All that we know about Muriel is to be found in J. S. P. Tatlock, 'Muriel: The Earliest English Poetess', *Publications of the Modern Language Association of America* 48 (1933), pp. 317–21. Her name implies that she was Norman, but the rave reviews her work received from such writers as Serlo and Baudri of Bourgeuil indicate that she was writing in Latin.

75. Brief accounts of all these writers (together with bibliographies) may be found in the useful compendium by Katharina M. Wilson, *An Encyclopedia of Continental Women Writers* (Garland Reference Library of the Humanities, 698; New York/London, 1991) (two volumes). Peter Dronke, *Women Writers of the Middle Ages: A Critical Study of Texts from Perpetua (d. 203) to Marguerite Porete (d. 1310)* (Cambridge, 1984), has sections on Constantia, Héloise, and Hildegard of Bingen, and one chapter (Chapter 4) on 'Personal Poetry by Women: the Eleventh and Twelfth Centuries'. The women of the Italian Renaissance are best discussed in M. L. King & A. Rabil, *Her Immaculate Hand. Selected Works By and About the Women Humanists of Quattrocento Italy* (Binghampton, NY, 1983), and M. L. King, *Women of the Renaissance* (Chicago/London, 1991). See also the interesting collection of papers in *Beyond Their Sex: Learned Women of the European Past*, ed. P. H. Labalme (New York/London, 1980).

76. See nn. 110–12 below.
77. After the thirteenth century, those houses which formerly had received only aristocratic women of the highest social status found themselves forced to lower their standards. The daughters of royal and baronial families gradually became fewer, and their place was taken by daughters of the local gentry. Lacock and Elstow are good examples, but there are a number of others. There were several reasons for this, but this is not the place to examine them. See Power, pp. 4–14.
78. VCH *Cambridgeshire*, vol. 2, p. 294.
79. VCH *Kent*, vol. 2, p. 181.
80. VCH *Wiltshire*, vol. 3, pp. 243, 249.
81. See Legge, 'Anglo-Norman as a Spoken Language' (n. 2), p. 109. See also *idem, Anglo-Norman Literature and Its Background* (Oxford, 1963; rpt. 1971), p. 266.
82. See Clanchy, *Memory to Written Record*, pp. 197–223.
83. See nn. 44 and 50 above.
84. VCH *Wiltshire*, vol. 3, p. 238.
85. See nn. 44–47 and 51–52 above.
86. See generally M. D. Legge, 'The French Language and the English Cloister', in *Medieval Studies Presented to Rose Graham*, ed. V. Ruffer & A. J. Taylor (Oxford, 1950), pp. 146–62.
87. See Orme, *Childhood to Chivalry*, pp. 121–8; *idem*, 'Education of the Courtier' (n. 10), pp. 169–70; and Parkes, 'Literacy of the Laity' (n. 43), pp. 289–90.
88. See LACOCK *MR* b.
89. Legge, 'Anglo-Norman as a Spoken Language' (n. 2), p. 116.
90. All are listed in Index II and there is no need to repeat that information here.
91. M. D. Legge, *Anglo-Norman in the Cloisters: The Influence of the Orders upon Anglo-Norman Literature* (Edinburgh, 1950), pp. 98–101; *idem, Anglo-Norman Literature and Its Background* (n. 81), pp. 223–4. The material in Legge's later book does not always supersede that in the earlier.
92. Legge, *Anglo-Norman Literature and Its Background*, pp. 107–8.
93. Legge, *Anglo-Norman in the Cloisters*, pp. 64–8; *idem, Anglo-Norman Literature and Its Background*, pp. 214–6.
94. See Power, pp. 25–8, for examples of other youngsters entering nunneries. Mary had done so in order to be a companion to her grandmother, Queen Eleanor of Provence.
95. See Legge, *Anglo-Norman in the Cloisters*, pp. 77–8; *idem, Anglo-Norman Literature and Its Background*, pp. 298–302.
96. See Legge, *Anglo-Norman in the Cloisters*, pp. 105–6; *idem, Anglo-Norman Literature and Its Background*, pp. 187–91.

97. See Legge, *Anglo-Norman in the Cloisters*, pp. 106–7; *idem*, *Anglo-Norman Literature and Its Background*, pp. 238–9; and SHAFTES-BURY *MR* b.

98. See Legge, *Anglo-Norman in the Cloisters*, pp. 82–4; *idem*, *Anglo-Norman Literature and Its Background*, pp. 226–7.

99. See Legge, *Anglo-Norman in the Cloisters*, pp. 91–6.

100. CAMPSEY 5. Eileen Power knew of the work by Clemence of Barking, but thought that Juliana Berners, the author of the *Boke of St Albans*, might also have been a nun (Power, pp. 239–40). This is not the case: see R. Hands, 'Juliana Berners and *The Boke of St. Albans*', *Review of English Studies* N.S. 18 (1967), p. 24.

101. See Legge, *Anglo-Norman Literature and Its Background*, pp. 66–72 (for Jarnik's edition, see p. 66, n. 1). She gives her name and her nunnery at lines 2677–9: 'Jo ki sa vie ai translatee / Par nun sui Clemence numee, / De Berkinge sui nunain' (*ibid.*, p. 68).

102. See n. 33 above and Legge, *Anglo-Norman Literature and Its Background*, pp. 60–6 (for Södergård's edition, see p. 60, n. 1).

103. *Ibid.*, pp. 67, 71.

104. See nn. 33 and 102 above.

105. See Legge, *Anglo-Norman Literature and Its Background*, pp. 264–6 (for Södergård's edition, see p. 264, n. 1). She gives her name at lines 4619–20 of the text: 'Ici escris mon non Marie, / Pur ce ke soie remembree' (*ibid.*, p. 265).

106. Louis Karl suggested Ely ('Notice sur l'unique manuscrit français de la Bibliothèque de duc de Portland à Welbeck', *Revue des langues romanes* 54 [1911], p. 216), but forgot that the Ely nuns had been exterminated by the Danes in 870. In *Anglo-Norman in the Cloisters*, pp. 51, 75, Dominica Legge suggested Canonsleigh, but later rejected this idea, on linguistic grounds, in favour of Chatteris (*Anglo-Norman Literature and Its Background*, p. 264).

107. A. T. Baker, 'Saints' Lives Written in Anglo-French: Their Historical, Social and Literary Importance', *Essays By Divers Hands, being the Transactions of the Royal Society of Literature of the United Kingdom*, N.S. 4, ed. E. Gosse (London, 1924), p. 122.

108. See Legge, *Anglo-Norman Literature and Its Background*, pp. 260–1. 'The original author', she adds, 'saw nothing strange in delivering an attack, enhanced by a subtle use of rhetoric, on the frail nature of woman (lines 1328–1336) in a work devoted to the praise of one of the species', and 'the nuns [at Campsey] had to endure being addressed as "seigniurs" at meal-times' (*ibid.*, p. 261).

109. Line 7 of the poem, conveniently reproduced (with an important commentary) in Legge, *Anglo-Norman Literature and Its Background*, p. 63.

110. Ö. Södergård (ed.), *La vie d'Edouard le Confesseur: Poème Anglo-Normand du XIIᵉ siècle* (Uppsala, 1948), p. 273, lines 5296–5320 (see also Legge, *Anglo-Norman Literature and Its Background*, pp. 61 [omitting lines 5300–04], 65, with a different translation.) In the prose version of this *Life* which appears in B.L., Egerton 745, this passage reads as follows (fol. 120v): 'If any of you wants to know who composed this book in French (*roumans*), you will know it only on condition that you pray God to pardon the sins of the person who composed it. This life was translated in the abbey of Barking. One of the handmaids of Jesus Christ translated it, but she should not be mentioned by name, for her name, as she well knows, is not worthy to be read in the life of so great a man as was the saintly King Edward. She begs that all those who read this book will not think [the saint] dishonoured because a woman has translated it; and she prays that all who read this life will pray God to forgive her presumption in being so rash as to translate so worthy a life.' The French text may be found conveniently in P. Meyer, 'Notice du Ms. Egerton 745 du Musée Britannique, Appendice: Vie en prose de saint Édouard, roi d'Angleterre', *Romania* 40 (1911), p. 60.
111. *In A Great Tradition: Tribute to Dame Laurentia McLachlan, Abbess of Stanbrook, by the Benedictines of Stanbrook* (London, 1956), p. 152.
112. We should note, however, that the desire for anonymity was not restricted to women. The unknown author of a late thirteenth-century verse life of St Francis likewise conceals his name: 'Pur ly pryez ke se entremyst / De translater en fraunceys / Ceste vie de Seynt Fraunceys, / Ke de ses pechez ayt pardun. / Suffist ke Deu ben set sun nun.' ('Pray for him who undertook to translate this life of St Francis into French, that his sins may be pardoned. It is enough that his name is well known to God.') (Legge, *Anglo-Norman Literature and Its Background*, pp. 258–9).
113. Parkes, 'Literacy of the Laity' (n. 43), p. 287.
114. See n. 5 above.
115. See n. 46 above.
116. See nn. 50–52 above.
117. See Adamson, 'Extent of Literacy in England' (n. 14); Hirsch, *Printing, Selling and Reading* (n. 62), pp. 147–53; Parkes, 'The Literacy of the Laity' (n. 43), pp. 275–97; and M. Keen, *English Society in the Later Middle Ages 1348–1500* (London, 1990), pp. 217–39.
118. See W. Everett, '*The Clensyng of Mannes Soule*: An Introductory Study', *Southern Quarterly* 13 (1975), pp. 268–9.
119. BARKING 11. Whether the work was actually written for Barking —or for any nunnery—remains uncertain. A. I. Doyle suggests that it might have been (A. I. Doyle, 'Books Connected with the Vere

Family and Barking Abbey', *Transactions of the Essex Archaeological Society* N.S. 25 [1958], p. 240); Everett argues against it ('*Clensyng*', pp. 269–71). I am not sufficiently familiar with the text of the *Cleansing* to make a judgement. *The Chastising of God's Children* also appears to have associations with Barking, but just how close those associations are remains unclear (see J. Bazire & E. Colledge [ed.], *The Chastising of God's Children* [Oxford, 1957], pp. 34–7).

120. It may not be. It is not written in the same hand as the ownership-inscription (see BARKING 11; Bazire & Colledge, *Chastising*, pp. 36–7; Everett, '*Clensyng*', p. 269), and its purport is not entirely clear.

121. BARKING 1.

122. See Deanesly, *Lollard Bible* (n. 45), pp. 321–5. The archbishop 'decreed and commanded that it should be made public as catholic, to the edification of the faithful, and the confutation of all false heretics or Lollards' (*ibid.*, p. 322).

123. Doyle, 'Books Connected with the Vere Family and Barking Abbey' (n. 119), p. 240. If, as I believe, some of the books owned by William Pownsett in 1554 once formed part of the Barking library, it is possible that the nuns were also in the fore-front for printed texts of Latin theology and philosophy (see BARKING [APPENDIX]).

124. See Deanesly, *Lollard Bible*, p. 218.

125. DARTFORD 4b; LONDON (ALDGATE) 2b.

126. See Deanesly, *Lollard Bible*, p. 346; M. T. Brady, 'The Pore Caitif: An Introductory Study', *Traditio* 10 (1954), pp. 529–48; and *idem*, 'Lollard Interpolations and Omissions in Manuscripts of *The Pore Caitif*', in *De Cella in Seculum: Religious and Secular Life and Devotion in Late Medieval England*, ed. M. G. Sargent (Cambridge, 1989), pp. 183–203.

127. DARTFORD 1c, 7n; LONDON (ALDGATE) 6; SHAFTESBURY 2f (the *Charter* only).

128. THETFORD 1.

129. *Visitations of the Diocese of Norwich A.D. 1492–1532*, ed. A. Jessopp (Camden Society, N.S. 43; London, 1888; rpt. New York, 1965), p. 91.

130. She was abbess of Denney from 1512 to 1539. For her life after that, see DENNEY 2.

131. DENNEY 2. For a brief account of the work, see Deanesly, *Lollard Bible*, pp. 215–6.

132. See VCH *Cambridgeshire*, vol. 2, p. 301.

133. For the date of Tyndale's version, see Charles Fantazzi's introduction to his excellent translation of the *Enchiridion* in the *Collected Works of Erasmus, Vol. 66*, ed. J. W. O'Malley (Toronto/Buffalo/

London, 1988), p. 6. The date of 1518 given in VCH *Cambridgeshire*, vol. 2, p. 301 is too early. The Latin original (of which a copy might possibly have been at Barking [see BARKING (APPENDIX) 4]) was first published with two other works in 1503 and, as an independent edition, in 1515. Tyndale's translation has not survived, though it may have influenced the version published by Wynkyn de Worde in 1533 (*Collected Works, Vol. 66*, p. 6).

134. See *LP*, vol. 4/2, pp. 1833–4 (no. 4282). Monmouth, in fact, had two copies of the book: he had given or lent the other one to 'a friar of Greenwich', but thought that it was now in the possession of the bishop of Rochester (*ibid.*)

135. *Ibid.* See further G. Walker, 'Heretical Sects in Pre-Reformation England', *History Today* 43 (1993), pp. 46–7, who concludes that 'there is enough in [Monmouth's] story to suggest that he may have been telling the truth, in part at least' (p. 47).

136. See Chapter 2, n. 4. It is interesting to note that although about three-quarters of all incunables were in Latin, more than half of those printed in England were in English (Hirsch, *Printing, Selling and Reading* [n. 62], pp. 132, 134).

137. The best account of Whytford's works is to be found in J. Hogg, *Richard Whytford's The Pype or Tonne of the Lyfe of Perfection, Vol. 1, Pt. 2* (Salzburg Studies in English Literature, 89/1, pt. 2; Salzburg, 1989). For a list of works definitely by Whytford, see *ibid.*, pp. 50–61; those which he might have written are listed on pp. 61–2. The question of his authorship of *The Following of Christ* is fully discussed on pp. 79–99. D. Crane, 'English Translations of the *Imitatio Christi* in the Sixteenth and Seventeenth Centuries', *Recusant History* 13 (1975), pp. 79–100, argues for Whytford as translator (see especially p. 95, n. 7). I can make no contribution to the discussion.

138. This work is fully discussed in Chapter 5 (pp. 190–219) of Hogg's study cited immediately above.

139. See VCH *Middlesex*, vol. 1, p. 186, n. 14 and SYON B.1. The work is preserved in Cambridge, U.L., Dd.2.33, fols. 5–193 (s.xvi[in]): see P. S. Jolliffe, 'Middle English Translations of *De Exterioris et Interioris Hominis Compositione*', *Mediaeval Studies* 36 (1974), pp. 259–77.

140. See H. S. Bennett, 'Notes on Two Incunables: *The Abbey of the Holy Ghost* and *A Ryght Profytable Treatyse*', *The Library* Ser. 5, 10 (1955), pp. 120–1; A. I. Doyle, 'Thomas Betson of Syon Abbey', *The Library*, Ser. 5, 11 (1956), pp. 115–8; and M. C. Erler, 'Syon Abbey's Care for Books: Its Sacristan's Account Rolls 1506/7–1535/6', *Scriptorium* 39 (1985), p. 294.

141. See VCH *Middlesex*, vol. 1, p. 187, and J. T. Rhodes, 'Syon Abbey and its Religious Publications in the Sixteenth Century', *Journal of*

Ecclesiastical History 44 (1993), p. 20. The nun in question might have been from Denney (see *ibid.*, p. 20, n. 50).

142. See *ibid.*, p. 22, and p. 16, n. 35.

143. Darker's hand is distinctive and is illustrated in M. B. Parkes, *English Cursive Book Hands 1250–1500* (Oxford, 1969; rpt. Berkeley/Los Angeles/London, 1980), pl. 8(ii). Parkes' commentary includes a list of other manuscripts copied by Darker. Those included in Part II of this study are SYON A.19, A.29, and B.3.

144. See R. W. Chambers, *On the Continuity of English Prose from Alfred to More and His School* (London, 1932; rpt. 1950), p. cxxxii. See also nn. 94–99 above. Another good example is Osbern Bokenham's *Legendys of Hooly Wummen*, ed. M. S. Serjeantson (EETS/OS, 206; London, 1938), which was written for an unnamed nunnery in East Anglia. A. I. Doyle, 'Books Connected with the Vere Family and Barking Abbey' (n. 119), p. 236, n. 8, has suggested that the nunnery might have been Denney.

145. The authors and titles listed in nn. 137–142 are not and are not intended to be exhaustive. For more complete accounts of publications at, by, and for Syon, see VCH *Middlesex*, vol. 1, pp. 186–7; J. Hogg, 'The Contribution of the Brigittine Order to Late Medieval English Spirituality', in *Analecta Cartusiana* 35 (*Spiritualität Heute und Gestern: Internationaler Kongress vom 4. bis 7. August 1982*, Band 3; Salzburg, 1983), pp. 153–74 (which is primarily concerned with Whytford), and Rhodes, 'Syon Abbey and its Religious Publications', pp. 11–25. That still other works in English were to be found in the library of the Syon sisters is not in question. The titles of some of them are mentioned by the author of *The Mirror of Our Lady* and include Rolle's English Psalter (*Myroure*, ed. Blunt [n. 18], p. 3), 'Englysshe bibles' (*ibid.*), and 'saynt Mawdes boke' (p. 33 and elsewhere). 'Saint Maud's book' is a common title for the English translation—*The Book of Ghostly Grace*—of the *Liber specialis gratiae* of Mechtild of Hackeborn. A 'shorte lesson' from this treatise is included in the *Myroure* (pp. 276–7). My main concern in these chapters, however, is with surviving volumes, and my brief notes on Syon are *not* intended to be a comprehensive study. A great deal of work remains to be done of this extraordinarily interesting house.

146. See M. Bateson, *Catalogue of the Library of Syon Monastery Isleworth* (Cambridge, 1898), p. ix.

147. R. Lovatt, 'The Library of John Blacman and Contemporary Carthusian Spirituality', *Journal of Ecclesiastical History* 43 (1992), p. 226. 'As the intellectual distinction of the brethren increased across the century [Lovatt continues], so the books which they gave to the

library reveal a noticeable decline in the representation of English authors and their replacement by foreign writers, and an almost total absence of works in the vernacular. The change is the more striking because the sisters of Syon retained their appetite for vernacular spiritual writings and in this respect it would seem that their tastes became increasingly divorced from those of the brethren' (*ibid.*).

148. V. Gillespie, 'Vernacular Books of Religion', in *Book Production and Publishing in Britain 1375–1475*, ed. J. Griffiths & D. Pearsall (Cambridge, 1989), p. 318. See also the earlier study by H. S. Bennett, 'The Production and Dissemination of Vernacular Manuscripts in the Fifteenth Century', *The Library*, Ser. 5, 1 (1946–47), pp. 167–78.

149. By 'spirituality' I do not just mean 'mysticism' (whatever that may be), and English writings on spirituality are not restricted to the works of the fourteenth-century English 'mystics'. Any 'vernacular guide to godliness' (if I may again quote Gillespie [*Book Production and Publishing in Britain 1375–1475*, p. 317]) may be included in the category.

150. Though more was going on than some have supposed: see Doyle, 'Book Production by the Monastic Orders in England (c. 1375–1530)' (n. 66), pp. 1–19, and *idem*, 'Publication by Members of the Religious Orders', in *Book Production and Publishing in Britain 1375–1475*, pp. 109–23.

151. The evidence for this will be presented in my 'Monastic Libraries: 1400–1557', in *A History of the Book in Britain, Vol. III: 1400–1557*, ed. L. Hellinga & J. B. Trapp (forthcoming).

152. In counting the books (a tedious exercise which I cannot recommend), I excluded non-monastic cathedrals, dioceses, parishes, parish churches, collegiate churches, hospitals, university colleges, guilds, and secular institutions. Printed books account for about 6.5% of the total.

153. Contrary to what one might expect, this figure is increased, not decreased, if one excludes the forty-eight volumes listed under SYON (Section A). The total number of manuscripts and printed books is then 96; the total number of fifteenth- and sixteenth-century manuscripts (excluding those from Syon) is 51; the percentage is 53%.

154. With regard to printed books, with the exception of Durham, the figures are paltry: five volumes from Christ Church (1.5%), three from Bury (1.1%), one from St Augustine's (0.4%), and five from Worcester (1.3%). Over 630 books and manuscripts survive from Durham, and of these about 140 (22%) are printed books (see A. I. Doyle, 'The Printed Books of the Last Monks of Durham', *The*

Library, Ser. 6, 10 [1988], p. 203). Further discussion of this matter will be found in my 'Monastic Libraries: 1400–1557' (n. 151).

155. *The Cloud of Unknowing and The Book of Privy Counselling*, ed. P. Hodgson (EETS/OS, 218; London, 1944), p. 162, lines 17–19.
156. *Ibid.*, p. 137, line 16.
157. *Ibid.*, p. 153, lines 13–15. See further W. A. Pantin, *The English Church in the Fourteenth Century* (Cambridge, 1955; rpt. Toronto/ Buffalo/London, 1980), pp. 251–2, but Pantin's designation of these texts as 'anti-intellectual' is misleading. Rolle and the others are not saying that scholarship is wrong or to be avoided, but only that conceptual knowledge must be distinguished from experiential knowledge, and that learning, on its own, will not lead a person to the experience of God. To know that the composition of water is H_2O is undeniably of great scientific value, but it will not help you if you are dying of thirst in the desert.
158. Forde, Rievaulx, and possibly Buckfast. This is clearly not the place for an extended discussion of this question.
159. See Chapter 1, n. 123.
160. See D. N. Bell, 'The Books of Meaux Abbey', *Analecta Cisterciensia* 40 (1984), p. 28. When Thomas de Burton wrote his great chronicle of Meaux, he had already retired to Fountains (*ibid.*, p. 25).

PART II
A LIST OF MANUSCRIPTS
AND PRINTED BOOKS
FROM ENGLISH NUNNERIES

ABBREVIATIONS

Allen
: H. E. Allen, *Writings Ascribed to Richard Rolle, Hermit of Hampole* (New York, 1927; rpt. 1966).

Aungier
: G. J. Aungier, *The History and Antiquities of Syon Monastery, the Parish of Isleworth, and the Chapelry of Hounslow* (London, 1840).

Bloomfield
: M. Bloomfield, *et al.*, *Incipits of Latin Works on the Virtues and Vices, 1100–1500 A.D.* (Cambridge, Mass., 1979).

Bossuat
: R. Bossuat, *Manuel bibliographique de la littérature française du moyen âge* (Melun, 1951; rpt. Nendeln/Liechtenstein, 1971), with supplements for 1949–53 (with J. Monfrin) (Paris, 1955; rpt. Nendeln/Liechtenstein, 1971), 1954–60 (Paris, 1961), and 1960–80 (Part 1, by F. Vielliard & J. Monfrin) (Paris, 1986).

Bourdillon
: A. F. C. Bourdillon, *The Order of Minoresses in England* (British Society of Franciscan Studies, 12; Manchester, 1926).

Brown/Robbins
: C. Brown & R. H. Robbins, *The Index of Middle English Verse* (New York, 1943), with Supplement by R. H. Robbins & J. L. Cutler (Lexington, 1965).

Cavanaugh
: S. H. Cavanaugh, *A Study of Books Privately Owned in England: 1300–1450* (University of Pennsylvania, Ph.D. Diss., 1980; University Microfilms International).

Chevalier
: U. Chevalier, *Repertorium Hymnologicum* (Louvain, 1892–1921). Six volumes.

Collins
: A. J. Collins (ed.), *The Bridgettine Breviary of Syon Abbey*, (Henry Bradshaw Society, 96; Worcester, 1969).

Copinger	W. A. Copinger, *Supplement to Hain's 'Repertorium Bibliographicum'* (Leipzig, 1895–1902; repr. Milan, 1950).
Davis	G. R. C. Davis, *Medieval Cartularies of Great Britain* (London, 1958).
de Hamel	C. F. R. de Hamel, *Syon Abbey. The Library of the Bridgettine Nuns and their Peregrinations after the Reformation* (Roxburghe Club, 1991).
Duff	E. G. Duff, *Fifteenth Century English Books* (Oxford, 1917; rpt. Meisenheim, 1964).
Frere	W. H. Frere, *Bibliotheca Musico-Liturgica* (London, 1901–32).
GW	*Gesamtkatalog der Wiegendrucke* (Leipzig, 1925–38).
Hain	L. Hain, *Repertorium Bibliographicum* (Leipzig, 1826–38; repr. Milan, 1948).
HLF	*Histoire littéraire de la France* (Paris, 1865–1949; rpt. Nendeln/Liechtenstein, 1973–74).
Hoskin	E. Hoskins, *Horae Beatae Mariae Virginis* (London/New York, 1901; rpt. Farnborough, 1969).
Jolliffe	P. S. Jolliffe, *A Check-List of Middle English Prose Writings of Spiritual Guidance* (Toronto, 1974).
Kaeppeli	T. Kaeppeli, *Scriptores Ordinis Praedicatorum Medii Aevi* (Rome, 1970–).
Kaufmann	C. M. Kaufmann, *Romanesque Manuscripts 1066–1190* (London, 1975).
Ker	N. R. Ker, *Medieval Libraries of Great Britain* (London, 1964²). Supplement to the Second edition by A. G. Watson (London, 1987).
Ker/MMBL	N. R. Ker, *Medieval Manuscripts in British Libraries* (Oxford, 1969–92). Four volumes (the fourth volume was completed by A. J. Piper).
Ker/AS	N. Ker, *Catalogue of Manuscripts Containing Anglo-Saxon* (Oxford, 1957).
L/B/E	R. E. Lewis, N. F. Blake, & A. S. G. Edwards, *Index of Printed Middle English Prose* (New York/London, 1985).
LP	*Letters and Papers, Foreign and Domestic, of the Reign of Henry VIII*, ed. J. S. Brewer *et al.*, (London, 1862–1910).

Långfors	A. Långfors, *Les Incipit des poèmes français antérieurs au XVIᵉ siècle* (Paris, 1917; rpt. New York, 1970).
Martyrology	The *Martyrology of Syon*, compiled by Richard Whytford, and now preserved in the British Library as B.L., Add. 22285.
Morgan	N. J. Morgan, *Early Gothic Manuscripts (II): 1250–1285* (London, 1988).
Revell	P. Revell, *Fifteenth Century English Prayers and Meditations: A Descriptive List of Manuscripts in the British Library* (New York/London, 1975).
Römer	F. Römer, *Die Handschriftliche Überlieferung der Werke des heiligen Augustinus, Bd. II: Grossbritannien und Irland* (Vienna, 1972).
STC	A. W. Pollard & G. R. Redgrave, *A Short Title Catalogue of Books Printed in England, Scotland, and Ireland 1475–1640* (London, 1976 [revd. ed.]).
Schneyer	J. B. Schneyer, *Repertorium der lateinischen Sermones des Mittelalters* (*Beiträge zur Geschichte der Philosophie und Theologie des Mittelalters* XLIII: 1–11; Münster i. W., 1969–90).
Schulte	J. F. von Schulte, *Die Geschichte der Quellen und Literatur des canonischen Rechts von Gratian bis auf die Gegenwart* (Stuttgart, 1875).
Sonet	J. Sonet, *Répertoire d'Incipit de prières en ancien français* (Geneva, 1956), with supplements by K. V. Sinclair (Hamden, CN, 1978; Westport, CN, 1979), and P. Rézeau (Paris, 1986).
Stegmüller	F. Stegmüller, *Repertorium Biblicum Medii Aevi* (Madrid, 1940–80).
Test. Ebor.	*Testamenta Eboracensia: A Selection of Wills from the Registry at York* (*Surtees Society* 4, 30, 45, 53, 79, 106; Durham/London, 1836–1902). Vol. 1 was edited by J. Raine; vols. 2–5 by J. Raine, Jr.; and vol. 6 by J. W. Clay.
VCH	Victoria County History.
Walther	H. Walther, *Initia Carminum ac Versuum Medii Aevi Posterioris Latinorum* (*Carmina Medii Aevi Posterioris Latina*, I; Göttingen, 1959–69).

Watson   See s.v. Ker above.
Watson/*London*   A. G. Watson, *Catalogue of Dated and Datable*
                   Manuscripts c.700–1600 in the Department of
                   Manuscripts, The British Library (London, 1979).
Watson/*Oxford*   A. G. Watson, *Catalogue of Dated and Datable*
                   Manuscripts c.435–1600 in Oxford Libraries (Ox-
                   ford, 1984).

In the following list, the location of the nunneries is given
according to the older counties of England, not the modern
administrative divisions. This is not antiquarian conservatism,
but reflects the invaluable (though sometimes outdated) accounts
in the various volumes of the VCH.

The inscriptions transcribed below are restricted to those
of immediate relevance to this present enquiry.

THE LIST

AMESBURY (Wiltshire), *Priory and later abbey of BVM and St Mellor (Cell of Fontevrault)* (Benedictine Nuns).

1 ?Cambridge, U.L., Ee.6.16 s.xiv

Hours of the Virgin (fol. 17–127), preceded by variant offices for Advent and a Calendar, and followed by other additional services, the Penitential Psalms, a Litany, further Hours (including those of St Mellor or Melorus, patron of Amesbury), Psalms 1–19, Hours of the Cross, various prayers, the Office of the Dead, Hours of St John the Baptist, Psalms 113–147, prayers in French (Sonet 2718, 2929, 3650), three prayers in Latin, and a hymn in French to the Holy Spirit. On fols. 8 and 9 are hymns to St Anne in Latin and French (Sonet 2496), and on fol. 16 a hymn to St Francis in French (Sonet 544). The French material in this manuscript is discussed by Paul Meyer in *Romania* 15 (1886), pp. 271–2, who also provides an edition of the hymn to St Francis. The hymn to the Holy Spirit (Sonet 1818) has been edited by S. H. Thomson in *Medium Aevum* 8 (1939), pp. 38–9. The manuscript is no. 781 in Frere.

(fol. 9 [s.xiv]) *Aue noster sanctissime Roberte, sacerdos Dei electe, funditur et constitutor tocius ordinis Fontiseuraddi.* Robert of Arbrissel, who died in 1117 and was actually a *beatus*, not a saint, founded the Order of Fontevrault at Fontevrault (in the south of France), in about 1100.

2 London, B.L., Add. 18632 s.xv

a (fol. 5) John Lydgate, *Siege of Thebes* (Brown/Robbins 3928). **b** (fol. 34) Thomas Hoccleve, *De regimine principum* (Brown/Robbins 2229). The fly-leaves of this manuscript (fols. 2 and 101) contain fragments of the household accounts of Elizabeth de Burgh, countess of Ulster. The accounts cover parts of the years 1356–9 and are of interest in mentioning payments made to Geoffrey Chaucer when he was a page in her household. A complete edition of the accounts by E. A. Bond is printed in *Life-Records of Chaucer*, ed. E. A. Bond &

M. D. Selby (Chaucer Society, 2nd Ser., 21; London, 1886), vol. 3, pp. 97–113. The sections relating specifically to Chaucer, together with a full discussion, may be found in *Chaucer Life-Records*, ed. M. M. Crow & C. C. Olsen (Oxford, 1966), pp. 13–18.

(fol. 99v [s.xvi[1]]) *Istum librum dominus Richardus Wygyngton, capellanus, dedit prioresse et conuentui monasterii Ambrosii Burgi in uigilia natiuitatis beate Marie uirginis Anno Domini m<illesim>o quingentesimo octauo, ut ipse ex caritate orent pro ipso et amicis suis. Et si aliquis istum librum a monasterio alienauerit, anathema sit.* Nothing is known of Richard Wiggington. The transcript of this inscription on fol. 100 of the manuscript contains three errors.

3 London, Private Collection, s.xiv

Four folios of a breviary.

The fragment contains prayers for the Octave of St Mellor and nine readings for St Frideswide.

4 ?Oxford, Bod. Lib., Add. A.42 (S.C. 30149) s.xv[ex]

An (unprinted) exhortation addressed to 'My deare susterys Mary and Anne wyth all the other devouth dyscyples of the scole of cryste in youre monastery of Amysbury, be grace and the blessyng of oure lorde euyrlastyng. Amen.' (Jolliffe H.22 = O.35). The last folios of this manuscript (fols. 21–30) have been remounted. The prioress at the time was Christiana, but she is not listed in VCH *Wiltshire*, vol. 3, p. 258.

Although the exhortation is addressed to the nuns of Amesbury, we cannot be absolutely certain that this particular manuscript came from the house.

5 ?Oxford, Bod. Lib., Liturg. misc. 407 (S.C. 29071) s.xiii[in]–xiv

The earlier part of this manuscript (s.xiii[in]) contains a Psalter, preceded by a Calendar (with a table) and followed by Canticles with the Athanasian Creed. There is no Litany. The Hymnary (fols. 223–55 [without music]), which contains French rubrics, was added in the second half of the 14th century, at which time certain additions were made to the Calendar. The manuscript is no. 178 in Frere.

The manuscript may have been written at Fontevrault (see 1 above), the mother-house of Amesbury. The association with Amesbury depends on liturgical and calendrical evidence (St Mellor's name appears in blue in the Calendar [fol. 5v]): see further the notes to S.C. 29071.

6 Windsor Castle, Jackson Collection, 3 (4 fols.) s.xiii
   Four folios of a Breviary.
   The fragment contains offices for St Mellor and a prayer to
   St Edith.

ANKERWYKE (Buckinghamshire), *Nunnery of St Mary Magdalen*
(Benedictine Nuns).

1 Cambridge, Gonville & Caius Coll., 390 s.xv
   a (fol. 1) *Treatise of the Seven Points of True Love and Everlasting Wisdom* (L/B/E 465). This is an English translation
of the Latin version (*Horologium sapientiae*) of Heinrich Suso's
Büchlein der ewigen Weisheit (*Little Book of Eternal Wisdom*). **b**
(fol. 56v) *The Life and Martyrdom of St Catherine of Alexandria*
(L/B/E 28 [ending imperfectly]). This is the Life of St Catherine extracted from the *Golden Legend*.
   (fol. 32v [s.xvi^1]) *Thys ys my boke. God geue me grase to
foolow the good and godli counseyll therin. Alicia Lego. Ihesu haue
marsy on me, myserbel synner.* In the report of the visitation by
Bishops Atwater and Langland to Ankerwyke on 25 May 1519
there is mention of a Domina Alicia Leg' who, with Domina
Magdalena Downe (prioress at the time of the Dissolution),
is described as *tacite non expresse sunt professe,* i.e. they were
ready to make their profession but had not yet been professed (*Visitations in the Diocese of Lincoln, 1517–1531,* ed. A. H.
Thompson [Lincoln Record Society, 35; Hereford, 1944], vol. 2,
p. 70). She appears to have been the daughter of William Lego,
barber-surgeon, who was buried in the church of the Grey
Friars in London. Anne, another daughter, was also a nun
(see C. L. Kingsford, 'Additional Material for the History of
the Grey Friars, London', in *idem* [ed.], *Collectanea Franciscana,
II* [British Society of Franciscan Studies, 10; Manchester, 1922],
p. 138 [will dated 15 August 1530]).

Miscellaneous Records
   a When Bishop Alnwick visited the priory on 10 October
1441 Dame Margery Kyrkeby or Kirby reported 'quod habeban-
tur in domo pulchra psalteria in numero x, quorum quedam
priorissa donauit et alienauit. Fatetur [*viz.* prioriﬀa] se acco-
modasse tria, vnum priorisse de Bromhale; negat absque consensu conuentus' ('that there used to be ten beautiful psalters
in the house, some of which the prioress has given away and

alienated. [The prioress] admits that she has lent three—one [of them] to the prioress of Bromhall—[but] she denies [that she did so] without the consent of the convent' (*Visitations of Religious Houses in the Diocese of Lincoln, Vol. 2: Records of Visitations held by William Alnwick, 1436–1449*, ed. A. H. Thompson, [Lincoln Record Society, 14; Horncastle, 1918], vol. 2/1, p. 2). The prioress of Ankerwyke at this time was Clemence Medford who had earlier been a nun at Bromhall (the two nunneries were only about six miles apart), and the prioress of Bromhall was probably Alice Burton (VCH *Berkshire*, vol. 2, p. 81). When Clemence Medford died in 1442, she was succeeded by Margery Kirby.

b In the report of their visitation on 25 May 1519, Bishops Atwater and Langland reported 'ij libros missales impressos' in the church (*Visitations in the Diocese of Lincoln* [see 1 above], vol. 2, p. 71). *Impressos* indicates that the missals in question were printed books.

ARDEN (Yorkshire, N.R.), *Priory of St Andrew* (Benedictine Nuns).

Miscellaneous Records

In his will dated 27 April 1481 (probated 7 March 1482–3), William Overton of Helmsley bequeathed to his niece Elena, 'moniali in Arden, v marcas, et unum Primarium magnum cum coopertorio de damask coloris blodii' (*Test. Ebor.*, vol. 3, p. 262). Five marks was £3:6:8, about eight months' wages for an un-skilled labourer at the time.

ARTHINGTON (Yorkshire, W.R.) *Priory of BVM* (Cluniac Nuns).

Miscellaneous Records

In her will dated 27 March 1448 (probated 1 April 1448), Agnes Stapilton, widow of Sir Brian Stapilton/Stapleton of Car-leton, bequeathed 'Item . . . monialibus de Arthyngton, xxs., et librum meum vocatum *Prik of conscience*' (J. W. Clay [ed.], *North Country Wills . . . 1383–1558* [Surtees Society, 116; Durham/Lon-don, 1908], p. 48 [Cavanaugh, pp. 815–6]).

The volume recorded is the popular *Prick of Conscience*, sometimes attributed (probably incorrectly) to Richard Rolle (see Allen, pp. 372–97 [where this bequest is mentioned]; Brown/Robbins 3428).

BARKING (Essex), *Abbey of BVM and St Ethelburga* (Benedictine Nuns).

In the list below, manuscripts 2, 6, and 10–13 are recorded in M. R. James, 'Manuscripts from Essex Monastic Libraries', *Transactions of the Essex Archaeological Society* N.S. 21 (1937 [for 1933]), p. 35, and manuscripts 1, 2, 7, and 10–14 in N. R. Ker, 'More Manuscripts from Essex Monastic Libraries', *Transactions of the Essex Archaeological Society* N.S. 23 (1945), pp. 301–2, 305, 310.

1 Beeleigh Abbey, Miss C. Foyle s.xv[in]

a (fol. 3) Nicholas Love, *Mirror of the Blessed Life of Christ (Speculum vitae Christi)* (L/B/E 553). This is a translation of *ps.-*Bonaventure, *Meditationes vitae Christi*. **b** (fol. 169v) William Flete, *De remediis contra temptationes* (a variant of the first Middle English version) (Jolliffe K.8.[a]; L/B/E 230, 528). The first three folios of the manuscript contain two devotional excerpts in English and a brief treatise in Latin *de peccatore, inc.* 'Narratur in Daniele'. This is not listed in Bloomfield. On fol. 4v, after the table of contents for the *Mirror*, are the Latin verses 'Balsamus et munda cera' (Walther 2058) which appear in numerous manuscripts; and at the end of the volume (fol. 177) is another brief and unidentified Latin text, *inc.* 'Scribitur Mathei quinto capitulo'. I am indebted to Miss Christina Foyle of Beeleigh Abbey for providing me with a full description of this manuscript.

(fol. 4v [s.xv[in]]) *Iste liber constat domine Sibille de Felton, abbatisse de Berkyng.* (fol. 178 [s.xv]) *Mistris Agnes Gowldewell me possidet ex dono Margarete Scroope quondam monache monasterii de Berckynge.* (fol. 179v [s.xv]) *Mystris Gowldewell me possidet teste Streete.* The inscriptions on fols. 178 and 179v are in the same hand. Sybil de Felton (or Sybil Morle) was abbess of Barking from 1393 to her death in 1419. She was born in 1359, the second daughter of Sir Thomas Felton, K.G. (whose *obit* appears in the Calendar in no. **14** below [3 May]) and his wife, Joan, the daughter of Sir Richard Walkefare. Sybil was married to Sir Thomas Morley and entered Barking after his death (VCH *Essex*, vol. 2, p. 121). See also nos. **11, 14** and **15** below. Margaret Scroope, Scrope, or Scrowpe was first chantress at the election of the last abbess of Barking, Dorothy Barley, in

1527 and received a pension after the abbey was dissolved in November 1539 (*ibid.*, p. 123). She was a cousin of Elizabeth de Vere, Countess of Oxford (see no. **13** below and A. I. Doyle, 'Books Connected with the Vere Family and Barking Abbey', *Transactions of the Essex Archaeological Society* N.S. 25 [1958], p. 241, n. 1).

2 Cambridge, Trinity Coll., 1226 (O.3.54) s.xv

Hymnary (with music) for *proprium de tempore, proprium sanctorum,* and *commune sanctorum* (imperfect at end). The Hymnary (which begins on fol. 13) is preceded by matins of the dead and the ferial office and followed by a few canticles and antiphons. A description of the manuscript is provided in J. B. L. Tolhurst (ed.), *The Ordinale and Customary of the Benedictine Nuns of Barking Abbey* (Henry Bradshaw Society, 65–66; London, 1927–28), vol. 1, p. x.

Three hymns for St Ethelburga and one for St Erkenwald clearly indicate a Barking provenance. See also Ker, 'More Manuscripts from Essex Monastic Libraries', p. 305.

3 ?Cardiff, Public Lib., 1.381 fos. 81–146 s.xii^{in}–xiii

A collection of seven *vitae sanctorum* as follows: **a** (fol. 81) Goscelin, Life of St Ethelburga (*BHL* 2630b). **b** (fol. 94) Life of St Hildelitha (*BHL* 3942). **c** (fol. 97) Life of St Edward the Martyr (*BHL* 2418). **d** (fol. 102v) Goscelin, Life of St Edith (*BHL* 2388). **e** (fol. 121) Ricemarch, Life of St David (*BHL* 2107). **f** (fol. 130) Hildebert of Lavardin, Metrical Life of St Mary of Egypt (*BHL* 5419; Walther 18159). **g** Life of St Ebrulfus (*BHL* 2377).

The appearance of *vitae* of St Ethelburga and St Hildelitha, who was appointed second abbess of Barking c. 717, leave little doubt that this manuscript was once at the abbey. Other descriptions of the manuscript are noted by Ker in Ker/*MMBL*, vol. 2, p. 347.

4 ?Cardiff, Public Lib., 3.833 s.xiii^{ex}

a (fol. 1) Defensor of Ligugé, *Scintillarium* (*CPL* 1302). **b** (fol. 46) Brief anonymous theological tracts and commonplaces, including an anonymous *De sacramento altaris*, ps.-Jerome, *De xv signis* (this is actually an extract from Peter Comestor, *Historia scholastica, cap. 141 in evangelia* [*PL* 198: 1611A–C]), *De decem plagis Egypti* (Walther 14585), and an extract from Augustine's *De doctrina christiana* (*PL* 34: 82–90). **c** (fol. 61) John Beleth, *Summa de ecclesiasticis officiis* (ed. H. Douteil, *CCCM* 41, 41A

[1976]). One quire is now lost. **d** (fol. 150) *Summa de vitiis et virtutibus* (Bloomfield 5449), attributed in this manuscript to Stephen Langton. This is followed (fol. 164) by a few theological notes.

(fol. 1 [s.xiii^ex]) *Liber sancte Adelburge de <Barking>, qui ipsum alienauerit, anathema sit. Amen.* <Barking> has been thoroughly erased, but it can hardly be anywhere else.

5 London, B.L., Add. 10596, fols. 25–83 s.xv

a (fol. 25) Wycliffite translation of the book of Tobit in the revision traditionally ascribed to John Purvey (L/B/E 119). **b** (fol. 47v) *Magnificat* and *Benedictus*, both in the later Wycliffite version. **c** (fol. 49) An anonymous and unprinted 'deuout meditacioun . . . on the godenes of oure blessid lord' (Revell 6). **d** (fol. 54v) Prayers (unprinted) in English to Jesus, Michael, Gabriel, Raphael, one's guardian angel, all angels and evangelists, patriarchs, holy innocents, martyrs, confessors, virgins, maidens, and all saints (see Revell 263, 323–9, 331–8, and P. Brown & E. D. Higgs, *Index of Middle English Prose, Handlist V* [Cambridge, 1988], pp. 24–34). **e** (fol. 77) Wycliffite translation of the book of Susanna in the revision traditionally ascribed to John Purvey (L/B/E 119). **f** (fol. 82v) Two pages of prayers (in Latin) to *mater Ethelburga*, patroness of Barking (imperfect at beginning and end).

(fol. 82 [s.xv]) *Iste liber constat Matilde Hayle de Berkinge*, followed by *Iste liber constat D<omine> Marie Hastyngs de Berkynge*. The Hayle inscription is beautifully written in red at the head of the folio; the Hastings inscription is written in black at the foot in a later and less formed hand. Nothing is known of either nun.

6 ?London, B.L., Cotton Julius D.viii fols. 40–47v s.xv

This ys the Charthe longynge to the office off the Celeresse of the Monestary of Barkynge as heraffter folowethe, printed in William Dugdale, ed. J. Caley, H. Ellis, & B. Bandinell, *Monasticon Anglicanum* (London, 1817–30), vol. 1, pp. 442–5 (but the orthography of the manuscript is only approximately reproduced). A summary of the document may be found in E. E. Power, *Medieval English Nunneries* (Cambridge, 1922; rpt. New York, 1964, 1988), pp. 563–8. It is possible that the version in the Cotton manuscript is a translation of an earlier text in Latin or French.

It is not certain that these specific folios of Cotton Julius D.viii came from Barking, but there can be no doubt that the original *Charthe* or Charter came from the house. It is included in James, 'Manuscripts from Essex Monastic Libraries', p. 35, but not in Ker or Watson.

7 London, B.L., Cotton Otho A.v s.xiv^ex

This manuscript originally contained a paschal table, a Calendar, and an explanation of the Calendar in English, but most of the manuscript was destroyed in the Cotton Fire of 1731. Only five damaged folios remain: two of the Calendar (for January, February, July, and August) and three of the table, including a *Tabula equacionis duodecim domorum ad meridiem Oxonie*.

What survives of the Calendar is almost identical to that in no. **14** below, and there is no doubt that the manuscript was at Barking. See further Tolhurst (ed.), *Ordinale and Customary* (see no. **2**), vol. 1, pp. ix–x.

8 London, Lambeth Palace, 1495.4 (printed book)

Vitas patrum (in English, and attributed to Jerome), printed by Wynkyn de Worde, Westminster, 1495 (*STC* 14507; Duff 235).

(fol. 1 [s.xvi^1]) *Thys bouke belongyth to Martha ffabyan*. (fol. CCCxlvij) *This bouke belongyth to Martha ffabyan*. Martha Fabyan was a nun at the time of the surrender of Barking in 1539 (VCH *Essex*, vol. 2, p. 120; *LP*, vol. 15, p. 547).

9 ?Nijmegen, U.L., 194, fols. 41–104 s.xv

A collection of prayers and devotional material in Latin and English, beginning with prayers (in Latin) to five saints, including Ethelburga and Hildelitha (cf. no. **3** above). These are followed by prayers to the Virgin, a prayer (in English) before taking communion, Hours of the Holy Spirit (fol. 61–72 and 86–104v), the Fifteen Oes of St Bridget (fol. 105r), the Psalter of St Jerome (fol. 114), Psalms 21–30, and numerous other prayers and salutations to the sacrament, the crucifix, the Virgin, and a variety of saints, both in Latin and English (including another copy of Brown/Robbins [Suppl.] 790.5). The collection ends (fol. 180) with prayers to the nine orders of angels. I am indebted to Drs. L. H. L. Stapper of the Katholieke Universiteit Nijmegen for providing me with a full description of this manuscript.

The prayers to St Ethelburga and St Hildelitha, together with feminine grammatical forms (e.g. *peccatrici* [fol. 163]), almost certainly indicate a Barking provenance.

10 Oxford, Bod. Lib., Bodl. 155 (S.C. 1974) s.x/xi

The four gospels (in Latin) with Jerome's prefaces and the 'Ammonian' sections of Eusebius in the margins. At the end is a list of liturgical gospels for the year preceded by an *argumentum*. The manuscript, no. 227 in Frere, is incomplete in three places, including the beginning.

On fol. 196v is a s.xi list (in Anglo-Saxon) of lands held by Gilebeard (= Gilbert) in Stifford, Essex (see Ker/*AS*, pp. 357–8 no. 303), and a late s.xii copy of an attestation (in Latin), originally issued by Abbess Aelfgiva, recording the gift of a tithe of land to the abbey of Barking. Both documents are printed, with numerous inaccuracies, in G. Hickes, *Linguarum Vett. Septentrionalium Thesaurus Grammatico-Criticus et Archaeologicus* (Oxford, 1705; rpt. Menston, 1970), vol. 1, Dissertatio Epistolaris, pp. 10–11.

11 Oxford, Bod. Lib., Bodl. 923 (S.C. 27701) s.xiv[2]

The Cleansing of Man's Soul (Jolliffe E.14), edited from this manuscript by C. L. Regan (Harvard Univ., Ph.D. Diss., 1963).

(fol. 153v) *Anno domini 1401*, followed on the next line and in a different hand by *Iste liber constat Sibille de Feltoun, abbatisse de Berkyng*. For Sybil de Felton, see no. 1 above; for the significance of the date in this inscription, see *The Chastising of God's Children*, ed. J. Bazire & E. Colledge (Oxford, 1957), pp. 36–7, and Part I of this study, Chapter 3, nn. 119–20.

12 Oxford, Bod. Lib., Laud lat. 19 s.xii [b.3]

a (fol. 1v) Song of Songs, with gloss. This ends on fol. 31v. Fol. 32r is blank, and fols. 32v–33v contain theological excerpts designed to introduce the gloss on Lamentations which follows. **b** (fol. 34v) Lamentations, with gloss.

(fol. 1 [s.xiii[1]]) *Hic est liber sacratissime Dei genitricis Marie, et beate Aethelburge uirginis Berkingensis ecclesie, quem qui abstulerit aut super eo fraudem fecerit, anathematis mucrone feriatur*. The press-mark (b:3) appears on the spine and on the front pastedown: on the spine we have *b : cantica canticorum glos<ata> : 3* (the title is s.xiii; the press-mark has been added later); on the paste-down is *Cantica cant<icorum> glosat<a> .b.iij* (s.xiii). The inscription on the spine and the *ex libris* inscription are both

illustrated in Ker, 'More Manuscripts from Essex Monastic
Libraries', pls. IIa and b.

13 Oxford, Magdalen Coll., lat. 41 s.xv

This manuscript contains a large collection of devotional
and moral works in French. Precisely the same collection
is to be found elsewhere: e.g. Paris, Bib. Nat., Fr. 916, 918
(containing only the first part of the collection [items **a** to **n**,
with the table to item **o**]), 19271 (lacking the first folio), and
22921. Much of the material remains unprinted.

a (fol. 2, following a list of contents on fol. 1) *Les lamentations
saint Bernart* (imperfect at the beginning). A comparison with
the complete manuscripts (Paris, Bib. Nat., Fr. 916, 918, and
22921) enables us to identify these *ps.*-Bernardine *Lamentations*
as those beginning 'Ly livres en quoy nous devons especialement lire sans nul entrelaissement'. The mutilated version in
the present manuscript begins with 'les estoilles. Et apres,
Pulcra es et decora. Et telle la mere comme le filz'. The work
ends (fol. 9v) with a prayer to St Augustine and a prayer
to Christ. **b** (fol. 10v) *Comment saint Bernart reprent et chastie
ceulz qui nont compassion de la mort Jhesucrist, inc.* 'Or reprent
ci et chastie saint Bernart . . . Dist ilhoms qui es tu et quel tuer
as tu qui nas compassion de la mort ton seigneur?' (in the
other manuscripts of the collection, this is considered to be
part of the preceding *Lamentations*). **c** (fol. 14v) *Les meditacions
saint Bernart* = a translation of the *ps.*-Bernardine *Meditationes
piisimae de cognitione humanae conditionis* (*PL* 184: 485–508;
Bloomfield 3126). **d** (fol. 38) *Les contemplacions St. Augustin*
= a translation of the *ps.*-Augustinian *Meditationes* of which
the preface begins 'Pource que nous sommes mis ou my lien
des las de ligier nous nous refroidons des de sirs celestielx'. **e**
(fol. 65) *Une oroison de saint Augustin a Dieu* = a translation of
chapter 40 of the *ps.*-Augustinian *Meditationes* printed in *PL* 40:
838–40 (Sonet 1591). **f** (fol. 65v) *Les meditacions saint Augustin
en pensant a Dieu* (Sonet 2028). **g** (fol. 67) *Ci apres sensuit comment on doit Dieu amer, inc.* 'Fin amant sont appele cil et celles
qui Dieu aiment'. **h** (fol. 71) *La voie par quoy nous devons aler
en paradis, inc.* 'La voie par quoy nous devons aler en paradis,
cest la voie damour'. **i** (fol. 78v) *Ci apres sensuit lordenance du
char Helye le prophete, inc.* 'La sainte escripture dist que Helyas
li prophetes averta ou ciel par estourbeillon'. **j** (fol. 81) *Un
preschement de notre Seigneur.* This is a sermon of Maurice of

Sully on Mt 13:24 (the Parable of the Sower): see P. Meyer, *Romania* 23 (1894), p. 185. **k** (fol. 82v) *Ce sont les vij. choses, que cuer en qui Dieu habite doit avoir, inc.* 'Cuers en qui Dieu habite doit avoir ces choses. Il doit estre amer en contricion'. **l** (fol. 84v) *Comment iiij pechiez mortelz sont segnefiez per iiij bestes sauvages, inc.* 'De nulle viande ne mengust Dieux si voulentiers comme de pechie'. **m** (fol. 85v) *De la demande que fist la mere saint Jehan et saint Jaque a nostre seigneur Jhesucrist, inc.* 'Quant nostre sires Jhesucrist aloit par terre avec ses apostres'. **n** (fol. 86) *Le livre de la misere de lomme* = a translation of Innocent III, *De miseria humanae conditionis* (Bloomfield 1753). **o** (fol. 121) *Xij des tres grans proffis esperituelz, que les tribulacions font a ceulz qui benignement et en pacience les recoivent* = a translation of the *De XII utilitatibus tribulationis* attributed sometimes to Peter of Blois and sometimes to Adam the Carthusian, but possibly by Hugh of Saint-Cher. For an English version, see Jolliffe J.3.[b] and L/B/E 142. **p** (fol. 147) *Aucuns bons enseignemens pour eschiver les pechiez de luxure davarice et daccide, inc.* 'Il sont .viij. choses qui donnent occasion de cheoir ou pechie de luxure'. **q** (fol. 147v) *Comment on se doit garder contre aucunes temptacions, inc.* 'Nous trouvons on viez testament dun roy ot nom nas qui assist une cite qui avoit a nom Iabes'. **r** (fol. 150) *De la age Adam et comment il envoia Seth son filz en paradis terrestre, inc.* 'Apres ce que Adam nostre premier pere fut gete hors de paradis terrestre'. **s** (fol. 152) *Cest la devise de la messe, inc.* 'Quant on sonne la messe si doit on penser que sont li message au roy de paradis'. **t** (fol. 155) *Cest lordenance comment on se doit confesser, inc.* 'Quiconques se veult a droit confesser, il ne doit pas venir despourvenement devant son confesseur'. **u** (fol. 160) *Les enseignemens que li bons roys saint Loys fist et escript de sa main et les envoia de Carthage, ou il estoit au roy Phelippe son filz* = Louis IX, *Les enseignements à Philippe*: edited by D. O'Connell, *The Teachings of Saint Louis: A Critical Text* (Chapel Hill, 1972). O'Connell does not list this manuscript. **v** (fol. 161v) *Les enseignemens que li bons roys saint Loys fist et escript de sa main et les envoia de Carthage, ou il estoit a la royne de Nauarre sa fille* = Louis IX, *Les enseignements à Isabelle*: edited by D. O'Connell, *The Instructions of Saint Louis: A Critical Text* (Chapel Hill, 1979). Again, O'Connell does not list this manuscript. **w** (fol. 163v) *Cest la fin du bon roy saint Loys, que il ot a sa mort que levesque de Thunes envoia a Thibaut, Roy de Nauarre*

= the letter sent by Thibaut V, King of Navarre, to Eudes de Châteauroux, cardinal-archbishop of Thunes, narrating the events surrounding the death of Louis IX: see *HLF*, vol. 21, pp. 808–10, and vol. 19, pp. 228–32. **x** (fol. 164) *Cest cy endroit lordenance de madame la contesse Dalensson et de Bloys que elle ot a son trespassement* = the *Relation anonyme des derniers moments de Jeanne, comtesse d'Alençon et de Blois,* printed in E. Martène & U. Durand (ed.), *Veterum Scriptorum et Monumentorum . . . Amplissima Collectio* (Paris, 1724; rpt. New York, 1968), vol. 6, cols. 1219–38. Jeanne was the only daughter of Jean de Châtillon, Count of Blois and Chartres, and married Pierre, Count of Alençon, the fifth son of Louis IX. She died on 29 January 1292 (1291 [Old Style] according to the manuscript). For an account of her life and a full discussion of the *Relation,* see *HLF*, vol. 20, pp. 107–13. **y** (fol. 177v) *Le livre maistre Hugues de St. Victor, de larre de lame* = a translation of Hugh of Saint-Victor, *Soliloquium de arra animae* (R. Goy, *Die Überlieferung der Werke Hugos von St Viktor* [Stuttgart, 1976], pp. 277–329). **z** (fol. 204v) *Grant plente de bons proverbs et veritables qui ne sont pas en rime, ains sont en prose, que Seneques li philosophes fist* = Ps.-Seneca, *Proverbia*: see J. Morawski, *Romania* 48 (1922), p. 481, n. 1. **aa** (fol. 207v) *Les dis et proverbes des sages et premierement Catons dist* = *Proverbes des sages/Dits des philosophes* (Långfors p. 231 'N'est pas sire de son pais'). **ab** (fol. 209v) *Le dit des philosophes dalixandre quant il fu mort* = *Dits des philosophes* (Långfors p. 158 'Hier Alixandres faisoit son tresor d'or'). **ac** (fol. 210) *Le livre qui est appele, Je vois morir* = *Le miroir du monde* (Långfors p. 187 'Je vois morir, venez avant'). **ad** (fol. 214) The *Pater noster* in French. **ae** (fol. 214v) *La meditacion de la mort* (Sonet 2724). **af** (fol. 218) Acrostic verses by Augustin Bongenou (Sonet 193). The first letters of the lines spell out the name of the poet.: Bongenou Augustin me.

(fol. 218v [s.xv²]) *Memorandum that Elizabeth Veer sumtyme Countes of Oxforde the xxvj. day of ffeuerer the yere of lorde m.cccc.lxxvij [? possibly lxxiiij], yave this Boke to the monastery of Berkyng, on whos sowle oure lorde haue mercy. Amen.* The last three or four figures of the date are badly rubbed and hardly legible, though some later reader has 'clarified' them to read vij. Ker preferred to transcribe them as 1477 and Doyle as 1474 (see Doyle, 'Books Connected with the Vere Family and

Barking Abbey', p. 235, n. 7). I am inclined to agree with Ker. For Elizabeth Vere and her gifts to Barking, see *ibid.*, pp. 233–8.

14 Oxford, University Coll., 169 s.xiv/xv

An Ordinal, preceded by an incomplete Calendar (November and December are wanting), for the use of the nuns of Barking. It includes primarily antiphons, psalms, chapters, hymns, and collects for the day offices, and additional material for the night office. At the end of the volume (fol. 208) is a directory for processions, various *ordines*, including an *ordo* (in French [incomplete]) for *La eleccion dune Abbesse*, an *ordo de professione monialis*, an *ordo ad benedicendam abbatissam*, an *ordo* (in French) for the annointing of an abbess, *La receite des porcions qe la chambre doit receiver cest assevoir*, a list (in French) of the abbesses of Barking with their places of burial, and, in a late s.xv cursive hand in English, an *ordo* 'whan a pryores shall be made Thabbes' and a list of ordinations performed in 1507 and 1509 by Richard FitzJames, bishop of London from 1506 to 1522. An edition of the entire manuscript was published by J. B. L. Tolhurst, *The Ordinale and Customary of the Benedictine Nuns of Barking Abbey* (Henry Bradshaw Society, 65–66; London, 1927–28). It is no. 482 in Frere.

(fol. 6v [s.xv^{in}]) *Memorandum quod anno Domini millesimo quadragintesimo quarto domina Sibilla, permissione diuina abbatissa de Berkyng, hunc librum ad usum abbatissarum in dicta domo in futurum existencium concessit et in librario eiusdem loci post mortem cuiuscumque in perpetuum commoraturum ordinauit, donec eleccio inter moniales fiat, tunc predictus liber eidem electe in abbatissam per superiores domus post stallacionem deliberetur.* For Sybil de Felton, see no. **1** above.

15 Paris, B.N., Fr. 1038 s.xiii/xiv

a (fol. 1) *Vies des pères* (Bossuat p. 322). This is the prose translation of the *Vitas patrum* (*BHL* 6524 foll.) prepared for Blanche of Navarre, Comtesse de Champagne, sometime between 1199 and 1229. After a prologue (in verse) it begins with the life of Paul the Hermit, and includes the *Historia monachorum in Aegypto* (*BHL* 6524), *Verba seniorum* (*BHL* 6525), *Excerpta Cassiani et Sulpicii Severi* (*BHL* 6526), and a variety of saints' lives (see *BHL* p. 943). A full and detailed description may be found in *HLF*, vol. 33, pp. 292–314. **b** (fol. 110) *Les voyages de saint Antoine.* This is a translation of the *Itinerarium*

S. Antonini martyris, an account of a pilgrimage to Palestine by Antoninus of Placentia in the sixth century (the translator has confused Antoninus with Antony) (see *HLF*, vol. 33, p. 312; there are numerous editions). c (fol. 114) *Ps.*-John of Damascus, *L'Histoire de Barlaam et Josaphat* (Bossuat 3216, 6624; *BHL* 979 [the Latin original]). d (fol. 162) Adso of Montier-en-Der, *La légende de l'Antéchrist*, the prose translation made in the first half of the thirteenth century (see P. Meyer, *Romania* 17 [1888], pp. 382–3, and *HLF*, vol. 6, pp. 477–81; Bossuat p. 299). e (fol. 164) A brief text entitled *Si comme Nostre Sires vendra jugier le monde, inc.* 'Quant .xl. jorz seront passez appres la mort Antecrist'. f (fol. 164) *L'assomption de Notre Dame* (see Bossuat 3089 *bis*–92). This is a translation of *ps.*-Melito of Sardis, *Transitus beatae Mariae Virginis, versio latina B* (Stegmüller 164,5; *BHL* 5352). It occurs in numerous manuscripts. On the last fly-leaf of the volume there has been added in a s.xv hand a receipt (in English) for making *aqua vitae*.

(fol. 4 [s.xv[in]]) *Cest liuere achata dame Sibille de Feltonne, abbesse de Berkyng, de les executurs de dame Philippe Coucy, duchesse d'Irland et contesse d'Oxenford.* For Sybil de Felton, see no. 1 above. Philippe de Coucy was born in 1367, the second daughter of Enguerrand VII, Sire de Coucy, and Isabella, daughter of Edward III of England. She married Robert de Vere, ninth earl of Oxford (it was a tumultuous marriage), and died in 1411. She styled herself Duchess of Ireland to her death. After Sybil Felton's death, the book passed into the hands of the bibliophile Charles d'Orléans, and when he died in 1465 it became the property of his widow, Marie de Clèves. After her death it eventually became part of the royal collection and then of the Bibliothèque nationale. See Doyle, 'Books Connected with the Vere Family and Barking Abbey', p. 241.

APPENDIX

In two manuscripts at present preserved in the Essex Record Office—MSS D/DP F234 and D/DP F235—are copies of the will and probate inventory of William Pownsett of Eastcheap who was steward of the estates of Barking Abbey in the years immediately preceding its Dissolution in 1539. Pownsett himself died in March 1554 and we may presume that the inventory of his goods was made shortly after his death. Included in the 'Inventory at East Chepe' is a list of twenty-nine books, with valuations, headed 'Certayne bookes yn the Abbey of Barkynge', and it is possible, though not certain, that some or all of these books once formed part of the nuns' library.

There are, however, problems. First of all, as has already been mentioned, the books are included in the inventory of Pownsett's house at Eastcheap, and the executors' account in MS D/DP F235 specifically refers to the books as 'Pownsett's books left in the abbey of Barking at his death' (fol. 15)—though where they were left is problematical, for by 1554 most of the abbey buildings had been dismantled and the stones reused elsewhere. It is therefore possible that the books in the list had never formed part of the Barking library, but were Pownsett's own property which he had kept in his quarters at the abbey. The law books ([APP.] 7, 8, 14, 16a) would certainly fit into this category and, if Pownsett were of a pious or philosophical disposition, so might many of the others. The fables of Aesop could have served him for welcome recreation.

On the other hand, after the surrender of the abbey in 1539 the books of the library were destroyed or dispersed, and it is possible that some of them, for sentimental if not religious reasons, were acquired by the former steward. If this were the case, it would account for such volumes as the *De modo confitendi*, the *postillae* of Nicholas of Lyra, the *Cathalogus sanctorum*, Haimo's commentary on the Pauline epistles, and a number of others.

In other words, we cannot be certain whether the books listed in the Pownsett inventory belonged to the deceased steward or the suppressed nunnery; and if, as I suspect, they represent a mixture of the two, we cannot be certain of what belonged to whom. The inventory, therefore, must be treated with caution, and for that reason it is here presented as an Appendix to the list of surviving manuscripts from Barking. What we cannot and must not say, however, is that because the majority of the books are in Latin, they could not have formed part of the nuns' library. The fallacy of that argument has, I hope, been demonstrated in the first part of this study.

Some of the titles in the list are too vague to permit precise identification (e.g. [APP.] 8, 10) and some are garbled (e.g. [APP.]

3, 9, 17a: this, undoubtedly, is the result of one person reading out the titles and another attempting to write them down), and I suspect that all the volumes listed were printed books rather than manuscripts.

For further discussion of the matter, the reader is referred to *English Benedictine Libraries: The Shorter Catalogues*, ed. R. Sharpe *et al.* (Corpus of British Medieval Library Catalogues, 4; London, 1995), item B7. I am greatly indebted to Dr Richard Sharpe for drawing my attention to this interesting list and for his generosity in providing me with a transcript.

Certayne bookes yn the Abbey of Barkynge.

(APP.) **1** In primis **a** Virgill and **b** Tullis officis with a
comment   xxd.
(APP.) **2** Item **a** a booke de modo confitendi and **b** a
bybble in lattyn   iij s. iiij d.
(APP.) **3** Item a booke de causa boemica   iiij d.
(APP.) **4** Item an enchiridion militis Christi   xij d.
(APP.) **5** Item Isopps fabels   ij d.
(APP.) **6** Item a booke called Gemma predicantium   viij d.
(APP.) **7** Item a book called Vocabulus utriusque iuris   xij s.
(APP.) **8** Item ij bookes **a** one of the decres of the lawe,
b the other of the distinctions of the law   iij s. iiij d.
(APP.) **9** Item a booke de epistola Nicholai lier   viij d.
(APP.) **10** Item ij bookis of Sermones   x d.
(APP.) **11** Item one booke called Destructorium vitiorum viij d.
(APP.) **12** Item one booke called Cathalogus Sanctorum   xij d.
(APP.) **13** Item a book called Hamo super epistolas Pawli xx d.
(APP.) **14** Item **a** one book called casus Barnerdi & **b**
an other called Racionale diuinorum officinorum   xij d.
(APP.) **15** Item a book super epistolas chanonicas   viij d.
(APP.) **16** Item **a** one called summa Hostensis and
b nother called testus Sentenciarum   xvj d.
(APP.) **17** Item **a** a book called decem libri ethnorum,
b an other called opus aureum sanctorum, and **c**
another called summa aurea   xviij d.
(APP.) **18** Item one book called Tartaret   vj d.
(APP.) **19** Item a book called Thomas primus opus
Dionisii   ii s.

(APP.) **20** Item a book called Dionisyus super spalmos   ij s.
(APP.) **21** Item a book called Dionysyus super iiij^or
  Euangelia   ij s.

The identification of the volumes is as follows: (APP.) **1**
a Probably one of the numerous printed editions of the *opera
omnia* of Virgil (pr. Strasbourg, 1468 &c.; Copinger 5996 foll.);
b Cicero, *De officiis*, with a commentary (pr. Cologne, c. 1465
&c.; *GW* 6914–74). **2 a** If, as I suspect, the volumes in this list are
printed books, this entry probably refers to the *De modo confitendi*
(and other similar titles) of Matthew of Kraków (pr. Paris, c.
1510 &c.; Bloomfield 4945). The work was commonly attributed
to Aquinas or Bonaventure and regularly printed under their
names. Nevertheless, the title is not uncommon and we cannot be
certain of this identification; **b** a Latin Bible (see *GW* 4201 foll.). **3**
I cannot identify this item. **4** Erasmus, *Enchiridion militis Christiani*
(pr. Louvain, 1515 &c.). **5** Undoubtedly Caxton's translation of
the fables of Aesop first published in 1484 (*GW* 376–8; Duff 4–
6). **6** Nicolas Denyse, *Gemma praedicantium* (pr. Caen, 1507 &c.;
H. Caplan, *Mediaeval Artes Praedicandi: A Hand-List* [Ithaca, N.Y.,
1934], no. 228). **7** The anonymous *Vocabularius iuris utriusque*, a
popular and widely read legal treatise (pr. Basel, c. 1475 &c.;
Copinger 6354 foll.). **8 a–b** The content of these law books is not
in doubt, but the descriptions do not permit precise identification. Nor is it clear in what language the books were written. **9**
Certain of the *postillae* of Nicholas of Lyra (Stegmüller 5833 foll.),
almost certainly in printed form (see Hain 10363 foll.), but we
cannot be certain which *postillae* are listed. **10** Two collections
of unidentified sermons. **11** Alexander Carpenter, *Destructorium
vitiorum* (pr. Paris, 1516 &c.; Bloomfield 3612). Printed editions of
this work are very common; manuscripts are rare. **12** Presumably
some sort of Martyrology, but the entry reads more like a description than a title. **13** Haimo of Auxerre (*ps.*-Haimo of Halberstadt),
Commentary on the Pauline Epistles (pr. Strasbourg, 1519 &c.;
Stegmüller 3101–14). **14 a** Bernard Bottone of Parma, *Casus longi
super Decretales* (pr. s.l., 1475 &c.; *GW* 4092–4105; Schulte 2: 115–
6); **b** William Durandus, *Rationale divinorum officiorum* (pr. Mainz,
1459 &c.; Schulte 2: 155). **15** An unidentifiable commentary on
the canonical epistles. **16 a** Henry of Ostia, *Summa super titulis
Decretalium* (pr. Rome, 1473 &c.; Schulte 2: 125–7); **b** Peter Lombard, *Sententiarum libri IV* (pr. Strasbourg, s.d. &c.; Hain 10183

foll.). **17 a** Aristotle, *Ethica*, in one of the medieval Latin translations (see *GW* 2359–80); **b** James/Jacob of Voragine, *Legenda
aurea* (pr. Louvain, s.d. *&c.*; Copinger 6380 foll.); **c** William of
Auxerre, *Summa aurea super quatuor libros Sententiarum* (pr. Paris,
s.d. *&c.*; F. Stegmüller, *Repertorium commentariorum in Sententias
Petri Lombardi* [Würzburg, 1947], no. 281). **18** Either the commentary on the *Summulae logicales* of Peter of Spain or one of
the Aristotelian commentaries of Peter Tartaret/Petrus Tartaretus
(Hain 15333 foll.). **19** Thomas Gallus of Verceil, Paraphrases of
the *ps.*-Dionysian *corpus* (pr. Strasbourg, 1502). **20** Dionysius the
Carthusian (Denys van Leeuven, Denys Ryckel), Commentary on
Psalms (pr. Cologne, 1531 *&c.*; Stegmüller 2095). **21** Dionysius the
Carthusian, Commentary on the Four Gospels (pr. Cologne, 1532
&c.; Stegmüller 2122–25).

BREWOOD BLACK LADIES (Staffordshire), *Priory of BVM*
(Benedictine Nuns).

Miscellaneous Records
William Dugdale, ed. J. Caley, H. Ellis, & B. Bandinell, *Monasticon Anglicanum* (London, 1817–30), vol. 4, pp. 500–01, prints an
inventory of the priory taken at the time of its dissolution (1538).
One book is recorded:
> *The Churche* (p. 500)
> on masboke.

BROADHOLME (Nottinghamshire), *Priory of BVM* (Premonstratensian Canonesses).

Miscellaneous Records
   In his will dated 21 January 1374 (probated 19 March
1374), William de Blythe, archdeacon of Norfolk and canon of
Chichester, bequeathed 'Item . . . domine priorisse de Brodholme
meum bonum psalterium ad orandum pro anima mea et volo
quod ipsa habeat ad totam vitam suam et postea remaneat domui perpetualiter' (Cavanaugh, pp. 103–4, from Lambeth Palace,
Reg. Whittlesey, fols. 129v–130). The identity of the prioress of
Broadholme at this time is unknown.

BROMHALL (Berkshire), *Priory of St Margaret* (Benedictine
Nuns).

Miscellaneous Records
See ANKERWYKE, *Miscellaneous Records* **a**.

BRUISYARD (Suffolk), *Abbey of the Annunciation of BVM* (Franciscan Nuns).

1 ?London, B.L., Sloane 2400 s.xiii

Psalter, preceded by a Calendar and followed by Canticles, Athanasian Creed, a Litany, and six brief prayers (in Latin). A few additional Latin prayers have been added on fols. 165r–166v in later hands.

(fol. 1v [s.xv]) *ffelbrigg.* (fol. 2v [s.xv]) *Iste liber est: Sororis Anne ffelbrygge ad terminum vite, post cuius decessum pertinebit conuentui Minorissarum de Bruszerde.* Anne Felbrygge was the daughter of Sir Simon Felbrygge, standard-bearer to Richard II, and his wife Margaret, daughter of the duke of Silesia. The Felbrygge arms are painted on the edges of the Psalter. Sir Simon died in February 1442/3 and his wife on 27 June 1416: their *obits* appear in the Calendar on fols. 3r, 5v, and 7v. Anne also received 8 marks (£5.6.8) *per annum* by her father's will. This is roughly equivalent to the yearly wage of a skilled mason. See further Bourdillon, pp. 38, 52. We might also note that this beautiful Psalter is one of the few surviving books decorated with embroidery. The Annunciation is depicted on the front cover (about 8.25" x 5.75") and the Crucifixion on the back (about half-an-inch larger). Whether these are the work of Anne Felbrygge herself we cannot say.

2 Oxford, Bod. Lib., Tanner 191 (printed book)

The Royal Book, printed by Wynkyn de Worde, London, 1507 (*STC* 21430). This is an English translation of the *Somme le roi* or *Somme des vices et des vertus*, a manual of moral instruction prepared in 1279 at the request of Philip III the Bold by his confessor, Frère Laurent d'Orléans (Bossuat 3598–3606).

(fol. H.iiij[v] [s.xvi[1]]) *Iste liber pertinet domine Margerie Bakon, Minorisse de Broseyard, ex dono fratris Thome Monger.* Nothing is known of Margerie Bakon and she is not mentioned by Bourdillon.

Miscellaneous Records

a H. Harrod, 'Extracts from Early Wills in the Norwich Registries', *Norfolk Archaeology* 4 (1855), pp. 317–39, records a bequest made to Bruisyard in 1481 by Margaret Purdans of St Giles', Norwich, widow, as follows: 'to the convent of Nuns at Brosyerd, after the decease of the Lady Margaret Yaxley, I give a book called *Le doctrine of the herte*' (p. 335). Margaret Yaxley was a nun at Bruisyard in 1480 (see *ibid.* p., 335 fn. [Bourdillon, p. 92, misreads Yaxley as Zaxle]).

For *The Doctrine of the Heart*, see Jolliffe H.1 = O.3.

b In his will dated 20 August 1501, Sir Walter Quyntyn, 'preest in the pisshe of seynt Nicholas in Ippiswyche dwelling', bequeathed 'to the noonys of Brosyerde a booke called *Legenda aurea* in Englisshe' (F. Haslewood, 'Will of Sir Walter Quyntyn, of Ipswich', *Proceedings of the Suffolk Institute of Archaeology and Natural History* 7 [1889], p. 111).

For the Middle English versions of the *Golden Legend*, see L/B/E 682. The first printed edition was published by Caxton in 1484 (Duff 408; *STC* 24823).

BUCKLAND MINCHIN (Somerset), *Priory of St John the Baptist* (Nuns of St John of Jerusalem).

1 London, Soc. of Antiquaries, 713 s.xiii/xiv

Psalter, preceded by a Calendar (lacking May–August) and followed by Canticles, the Athanasian Creed, and fragments of the Office of the Dead. At the end of the volume (fol. 174) is an unrelated legal fragment (s.xiv/xv). The Psalter was written in the South Netherlands at the end of the thirteenth or beginning of the fourteenth century, but by the fifteenth century was in the possession of the sisters at Buckland. At that time the house belonged to the Order of St John of Jerusalem. Prior to c. 1180 and after 1500 it was Augustinian (see D. Knowles and R. N. Hadcock, *Medieval Religious Houses: England and Wales* [New York, 1972 (revd. ed.)], p. 284). I am indebted to Adrian James, Assistant Librarian of the Society of Antiquaries, for a description of this volume.

(fol. 5 [s.xv]) *Iste psalterium constat sororum de Bokland.*

BURNHAM (Buckinghamshire), *Abbey of BVM* (Augustinian Canonesses).

Miscellaneous Records

In his will of 1392, John de Bannebury, former fellow of Merton College and rector of the third portion of Waddesdon (Buckinghamshire), bequeathed 'to Agnes, abbess of Burnham, my portiforium' (A. Gibbons, *Early Lincoln Wills. An Abstract of All the Wills and Administrations Recorded in the Episcopal Registers of the Old Diocese of Lincoln, . . . 1280–1547* [Lincoln, 1888],

p. 27 [Cavanaugh, p. 70]). The Agnes in question was Agnes Frankleyn, who resigned her abbacy the following year (VCR *Buckinghamshire*, vol. 1, p. 384).

CAMPSEY (Suffolk), *Priory of BVM* (Augustinian Canonesses).

1 Cambridge, U.L., Add. 7220 s.xiii[1]

Psalter, preceded by a Calendar and followed by a complete set of Canticles with the Athanasian Creed (ending imperfectly).

(fol. 2 [s.xiv[1]]) *Cest liuere est a covent de Campisse*. The s.xv pressmark—O.E..94.—appears on fol. 8: O.E. is written at the top of the page in the middle, and .94. at the top right. I am indebted to Miss Jayne Ringrose of Cambridge University Library for a description of this manuscript. I have also followed her suggestion as to its date.

2 Cambridge, Corpus Christi Coll., 268 s.xv

a (fol. 2) *A Comfortable Treatise to Strengthen and Comfort Creatures in the Faith* (Jolliffe K.13). **b** (fol. 10) Walter Hilton, *The Ladder of Perfection*, Book I (L/B/E 255). **c** (fol. 54) *Treatise of the Seven Points of True Love and Everlasting Wisdom* (L/B/E 465). This is an English translation of the Latin version (*Horologium sapientiae*) of Heinrich Suso's *Büchlein der ewigen Weisheit* (*Little Book of Eternal Wisdom*). **d** (fol. 98) Walter Hilton, *The Ladder of Perfection*, Book II (L/B/E 255).

(fol. 169v [s.xv[2]]) *Memorandum that I, Elizabeth Wylby, . . . N<onne> of <Camp>essey, gyffe thys boke* (the rest of the inscription has been cut off the bottom of the leaf). Elizabeth Wylby is listed as a nun of Campsey in episcopal visitations of 1 August 1514 (as Elizabeth Willughby) and 27 June 1526 (as Elisabeth Willoughbie) (*Visitations of the Diocese of Norwich, A.D. 1492–1532*, ed. A. Jessopp [Camden Society, N.S. 43; London, 1888; rpt. New York, 1965], pp. 133, 219). The same nun gave an untraced copy of the *Chastising of God's Children* to Dame Catherine Symonde, to pass from her to another sister of Campsey (see no. **6** below).

3 London, B.L., Add. 40675 s.xiv

a (fol. 2) Psalter (abbreviated), preceded by the *Suscipere dignare* prayer adapted for female use, and followed by Canticles, Athanasian Creed, and the Office of the Dead. On fols. 33v and 34r, originally blank, two hymns have been added

(Chevalier 3733–4 and 27196). **b** (fol. 35) Hymnary. **c** (fol. 63) Hours of St John the Baptist and (fol. 66) of St Mary Magdalene. **d** (fol. 69) Metrical Psalters of the Holy Spirit (see C. Blume & G. M. Dreves [ed.], *Analecta Hymnica Medii Aevi* [Leipzig, 1900], vol. 35, p. 7) and of the Holy Cross (edited in *ibid.*, pp. 12–25). **e** (fol. 109) A long prayer in French (ending on fol. 110v), partly in verse, *inc.* 'Tres duz sire et tres duz ihu crist', not recorded in Sonet.

(fol. 34 [s.xv]) *Cest liuere est a couent de Campisse.* The s.xv pressmark—d.d..141.—appears on the next folio (fol. 35). On fol. 111 appears the anathema in a later hand: *Qui librum furatur, per collum pendere datur.*

4 London, B.L., Arundel 396 x.xv

a (fol. 1) John Capgrave, *The Life of St Catherine* (Brown/ Robbins 6). **b** (fol. 118) A paschal table from 1446 to 1649 with interlinear Latin verses, *inc.* 'Robustus iudas horam, nunc eripiens est'. The table is preceded by instructions (in Latin) on how to use it. **c** (fol. 121) John Lydgate, *Interpretacio misse* (Brown/Robbins 4246).

(fol. 130v [c. 1500]) *Iste liber est ex dono domine Katerine Babyngton, quondam subpriorisse de Campseye, et si quis illum alienauerit sine licencia vna cum consensu dictarum conuentus, malediccionem Dei omnipotentis incurrat et anathema sit. Dictarum* should perhaps have been followed by something like *sanctimonialium.* Catherine Babington was sub-prioress of Campsey in 1492 (VCH *Suffolk*, vol. 2, p. 115; *Visitations of the Diocese of Norwich* [see no. 2], p. 36 [visitation of 24 January 1492]).

5 London, B.L., Add. 70513 (formerly Loans 29/61, and prior to that, Welbeck Abbey, Duke of Portland, I.C.1) s.xiv

a (fol. 1) Nicolas Bozon, Life of St Elizabeth of Hungary (Bossuat 3414). **b** (fol. 4) *idem* (attrib.), Life of St Paphnutius (Bossuat 3345). **c** (fol. 6) *idem*, Life of St Paul the Hermit (Bossuat 3363). **d** (fol. 9) Guernes de Pont-Sainte-Maxence, Life of St Thomas of Canterbury (Bossuat 3385 [imperfect at the beginning]). **e** (fol. 50v) William the Norman/Guillaume le Clerc, The Romance of St Mary Magdalen (two editions noted by Karl, p. 213; omitted in Bossuat). **f** (fol. 55v) Life of St Edward the Confessor (Bossuat 3248 [some fragments were edited by Paul Meyer in *Romania* 40 [1911], pp. 64–7]). **g** (fol. 85v) 'Maheu', Life of St Edmund of Canterbury (Bossuat 3247).

I am convinced by the arguments of R. Vaughan, *Matthew Paris* (Cambridge, 1958), pp. 168–81 and C. H. Lawrence, *St Edmund of Abingdon: A Study in Hagiography and History* (Oxford, 1960), pp. 70–1, that 'Maheu' was Matthew Paris, and that this Anglo-Norman *Life* was a translation by Matthew of his earlier Latin version. **h** (fol. 100v) Marie, Life of Saint Audrey (= Etheldreda), ed. O. Södergård, *La vie Sainte Audrée* (Uppsala, 1955; omitted in Bossuat). **i** (fol. 134) Life of St Osyth/Osgitha (Bossuat 3344). **j** (fol. 147) Simon of Walsingham, Life of St Foi (Bossuat 3416). **k** (fol. 156v) Life of St Modwenna (Bossuat 6644). **l** (fol. 222) Life of St Richard of Chichester, sometimes attributed to Peter of Peckham (Bossuat 3372). **m** (fol. 246) Clémence of Barking, Life of St Catherine of Alexandria (Bossuat 3401 [Jarnik did not know of the Welbeck manuscript]). A full description of the manuscript may be found in S. A. Strong, *A Catalogue of Letters and Other Historical Documents Exhibited in the Library at Welbeck* (London, 1903), pp. 5–8 (with facsimile), or, better, in L. Karl, 'Sur l'unique manuscrit français de la Bibliothèque du duc de Portland à Welbeck', *Revue des langues romanes* 54 (1911), pp. 210–29. Copies of Strong's catalogue are rare. Items **f**, **h**, and **m** are discussed in Part I, Chapter 3, of this study.

fol. 1 [s.xv]) *Cest liuere est a Couent de Campisse.* (fol. 265v) *Ce liure <est> deviseie a la priorie de Kampseie de lire a mengier.*

Untraced Books

6 Ker, 28, reports a printed book listed in the catalogue of the Harleian Sale in 1744: *The Chastysing of Goddes Chyldern*, printed by Wynkyn de Worde, Westminster, 1493 (*GW* 6583; *STC* 5065; Duff 85).

According to the *Catalogus Bibliothecae Harleianae* (1744), vol. 3, no. 1560, 'On the last leaf, there is a *Memorandum*, written by a Nun of *Campessey*, named *Elyzabeth Wyllowby*, That she gives this Book to Dame Cateryne Symonde, under the Condition, That, in no wise, she sell it, or give it from the house of *Campessey*: But she shall give it to one of the Sisters.' Elizabeth Willowby was also the donor of no. **2** above. Cateryne/Katerina Symonde/Symond/Symondes/Symon is listed as a nun of Campsey in episcopal visitations of 1 August 1514, 27 June 1526, and 25 June 1532, by which date she had risen to the position of subprioress (*Visitations of the Diocese* *of Norwich* [see no. 2], pp. 134, 219, 290). By the time of the visitation of 1532, Elizabeth Willowby has disappeared from the scene.

Miscellaneous Records

F. Haslewood, 'Inventories of Monasteries Suppressed in 1536', *Proceedings of the Suffolk Institute of Archaeology and Natural History* 8 (1894), pp. 83–116, prints a number of inventories of religious houses in Suffolk. Included among them is an inventory of Campsey dated 29 August 1536. The following book is recorded:

In the Church att the High Alter (p. 113)
Item an older masse bok ij cruetts lytell worthe att vj^d.

CANONSLEIGH (Devon), *Abbey of BVM, St John the Baptist, and St Etheldreda* (Augustinian Canonesses).

1 London, B.L., Cotton Cleopatra C.vi s.xiii^{in}

Ancrene Riwle (L/B/E 559), edited from this manuscript by E. J. Dobson, *The English Text of the Ancrene Riwle* (EETS/OS, 267; London, 1972), who provides a full description on pp. xx–xxv. At the end of the volume (fol. 199–201) are three folios of miscellaneous material, including verses in Latin to St Etheldreda, patroness of Canonsleigh, other verses in Latin (Walther 17963) and French (Långfors, p. 335 'Ky voet amer saunz pesaunce', edited by A. Långfors in *Romania* 55 [1929], pp. 551–2 [fourteen lines]), and notes on numerals.

(fol. 3 [a flyleaf]) *Datus abbatie et conuentu de Legh', per dame M<atilda> de Clar'*. According to Dobson, p. xxii, this inscription is written in a hand 'of about 1300'. Ker dates it s.xiii^{ex}. Matilda de Clare, Countess of Gloucester, was responsible for the re-foundation of Leigh or Canonsleigh as a house for Augustinian Canonesses. It had previously been for Canons. The date of the re-foundation was 1284 and Matilda died before 1289.

CARROW (Norfolk), *Priory of BVM and St John* (Benedictine Nuns).

1 Baltimore, Walters Art Gallery, 90 s.xiii

Psalter, preceded by *memoriae* of the saints and a Calendar, and followed by Canticles, a Litany, the Office of the Dead, Hours of the Virgin (Sarum Use), and (fol. 298) a *Psalterium beatae Mariae* (Chevalier no. 2037, preceded by Chevalier no. 19948). This is the so-called Carrow Psalter, a well-known illuminated manuscript, in which the *memoriae* are accompanied by some fifty full-page miniatures. A full description by M. R. James may be found in *A Descriptive Catalogue of the Second Series of Fifty Manuscripts (nos. 51–100) in the Collection of Henry Yates Thompson* (Cambridge, 1902), pp. 2–11 no. 52. See also Morgan no. 118. According to James, the artist of the miniatures was not strong in rendering expression: 'most of his Apostles wear a look of apologetic deprecation, or of settled melancholy' (p. 7).

(fol. 1 [s.xv]) *Istud psalterium pertinet domui de Carehowe.* This inscription is in the same hand as that in no. 3 below. The Psalter was not written at Carrow, and the kneeling man depicted in the historiated initial which begins the *Psalterium beatae Mariae* probably represents the original owner.

2 Madrid, Bibl. Nac., 6422 s.xiii²

Psalter, preceded by a Calendar and followed by Canticles, Litanies, the Office of the Dead and *Commendatio animarum*. For full descriptions, see J. Janini & J. Serrano, *Manuscritos litúrgicos de la Biblioteca Nacional* (Madrid, 1969), pp. 87–88 no. 65, and Morgan no. 120. Morgan points out that this manuscript and no. 1 above were probably produced in Norwich. The manuscript is not included in Ker or Watson.

The Benedictine Calendar contains feasts characteristic of Carrow (see Morgan, vol. 2, p. 90) together with the *obit* of *A. de Monte Kensi, priorissa de Karhowe* (14 July). An Agnes de Monte Ganisio or Gavisio is recorded as prioress of Carrow in 1224 (VCH *Norfolk*, vol. 2, pp. 352, 354), but I am uncertain as to the correct spelling of her name and I have not examined this manuscript. Some of the initials in the Psalter contain heraldic decorations, among which are the arms of the Warenne family: Muriel de Warenne was a nun at Carrow in the thirteenth century and the family made several benefactions to the priory (see VCH *Norfolk*, vol. 2, p. 352).

3 Reykjavik, Nat. Mus., 4678 + Nat. Lib., IB 363 8vo + Nat. Lib., Lbs. frag. 51 s.xiv

Three fragments of a Psalter. Nat. Mus. 4678 is a single leaf from the beginning of the Psalter containing a miniature of the crucifixion; Nat. Lib. IB 363 8vo is a fragment of a sixteenth-century collection of prayers in Icelandic with which is bound one leaf from the Psalter; Nat. Lib. frag. 51 is a single folio containing Psalm 17: 26–35. I am indebted to Sjöfn Kristjánsdóttir of the National Library of Iceland for this information. Further discusion of the relationship of this Psalter to other East Anglian Psalters in general and the Tickhill Psalter group in particular (including no. 1 above) may be found in Selma Jónsdóttir, 'Enskt saltarabrot á Íslandi', in *Andvari*, 1967, pp. 159–70, *idem*, 'Heilagur Nikulás í Árnasafni', in *Afmaelisrit Jóns Helgasonar, 30. júní 1969* (Reykjavík, 1969), pp. 260–67 (with English summary, 'St. Nicholas in Iceland: A Fragment of an English Psalter', on pp. 268–9), and *idem*, tr. P. Foote, *Illumination in a Manuscript of Stjórn* (Reykjavík, 1971), pp. 31–45.

(Nat. Mus. 4678 *recto* [s.xv]) *Istud psalterium pertinet domui de Carehowe*, in the same hand as no. 1 above. This leaf is illustrated in Jónsdóttir, *Illumination in a Manuscript of Stjórn*, pl. 19, but the inscription is hardly legible.

CASTLE HEDINGHAM (Essex), *Priory of BVM, St James, and Holy Cross* (Benedictine Nuns).

1 ?London, B.L., Egerton 2849 s.xiii
Mortuary Roll of Lucy (probably Lucy de Vere), foundress and first prioress of Castle Hedingham. She may have been the wife of Aubrey de Vere, first Earl of Oxford (see VCH *Essex*, vol. 2, p. 122), but this is not certain. Sally Thompson, *Women Religious* (Oxford, 1991), pp. 180–1, suggests she was de Vere's daughter. The roll begins with three illustrations (two of them are of Lucy: in the second, her soul is being carried to heaven by angels, and in the third, her encoffined body is being censed and asperged). Then comes a copy of the circular letter of Agnes, the second prioress, announcing her predecessor's death and asking for prayers for her soul. Finally, we have the replies from 122 houses acceding to her request and asking for prayers in return. The manuscript dates from a few years after 1226 (see Watson/*London*, vol. 1 no. 613 and Morgan, p. 103, who also provides a description of the manuscript [no. 56]). It is not included in Ker or Watson.

There can be little doubt that the roll was made for Castle Hedingham and kept at the nunnery.

Miscellaneous Records

R. C. Fowler, 'Inventories of Essex Monasteries in 1536', *Transactions of the Essex Archaeological Society* N.S. 9 (1903–06), pp. 280–92, 330–47, 380–400, prints a number of inventories of religious houses in Essex. Included among them is an inventory of Castle Hedingham dated 13 June 1536. The following books are recorded:

In the Quyre (p. 291)

Item ii. masse books—ii*s*. (with the marginal comment: One sold)

Item vi. books of parchment at—ii*s*.

CHESHUNT (Hertfordshire), *Priory of St Mary* (Benedictine Nuns).

Miscellaneous records

John E. Cussans, *History of Hertfordshire, Vol. 2: Hertford Hundred* (London, 1876; rpt. Menston, 1972), pp. 267–71 (Appendix II), prints an inventory of Cheshunt taken at the Dissolution and dated 28 May 1536 (K.R. Church Goods 12/30). The following books are recorded:

In the Quyre (p. 267)

Item x bookes lyinge in the Quyre at (xx^s. x^s.) (the two amounts are written one above the other and bracketed together on the left, and the whole entry has been scored through)

In the Dortor (p. 268)

Item a Masse booke in parchement at lxvj^s. viij^d. (this entry has also been scored through)

In . . . my Ladys Chamber (p. 270)

Item ij Chestes in my Ladys Chamber, wherof one of them ys full of Evydence [Deeds] praysed at xij^d.

CHESTER (Cheshire), *Priory of BVM* (Benedictine Nuns).

1 San Marino, Huntington Lib., EL 34 B.7 s.xv/xvi

Processional, containing processions for the *temporale* and *sanctorale* combined, and ending with the procession for the dedication of a church. The Processional is followed (fol. 70v) by a Christmas carol, various prayers (some in English), benedictions, antiphons of the Virgin, and more prayers in

English (including Brown/Robbins 2471, 2474, 2560, 2931, and 3238). At the beginning of the manuscript is the antiphon and response from the service for the consecration of nuns, and at the end there have been added a petition for acceptance into the community and another prayer, both in Latin. An edition of the entire manuscript (from fol. 7 onwards) has been published by J. W. Legg, *The Processional of the Nuns of Chester* (Henry Bradshaw Society, 18; London, 1899). For a facsimile of fol. 42, see *Aspects of Medieval England: Manuscripts for Research in the Huntington Library. An Exhibition Prepared for the Medieval Academy of America, 14 April 1972* (San Marino, 1972), no. 40.

(fol. 85v [s.xvi[in]]) *This booke longeth to Dame Margery Byrkenhed of Chestre.* This inscription appears to be in the same hand as the text, but nothing is known of Margery Birkenhead.

DARTFORD (Kent), *Priory of BVM and St Margaret* (Dominican Nuns).

1 Downside Abbey, 26542 s.xv[2]

    a (fol. 1) Walter Hilton (?), *Pricking of Love* (L/B/E 46). This is an abridged translation of *ps.*-Bonaventure, *Stimulus amoris*. **b** (fols. 90v, 92v, 92r) A brief (unprinted) devotional piece on 'How a man shal knowe whiche is the speche of the flesshe in his hert' (Jolliffe F.12). Fol. 93 is blank. **c** (fol. 94) *Poor Caitiff* (Jolliffe B). **d** (fol. 168v) An extract (in Latin) from the *Speculum spiritualium* (fols. 131–2 of the 1510 Paris edition). **e** (fol. 172) *Ps.*-Augustine, *Sermo (app.)* 265 (*PL* 39: 2237–40). For a full description of this manuscript, see A. Watkin, 'Some Manuscripts in the Downside Abbey Library (continued)', *Downside Review* 59 (1941), pp. 75–83.

    (fol. iii[v] [s.xvi[in]]) *This boke is youe to Betryce Chaumbir', and aftir hir decese to sustir Emme Wynter and to sustir Denyse Caston', nonnes of Dertforthe, and so to abide in the saam hous of the nonnes of Dertforthe for euere. To pray for hem that yeue it.* The last sentence is in a different hand, and whoever wrote it has added *Ave Maria* and *Jh<es>u Amen* at the beginning of the inscription. Emma Winter was the owner of nos. **5** and **8** below, but I have found no record of the other two nuns.

2 Dublin, Trinity Coll., 490 (E.2.15) s.xv

    The *Brut Chronicle* (L/B/E 374 [the original version]). The edition by F. W. D. Brie, *The Brut or the Chronicles of England*

(EETS/OS, 131, 136; London, 1906, 1908), utilizes this manuscript.

(flyleaf *verso* [s.xv]) *Iste liber constat religiosis sororibus de Dertford.*

3 ?London, B.L., Arundel 61 s.xvi

Rentale of the priory of Dartford, drawn up between 20 November 1507 and 1 November 1508 by Prioress Elizabeth Cressener. The document contains a meticulous listing of all the lands and properties owned by the convent in Kent and (partly) in Norfolk, together with the rents and services due. The first folio is much damaged.

Elizabeth Cressener was prioress of Dartford from 1488 or 1489 to her death in 1537 (VCH *Kent*, vol. 2, p. 189). She was clearly a very careful administrator. This manuscript is not included in Ker or Watson.

4 London, B.L., Harley 2254 s.xv

a (fol. 1) Walter Hilton (?), *Pricking of Love* (L/B/E 46 [see no. 1a above]). b (fol. 73) Walter Hilton, *Mixed Life (Vita mixta)* (L/B/E 147).

(fly-leaf i^v [s.xv^2]) *Thys boyk longyth to Dame Alys Braintwath the worchypfulle prioras of Dartforde,* followed (in later hands [s.xvi^1]) by *Jhesu mercy, Orate pro anima domina (sic) Elizabith Rede huius loci,* and *Orate pro anima Johanne Newmarche.* Alice Brainthwaite is mentioned as prioress of Dartford in 1461, 1465, and 1467. The same name occurs again in 1475 and 1479 (see VCH *Kent*, vol. 2, p. 189). She also owned no. 9 below. Of Elizabeth Rede and Joan Newmarch I know nothing.

5 London, Soc. of Antiquaries, 717 s.xv

Office of the Dead (fol. 14v), preceded by the Penitential Psalms, a Litany, and a *memoria* of St Christina, and followed (fol. 55) by other processional offices.

(fol. 55 [s.xv]) *Orate pro anima sororis Emme Wyntyr qui fieri fecit istum librum.* Emma Winter also owned nos. 1 above and 8 below.

6 ?Oxford, Bod. Lib., Bodl. 255 (S.C. 3010) fols. 1–44 s.xv/xvi

An unprinted commentary in English on the *Rule of St Augustine, inc.* 'The commaundementes off Almyghty God be rede unto vs to thentent they myght be understand'. In the manuscript, the commentary is entitled *De vita religiosorum* (in red). Below that (in black) is *Hec sunt que ut observantibus precipimur in monasterio constituti.*

On fol. 44r, covering the whole page, are the arms of Prioress Elizabeth Cressener (see no. 3). They are fully described in the notes to S.C. 3010.

7 Oxford, Bod. Lib., Douce 322 (S.C. 21896) s.xv

a (fol. 2) John Lydgate, *Calendar* (Brown/Robbins 1721), followed by two anonymous poems (Brown/Robbins 1781 and 1460) and a prayer in verse (Brown/Robbins 2352). **b** (fol. 10) *Petty Job*, here attributed to Richard Rolle (Allen, pp. 369–70; Brown/Robbins 1854), followed by two anonymous poems (Brown/Robbins 561 and 741) and part of the *Good Confession* (Jolliffe C.21; L/B/E 309). **c** (fol. 19v) John Lucas, *Death's Warning to the World* (Brown/Robbins 3143). **d** (fol. 20) *Treatise of the Seven Points of True Love and Everlasting Wisdom* (Jolliffe L.8.[b]; L/B/E 465). This is an English translation of the fifth chapter of the Latin version (*Horologium sapientiae*) of Heinrich Suso's *Büchlein der ewigen Weisheit* (*Little Book of Eternal Wisdom*). **e** (fol. 25v) An extract from an English version of the *Somme le roi* of Frère Laurent d'Orléans (see BRUISYARD 2). **f** (fol. 26v) *Book of the Craft of Dying* (Jolliffe L.4.[a]; L/B/E 234), sometimes attributed (incorrectly) to Richard Rolle. This is also heavily based on Chapter V of Suso's *Horologium sapientiae*. **g** (fol. 39) *A Treatise of Ghostly Battle* (Jolliffe H.3; L/B/E 120). **h** (fol. 52v) *A Ladder of Four Rungs* (a translation of the *Scala paradisi* of Guigo II of La Chartreuse) (Jolliffe M.1 = O.2; L/B/E 76). **i** (fol. 62v) *A Little Short Treatise* (Jolliffe J.2.[c]; L/B/E 287). This is a translation of *De patientia tribulationum* attributed by Bale to Adam the Carthusian. As usual, this precedes the next item: **j** (fol. 64) *The Twelve Profits of Tribulation* (Jolliffe J.3.[b]; L/B/E 142). This is a translation of the *De XII utilitatibus tribulationis* attributed sometimes to Peter of Blois and sometimes to Adam the Carthusian, but possibly by Hugh of Saint-Cher. It is preceded, as is common, by a Latin passage *de patientia infirmitatis, inc.* 'Si sciret homo'. **k** (fol. 78) Richard Misyn, *The Mending of Life* (a translation of the *Emendatio vitae* of Richard Rolle) (L/B/E 652). **l** (fol. 94) An English translation of the *ps.*-Augustinian *Meditatio Sancti Augustini* (Jolliffe I.32; L/B/E 574). **m** (fol. 98) *The Confession of St Brendan* (Jolliffe C.31; L/B/E 311). **n** (fol. 100r–v) the *Charter* (imperfect) from the *Poor Caitiff* (Jolliffe B; L/B/E 166). Other minor items are listed by Jolliffe at G.9, G.29, L.1, and M.15. Full descriptions may be found in the *Catalogue of the Printed Books and Manuscripts Bequeathed by Francis Douce, Esq., to the Bodleian Library* (Oxford, 1840), pp. 55–7; L. Braswell, *The Index of Middle English Prose, Handlist IV* (Cambridge, 1987), pp. 74–85; and Doyle, 'Books Connected with the Vere Family and Barking Abbey' (see BARKING 1), pp. 222–8.

(fol. i [s.xv]) *These booke, in whome is contente dyuers deuoute tretis, and specyally the tretis that is callid Ars moriendi, ys of the gifte of Wylliam Baron Esquyer to remayne for euyr to the place and nonrye of Detforde, and specially to the vse of dame Pernelle Wrattisley, sister of the same place, by licence of her abbas, the whiche Pernelle is nece to the for seyde gentylman William Baron.* William Baron, whose escutcheon appears on fol. 10, was an officer of the Royal Exchequer and active in London between 1430 and 1470. According to A. I. Doyle, 'Books Connected with the Vere Family and Barking Abbey', pp. 228–9 (and also the notes to S.C. 21896), Pernelle (or Petronilla) Wrattisley was more probably his grand-daughter than his niece.

8 ?Oxford, Bod. Lib., Rawl. G.59 (S.C. 14790) s.xv

Ps.-Cato, *Disticha Catonis*, in Latin (ed. M. Boas [Amsterdam, 1952]) together with a translation in English verse, *inc.* 'When I avy3sed me ryght hertely/How dyverse men even grevously.' This is a variant version of the anonymous Northern translation of *ps.*-Cato (see C. Brown, *A Register of Middle English Religious and Didactic Verse* [Oxford, 1916–20], vol. 2, p. 377 no. 2534, and Brown/Robbins 3957). Watson, p. 15, says that the translation is in French, but this is not the case.

(fol. 13 [s.xvi[in]]) *Suster Emme Wyntyr.* Sister Emma Winter also owned nos. 1 and 5 above.

9 Taunton, Somerset County Record Office, DD/SAS C/1193/68 (formerly Taunton, Castle Mus., 2) s.xv

Hours of the Virgin (Dominican Use), preceded by a Sarum Calendar and followed by various prayers, a Litany, the Office of the Dead, *Commendatio animarum*, the Penitential Psalms and Gradual Psalms. A few prayers in Latin and a short devotional piece in English have been added on the fly-leaves in a later (s.xv[2]) hand.

(fol. 103v [s.xv^ex]) *Omnipotens domine, pro tua pietate miserere anime famule tue, et a contagiis mortalitatis exutam, in eterne saluacionis partem restitue. Orate pro anima sororis Alicie Brainthawyt qui* (sic, for *que*) *dedit nobis istum librum.* Alice Brainthwaite also owned no. 4 above.

DENNEY (Cambridgeshire), *Abbey of St James and St Leonard* (Franciscan Nuns).

1 Cambridge, U.L., Add. 8335 s.xv
The Northern Homily Cycle in English verse. This manuscript, formerly belonging to the Marquess of Bute, contains an East-Midland revision of the original cycle. There are 61 homilies, all of which are listed in C. Brown, *A Register of Middle English Religious and Didactic Verse* (Oxford, 1916–20), vol. 1, pp. 460–6. See also Brown/Robbins 733–6. The edition of J. Small, *English Metrical Homilies* (Edinburgh, 1862) was prepared without knowledge of the Bute Manuscript. See further T. Heffernan, 'The Rediscovery of the Bute Manuscript of the *Northern Homily Cycle*', *Scriptorium* 36 (1982), pp. 118–29, and M. Corbett, 'An East-Midland Revision of the Northern Homily Collection', *Manuscripta* 26 (1982), pp. 100–7.

(p. 2 [s.xv]) *Iste <liber> . . . sororum minorum s<anct>i Leonar<di> Denay.* This inscription has been erased, but is partly visible under ultra-violet light. The abbey may not have owned the book for long. On p. 382 is a s.xv ownership inscription of Thomas Calbot, a merchant of Lynne. It is possible that the volume was pledged as a security in the late fifteenth century, but by whom is unknown (see the Sotheby's sale catalogue for 13 June 1983 [The Marquess of Bute Sale], p. 37).

2 Oxford, Bod. Lib., Hatton 18 (S.C. 4109) s.xv
William of Nassington, *Speculum vitae* (Brown/Robbins 245).

(fol. 210v [s.xvi^in]) *Iste liber est uenerabilis domine dompne Elesabeth Throgkmorten, abbatisse de Denney, teste Thoma Gylberd in eodem monasterio olim manenti.* Elizabeth Throckmorton was the last abbess of Denney (Bourdillon, pp. 52, 83, 88; VCH *Cambridgeshire*, vol. 2, p. 302), and after the dissolution of the house, she retired to her family seat at Coughton in Warwickshire where, with two or three of her nuns, she continued to

live the life of a minoress until her death in 1547 (Bourdillon, p. 83). A second inscription shows that the book passed
into the hands of John Fakun, 'presumably he who was vice-
warden of the Grey Friars and signed the surrender' (VCH
Cambridgeshire, vol. 2, p. 302). Elizabeth Throckmorton also
had in her possession at one time a copy of William Tyndale's
translation of the *Enchiridion militis christianae* of Erasmus: the
details of the matter are recounted in Part I, Chapter 3, of this
study.

Miscellaneous Records
   In her will dated 27 March 1448 (probated 1 April 1448),
Agnes Stapilton, widow of Sir Brian Stapilton/Stapleton of Car-
leton, bequeathed 'Item . . . Abbatisse de Denney, unum cruci-
fixem (*sic*) et unum librum de Frensshe' (*North Country Wills* [see
ARTHINGTON, *Miscellaneous Records*], p. 48 [Cavanaugh, pp.
815–6]). The abbess in question was almost certainly Katherine
Sybyle (VCH *Cambridgeshire*, vol. 2, p. 302).

DERBY (Derby), *Priory of BVM, King's Mead* (Benedictine Nuns).

1 London, B.L., Egerton 2710 s.xiii
   a (fol. 2) An Anglo-Norman verse paraphrase of the Bible
(Långfors p. 13 'Al rei de glorie'; Bossuat 3009). b (fol. 112)
Herman de Valenciennes, *La passion du Christ* (extracted from
his verse rendering of the Bible) (Långfors p. 227 'Mout par
fu'; Bossuat 3017). c (fol. 126) The Gospel of Nichodemus
(Bossuat does not list this version, but Paul Meyer, 'Notice
du ms. Egerton 2710 du Musée britannique', *Bulletin de la
société des anciens textes français* 15 [1889], pp. 87–8, provides
a brief discussion). Appended to the end of the gospel (fols.
132v–134r) is a French version of the *Cura sanitatis Tiberii* (the
legend of Veronica [*BHL* 4218–20]). This is not uncommon. d
(fol. 134) The metrical sermon *Grant mal fist Adam* (Långfors
p. 153; Bossuat 3536). e (fol. 136) Herman de Valenciennes,
L'Assomption de Notre Dame (Långfors p. 377 'Seignurs ore
escutez, ke Deu vous beneie'; Bossuat 3089, 3091). f (fol. 139)
Three passions (in prose): the first of St John, the second of St
Peter and St Paul, the third of St Bartholomew (see Meyer, *op.
cit.*, pp. 92–4). g (fol. 145) Guichard de Beaulieu, *Le sermon du
siècle* (Långfors p. 134 'Entendez [en]vers mei'; Bossuat 3537).

h (fol. 148v) Passion of St Lawrence (in verse) (Långfors p. 213 'Maistre, a cest besoing'; Bossuat 3330). The edition by D. W. Russell, *La vie de Saint Laurent* (Anglo-Norman Text Society, 34; London, 1976) is based on Paris, Bib. Nat., Fr. 19525, but includes variants from this manuscript. **i** (fol. 151v) The Lord's Prayer (in French), together with an incomplete commentary (Sonet 2853, 3224). For a complete description of this manuscript, see P. Meyer, 'Notice du ms. Egerton 2710 du Musée britannique', *Bulletin de la société des anciens textes français* 15 (1889), pp. 72–97. See also J. Vising, *Anglo-Norman Language and Literature* (London/Oxford, 1923), p. 42 no. 9.

(fol. 83v [s.xv] *Thys bok gaf(?) here(?) of Boht(?) to ye nuns of Derbe*. This inscription is written in a dreadful scrawl and the words from *gaf* (?) to *Boht* (?) are unintelligible to me. What I have transcribed as *here* might possibly be *geve*.

EASEBOURNE (Sussex), *Priory of BVM* (Easebourne was founded as a Benedictine house, but became a priory of Augustinian Canonesses at an uncertain date, perhaps in the course of the 15th century).

Miscellaneous Records

a W. H. Blaauw, 'Episcopal Visitations of the Benedictine Nunnery of Easebourne', *Sussex Archaeological Collections* 9 (1857), pp. 10–13 transcribes and translates a *visus* of the priory dated 27 May 1450. The following books are recorded as being in the church (p. 12):

In primis in ecclesia: . . . **1** ij Missalia, **2** ij Portiforia, **3** iiij Antiphonaria, **4** i Legenda grossa, **5** viij Psalteria, **6** i Collectane, **7** i Troparium, . . . **8** i Biblia gallicana, **9** ij Ordinalia in gall<ico>, **10** i Librum euangelii, **11** i Martirologium.

b In a will drawn up in 1451, Mercy Ormesby, wife of Arthur Ormesby of Ormsby, Lincolnshire, bequeathed 'priorisse de Esbourne **1** vnum primarium copertum cum panno blodio intermixtum auro et **2** vnum librum Anglie vocatum the Chastesing of goddes childern, in perpetuum permansurum predicte domum de Esbourne' (H. R. Plomer, 'Books Mentioned in Wills', *Transactions of the Bibliographical Society* 7 [1902–04], p. 116 [Cavanaugh pp. 619–30]).

Item **b.2** is *The Chastising of God's Children* (L/B/E 343).

EDINBURGH, *Convent of St Catherine of Siena* (Dominican Nuns).

1 ?Edinburgh, U.L., 150 s.xvi

   a (fol. 1) Gospels for *proprium de tempore, proprium sancto-rum,* and *commune sanctorum,* followed by a rubric and a table in Scots. **b** (fol. 24) *Constitutiones sororum Ordinis Predicatorum.* An edition of the manuscript was published by J. Maidment, *Liber Conventus S. Katherine Senensis prope Edinburgum* (Ab-botsford Club, 21; Edinburgh, 1841).

2 Edinburgh, Nat. Lib. of Scotland, H8.f17 (printed book)

   Psalterium Davidicum, cum aliquibus canticis ecclesiasticis, lita-niae, hymni ecclesiastici, printed at Paris, 1552. See J. Durkan & A. Ross, *Early Scottish Libraries* (Glasgow, 1961), p. 86.

   (title-page [s.xvi2]) *This buk pertenis to sister Marione Crafurde in the place of the Senis besyde Edinburgh.*

ELSTOW (Bedfordshire), *Abbey of BVM and St Helen* (Benedictine Nuns).

1 London, B.L., Royal 7 F.iii AD 1191–92

   a (fol. 1) Peter Comestor, *Historia scholastica* (Stegmüller 6543–65). **b** (fol. 165v) Richard of Saint-Victor, *Allegoriae in Vetus Testamentum* (Stegmüller 7318).

   (fol. 196v [s.xii^ex]) *Scriptus est liber iste anno tertio coronationis Regis Ricardi, quem scribere fecit C. de Chanuill, bone memorie abbatissa beate Marie de Helenestow, in eruditionem et profectum conuentus sui et ceterorum inspicientium. Conuertantur igitur pre-fate abbatisse opera sua bona in salutem anime sue intercedentibus pro ea meritis et precibus gloriosissime Dei genitricis semper uirginis Marie, et post huius uite cursum, eterne retributionis brauium per-cipiat, cumque sanctis et electis Dei in eterna felicitate perhenniter iocundari mereatur, parante Domino nostro Ihesu Christo qui uiuit et regnat per omnia secula seculorum. Amen.* Cecily de Chanvill was abbess of Elstow in the last decades of the twelfth cen-tury and seems to have had a troubled abbacy, being much involved with lawsuits (see VCH *Bedfordshire,* vol. 1, pp. 353–4, 357). A facsimile of the inscription may be found in volume 4 of the Warner/Gilson catalogue of the Royal and King's collections, pl. 56b. See also Watson/*London,* vol. 1 no. 878, and vol. 2 pl. 109 (fol. 118).

ESHOLT (Yorkshire, W.R.), *Priory of BVM and St Leonard* (Cistercian Nuns).

Miscellaneous Records

In her will dated 27 March 1448 (probated 1 April 1448), Agnes Stapilton, widow of Sir Brian Stapilton/Stapleton of Carleton, bequeathed 'Item . . . monialibus de Ayssheholt, xxs., et librum meum vocatum *Chastisyng of goddeschildern*' (*North Country Wills* [see ARTHINGTON, *Miscellaneous Records*], p. 48 [Cavanaugh, pp. 815–6]).

The book is *The Chastising of God's Children* (L/B/E 343).

FLIXTON (Suffolk), *Priory of BVM and St Catherine* (Augustinian Canonesses).

1 Cambridge, U.L., Ee.3.52 s.xv

The first volume of a bible in French, containing the books from Genesis to Job (including, of course, Tobit). Intermingled with the text is a French commentary. The inscription (transcribed below) indicates that the priory also possessed a second volume, but it has not been identified. The manuscript is described in S. Berger, *La Bible française au moyen âge* (Paris, 1884; rpt. Geneva, 1967), pp. 407–8, with additional notes by Paul Meyer in *Romania* 15 (1886), pp. 265–7. Meyer demonstrates that the second (lost) volume included the New Testament as well as the remainder of the Old.

(fly-leaf i [s.xv]) *Nota quod anno Domini M° CCCC° XLII° obiit uenerabilis armiger Thomas uidelicet Croftys in conuentu monialium de Bungey, die mensis Ianuarii uicesima secunda, qui comunitati canonicarum de Flyxton contulit simul et donauit Vetus Testamentum in duobus uoluminibus gallici ydyomatis, ad singulare solacium priorisse sororumque suarum presencium et futurarum.* Bungay (VCH *Suffolk*, vol. 2, pp. 81–3) is only three miles from Flixton. The prioress of Flixton in 1442 was probably Maud Rycher (*ibid.*, p. 117).

Miscellaneous Records

F. Haslewood, 'Inventories of Monasteries Suppressed in 1536', *Proceedings of the Suffolk Institute of Archaeology and Natural History* 8 (1894), pp. 83–116, prints a number of inventories of religious houses in Suffolk. Included among them is an inventory of Flixton dated 21 August 1536. The following books are recorded:

In . . . the Quire (p. 89)
Item diu<er>s Bokes of the<r> use lytell worth att ij^s.

GODSTOW (Oxfordshire), *Abbey of BVM and St John the Baptist* (Benedictine Nuns).

1 Manchester, Chetham's Lib., 6717 (Mun.A.6.74) s.xv
Psalter, followed by Canticles, Litanies, Hours of the Virgin (Sarum Use), *Salve regina* and other hymns to the Virgin, Hours of the Holy Spirit, Hours of the Holy Trinity, prayers, the Office of the Dead and *Commendatio animarum*, the Fifteen Oes of St Bridget (fols. 143–6), and a long hymn to the Virgin (Chevalier 2215). There is no Calendar. The manuscript is no. 633 in Frere.

(fol. 148v [s.xv]) *Istud psalterium dedit Iohannes Gyste armiger ad vsum monialium monasterii Sancti Iohannis Baptiste de Godestow, et si quis illud alienauerit a dicto monasterio anathema sit. Amen.*

2 Oxford, Bod. Lib., Rawl. B.408 s.xv
Cartulary of Godstow (in English) begun after 1467 and written by 'a pore brodur and welwyller to the goode Abbas of Godstowe, Dame Alice Henley, and to all hyr couent.' Alice Henley died in 1470. The cartulary, an English abstract of P.R.O., Exch., K.R. (Misc. Bks. i.20 [AD 1404]) (Davis no. 462), is preceded by a Calendar and a few devotional pieces and was edited from this manuscript by A. Clark, *The English Register of Godstow Nunnery, Near Oxford* (EETS/OS, 129, 130, 132; London, 1905–11). See Davis no. 463.

GORING (Oxfordshire), *Priory of BVM* (Augustinian Canonesses).

1 Cambridge, Trinity Coll., 244 (B.11.5) s.xiii
Psalter, preceded by a Calendar and followed by Canticles and a Litany.

(fol. vii^v [s.xiii]) *Istum librum contulerunt Robertus Heryerd et Iohanna uxor eius priorisse et conuentui ecclesie sancte Marie de Gorynges, ut ipse orent pro statu predictorum Roberti et Iohanne tam in uita quam in morte. Et pro animabus Thome Aldryngton, Edmundi, Iohanne, Ricardi, Alicie, Hugonis, Agnetis et omnium fidelium defunctorum ut ipse per Dei misericordiam in pace requiescant. Amen.*

GREENFIELD (Lincolnshire), *Priory of BVM* (Cistercian Nuns).

Miscellaneous Records

In his will dated 9 April 1391, William de Thorp, knight, bequeathed 'to Margery his sister, a nun of Grenefeld, ten marks and a psalter' (R. R. Sharpe, *Calendar of Wills Proved and Enrolled in the Court of Husting, London* [London, 1890], vol. 2, p. 326). Ten marks was 6.13.4.

Note

According to G. F. Warner & J. P. Gilson, *Catalogue of Western Manuscripts in the Old Royal and King's Collections in the British Museum* (London, 1921), vol. 2, p. 172, B. L., Royal 15 D.ii probably belonged to Greenfield nunnery. This is possible, but far from certain (the manuscript is rejected by Ker); more important is the fact that the s.xv book-list which appears on fol. 211 of this volume (transcribed, with some inaccuracies, in Warner & Gilson, p. 171) is not a list of books belonging to Greenfield, but a list of books belonging to Cicely Welles, third daughter of Edward IV, who at one time also owned this manuscript.

HAMPOLE (Yorkshire, W.R.), *Priory of BVM* (Cistercian Nuns).

1 San Marino, Huntington Lib., EL 9 H.17 s.xiv^2

  a (fol. 2) Hymns, Hours of the Passion, Short Office of the Cross (ascribed in the rubric to Pope John XXII [1316–34]) accompanied by the Hours of the Passion in French verse (Långfors p. 397 'Sire Jhesu, ky par toun doux playser'; Sonet 2043 [ascribed in the rubric to Pope Urban IV (1261–64)]), Hours of the Virgin (Dominican Use), the Psalter of St Jerome, and a Calendar. **b** (fol. 42) Psalter, followed by the ferial Canticles, a Litany, and the Office of the Dead. The volume is sometimes referred to as the Vernon Psalter and is fully described in C. W. Dutschke, *Guide to Medieval and Renaissance Manuscripts in the Huntington Library* (San Marino, 1989), vol. 1, pp. 30–3. For the illustrations, see L. F. Sandler, *Gothic Manuscripts 1285–1385* (Oxford, 1986) no. 53.

  (fol. 36 [s.xiv^2]) *Domina Issabella de Vernun dedit istud psalterium conuentui de Hanpul, qui alienauerit excomunicatus est.* Isabel de Vernon was presumably a member of the family of that name which held lands in Staffordshire and Derbyshire. She may possibly be the women represented in the historiated initial on fol. 175v.

Miscellaneous Records

In his will dated 6 November 1467 (probated 26 January 1474–5), Robert Est of York bequeathed 'Domui sanctimonialium de Hampaule Psalterium glosatum, de propria scriptura Beati Ricardi, heremitae, ibidem jacentis' (*Test. Ebor.*, vol. 3, p. 160).

This most interesting bequest refers to Rolle's own copy of his English Psalter (Allen, pp. 169–77; Stegmüller 7303).

HARROLD (Bedfordshire), *Priory of St Peter* (Augustinian Canonesses).

1 London, Private Collection (P. Getty, Jr.), 1 (formerly Bristol, Baptist Coll., Z.c.23) s.xii[ex]

Psalter, preceded by a Calendar with computistical tables (including Walther 5057) and followed by the ferial Canticles, a Litany, and various prayers.

This manuscript was orginally written in the late 12th century by or for a priest in Kent, but by the early 13th century it was in the possession of Harrold. At that date nineteen documents of s.xii–xiii relating to a claim by the priory of Harrold to the church at Stevington in Bedfordshire were copied on fols. 143v–5v. These have been edited by C. R. Cheney, 'Harrold Priory: A Twelfth-Century Dispute', *Bedfordshire Historical Record Society* 32 (1952), pp. 1–26, reprinted in his *Medieval Texts and Studies* (Oxford, 1973), pp. 285–313. See Davis no. 472.

HEYNINGS (Lincolnshire), *Priory of BVM* (Cistercian Nuns).

1 Lincoln, Cathedral Chapter Lib., 199 s.xii

a (fol. 4) Honorius Augustodunensis, *Gemma animae* (*PL* 172: 541–738), preceded by a collection of theological *sententiae*. b (fol. 147) *Ps.*-Hugh of Saint-Victor, *Speculum ecclesiae* (*PL* 177: 335–75), followed by a group of brief texts by *ps.*-Marbod and Isidore of Seville (L. Thorndike & P. Kibre, *A Catalogue of Incipits of Medieval Scientific Writings in Latin* [Cambridge, Mass., 1963], cols. 226, 654, 901). c (fol. 183) Philippe de Thaun, *Li cumpoz* (Bossuat 2856). d (fol. 213) Homiliary, based on the Carolingian homiliary of Saint Père de Chartres. For a full account, see R. M. Thomson, *Catalogue of the Manuscripts of Lincoln Cathedral Chapter Library* (Cambridge, 1990), pp. 159–61. e (fol. 345) *Vita S. Rumuoldi* (*BHL* 7385). f (fol. 349) Abbo of

Fleury, *Passio S. Edmundi* (*BHL* 2392 [excerpts only]), followed
by three folios of a Breviary for secular use.

(fol. 354v [s.xv]) *Iste liber constat domui beate Marie de Heuyn-
ningis.*

Miscellaneous Records

In her will probated 12 August 1412, Elizabeth Darcy,
widow of Philip Lord Darcy (who died in 1399), bequeathed 'to
Heynynges chapel a great missal; et volo quod meum portiforium et meum magnum psalterium sint infixa cum una cathena
ferri in capella de Henynges et ibidem remaneant' (A. Gibbons,
*Early Lincoln Wills. An Abstract of All the Wills and Administrations
Recorded in the Episcopal Registers of the Old Diocese of Lincoln, . . .
1280–1547* [Lincoln, 1888], pp. 117–8 [Cavanaugh, p. 229]).

HIGHAM (Kent), *Priory of St Mary* (Benedictine Nuns).

1 ?Cambridge, St John's Coll., 271 s.xiii[ex]

Mortuary Roll of Amphelisa, prioress of Higham (or Lillechurch). There is a full description of the roll in C. E. Sayle,
'The Mortuary Roll of the Abbess of Lillechurch, Kent', *Proceedings of the Cambridge Antiquarian Society* 10 (1901–04), pp.
383–409, but both Sayle and James (in his catalogue of the
St John's College manuscripts) identify Amphelisa with Amphelisa or Amfelisia de Dunlegh, prioress of Lillechurch from
1275 to her death in 1295 (VCH *Kent*, vol. 2, p. 146). Sally
Thompson, however, in her *Women Religious* (Oxford, 1991),
p. 11, n. 26, shows that the Amphelisa in question was an
earlier Amphelisa, not recorded in VCH, who was prioress at
the end of the twelfth or beginning of the thirteenth century.
The roll is just over thirty-seven feet long and contains entries
for 372 houses visited by the roll-bearer. All are listed by
Sayle, together with their dedications (invariably included
in the roll), and their modern location, county, and Order.
Alphabetical indexes are provided on pp. 400–9.

As with the mortuary roll from Castle Hedingham, it is
probable that the Higham roll was made for the priory and
kept there.

Miscellaneous Records

Robert F. Scott, *Notes from the Records of St John's College,
Cambridge. Third Series* (privately printed, 1906–13 [first published in *The Eagle* (the college journal), vol. 32, no. 154 for March

1911]), pp. 403–8, prints an inventory of Higham dated 16 July 1525. One book is recorded:

De iocalibus et alijs ornamentes Ecclesie (p. 406)

A boke of gospelles couered with siluer and ouer gilte with stones of cristall.

HORTON (Dorset), *Abbey of St Wolfrida* (Benedictine Nuns).

1 El Escorial, e.ii.1 s.xi[in]

Boethius, *De consolatione philosophiae* (*CPL* 878), with marginal commentary and interlinear glosses. A microfilm of the manuscript is available in the Bodleian Library.

(fol. 1 [s.xi]) Þas boc syllþ aelfgyþ gode into horetune. See Ker/*AS*, pp. 152–3, no. 115.

ICKLETON (Cambridgeshire), *Priory of St Mary Magdalen* (Benedictine Nuns).

1 Cambridge, St John's Coll., 506 and T.9.1 AD 1516

This is a composite volume, part manuscript and part printed book. There are 31 manuscript folios at the beginning and 42 at the end. The printed book is the *Psalterium cum Hymnis secundum Usum et Consuetudinem Sarum et Eboracensis*, printed at Paris, 1516 (*STC* 16259). The manuscript sections contain a Litany and a series of commemorations, prayers, and liturgical offices in Latin. On fol. 42 is a note, in English and in a later hand, on the seven archangels.

(end fly-leaf [s.xvi[1]]) *Thys bowke belonges vnto Dame Elizabeth Trotter, prophessyd noyne in the abbay of Ikelyngton in the dyocesse of Ely.* This inscription appears to be in the same hand as the manuscript sections of the volume. Of Elizabeth Trotter I know nothing.

KILBURN (Middlesex), *Priory of St Mary and St John the Baptist* (probably Benedictine, but possibly Augustinian Canonesses).

Miscellaneous Records

William Dugdale, ed. J. Caley, H. Ellis, & B. Bandinell, *Monasticon Anglicanum* (London, 1817–30), vol. 3, pp. 424–5, prints part of an inventory of the priory dated 11 May 1536. The following books are recorded:

The Chamber next to the Chirche (p. 424)

Item, two bookes of Legenda Aurea, the one in prynt, and the other wryten, bothe Englyshe, iiij[d].

(For the *Golden Legend* in English, see BRUISYARD, *Miscellaneous Records*, **b**.)

   The Inventory of the Chirche Stuff (p. 425)

   Item, two masbookes, one old writen, and the oder print, atxx^d.

   Item, four processions in parchement, iij^s. and paper, x^d.

   Item, two Legendes, viij$^{d.}$ the one in parchement, and thoder in paper.

   Item, two chestes w^t. diverse bookes perteininge to the chirche, bookes of no value.

KINGTON ST MICHAEL (Wiltshire), *Priory of BVM* (Benedictine Nuns).

1 Cambridge, U.L., Dd.8.2 s.xv^{ex}

   a (fol. 2) A brief list of English kings from Arviragus to Henry VII together with their places of burial. **b** (fol. 3v) An *ordo* (in English) 'to resseyve brothers and sisters' into Kington. Such brother and sisters might be thought of as Honorary Members of the priory, though the only resident brother was the chaplain. This is followed by an *ordo* (again in English, with Latin rubrics) 'to resseyve a minchin [= nun].' **c** (fol. 5) Prayers to the Virgin, to angels and saints, and two metrical prayers, all in English. The metrical prayers are Brown/Robbins 241 and 3231 (omitting *Crist*). **d** (fol. 5v) A letter of Thomas Langton, bishop of Salisbury (1485–93), appointing Catherine Moleyns prioress of Kington, her predecessor having been forced to resign in 1492 (see J. E. Jackson, 'Kington St Michael', *Wiltshire Archaeological and Natural History Magazine* 4 [1858], pp. 56–60). This is followed by a detailed list of priory lands, monastic revenues, and prayers for benefactors. **e** (fol. 8) The obituary Calendar of Kington compiled by Catherine Moleyns in 1493 (Davis no. 515). This is the most important part of the manuscript and is followed by a list of gifts made to the monastery by John Baker (see below). An abbreviated version of the *Obituary* was published by Jackson, 'Kington St Michael', pp. 60–7. **f** (fol. 21) The second part of the volume contains eighteen folios of services for the sick, *Commendatio animarum*, and Hours of the Virgin. The manuscript is no. 855 in Frere.

(fol. 5 [s.xv^ex]) *John Baker of Briggewater./ Christe help the nowe and euer. Amen./ And Dame Kateryne Moleyns also/ To the blysshe of heuen that she may go. Amen.* John Baker's name also appears on fol. 1v together with *Jesu haue mercy on the soule of John Baker.* He and his wife were received as brother and sister of Kington on Lady Day 1498. On fol. 10 of the *Obituary* appears a list of gifts made to the priory by Baker when Catherine Moleyns was prioress: included among them is *This boke for to be there mortilage* (*mortilage* is a variant spelling of *martiloge* or martyrology). Catherine Moleyns was formerly a nun of Shaftesbury and was probably a relative of Adam Moleyns, Dean of Salisbury in 1441, and Bishop of Chichester from 1445 to his death in 1450. She was elected prioress of Kington in 1492 and died in 1506 (VCH *Wiltshire*, vol. 2, pp. 260–1).

2 Oxford, Corpus Christi Coll., 220 s.xv

a (fol. 1) *A Little Short Treatise* (Jolliffe J.2.[c]; L/B/E 287). This is a translation of *De patientia tribulationum* attributed by Bale to Adam the Carthusian. **b** (fol. 5v) *The Twelve Profits of Tribulation* (Jolliffe J.3.[b]; L/B/E 142). This is a translation of the *De XII utilitatibus tribulationis* attributed sometimes to Peter of Blois and sometimes to Adam the Carthusian, but possibly by Hugh of Saint-Cher. It frequently follows the *Little Short Treatise* in the manuscripts and is preceded, as at DARTFORD 7j and elsewhere, by a Latin passage *de patientia infirmitatis.* **c** (fol. 24v) *Book of the Craft of Dying* (Jolliffe L.4.[a]; L/B/E 234), sometimes attributed (incorrectly) to Richard Rolle. See also DARTFORD 7f. **d** (fol. 42) *A Treatise of Ghostly Battle* (Jolliffe H.3; L/B/E 120). The fly-leaves of the manuscript are fragments of a roll of household accounts.

(fol. 3v [s.xvii]) *This boke was appertaininge to Marye Dennis sometymes Ladie Abbesse of a certen nunnery in Glocestershyre. She dyed in Bristowe 1593, a good olde maide, verie vertuose and godlye, and is buried in the churche of the Gauntes ane the grene.* Mary Dennis or Marie Denys was the last prioress of Kington (she was appointed in 1535 having formerly been a nun at Lacock [VCH *Wiltshire*, vol. 3, p. 314; *LP*, vol. 9, p. 47 no. 160]), and *Glocestershyre* is an error for Wiltshire (see Jackson, 'Kington St Michael', pp. 55–6 and VCH *Wiltshire*, vol. 3, p. 261). According to John Aubrey, ed. J. Britton, *The Natural History of Wiltshire* (London, 1847), p. 70, 'the last Lady Prioresse of

Priorie St. Marie . . . was the Lady Mary Dennys, a daughter
of the Dennys's of Pocklechurch in Gloucestershire; she lived
a great while after the dissolution of the abbeys, and died in
Somersetshire about the middle or latter end of the raigne of
King James the first.' The volume is not included in Ker or
Watson.

Miscellaneous Records

Listed among the gifts made to Kington by John Baker (see
no. 1 above, fol. 10) are 'a boke of seynts lyves yn Englisshe', 'the
mendynge and renewynge of an olde Masboke of theres', and 'a
feire Matyns Boke with Dirige and many good prayers.'

The 'boke of seynts lyves yn Englisshe' probably refers to
an English version of the *Golden Legend* (see BRUISYARD,
Miscellaneous Records, b).

LACOCK (Wiltshire), *Abbey of BVM and St Bernard* (Augustinian
Canonesses).

1 Lacock Abbey, Mrs A. D. Burnett-Brown s.xiv–xv

William Brito, *Dictionarium/Expositiones vocabulorum bibliae*
(ed. L. W. & D. A. Daly [Padua, 1975]).

The fly-leaves of this manuscript (fols. i, ii, 195) are fragments of a s.xiii *compotus* roll from Lacock and of a Lacock
cellaress's accounts from the same period.

2 ?Oxford, Bod. Lib., Laud lat. 114 s.xiii[ex]–xv

Psalter, preceded by a Calendar (with Latin verses [Walther
9771]) and followed by Canticles, Athanasian Creed, a Litany,
and various prayers. The manuscript is no. 170 in Frere.

The Calendar contains s.xv additions for an abbey of Augustinian nuns; St Bernard is written in red in the Calendar
and follows St Augustine in the Litany; and St Cyriac, the
patron of Lacock church (which had been appropriated by
the abbey in the early fourteenth century [VCH *Wiltshire*, vol.
3, p. 308]), appears in both the Calendar and the Litany. There
can be little doubt that the volume was once at Lacock.

Miscellaneous Records

a In his will dated 31 January 1398, Ralph Erghum, bishop
of Bath and Wells, bequeathed 'To Agnes, my sister, my beautiful
psalter which the Rector of Marnhull gave me, to have it for her
life, and after her death it shall remain to the house of Lacok,

and to the Abbess there at that time and it shall not be parted with' (F. W. Weaver [ed.], *Somerset Medieval Wills (Second Series) 1501–1530* [Somerset Record Society, 19; London, 1903], p. 295). Agnes de Wyke was abbess of Lacock from 1380 to her death in 1403 (VCH *Wiltshire*, vol. 3, p. 315). There are no grounds for identifying the bishop's Psalter with no. 2 above.

b In a letter dated 23 or 24 August 1535, John Ap Rice, the colleague of Thomas Legh, wrote from Edington and reported that 'the Ladies [of Lacock] have their rule, thinstitutes of their religion and ceremonies of the same writen in the frenche tonge which they understand well and are very perfitt in the same, albeit that it varieth from the vulgare frenche that is nowe used, and is moche like the frenche that the common Lawe in writen in' (W. Gilchrist Clark, 'The Fall of the Wiltshire Monasteries', *The Wiltshire Archaeological and Natural History Magazine* 28 [1894–96], pp. 296–7). The volume has not survived.

LANGLEY (Leicestershire), *Priory of St Mary* (Benedictine Nuns).

Miscellaneous Records

M. E. C. Walcott, 'Inventory of St Mary's Benedictine Nunnery, at Langley, Co. Leicestershire, 1485', *Transactions of the Leicestershire Architectural and Archaeological Society* 4 (1878), pp. 117–22, prints an inventory of Langley dated 1485. Two books are recorded:

For ye chyrch (p. 119)

. . . ij masse boks.

LILLECHURCH : see **HIGHAM**.

LITTLEMORE (Oxfordshire), *Priory of BVM and St Nicholas* (Benedictine Nuns).

1 Oxford, Bod. Lib., Auct. D.2.6 (S.C. 3636), fols. 1–155 s.xii
Psalter, preceded by a Calendar and a paschal table for 1064–1595 and followed by Canticles, *Pater Noster*, Apostles' Creed, *Gloria*, Athanasian Creed, a Litany, and various prayers. The Calendar (fols. 2–8) was originally written for St Alban's, perhaps in 1149 (see E. W. B. Nicholson, *Early Bodleian Music. Introduction to the Study of Some of the Oldest Latin Musical Manuscripts in the Bodleian Library* [London, 1913], p. lxxx,

with a facsimile of fol. 7v), and the Psalter (fols. 9–155) for
the Old Minster at Winchester, but by 1200 they had been
bound together (see the notes to S.C. 3636).

(fol. 1v [s.xv^{in}]) *Caucio priorisse de Lytelmore ja<cet> pro xl s.
et habet supplementum por<ti>forium cum vno signaculo argenteo
2º folio incipiatur.* On fol. 155 is the name of *Adam Basset de
Litlemore* in a s.xiii hand.

LONDON, *Priory of St Helen, Bishopsgate* (Benedictine Nuns).

Miscellaneous Records

In his will dated 20 June 1349, William de Thorneye, pep-
perer of London, bequeathed 'to the prioress and nuns of S.
Elena, London, his portifory and psalter' (R. R. Sharpe, *Calendar of Wills Proved and Enrolled in the Court of Husting, London*
[London, 1890], vol. 1, p. 650 [Cavanaugh, p. 857]). The identity
of the prioress at the time is uncertain: it may have been Eleanor
de Wynton (VCH *London*, vol. 1, p. 461).

LONDON, *Priory of St John the Baptist, in Holywell* (Augustinian
Canonesses).

1 Oxford, Bod. Lib., Douce 372 (S.C. 21947) s.xv

James of Voragine, *The Golden Legend*, 'the which is drawn
out of ffrensshe into Englisshe, the yere of oure lorde M.CCCC.
and xxxviij, bi a synfulle wrecche whos name I beseche Ihesu
Criste bi his meritis of his passionne and of alle these holie
seintis afore written, that hit may be written in the boke of
euerlastinge life. Amen.' (fol. 163). This is the earlier Middle
English version (L/B/E 682) of the *Golden Legend* translated
from the 1348 French version of Jean de Vignay (Bossuat p.
537). It contains about fifty *vitae*, beginning with the Life of
St Antony and ending with the Life of Adam and Eve. A
full description is provided by Carl Horstmann, *Altenglische
Legenden: Neue Folge* (Heilbronn, 1881; rpt. Hildesheim/New
York, 1969), pp. cxxx–cxxxii (where the manuscript is cited
incorrectly as Douce 872). The volume is badly mutilated.

(fol. 163v [s.xv²]) *[B]e hit remembryd that John Burton, [c]itizen
and mercer of London, past oute of this lyfe the xx. day of Nouember,
the yere of oure lorde Mill<esimo>. cccc.lx and the yere of Kynge
Herry the sixte after the conquest xxxix; and the said John Burton
bequethe to dame Kateryne Burton, his doughter, a boke callyd*

Legenda Sanctorum, the seyde Kateryne to haue hit and to occupye to hir owne use and at hir owne liberte durynge hur lyfe, and after hur decesse, to remayne to the prioresse and the couent of Halywelle for euermore, they to pray for the saide John Burton and Johanne his wife and alle crystene sawles. And who that lettithe the execucion [of thi]s bequest be the lawe standeth.

LONDON, *Abbey of BVM and St Francis, without Aldgate* (Franciscan Nuns).

1 Cambridge, Trinity Coll., 301 (B.14.15) s.xv^{in}
   The Doctrine of the Heart (Jolliffe H.1 = O.3).

   (end fly-leaf [s.xv^{in}]) *Hit ys to witt that dame Cristyne Seint Nicolas of the menoresse of London, dowghtyr of Nicolas Seint Nycolas, squier, geff this boke aftyr hyr dysses to the offyce of the [erasure] and to the offys of the abbessry perpetually; the whyche passed to God out of this worlde the yere of owre Lorde m.cccc.l.v., the ix day of Marche, on whoys soule God haue merci.* In 1455, the abbess of the London Minoresses was one Christina (Bourdillon, p. 87).

2 London, B.L., Harley 2397 s.xv
   a (fol. 1) Walter Hilton, *The Ladder of Perfection* (L/B/E 255). **b** (fol. 73) *idem, Mixed Life (Vita mixta)* (L/B/E 147). **c** (fol. 85v) Commentary (in English) on Psalm 91, possibly by Walter Hilton (L/B/E 115.5). The flyleaves of the manuscript (fols. 1*–4v* and 95–98) contain liturgical material (with music).

   (fol. 94v [s.xv]) *Dame Elyzabeth Horwode, abbas of the Menoresse off London, to her gostle comfforthe, bowght thys boke, hyt to remayne to the vse off the systerrs of the sayde place, to pray for the yene [= gain] and ffor the sowles off hyr ffader and her moder, Thomas Horwode and Beatryxe, and the sowle off Mayster Robert Alderton.* Elizabeth Horwood was one of the successors of Christina as abbess of the London Minoresses, but her precise dates are unknown (Bourdillon pp. 79, 87).

3 ?Oxford, Bod. Lib., Bodl. 585 (S.C. 2357), fols. 48–104 s.xv
   Rule for Enclosed Minoresses (L/B/E 797), followed (fols. 72–101) by much additional material of a similar nature, primarily concerned with the liturgy and the ordering of services. This is a translation of the Rule for Minoresses as amended by Urban IV in 1263. An edition of the text, together with the additional material and a useful introduction, was published by W. W.

Seton in *A Fifteenth-Century Courtesy Book and Two Franciscan Rules* (EETS/OS, 148; London, 1914), pp. 63–124.

For the association of the manuscript with the Aldgate nuns, see *ibid.*, pp. 72–3. There can be little doubt on the question.

4 Reigate, Parish Church, Cranston Library 2322 s.xv[ex]

Hours of the Virgin (fols. 7–56v) preceded by a Calendar and followed by a considerable amount of liturgical material including various *memoriae*, psalms, antiphons, litanies, the Office of the Dead and *Commendatio animarum*, an office for solemn profession, the *Salve regina*, and various prayers. On fols. 180–8 are the Fifteen Oes of St Bridget (in Latin) preceded by a long introduction in English (L/B/E 17).

(fol. 191 [s.xv]) *Memorandum that dam Annes Porter gafe to dam An Frenell Meneres wythe owte Algate of Lundun this boke to gyfe aftur hur deses with the licens of hur sufferen to hom that she wull. God safe An.*

5 Wellington (N.Z.), Turnbull Lib. s.xv[in]

Psalter, preceded by a Calendar and followed by Canticles, prayers, a Litany, collects, and the hymn *Veni Creator Spiritus.*

(fol. 2 [s.xv]) *M<emoran>d<um> that this Sawter was gevyn by Beterice Carneburgh unto Dame Grace Centurio to have it to her for terme of her lyfe, and aftir her discesse to remayne unto what syster of the Meneres that it shall plese the seme grace to gyf it, never to be gevyn awey, solde, nor lent, but onely to the Meneres, they to pray perpetually for the sawles named in this present Sawter.* Of Dame Grace Centurio I know nothing. For the 'sawles named' in the Psalter, see M. M. Manion, V. F. Vines, & C. F. R. de Hamel, *Medieval and Renaissance Manuscripts in New Zealand Collections* (Melbourne/London/New York, 1989), p. 119.

Untraced Books

6 Ker, p. 123, reports a copy of *Poor Caitiff* (Jolliffe B) (s.xv), sold at the Meade Falkner Sale at Sotheby's on 12 December 1932 (lot 387).

According to the auction catalogue, a partially defaced inscription on the last page (fol. 98) read as follows: *M<emoran>d<um> that I dame Margaret Hasley, ladi and sister of the Meneresie of London, have be the licence of my sovren geve this boke to the use of Dame Anne Bassynburne, sister of the same priory, and after hir death to the comforte of hir sisters, and not to be geve nor lent*

without the place aforesaid. On whose soule God have mercy. Amen.
Neither sister is named by Bourdillon.

Miscellaneous Records

a In her will dated 9 August 1399, Eleanor, duchess of
Gloucester, bequeathed to her daughter Isabel, a young Minorite
nun (she was sixteen on 23 April 1400), a collection of seven
books, as follows: 'Item jeo devise a ma fille Isabella soer de
les avantditz menuresses . . . Item **1** un bible de Frauncois en
deux volumes, ove deux claspes d'or enamaillez ove les armes
de Fraunce. Item **2** un livre de decretales en Francois. Item **3** un
livre de meistre histoires. Item **4** un livre *de vitis patrum*, & **5** les
pastorelx Seint Gregoire. Item **6** psautier veil tanque a la nocturn
de *Exultate* glosez, **7** autre livre novel du psautier gloses de la
primer, *Domine exaudi* tanque a *omnis spiritus laudet dominum*, &
sount les dites livres de Francois' (J. Nichols [ed.], *A Collection of
All the Wills . . . of the Kings and Queens of England* [London, 1780;
rpt. New York, 1969], p. 183. An odd macaronic translation of
this bequest may be found in N. H. Nicholas, *Testamenta Vetusta,
being Illustrations from Wills . . .* [London, 1826], pp. 148–9).

1 For French translations of the Bible, see Bossuat 3008–
9 and compare FLIXTON 1 above. **2** The book of Decretals
cannot be precisely identified, but apart from the dubious case
of the law books listed in the BARKING (APPENDIX), it is
the only volume of canon law so far traced to a nunnery. **3**
This entry is too vague to permit identification. **4** For French
versions of the *Vies des Pères*, see Bossuat 3449–54. **5** This entry
presumably refers to a French version of the *Regula pastoralis* of
Gregory the Great (*CPL* 1712), but none is recorded in Bossuat.
6–7 The glosses to these Psalters were presumably in French
(cf. Bossuat 3041–9). Eleanor also owned a number of other
books which she left to other daughters (see Nichols, pp. 177–
85; Nicholas, pp. 146–9). Isabel went on to become abbess of
the London Minoresses in 1421 (Bourdillon, pp. 41–2, 87).

b In his will dated 23 June 1415, Henry Lord Scrope of
Masham bequeathed 'Sorori meae Matildi, Minorissae Londo-
niae, . . . **1** unum parvum Librum cum Matutinis de Cruce coopertum cum panno de Serico viridi, & **2** i. parvum Librum cum
Matutinis de compassione Mariae Virginis & cum Matutinis de
Trinitate, & **3** unum Rotulum qui incipit *cum Matutinis Sanctae Annae*, & **4** unum Librum in Anglicis, qui vocatur *Stimulus*

conscientiae, coopertum in albo Corio' (T. Rymer, ed. G. Holmes, *Foedera* [The Hague, 1740 [3rd ed.]; rpt. Farnborough, 1967], vol. 4, pt. 2, p. 133).

Items **b.1** and **b.2** are Books of Hours containing the Hours of the Cross, the Hours of the Compassion of the Virgin, and the Hours of the Trinity. Item **b.3** I take to be a collection of private devotions, but a roll form for this type of material at this period is most unusual (see M. T. Clanchy, *From Memory to Written Record: England 1066–1307* [Oxford, 1993[2], pp. 135–44). Item **b.4** is the popular *Prick of Conscience,* sometimes attributed (probably incorrectly) to Richard Rolle (see Allen, pp. 372–97 [where this bequest is mentioned]; Brown/Robbins 3428).

MALLING (Kent), *Abbey of BVM and St Andrew* (Benedictine Nuns).

1 Blackburn, Museum & Art Gallery, 091.21040 s.xv[in]

Hours of the Virgin (Sarum Use) (fols. 8–52v), preceded by a Calendar and followed by the *Salve regina,* the Penitential Psalms, a Litany, *Vigiliae mortuorum, Commendatio animarum,* the Psalter of St Jerome, and various *salutationes.* Included are the Fifteen Oes of St Bridget (fols. 149v–58v) and (in another hand) a Middle English verse life of St Margaret (fols. 167–83) (Brown/Robbins 2672). Other devotional pieces (in Latin) have been added in a later hand (s.xv[ex]) on fols. i and 183v. For other accounts of this manuscript and references to facsimiles of selected folios, see Ker/*MMBL,* vol. 2, p. 91.

(fol. 7 [s.xvi[1]]) *Domina Elezabeth Hull, abbatissa Ecclesiae conu-entualis de Mallyng, Roffensi diocesi, in humanis dum agebat, viribus licet corporis ferme destituta, hunc legauit librum Margarete Nevyll, ipsius que fidem Ihesu Christo commendandam, obnixe baptismatis sacramento spospondens offerebat in Ecclesiam parochali de Meryworthe ministrato, xxvj[to] die Septembris, Anno domini Millesimo CCCCC XX°, cuius quoque patronus prefate indubitatus fuit pater Dominus Thomas Nevyle, Miles, Henrici Anglorum Regis, fideique defensoris invictissimi conciliariorum vnus erat octaui, ac domini Georgij Nevyle, ordinis de le Gartere militis, dominique Bergevenny fraterculus ac coniunx domine Katherine ffytzhugh, quorum in hanc commercio lucem matrimoniali procreata denique fuit. Nunc quoque (ut decet) sue astripotenti commatricis animam* *oraciun<cu>lis supplicat, suscipiat ille cuius corpus nature soluit debitum xv die [erasure] Anno domini Millesimo Quingentesimo vicesimo iiij°.* This long inscription was first transcribed (with one inaccuracy [*coniux* for *coniunx*] and one query) by F. J. Furnivall in 'The Nevile and Southwell Families of Mereworth in Kent, A.D. 1520–1575', *Notes and Queries*, Ser. 4, 2 (1868), p. 578. I have compared it with a photograph kindly made available to me by Adrienne Wallman, Keeper of Art in the Blackburn Museum and Art Galleries. The reading *oraciun<cu>lis* is uncertain. The actual text reads *orac[five minims]lis*, and Furnivall could only conjecture '? for *oracionibus*.' I cannot believe that the writer of this florid inscription, with his predilection for words such as *astripotens* (it is recorded in du Cange), would make such an error. Margaret Nevile, as we are told, was born on 26 September 1520, the only daughter and sole heir of Sir Thomas Nevile. Her godparents were Elizabeth Hull and the abbot of Boxley. She married Sir Robert Southwell on 1 May 1536, gave birth to three sons and two daughters, and after the death of her first husband on 26 October 1559, married William Plumbe on 13 November 1561. She died on 25 December 1575 at the age of 55. Further information on her family is provided by Furnivall in the article cited above, pp. 577–8.

Miscellaneous Records

In his will dated 12 October 1368 (probated 18 April 1372), Simon de Bredon, fellow of Merton College and canon of Chichester, bequeathed 'Item librum de gallico intitulatum Manuel de pecche . . . monialibus de Mallyng' (F. M. Powicke, *The Medieval Books of Merton College* [Oxford, 1931], p. 84 [Cavanaugh, p. 129]).

The book is the *Manuel de pechiez* (Bossuat 3591–93) commonly, though doubtfully, attributed to William of Waddington.

MARHAM (Norfolk), *Abbey of BVM, St Barbara, and St Edmund* (Cistercian Nuns).

Miscellaneous Records

VCH *Norfolk*, vol. 2, p. 370, quoting P.R.O., Ch. Gds. K.R. 11/7, reports 'a mass book and six other books' in the church at Marham.

MARKYATE (Hertfordshire), *Hermitage, later priory, of Benedictine Nuns.*

1 Hildesheim, S. Godehardskirche + Cologne, Schnütgen Mus., M694 (formerly Sürth bei Köln, Dr J. Lückger [one leaf only]) s.xii^{in}

Psalter (pp. 72–372), preceded by a Calendar, forty full-page miniatures, the Life of St Alexis (in French) (pp. 57–68; Bossuat 42–43), the *Responsum S. Gregorii secundino incluso rationem de pictoris interroganti* with a French translation (p. 68), and followed by Canticles, *Pater noster*, Apostles' Creed, *Gloria*, Nicene Creed, Athanasian Creed, Litany, and Prayers. This is the sumptuous St Alban's Psalter, produced at St Alban's c. 1123 for Christina of Markyate. A brief description of the manuscript may be found in Kaufmann no. 29 and a full account in C. R. Dodwell, F. Wormald, & O. Pächt, *The St Alban's Psalter* (London, 1960).

For the association of this volume with Christina, see *The Life of Christina of Markyate: A Twelfth Century Recluse*, ed. C. H. Talbot (Oxford, 1959; rpt. Oxford, 1987), pp. 22–7.

MARRICK (Yorkshire, N.R.), *Priory of BVM and St Andrew* (Benedictine Nuns).

1 New York, Publ. Lib., Spencer Collection, 19 s.xv^{in}

Dream of the Pilgrimage of the Soul (L/B/E 75). This is a Middle English translation of the *Pélerinage de l'âme* (Bossuat 4904–6) of Guillaume de Digulleville/Deguileville, a Cistercian monk at the abbey of Chaalis from 1316 to his death sometime after 1358. The manuscript is illustrated with twenty-six magnificent miniatures and a complete description, with six facsimiles, may be found in V. H. Paltsits, 'The Petworth Manuscript of *Grace Dieu* or *The Pilgrimage of the Soul*', *Bulletin of the New York Public Library* 32 (1928), pp. 715–21. The miniatures are also listed in the auction catalogue of the Lord Leconfield Sale, Sotheby's, 23 April 1928 lot 76.

(fly-leaf iii^v [s.xv]) *Iste liber constat monasterio sanctimonialium sancti Andree Apostoli de Marrycke. Si quis illum alienauerit, uendiderit seu furatus fuerit, sentenciam maioris excommunicacionis minime euadat et periculi eterne dampnacionis incurrat.* A very similar inscription is repeated on fol. 133v. Again on fly-leaf iii^v (c. 1500) we find *This boke belongs to the Nunnery of the Nuns of Marrycke* and *Here beginnith the boke cald Grace Deu, giffin vnto the monestarye of Marrik by Dame Agnes Radcliffe, on whose sowl Jhesu haue mercye. Amen. Per me Isabell Lumley.* Agnes Radcliffe was the daughter of Lord Henry Scrope and married Sir Richard Radcliffe, a favourite of Richard III, who was killed at the Battle of Bosworth on 22 August 1485. Agnes then attached herself to the nunnery at Marrick. Isabelle Lumley was her daughter. The volume was originally owned by Sir Thomas Cumberworth of Somerby in Lincolnshire. Further information on the various owners is provided by Paltsits in the article cited above, pp. 715–7.

MINSTER IN SHEPPEY (Kent), *Priory of BVM and (later) St Sexburga* (The priory seems to have alternated between Benedictine and Augustinian observance. From the end of the eleventh century to 1396 it was Benedictine; but from 1396 to 1536, Augustinian. See VCH *Kent*, vol. 2, pp. 149–50).

Miscellaneous Records

M. E. C. Walcott, 'Inventories of (I.) St. Mary's Hospital or Maison Dieu, Dover; (II.) The Benedictine Priory of St. Martin New-Work, Dover, for Monks; (III.) The Benedictine Priory of SS. Mary and Sexburga, in the Island of Sheppey, for Nuns', *Archaeologia Cantiana* 7 (1869), pp. 272–306, prints an inventory of Minster in Sheppey dated 27 March 1536. The following volumes are recorded:

In the church (p. 292)

ij bokes with ij sylver clapses the pece, and vj bokes with one sylver clasp a pece, l bokes good and bad.

In the vestry (p. 292)

vij bokes, whereof j goodly mase boke of parchement, and dyvers other good bokes.

In the lady chapel (p. 294)

an olde presse full of old boks of no valew.

In the parlour (p. 298)

a boke of Saynts lyfes.

The reference is probably to an English version of the *Golden Legend* (see BRUISYARD, *Miscellaneous Records*, b).

NEWCASTLE UPON TYNE, *Priory of St Bartholomew* (Benedictine Nuns).

Miscellaneous Records

In his will dated 13 May 1376 and probated the same day, William de London, citizen of Carlisle, bequeathed 'monialibus Sci. Barthol. Novi Castri super Tynam unum psaltarium (*sic*) et dimidiam marcam' (R. S. Ferguson, *Testamenta Karleolensia. The Series of Wills from the Prae-Reformation Registers of the Bishops of Carlisle 1353–1386* [Cumberland & Westmorland Antiquarian and Archaeological Society, E.S.9; Kendal/Carlisle/London, 1893], p. 115 [Cavanaugh, pp. 540–1]).

NUN APPLETON (Yorkshire, W.R.), *Priory of BVM and St John the Evangelist* (Cistercian Nuns).

Miscellaneous Records

In an undated will (c. 1470), John Lathum, a canon of Beverley, bequeathed 'Priorissae et Conventui de Appilton praedicta, ad usum capellani cantariae meae ibidem, et cum eis imperpetuum remansura, meum Portiforium magnum, . . . ac Missale meum de usu Eboracensi' (*Test. Ebor.*, vol. 3, p. 175). According to James Raine, Jr., the editor of the third volume of *Test. Ebor.*, Lathum 'was probably the greatest benefactor that the little nunnery of Appleton ever had' (p. 174 [note]).

NUN COTON (Lincolnshire), *Priory of BVM* (Cistercian Nuns).

1 London, B.L., Harley 2409 s.xv

This manuscript was originally at Swine, but was given by Dame Maud Wade, prioress of Swine, to Dame Joan Hyltoft of Nuncoton. For a description, see below s.v. SWINE B.2.

NUN MONKTON (Yorkshire, W.R.), *Priory of BVM* (Benedictine Nuns).

Miscellaneous Records

a In his will dated 14 August 1430 (probated 21 April 1431), William Stowe, Senior, of Ripon, a retainer in the household of Henry Percy, earl of Northumberland, bequeathed 'Item Priorissae de Monnkton unum parvum Psalterium' (*Test. Ebor.*, vol. 2, p. 13 [Cavanaugh, pp. 828–9]). The prioress at the time may have been Maud de Goldesburgh, but that is not certain (see VCH *Yorkshire*, vol. 3, p. 123).

b In her will dated 27 March 1448 (probated 1 April 1448), Agnes Stapilton, widow of Sir Brian Stapilton/Stapleton of Carleton, bequeathed 'Item . . . monialibus de Nunne Monkton. xxs., et librum meum vocatum *Vice and vertues* (*North Country Wills* [see ARTHINGTON, *Miscellaneous Records*], pp. 48–49 [Cavanaugh, pp. 815–6]).

The book is the *Book of Vices and Virtues* (L/B/E 668), an anonymous English translation of the *Somme le roi* of Frère Laurent d'Orléans (see BRUISYARD 2).

c In his will dated 20 February 1485–6, Thomas Hornby of York, *capellanus*, bequeathed 'Dominae Elizabethae Sywardby, moniali de Monkton, librum in Anglicis de Vita Domini nostri Jhesu Christi' (*Test. Ebor.*, vol. 3, p. 165 [note]). Elizabeth Sywardby's aunt, also called Elizabeth, had left her £6.13.4 if she would become a nun (*ibid.*, p. 165). She did so in 1470, and the interesting *expensae factae super et pro Elizabetha Sywardby facta moniali in Munkton* are recorded in detail in *ibid.*, p. 168. The books belonging to Elizabeth's aunt are recorded in *ibid.*, p. 163 and include a missal, a psalter, the *Revelations* of St Bridget (in English), two volumes entitled *De vita Christi* (one in English and one in Latin), *De mysterio passionis Domini* (in English), *De visitatione beatae Mariae virginis* (the language is not specified), Richard Rolle's *Meditatio passionis Domini*, and a book of offices.

The identity of this English *Life of Christ* is unclear. I suspect that it was Nicholas Love's *Mirror of the Blessed Life of Christ* (see BARKING 1), a best-seller in the fifteenth century, but there are obviously other possibilities.

d In his will dated 8 February 1479–80, John Burn, *capellanus* in the Church of York, bequeathed 'Priorissae et Conventui de Monkton j librum Anglicum de Pater Noster et aliis' (*Test. Ebor.*, vol. 3, p. 199 [note]).

The title of this volume is too vague to permit precise identification. The English *Pater noster* attributed to Richard Rolle (Stegmüller 7312,2; Allen, pp. 358–9) is only one of many possibilities.

e In her will dated 19 October 1502, Elizabeth Swinburne bequeathed 'meum optimum Primarium ad vendendum et distribuendum per aequales portiones conventui B<eatae> M<ariae> de Non Monkton et conventui S<anctae> Clementis Ebor.' (*Test. Ebor.*, vol. 4, p. 208).

NUNEATON (Warwickshire), *Priory of BVM of Nuns of Fonte-vrault.*

1 Cambridge, Fitzwilliam Mus., McClean 123 s.xiii^ex

   a (fol. 1) Robert Grosseteste, *Chasteau d'amour*. See S. H. Thomson, *The Writings of Robert Grosseteste, Bishop of Lincoln 1235–1253* (Cambridge, 1940; rpt. New York, 1971), pp. 152–5 no. 113. **b** (fol. 7v) A brief (unprinted) commentary in French prose on the Lord's Prayer. **c** (fol. 10) The Gospel of Nichodemus in French verse by 'Crestien' (Långfors p. 128 'En l'onur de la Trinité'; Bossuat 3070). **d** (fol. 30) William the Norman/Guillaume le Clerc, *Bestiary* (Långfors pp. 312–3 'Qui bien comence'; Bossuat 2878–9). **e** (fol. 66) A rhymed version of the Apocalypse in Latin and French (Långfors p. 197 'La vision de Jhesucrist' [the beginning of the poem is missing in this manuscript]; Bossuat 3076 *bis*). **f** (fol. 106) An incomplete copy of the *Officium beatae Mariae virginis* (in Latin). **g** (fol. 109) *Ps.*-Augustine, *Oratio* (adapted for female use and with a French rubric), *inc.* 'Deus propitius esto mihi peccatrici': see Römer, vol. 2/1, p. 374. **h** (fol. 110) A second copy of the commentary on the Lord's Prayer noted at b above. **i** (fol. 115) *Poema morale* (in English) (Brown/Robbins 1272). This volume is often cited as the *Nuneaton Book*.

   (fol. 1 [s.xiii/xiv]) *Iste liber constat Alicia Scheynton, et post ea<m> conuentu <de Nuneton>*. (fol. 8 [s.xiv^ex]) *Iste liber constat domine Margarete Sylemon et discipulas suas, et post mortem suam, conuentu de Nuneton*. Margaret Seliman was prioress of Nuneaton from c. 1367 to c. 1386 (VCH *Warwickshire*, vol. 2, p. 69). Alice Sheynton is otherwise unknown.

2 Douai, Bibl. mun., 887 s.xiii–xiv

   a (fol. 10) Alan of Tewkesbury, two sermons (Schneyer, vol. 1, p. 84 nos. 1–2) and a collection of his letters. The collection has been studied and the letters edited by M. A. Harris, 'Alan of Tewkesbury and His Letters', *Studia Monastica* 18 (1976), pp. 77–108 and 299–351. Harris also provides a brief history of the manuscript (pp. 103–5 [with a facsimile of fol. 36] and summaries of the two sermons (pp. 345–8). **b** (fol. 48) Gerald of Wales, *Topographia Hiberniae*, edited with the *Expugnatio Hibernica* by J. F. Dimock in Rolls Series 21/5 (London, 1867), pp. 3–202 (*Topographia*), 207–404 (*Expugnatio*). **c** (fol. 106) The letter of Hugh of Reading (= Hugh of Amiens = Hugh of Rouen) to Celestine II, printed in B. Pez, *Thesaurus Anecdotorum Novissimus*, (Augsburg, 1721–9), vol. 1/2, pp. 297–300. For the place of this letter in Hugh's work, see *HLF*, vol. 12, p. 655. **d** (fol. 108) Gerald of Wales, *Expugnatio hibernica* (see **b** above). A more recent edition of the *Expugnatio* was published at Dublin in 1978 by A. B. Scott and F. X. Martin. At the beginning of the volume are fragments of various conciliar and papal decrees and constitutions.

(paste-down [s.xiv]) *Liber ecclesie sancte Marie de Ayton.* The manuscript was given to the English College at Douai in the first half of the 17th century.

POLSLOE (Devon), *Convent of Benedictine Nuns.*

1 Oxford, Bod. Lib., Douce BB 200 (printed book)
Breuiarium seu Portiforium ad Usum Insignis Ecclesie Sarisburiensis, printed at Paris by Francis Regnault and Francis Byrckman, 1519 (*STC* 15816).

On the last leaf of the volume (originally blank) is a list of Polsloe nuns. With the exception of the first, all the names appear in the 1538 Pension List printed in G. Oliver, *Monasticon Dioecesis Exoniensis* (Exeter/London, 1846), p. 168. The leaf is headed *Polslow* and the list follows a few lines of devotional Latin. The first name is that of prioress Margaret Trow who died in 1535 (a later hand has added *dede* after her name), and the list has been updated in the years between her death and the surrender of the convent on 19 February 1538. The list reads as follows (the names as they appear in Oliver, p. 168, are added in parentheses): *Margaret Trow, lady of the place. dede* (in a later hand). *Dame Elnor Sydnam* (Elenor Sydnam) (originally followed by *supprioresse*, but *supprioresse* has been crossed out and *lady of the place* substituted in a later hand). *Dame Ane Carew* (Anne Carewe) (added in a later hand). *Dame Ales Sayer* (Ales Sawyer). *Dame Jone Kellye* (Johanne Kelley). *Dame Ibot Credo* (Ibott Crede). *Dame Jone Holwell* (Johanne Holwyn). *Dame Alys Worth* (Aleys Worthy). *Dame Anestas Roswell* (Anstys Ruswyll). *Dame Tomsyn Carew* (Tomesyn Carew). *Dame Elyzabeth Benet* (Elsabeth Benett). *Dame Jane Eton* (Jane Heton). *Dame Dorathe Cooke* (Dorothe Cooke). *Dame Elyzabeth Ashly* (Elsabeth Assheley). By 1538 Eleanor Sydnam was

prioress, Anne Carew was subprioress, and another nun—
Radygunde Tylley—had joined the convent.

Miscellaneous Records

In his will dated 8 June 1418, Thomas Reymound leaves to
the prioress and convent of Polsloe the sum of twenty shillings
and a copy of the *Liber gestorum Karoli, regis Francie* (F. C. Hingeston-Randolph, *The Register of Edmund Stafford [A.D. 1395–1419]:
An Index and Abstract of Its Contents* [London, 1886], p. 419 no.
55 [Cavanaugh, p. 715]).

The obvious identification of the volume is *ps.*-Turpin, *Gesta
Karoli Magni* or *Historia Karoli Magni et Rolandi* (edited most
recently by H. W. Klein [Munich 1986]), but there was a
substantial amount of material pertaining to the Cycle of
Charlemagne in circulation and we cannot be certain of this.
There is no reason to believe that the book was not in Latin:
bequests of books written in French normally give the title in
that language or, if the bequest be written in Latin, add 'in
gallico'.

REDLINGFIELD (Suffolk), *Priory of BVM and St Andrew* (Benedictine Nuns).

Miscellaneous Records

a M. E. C. Walcott, 'Inventories and Valuations of Religious
Houses at the Time of the Dissolution, from the Public Record
Office', *Archaeologia* 43 (1871), pp. 201–49, notes that in 1537 Sir
Edmund Bedingfield purchased from Redlingfield 'j antiphoner
with a grayle in the quyer of the use of Sarum vjs. viij d.' (p.
245) An Alicia Bedyngfeld or Bedyngfeild is listed as a nun of
Redlingfield in episcopal visitations from 7 August 1514 to 5
July 1532 (*Visitations of the Diocese of Norwich, A.D. 1492–1532*
[see CAMPSEY 2], pp. 138, 139, 183, 221, 297). An Elizabeth
Bedingfeld was a nun at Bungay, about eighteen miles south
of Redlingfield, in 1526 (*ibid.*, p. 261), and the family was well
known for its adherence to the Old Religion.

b F. Haslewood, 'Inventories of Monasteries Suppressed in
1536', *Proceedings of the Suffolk Institute of Archaeology and Natural
History* 8 (1894), pp. 83–116, prints a number of inventories of
religious houses in Suffolk. Included among them is an inventory
of Redlingfield dated 26 August 1536. The following books are
recorded:

In the Churche att the High Alter (p. 95)
Item a messe boke att xij^d.
In the Quire (p. 95)
Item iiij bokes of ther use lytell worth att [blank].

ROMSEY (Hampshire), *Abbey of BVM and St Elfleda* (Benedictine Nuns).

1 London, B.L., Lansdowne 436 s.xiv^in
   a (fol. 2) A brief (unprinted) chronicle of English history from Hengist to Egbert, *inc.* 'Insula ista que nunc Anglia dicitur, quondam propter inhabitantes Britones Britannia maior dicebatur'. **b** (fol. 6) Forty-three *vitae* of English saints in Latin, beginning with Augustine of Canterbury and ending with Wulfric of Hazelbury. A complete list, together with *incipits*, *explicits* and references to *BHL*, is provided by Paul Grosjean in 'Vita S. Roberti Novi Monasterii in Anglia Abbatis', *Analecta Bollandiana* 56 (1938), pp. 335–9. The article includes an edition of the *vita* of Robert of Newminster (no. 40 [fols. 116–121v] = *BHL* 7268). The surviving collection is imperfect both at the beginning and the end, and once included *vitae* of four other saints: Aldhelm, Patrick, Guthlac, and Adalbert (see Grosjean, p. 339).
   (fol. 1 [s.xv]) *Iste liber est de librario ecclesie [sup. lin.] sancte Marie et sancte Ethelflede uirginis de Romesey.*
2 London, Royal Coll. of Physicians, 409 s.xiii
   The 'Wilton Psalter' was taken from Wilton by Ralph Lepton, rector of Alresford and Kings Worthy, and given to Elizabeth Langrege, a nun of Romsey, in 1523. For a description of the Psalter, see below s.v. WILTON 2.
   The record of the transfer from Wilton to Romsey reads as follows (fols. 144r–v [s.xvi^1]): *The xth day of October yn the yere of our Lord God oon thousand fyve hundreth and XXIII, the XVth yere of Kyng Henry the VIIIth and the XXIIIth yere of the translacion of my lord Rychard Foxe, Bysshop of Wynchestre, maistre Raufe Lepton, parson of Alresford and of Kynges Worthy, servaunt and chapelayne to my sayde lord Richard, gaue thys boke to Elisabeth Langrege, whos granfader, John Warner gentylman, was uncle to my lady Dame Anne Westbroke, abbes of Romsey; to the saide Elizabeth, mynchynne of Romsey, the said maister Raufe was grete uncle unto. Aboue, that the said maister Raufe gaue first*

at the veyllyng of the saide Elizabeth: in money, ffyve poundes deliuered to John Raye, baylyff of Romsey; aboue, that the saide maister Raufe gaue to the saide Elizabeth oon goblet of syluer, all gylted, couered with thre lyons on the fote, and two sponys, the oon crystable garnysshed with siluer gylted with an image on the ende, the other all whyte. According to the *Registra Stephani Gardiner et Johannis Poynet, episcoporum Wintoniensium,* ed. H. E. Malden & H. Chitty (Canterbury and York Society, 37; London, 1930), p. 39, an 'Elizabetha Langriche, xvij annorum . . . etatis' was one of nine nuns professed at Romsey on 27 July 1534 in the presence of John Draper, bishop of Neapolis (the bishop of Winchester's suffragan). She was not the youngest: two were fourteen and one was fifteen. The oldest was thirty-one. Anne Westbrooke, formerly 'sexteyn' of Romsey, was elected abbess in 1515 and died in 1523. Her successor, Elizabeth Ryprose, was the last abbess (VCH *Hampshire and the Isle of Wight,* vol. 2, pp. 131, 132).

SAINT MARY DE PRÉ (Hertfordshire), *Priory of St Mary de Pré* (originally a conventual leper hospital, but from about the middle of the 14th century, a priory of Benedictine Nuns).

Miscellaneous Records

In the early 1350s, when the house was in transition from leper hospital to priory, Thomas de la Mare, abbot of St Albans from 1349 to 1396, made enquiry into conditions there. He found that the nuns 'pro magna parte primitus illiteratae fuerunt, et servitium nullum dixerunt; sed in loco cujuslibet Horae certas Orationes Dominicas et Salutationes Angelicas. Ordinavit igitur, ut servitium praesentes addiscerent, et futurae, et, Horas diurnas, pariter et nocturnas, observando in choro, de die et de Dominica servitium dicerent sine nota, cum Officiis Mortuorum certis temporibus decantandis. Et quia non habebant libros ad dicendum vel cognoscendum servitium, dedit eis libros Conventus de custodia Praecentoris, Portiforia, videlicet, vel Ordinalia, ad numerum sex vel septem.

Tituli librorum isti sunt: Ordinale sine titulo, quod Subcellerarius solebat habere, Ordinale quod jacebat in Capella Dormitorii, pro hiis qui non interfuere Matutinis, Ordinale de dono Alexandri Dyper, Ordinale de dono Walteri Eleemosynarii, Ordinale Johannis Merdeley, Ordinale de dono Garini Abbatis,

Ordinale [blank]' (the nuns 'were, for the most part, originally
illiterate and said none [of their] Offices: in place of any of the
Hours, [they would substitute repetitions of] the Lord's Prayer
or the Angelic Salutation. He therefore ordered that from that
time onwards they should learn all the Offices, both the day
Hours and those of the night, that they should observe them
in choir, and that on weekdays and Sundays they should say
the Office without music, but that at certain times they should
sing the Office of the Dead. And because they had no books
wherewith to say or learn the Office, he gave them books from
[his own] monastery which were in the keeping of the precentor,
namely, a total of six or seven *Portiforia* or *Ordinalia*. These are
the the titles of the books: an Ordinal without title which used
to be in the possession of the Sub-Cellarer; an Ordinal which
was lying in the Dormitory Chapel for the use of those who
could not attend Matins; an Ordinal given by Alexander Dyper;
an Ordinal given by Walter the Almoner; an Ordinal of John
Merdeley, an Ordinal given by Abbot Warin, [and] and Ordinal
[blank]') (*Gesta Abbatum Monasterii Sancti Albani*, compiled by
Thomas Walsingham, ed. H. T. Riley [Rolls Series 28/4 (vol. 2 of
the *Gesta*); London, 1867], vol. 2, pp. 401–2).

SHAFTESBURY (Dorset), *Abbey of BVM and St Edward* (Benedictine Nuns).

1 Cambridge, Fitzwilliam Mus., 2–1957 s.xvi[in]
     Hours of the Virgin (fols. 34–52), preceded by a Calendar
and the liturgy for Prime throughout the year, and followed
by the *Salve regina*, various *memoriae*, the Penitential Psalms,
a Litany, collects and prayers, the Votive Office of the Virgin,
the Office of the Dead (with music) and *Commendatio animarum*
(also with music). A Latin prayer has been added on fol. 1v,
and versicles and responses for the Penitential Psalms on fols.
133–4. This is the volume recorded in T. Wright & J. O. Halliwell, *Reliquiae Antiquae* (London, 1843; rpt. New York, 1966),
vol. 2, p. 117, as a 'handsome Latin breviary, in the possession
of Henry Walter, Esq. of The Willows, near Windsor.' It was
originally made for Elizabeth Shelford, the penultimate abbess
of Shaftesbury. She was appointed in 1505 and died in 1528
(see VCH *Dorset*, vol. 2, p. 79, and F. Wormald & P. M. Giles,
*A Descriptive Catalogue of the Additional Illuminated Manuscripts
in the Fitzwilliam Museum* [Cambridge, 1982], p. 516).

(fol. 132v [c. 1550]) *Iste liber pertinet domine Alicie Champnys moniali monasterii Shastonie, quem dicta Alicia emit pro summa decem solidorum de domino Richard<o> Marshall, re<c>tore ecclesie parochialis sancti Rumbaldi de Shastina predicta.* In the transcript of this inscription in the Wormald/Giles catalogue, p. 520, *moniali monasterii* is incorrectly rendered as *monachiali* (!). It is correctly transcribed in S. de Ricci & W. J. Wilson, *Census of Medieval and Renaissance Manuscripts in the U.S. and Canada* (New York, 1935; rpt. 1961), vol. 1, p. 2. Alice Champnys was a novice at the time of the election of Elizabeth Shelford and was still alive in 1553 (Wormald/Giles, pp. 516–7). The arms of the abbey appear on fol. 78v.

2 Cambridge, U.L., Ii.6.40 s.xv

a (fol. 5) *Contemplations of the Dread and Love of God (Fervor amoris)* (Allen, p. 357; Jolliffe H.15; L/B/E 362). **b** (fol. 58v) *An Information on the Contemplative Life and Active, as it is drawn out of the Revelation of St Bride* (Jolliffe H.13 = O.23). **c** (fol. 75) *A Treatise of Perfect Love* (Jolliffe G.8). **d** (fol. 76v) *A Treatise of Tribulation* (Jolliffe G.13). **e** (fol. 95) *The Pater Noster of Richard the Hermit* (Jolliffe M.3 [b] = 0.9 [b]; L/B/E 150; Stegmüller 7312,2; Allen, pp. 358–9). **f** (fol. 191) The *Charter* from the *Poor Caitiff* (Jolliffe B; L/B/E 166). **g** (fol. 198) Richard Rolle, *Epistle on the Commandment of God*, written to a nun of Hampole (Allen, pp. 251–6; L/B/E 660). **h** (fol. 207v) *A Devout Meditation of Richard Hampole* (L/B/E 202). This is actually an interpolated version of selected sections of the *Mirror of Holy Church (Speculum Ecclesiae)* of St Edmund Rich of Abingdon (see Allen, pp. 362–3). At the beginning of the volume (fols. 1–2) are a few Latin prayers.

(fols. 2r and 4v [s.xv]) *Iste liber constat domine Johanne Mouresleygh*, who is recorded as a nun of Shaftesbury in 1441 and 1460 (see J. Hutchins, *The History and Antiquities of the County of Dorset* [Westminster, 1861–70³], vol. 3, p. 30).

3 ?London, B.L., Add. 11748 s.xv

a (fol. 3) Walter Hilton, *The Ladder of Perfection* (L/B/E 255). This is followed (fol. 138v) by the beginning of a Latin version of *The Vision of St John of the Sorrows of the Virgin* (fifteen lines only), *inc.* 'Vidit gloriosissimam Virginem ineffabiliter decoratam'. **b** (fol. 140) Richard Rolle, *Of the Virtue of the Holy Name of Jesus (Oleum Effusum)* (Allen, pp. 66–68;

L/B/E 506). This is an English translation of part of the fourth section of Rolle's commentary on the Song of Songs. **c** (fol. 143) Nicholas Love, *The Rule of Life of Our Lady* (L/B/E 22). This is an English translation of the second chapter of *ps.-*Bonaventure, *Meditationes vitae Christi*. **d** (fol. 144v) *The Arms of Christ* (an English poem on the instruments of the Passion) (Brown/Robbins 2577). The edition by R. Morris in *Legends of the Holy Rood* (EETS/OS, 46; London, 1871), pp. 170–96, utilizes this manuscript.

(fol. 1 [s.xv]) *Hunc librum et librum vocatum Gracia Dei qui est in custodia Willelmi Carente habeant abbatissa et conventus Shafton<iensis> in succursum anime Johannis Horder.* William Carent (c. 1396–1476), a wealthy Dorset landowner, was steward of Shaftesbury Abbey. For the 'librum uocatum Gracia Dei', see *Miscellaneous Records* a below.

4 London, B.L., Cotton Nero C.iv s.xii

Psalter in Latin and French, preceded (fol. 40) by a Calendar and followed by a complete set of Canticles, *Gloria*, Lord's Prayer, and Athanasian Creed, all of which (with very minor exceptions) are in both Latin and French (Sonet 2577, 2636, 2719, 2737, 2754, 2857, 2986, 2995, 3021, 3149, 3152, 3165, 3401, 3515, 3697, 3787, 3817). The Creed is followed by a Litany and various Latin prayers to the Virgin, St Michael, St Swithun, and so on. The last four of these prayers have French translations. On fol. 140v is the so-called *Oratio S. Augustini* in Latin (see Römer, vol. 2/1, p. 376, where this manuscript is recorded). This is the famous Winchester Psalter (or St Swithun's Psalter) which has been discussed in numerous studies of twelfth-century English art from E. M. Thompson, *English Illuminated Manuscripts* (London, 1895), pp. 29–33 to the most recent account by K. E. Haney, *The Winchester Psalter: An Iconographic Study* (London, 1986). At the beginning are thirty-eight magnificent full-page miniatures. See also Watson/*London*, vol. 1 no. 539, and vol. 2 pl. 66 (fol. 114v). Watson dates the manuscript to 1121/29 x 1161.

The Psalter almost certainly originated at Winchester (St Swithun's) (the suggestion of Hyde Abbey is far less likely [see Kaufmann, p. 105]), where it was probably executed for Bishop Henry of Blois, bishop of Winchester from 1129 to 1171. Early additions to the Calendar (e.g. 14 April: *dedicatio*

ecclesie monasterii Schestonie) indicate that it soon passed into
the keeping of Shaftesbury.

5 London, B.L., Lansdowne 383 s.xii

Psalter, preceded by a Calendar, a table of epacts, three
folios of Latin prayers, six full-page miniatures (two others
follow the Psalter text), and an office entitled *In parasceue ad
crucem adorandam*. The Psalter is followed by Canticles, the
Athanasian Creed, *Gloria, Pater noster*, a Litany, and various
prayers to the Trinity, the Holy Spirit, the Virgin, St Michael, St
Peter, and so on. The illustrations are fully discussed in Kaufmann no. 48 (whether they were produced by the Shaftesbury
nuns remains uncertain), who also provides a full bibliography. See also Watson/*London*, vol. 1 no. 850, and vol. 2 pl.
97 (fol. 169). Watson dates the manuscript to before 1173. The
first flyleaf (fols. 1r–v) contains a fragment of a French metrical translation of Henry of Sawtrey's *Purgatorium S. Patricii*
(see H. L. D. Ward & J. A. Herbert, *Catalogue of Romances in
the Department of Manuscripts in the British Museum* [London,
1883–1910; rpt. 1962], vol. 2, pp. 474–6 [with edited excerpts]).

Evidence from the Calendar and Litany clearly indicates
a Shaftesbury provenance (the arguments are presented in
Kaufmann, p. 82), and the kneeling nun who appears in
the miniatures on fols. 14v and 165v presumably represents
the unknown abbess who commissioned the manuscript (see
Kaufmann, p. 83).

6 London, Lambeth Palace, 3285 (formerly Steyning, Sir Arthur
Howard, and Wellington, J. Hasson) s.xv[in]

Psalter, preceded by a Calendar and followed by a Litany
and seven prayers. There are no Canticles, but the Athanasian
Creed has been added at the end in a different and later hand
(fols. 191–3). Fly-leaves ii[v]–iv[v] contain a long prayer in Latin.
The illuminated title-page is a nineteenth-century addition.

This small and beautiful Psalter was originally made for
Edmund Audley, bishop of Salisbury from 1502 to his death in
1524, who gave it to his niece Anne Audley, a nun of Shaftesbury, as indicated by the inscription on fol. 191 (s.xvi[1]): *Liber
iste pertinet domine Anne Awdeley, moniali monasterii Shaston',
ex dono reuerendi domini domini (sic) Edmundi Awdeley, Sarum
episcopi ac auunculi predicte domine*. The name *Anne Awdley* also
appears on fol. ii.

7 ?Salisbury, Cathedral, 150 s.x[ex]

Psalter, preceded by a Calendar with various tables and followed by Canticles, *Gloria*, *Pater noster*, *Credo*, Athanasian Creed, a Litany, and the Office of the Dead. The volume contains a continuous interlinear gloss to the psalms and the Canticles in Anglo-Saxon and has been edited by C. & K. Sisam, *The Salisbury Psalter*, (EETS/OS, 242; London, 1959). For a full description of the manuscript, see *ibid.*, pp. 1–7. See also Ker/*AS*, pp. 449–51 no. 379.

Ker assigned this manuscript to Salisbury, but the Sisams adduce sound evidence from the Calendar, Litany, and use of feminine grammatical forms for a Shaftesbury provenance: see *The Salisbury Psalter*, p. 12, for the arguments.

Miscellaneous Records

a The inscription in no. 3 above refers to 'a book called *Gratia Dei*' which was also left to Shaftesbury Abbey by William Carent. The reference is to the *Dream of the Pilgrimage of the Soul* (L/B/E 75), the English translation of Guillaume de Digulleville's *Pélerinage de l'âme* (Bossuat 4904–6) (see MARRICK 1 above).

b Oxford, Bod. Lib., French e.22 (s.xvi[1]) contains an Anglo-Norman rhymed Apocalypse with prologue and commentary, and, at the end, a brief dissertation (49 lines) on 'Les set mortel pechez'. The manuscript was formerly owned by Sir John Fox and was bought by the Bodleian Library in 1946. The author of the work was William Giffard, chaplain to the nuns of Shaftesbury Abbey in the second half of the thirteenth century. He was presumably related to Mabel Giffard, abbess of Shaftesbury from 1291 to 1302 (VCH *Dorset*, vol. 2, p. 79), and Mabel was the sister of Walter Giffard, archbishop of York, and Geoffrey Giffard, bishop of Worcester. The family was notorious for its nepotism. The work has been edited from this manuscript by O. Rhys, *An Anglo-Norman Rhymed Apocalypse with Commentary* (Anglo-Norman Text Society, 6; Oxford, 1946; rpt. New York, 1967) (Bossuat 3076 *bis*), and Rhys's edition contains a long introduction by Sir John Fox which includes a detailed description of the manuscript. This introduction supersedes Fox's earlier study, 'An Anglo-Norman Apocalypse from Shaftesbury Abbey', *Modern Language Review* 8 (1913), pp. 338–51. There is no doubt that Giffard wrote the work for the Shaftesbury nuns, probably at the very end of the thirteenth century, and we may assume with some confidence that they once possessed a copy. Sir John Fox was of the opinion that his own manuscript was the volume in question, but although that is quite possible, there is no sound evidence for this assumption.

SINNINGTHWAITE (Yorkshire, W.R.), *Priory of BVM* (Cistercian Nuns).

Miscellaneous Records

In her will dated 27 March 1448 (probated 1 April 1448), Agnes Stapilton, widow of Sir Brian Stapilton/Stapleton of Carleton, bequeathed 'Item . . . monialibus de Synynghwayte, xxs., et librum meum vocatum *Bonaventure*' (*North Country Wills* [see ARTHINGTON, *Miscellaneous Records*], p. 48 [Cavanaugh, pp. 815–6]).

The volume in question is almost certainly Nicholas Love's *Mirror of the Blessed Life of Christ*, a translation of the *Meditationes vitae Christi* commonly but incorrectly attributed to Bonaventure (L/B/E 553).

STAMFORD (Lincolnshire), *Priory of St Michael* (Benedictine Nuns).

1 Oxford, Bod. Lib., Arch. A.d.15 (printed book)

The Rule of Seynt Benet, printed by Richard Pynson, London, 1517 (*STC* 1859). This is an English translation of the *Regula S. Benedicti* prepared by Richard Fox, bishop of Winchester from 1501 to 1528.

(fol. G.vi^v [s.xvi^1]) *Iste liber constat dompne Margarete Stanburne, priorisse domus monialium sancti Michaelis iuxta Stamford.* The name *Domina Margareta Stanburne* also appears at the foot of folios E.1 and E.iiij. Margaret Stanburn or Stainbarn was prioress of Stamford in 1528 (VCH *Northamptonshire*, vol. 2, pp. 100, 101).

SWINE (Yorkshire, E.R.), *Priory of BVM* (Cistercian Nuns).

A) DONATION

Cambridge, King's College, 18 is a late 12th- or early 13th-century collection of works by Ambrose of Milan (see **B.1** below) and was at one time owned by the Augustinian priory of

Shulbrede in Sussex. At the end of the volume (fol. 104v) is an entry in a late 14th- or early 15th-century hand which records a donation of twelve books to the priory of Swine by Peter 'vicarius ecclesie de Swyn'. It seems probable, therefore, that after being at Shulbrede, the manuscript found its way into the keeping of the Swine nuns. The act of donation reads as follows (sections marked . . . are illegible):

Isti sunt libri quos Petrus vicarius ecclesie de Swyn dedit beate Marie virgini gloriose et priorisse et conuentui Abathie de Swyn.

1 In primis, liber Ianuensis de sermonibus dominicalibus per totum annum cuius ij folium incipit *amicus inter amicos*.

2 Item liber quidam vocatus Mariale cuius ij folium incipit *inpericiam meam*.

3 Item liber Ysidorus de summo bono cuius ij folio incipit *omnipotenciam*.

4 Item liber Ysidorus Ethimologiarum cuius ij folium incipit *ter queram*.

5 Item liber Ambrosii de bono mortis cuius ii folium incipit . . . *festinabat*.

6 Item liber qui vocatur Pars oculi . . . ecclesiam parochialem illum dedit.

7 Item quidam (?) liber . . . vocatur . . . curatorum.

8 Item quidam liber vocatus Historia scolastica cuius ij folium incipit *statim dispositum est*.

9 Item quidam liber beate Matildis virginis vocatus Liber spiritualis gracie.

10 Item quidam liber de epistolis canonicis cuius ij folium textus incipit sic, *nos verbo veritatis* [Jm 1:18].

11 Item quidam liber sancte Brigide regine cuius prologus sic incipit, *Inveniet . . . dignos*.

12 Item liber Marci euangeliste glosati cuius ij folium textus sic incipit, *Soluere corrigiam* [Mk 1:7].

Si quis istos libros superius scriptos vel aliquem illorum ab ista abathia de Swyn alienaverit vel iniuste detinuerit, nouerit se indignacionem omnipotentis Dei et beate virginis Marie, domine et patrone eiusdem loci, et omnium sanctorum Dei incursurum, et coram summo iudice in vltimo iudicio fraudibus suis eternitatis responsurum.

The identification of the volumes is as follows: **1** James of Voragine, *Sermones de tempore* (Schneyer, vol. 3, pp. 221–46). **2** An unidentified *Mariale*: see *Lexicon für Theologie und Kirche* (Freiburg, 1962), vol. 7, pp. 46–7. **3** Isidore, *Sententiae* (*CPL* 1199). **4** Isidore, *Etymologiae* (*CPL* 1186). **5** Ambrose, *De bono mortis* (*CPL* 129). **6** William of Paull, *Oculus sacerdotis*, Part I: see L. E. Boyle, 'The *Oculus sacerdotis* and Some Other Works of William of Pagula', *Transactions of the Royal Historical Society*, Ser. 5, 5 (1955), pp. 81–110; Bloomfield 1088, 2499, 3129, 3686. **7** Hardly any of this entry can be read and the volume cannot be identified. **8** Peter Comestor, *Historia scholastica* (Stegmüller 6543–65). **9** Mechtild of Hackeborn, *Liber specialis gratiae* (ed. L. Paquelin, *Revelationes Gertrudianae et Mechtildianae*, vol. 2 [Poitiers/Paris 1877]). **10** The canonical epistles. **11** Birgitta of Sweden, *Revelationes*. A new edition is in preparation under the direction of Birger Bergh of the University of Lund. **12** The gospel of Mark with glosses.

For a complete account of this donation, see D. N. Bell, *The Libraries of the Cistercians, Gilbertines and Premonstratensians* (Corpus of British Medieval Library Catalogues, 3; London, 1992), pp. 144–6 (Z.25).

B) MANUSCRIPTS

1 ?Cambridge, King's Coll., 18 s.xii/xiii

a (fol. 1) Ambrose of Milan, *De officiis ministrorum* (*CPL* 144). **b** (fol. 71v) *idem, De mysteriis* (*CPL* 155). **c** (fol. 79v) *idem, De sacramentis* (*CPL* 154). **d** (fol. 96v) *ps.*-Ambrose, *De lapsu virginis* (*CPL* 651), concluding with a *deploratio uirginitatis* which does not appear in the *PL* text.

On fol. 1, in the initial, appears the s.xii/xiii *ex libris* of the Augustinian priory of Shulbrede in Sussex (*Prioratus de Shulbrede*) to which the manuscript originally belonged. For its association with Swine, see the notes on the donation A immediately above. How it reached Swine is unknown.

2 London, B.L., Harley 2409 s.xv

a (fol. 1) *Contemplations of the Dread and Love of God (Fervor amoris)* (Jolliffe H.15; L/B/E 362). **b** (fol. 52) William Flete, *De remediis contra temptationes* (the first Middle English version) (Jolliffe K.8.[a]); L/B/E 230, 528). **c** (fol. 70) The Life of St

Catherine of Siena (in English). **d** (fol. 75v) *The Nine Points of Virtue* (Northern Version) (Brown/Robbins 1188).

(fol. 78v [s.xv²]) *Be yt remembryd that dame Mald Wade, priorys of Swyne, has gyven this boke to dame Joan Hyltoft in Nuncotom (sic).* Dame Mald or Matilda Wade resigned as prioress of Swine in 1482 (VCH *Yorkshire*, vol. 3, p. 182). Of Dame Joan Hyltoft I know nothing.

Miscellaneous Records

In his will dated 20 February 1485–6, Thomas Hornby of York, *capellanus*, bequeathed 'Dompnae Agneti Vavasour, moniali de Swyn, librum de Vita Katerinae, in Anglicis scriptum' (*Test. Ebor.*, vol. 3, p. 165 [note]). The same Agnes Vavasour had earlier been left 'libri Sanctae Brigidae' by Elizabeth Sywardby, perhaps her aunt (*ibid.*, 165).

The English *liber de vita Katerinae* might be *The Life and Martyrdom of St Catherine of Alexandria*, recorded above at ANKERWYKE 1b, or John Capgrave's metrical *Life* recorded at CAMPSEY 4a. The *libri Sanctae Brigidae* are certainly the *Revelations* of St Bridget of Sweden, but whether the volume was in English or Latin is not stated. Since they were owned by a woman and bequeathed to a woman, the English version is more probable.

SYON (Middlesex), *Abbey of St Saviour, BVM, and St Bridget* (Bridgettine Nuns).

As was mentioned in the first part of this study (Chapter 2, nn. 72–75), there were two libraries at Syon, one for the brothers and one for the sisters, and the extensive early sixteenth-century catalogue preserved in Cambridge, Corpus Christi College, MS 141, and edited by Mary Bateson, *Catalogue of the Library of Syon Monastery Isleworth* (Cambridge, 1898), is undoubtedly that of the brothers (see Bateson, pp. xiii–xv). A new edition of this catalogue is being prepared by Drs I. A. Doyle and V. Gillespie for the *Corpus of British Medieval Library Catalogues*. The lists of surviving books provided by Ker and Watson do not distinguish between the two libraries, but it is not too difficult to determine which volumes came from which collection.

Firstly, any books that can be identified with entries in the catalogue can only have belonged to the brothers, and these are not here our concern. Secondly, an examination of the inscriptions in the surviving volumes often indicates either the sex of the owner or the collection for which the book was intended. Thirdly, the use of masculine or feminine grammatical forms occasionally serves the same purpose. And fourthly, the actual content of a particular volume can sometimes indicate, with more or less certainty, the collection to which it belonged. See further Section C below. The dozen manuscripts which provide us with no indication as to whether they belonged to the sisters or the brothers are described in Section B.

It need hardly be added that many of the liturgical manuscripts listed below would not have been kept in the libraries at all, but in the abbey church, the cloister, or the nuns' own cells. By the time of the foundation of Syon in 1415 the old proscription against private ownership had been much weakened. 'Strictly', says Christopher de Hamel, 'the nuns were allowed no personal possessions whatsoever, but surely the rules were flexible enough to permit the keeping of a prayer-book on indefinite loan for private use in the cell or cloister' (de Hamel, p. 74). It is sometimes not clear, therefore, whether particular books should be regarded as quasi-personal or institutional property (ibid., p. 125).

Three of the volumes listed below are associated with James Grenehalgh and Joan or Joanna Sewell. James Grenehalgh was born in Lancashire c. 1465. He was a schoolmaster in Wells in 1488 and was ordained a priest in the same city in 1494. By 1499 he was a Carthusian at Sheen and seems to have acted as unofficial spiritual director to Joan Sewell, a nun of Syon, who was professed in the year 1500 (see **A.7**). The close relationship which developed between them, however, appears to have become rather too close, for Grenehalgh was removed from Sheen to the Charterhouse at Coventry in 1507 or 1508 under circumstances (says Michael Sargent) 'which suggest either that he was suspected of incontinence or that he was unable or unwilling to take correction from his superiors. . . . He may also have spent some time in the Charterhouses of London and Mount Grace, but finally died, still a guest within the Order, in 1529 or 1530, in the Charterhouse at Kingston-upon-Hull' (M. G. Sargent, *James Grenehalgh as Textual Critic* [Analecta Cartusiana, 85; Salzburg, 1984], vol. 1, p. 109 = *idem*, 'James Grenehalgh: The Biographical Record', in *Kartäusermystik und -mystiker:*

Dritter Internationaler Kongress über die Kartäusergeschichte und - spiritualität, Bd. 4 [Analecta Cartusiana, 55; Salzburg, 1982] p. 38). A full account of Grenehalgh and of his relationship with Joan Sewell may be found in Sargent (1984), vol. 1, pp. 75–109 and *idem* (1982), pp. 20–54.

Grenehalgh probably presented **A.43**, a printed edition of Walter Hilton's *Ladder of Perfection*, to Sewell at the time of her profession at Syon in 1500, and almost certainly sent her other manuscripts for her theological and spiritual edification. In these, Grenehalgh marked those passages to which he wished particularly to draw her attention with her monogram, J.S. Other manuscripts contain a combined monogram, J.G.S., which he may or may not have intended her to see. There are five books which contain these monograms: Cambridge, Emmanuel Coll., 35 (**A.7**); London, B.L., Add. 24461 (**A.21**); London, B.L., Add. 37790; London, B.L., Royal 5 A.v; and Philadelphia, Rosenbach Foundation, Inc. H491 (**A.43**). Of these, **A.43** certainly belonged to Joan Sewell, and **A.7** and **A.21** were probably at some time in her possession. What, then, of London, B.L., Add. 37790 and Royal 5 A.v? The latter contains only the combined monogram, J.G.S., and was presented to the Carthusians of Coventry by their prior, Robert Odyham. Grenehalgh, therefore, could have used this manuscript only after his removal to Coventry in 1507/8, and there is no reason to believe that Joan Sewell ever saw it. The combined monograms are no more than echoes of what, for Grenehalgh, must have been the happier, sunlit days of the past. As for London, B.L., Add. 37790, although the J.S. monogram appears on fols. 96v and 226r, it is crudely written, and I agree with Sargent that it is probably not in the hand of James Grenehalgh. The significance of these monograms, therefore, remains unclear, and although this manuscript may well have a Syon connection, I have not included it in the list which follows. A full description of both Add. 37790 and Royal 5 A.v may be found in Sargent, *James Grenehalgh as Textual Critic*, vol. 2, pp. 499–510 and 520–6.

Much work remains to be done on the libraries at Syon, and I have no doubt that, in due course, more manuscripts will be traced to the house. We might, however, mention three which appear to have connections with Syon, though at the moment I cannot state with certainty that they were in the possession of the sisters:

1. Durham, U.L., Cosin V.iii.16 (s.xv/xvi): a collection of sermons and *theologica* in Latin, including *ps.*-Bernard of Clairvaux, *Speculum peccatoris*, *ps.*-Peter of Blois, *De duodecim utilitatibus tribulationum*, extracts from the *Revelationes* of St Bridget, *ps.*-Albertus Magnus, *Novem virtutes*, Gerard of Vliederhoven, *Cordiale quatuor novissimorum*, extracts from the *Liber specialis gratiae* of Mechtild of Hackeborn, and a number of other shorter pieces. On fol. 118rv is a letter, addressed to 'Welbiloued Susturs in our lord Iesu Crist', which is clearly from one convent of nuns to another. Dr Ian Doyle, to whom I am greatly indebted for a full description of this interesting volume, is of the opinion that the style and script of this letter resemble those of Thomas Betson, the brothers' librarian at Syon (c. 1481–1516). It is not clear, however, that the document was intended as a covering letter for the whole volume (if it were, it is in an odd place), and it may have been added simply for its own intrinsic interest. On the other hand, the texts from St Bridget and Mechtild would certainly be appropriate for Syon.

2. Oxford, Bodl. Lib., Bodl. 346 (s.xvi[1]): the Latin version of the *Revelationes* of St Bridget. Interspersed in the text are a sermon and prayers of St Bridget, the *Epistola solitarii ad reges* of Alphonso Pecha of Guadalajara, later bishop of Jaen, and various papal letters approving the Bridgettine Rule and Constitutions. At the end (fol. 182v) is a comprehensive index to the *Revelationes* followed by a copy of the *Officium beatae Brigidae*. Watson, p. 65, lists this manuscript, on the basis of its content, as being certainly from Syon, but I feel this is too sanguine. I can go only as far as suggesting the probability of a Syon connection.

3. Oxford, Bodl. Lib., Laud misc. 602 (s.xv): Walter Hilton, *The Ladder of Perfection*. The front fly-leaf of this manuscript is the bottom part of letters patent for Syon Abbey, dated 26 October 1462 (*Calendar of the Patent Rolls Preserved in the Public Record Office, Edward IV-Richard III* [London, 1897–1901], vol. 1 [Edward IV, 1461–67 (1897)], p. 216).

In the following entries, de Hamel refers to Christopher de Hamel's indispensable essay *Syon Abbey. The Library of the Bridgettine Nuns and Their Peregrinations after the Reformation* (Roxburghe Club, 1991); de Hamel followed by a number (e.g. de Hamel, no. 14) refers to the list of Syon manuscripts in *ibid.*, pp. 114–24 (de Hamel does not enumerate the printed books).

Martyrology refers to the *Martyrology of Syon*, compiled by Richard Whytford, and now preserved in the British Library as B.L., Add. 22285. The survival of the *Martyrology* was due to the Syon nuns who took it with them to Europe after the suppression of their house and continued to add to it long after the Reformation; but since there can be no doubt that it was originally a volume belonging to the brothers, I have not included it here among the nuns' manuscripts.

A) *Books belonging to the Sisters*

1 Aberdeen, U.L., 134 (de Hamel, no. 65) + Oxford, Bod. Lib., Rawlinson C.941 (de Hamel, no. 14) s.xv[ex]

The Myrroure of oure Ladye (L/B/E 798). When J. H. Blunt published his edition of the text for the EETS/ES, 19 (London, 1873; rpt. New York, 1973), he did not know of the Oxford manuscript and therefore prepared half his version from the printed edition of 1530. The Aberdeen manuscript contains Part I of the work and ends on p. 174 of Blunt's edition; the Oxford manuscript, containing Parts II and III, begins on p. 175 and ends on p. 332. Blunt suggested that the author of the work was Thomas Gascoigne (see Blunt, p. ix), but although this suggestion is still widely accepted, it is almost certainly incorrect. Certain passages in the text indicate that the author was a brother of Syon. Collins, pp. xxxvii–xl, argues for Thomas Fishbourne, the first Confessor-General of Syon, but if this is correct, Fishbourne could not have used London, B.L., Harley 612 (as Collins suggests on p. xx, n. 3), since this manuscript was written after Fishbourne's death in 1428. A new edition of the *Myrroure* is at present being prepared by Dr Ann Hutchison.

(Aberdeen, U.L., 134, last leaf [s.xvi[1]]) *This booke belongyth to syster Elyzabeth Monton*, and *Love drede & pray. Your symple seruaunt R. Tailour.* (Oxford, Rawlinson C.941, fol. 139v) *Here endeth the booke called Our Ladyes Myrroure. E. M. Off charite prayeth fore y<ou>r wreched seruaunt Robert T. Wryter of this booke.* Underneath this last inscription is written *Thys boke ys [blank]* (s.xvi[1]). Elizabeth Monton, or E. M., is undoubtedly the 'Elizabeth Mountayne' who is listed among the Syon nuns at

the time of the election of Constancia Browne (see **A.45**) on
31 August 1518 (Aungier, p. 81). She does not appear in the
1539 Pension List (or any later list), and although her death
is recorded in the *Martyrology* fol. 47 on 17 July (*Elyzabeth
Monton, Soror*), the year is not given. A Robert Taylor was
Clerk of Works at Syon in the first decade of the sixteenth
century (see R. W. Dunning, 'The Building of Syon Abbey',
Transactions of the Ancient Monuments Society, N.S. 25 [1981], p.
21), but the name was not uncommon.

2 Alnwick Castle, Duke of Northumberland, 505a (formerly Sion
House, Duke of Northumberland) (de Hamel, no. 64) s.xvi^{in}

Processional (with music), written for the sisters of Syon,
with contents similar to those in **A.6** below (q.v.).

3 Ampleforth Abbey, C.V.130 (printed book)

*A Deuout Treatyse Called the Tree & XII. Frutes of the Holy
Goost*, two parts, the first part printed by Robert Copland and
the second by Robert Copland and Michael Fawkes, London,
1534–35 (*STC* 13608). For a full description of this copy, see J.
J. Vaissier (ed.), *A deuout treatyse called the tree & xii. frutes of
the Holy Goost* (Groningen, 1960), pp. xxxvi–xxxviii.

(title-page [s.xvi^1]) *Dorothe Coderynton*. Dorothy Codrington
or Codryngton was a nun of Syon at the suppression of the
house in 1539 (Aungier, p. 89) and was also there during
the Marian revival. Her name appears in the Marian Pension List of 1554/5 (Aungier, p. 99), and a Dorothy [surname
unknown] is listed among the nuns at the restored abbey in
1557 (Aungier, p. 97). She died on 26 April 1586 (*Martyrology*
fol. 36r, where her name appears as Dorothea Cutryngton).
Marginal notes in her hand appear throughout the treatise.
According to Aungier, p. 535, a more accurate spelling of her
name is Goodrington, and Dorothy Goodrington was formerly
married to John Goodrington (who died in 1518), and entered
Syon after his death. If this is indeed the same woman, she
must have married young or died old. Her maiden name was
Fetiplace, and she was the fourth daughter of Sir Richard
Fetiplace (see **A.34** below).

4 Brussels, Bibl. Royale, IV.481 (de Hamel, no. 80) s.xv^{ex}

Psalter, followed by Canticles, a Litany, and various prayers.
There is no Calendar. The first folio and seven others are
missing.

(end paste-down [s.xvi[1]]) *Elynor ffeteplace.* For Eleanor Fetyplace and other members of the Fetyplace family connected
with Syon, see **A.34**. The Litany is Bridgettine with only St
Anne being placed higher than St Bridget, and the prayers on
fol. 251v contain feminine forms. Watson, p. 64, identifies this
volume as the one sold by Messrs. Maggs in 1935, but I am
informed by Dr de Hamel that this is not the case. The Maggs
Psalter (**D.1** below) remains untraced.

5 Cambridge, U.L., Add. 7634 + London, Private Collection (de
Hamel, no. 71) s.xv

Two fragments from a Bridgettine Breviary. The parts of the
Offices which survive are mainly the psalms (with music). The
Breviary exhibits some unusual features and differs from other
similar volumes from Syon: details are provided by Collins in
his description of the Cambridge fragment (Collins, pp. xlix–l).
Dr de Hamel is of the opinion that the hand of this manuscript
is identical to that of the Bedford Hours (B.L., Add. 18850) and
that these fragments are all that remain of one of the two office
books given by the Duke of Bedford to the Syon nuns on 5
February 1426 (see *Miscellaneous Records* **a** below; de Hamel,
pp. 62–4 [with reproduction]).

Collins includes this volume with other Breviaries belonging to the sisters, and if the persuasive arguments of Dr de
Hamel are correct, there is no doubt that we are dealing with
one of the sisters' books.

6 Cambridge, U.L., Add. 8885 (formerly Bristol, Baptist Coll.,
Z.d.40) (de Hamel, no. 62) s.xv–xvi[1]

Processional (with music), with processional offices for
twelve feasts including two of St Bridget. The processional
is followed (p. 113) by a Litany, the office for the profession
of a Bridgettine nun, a dispensation by John Kemp, bishop of
London (1421–5), to the sisters of Syon, and various antiphons
(Collins, pp. 111–4). The rubrics are mainly in Latin. At the
end of the volume has been added (s.xv–xvi[1]) the Office of
St Augustine and other liturgical material. Dr de Hamel (de
Hamel, p. 85) has suggested that this manuscript may have
been the exemplar for a group of four other processionals from
Syon: **A.2**, **A.12**, **A.40**, and **A.45**. All are very similar in content,
and a complete reproduction of **A.45** has been published by
James Hogg (see **A.45** below).

(p. vi [s.xvi[in]]) *Anne Dyngue, O mater Dei, memento mei. Anne Amarson, O mater Dei, obliuiscere me.* The death of Anna Dygne is recorded in the *Martyrology* fol. 27r on 13 February 1517 (the marginal note *Admiss<a>* appears by her name). A 'Maria Digne, Soror' is also recorded (*Martyrology* fol. 51v), but the date of her death is not given. See further de Hamel, p. 142, n. 86. Anne or Anna Amersham was a nun of Syon in 1518 (Aungier, p. 82), but does not appear in any later list since she died 21 October 1533 and was buried in a tomb *iuxta gerras* at Syon (*Martyrology* fols. 60v, 191v no. 9). De Hamel, p. 86, suggests that the reason for both names appearing in the processional was because Anne Dyngue and Anne Amersham always walked together in processions and could therefore have shared the same book. We may compare **A.40** below. A *terminus a quo* for this volume is 1457 (de Hamel, p. 68), and there is a reproduction of one of the folios in *ibid.,* p. 87.

7 ?Cambridge, Emmanuel Coll., 35 (I.2.14) s.xv[in]

a (fol. 2) Richard Rolle, three sections from his commentary on the Song of Songs (Allen, pp. 62–83; Stegmüller 7307; edited by E. M. Murray, *Richard Rolle's Commentary on Canticles edited from MS Trinity College, Dublin, 153* [Fordham Univ. Diss., 1958]): *Oleum effusum* (fol. 2), *Adolescentule* (fol. 3v), and *Curremus in odorem* (fol.10). This is followed by part of *Epistola* 133 of Anselm of Canterbury (*PL* 159: 167–8; ed. F. S. Schmitt, vol. 5, pp. 359–62 [11.13–25]) and two chapters from the *Incendium amoris* which have been inserted in the text. **b** (fol. 19v) *idem, Judica me Deus* (Stegmüller 7300; edited and translated by J. P. Daly, *An Edition of the 'Judica Me Deus' of Richard Rolle* [Salzburg, 1984]). The text here is a shorter version of *Judica* A: see Allen, pp. 98–101 and Daly, pp. xxviii–xxxi. **c** (fol. 23) *idem, Super Mulierem fortem/De vita activa et contemplativa* (Allen, pp. 159–61; Stegmüller 7305). This is followed by Chapter 6 of the *Incendium amoris* under the title *De causa haereticorum et fide Trinitatis* (Deanesly [see **e** below], pp. 160–2). **d** (fol. 61) *idem,* Commentary on the Lord's Prayer (Allen, pp. 155–7; Stegmüller 7312,1; Bloomfield 8395). **e** (fol. 63) *idem, Incendium amoris,* edited by M. Deanesly, *The Incendium Amoris of Richard Rolle of Hampole* (Manchester, 1915; rpt. Folcroft, 1974) (Allen, pp. 209–29; Stegmüller 7314). **f** (fol. 100) Honorius Augustodunensis (*ps.*-Augustine), *De cognitione verae vitae* (*PL* 40: 1005–

32), attributed, as usual, to Augustine. **g** (fol. 124) Bonaventure, *Soliloquium de quatuor mentalibus exercitiis/ Meditationes imaginis vitae* (Bloomfield 2150). **h** (fol. 164) Richard Rolle, *De amore Dei contra amatores mundi* (Allen, pp. 203–9; Bloomfield 4980 [imperfect at the beginning]). **i** (fol. 194) Richard Rolle, *Melos amoris/Melum contemplativorum* (Allen, pp. 113–29). The version here consists of twenty-four extracts from the full text: see E. J. F. Arnould (ed.), *The Melos Amoris of Richard Rolle of Hampole* (Oxford, 1957), pp. lxxv–lxxvii.

This is the first of the Grenehalgh-Sewell manuscripts discussed in the introduction to this list of books from Syon. On fol. 21v appears the J.S. monogram (reproduced in Sargent, *James Grenehalgh as Textual Critic*, vol. 1, p. 118); on fol. 22 we find *Sewell Syonita Reclusa* (reproduced in *ibid.*, p. 119); and on fol. 174v we have the tragic *Sewellam renue* (reproduced in *ibid.*, p. 125 and discussed in *ibid.*, pp. 101 and 105). All three inscriptions are in the hand of James Grenehalgh. Joan Sewell was professed at Syon in 1500 (see **A.43**), appears in the 1518 list of Syon nuns (Aungier, p. 81), and died 2 July 1532, two or three years after Grenehalgh (*Martyrology* fol. 45r). Her tomb is listed among the *sepultura sororum iuxta gerras* at Syon (*Martyrology* fol. 191v no. 5). Ker, p. 187, rejects this manuscript, but I do not agree with this. See further Deanesly, pp. 79–83, who also provides a detailed description of the first part of the manuscript (pp. 12–15). A full description may be found in Sargent, *James Grenehalgh as Textual Critic*, vol. 2, pp. 478–87.

8 Cambridge, Magdalene Coll., 11 (F.4.11) (de Hamel, no. 20) s.xv^{in}

a (fol. 1) Bridgettine Breviary (with English rubrics), beginning with a Calendar and followed (fol. 61v) by directions for the year, directions for principal feasts, an English version of Alfonso da Vadaterra's *Prologus in sermonem angelicum de excellentia Virginis Mariae* (in printed editions of the *Revelations*, this prologue follows the *Regula S. Salvatoris*), an 'ordinal of processions to be had and song bi sustres of the sayd ordyr and monasteri', and various prayers. **b** (fol. 109) Psalter, followed by Canticles and a Litany. An edition of part **a** of the manuscript has been published by A. J. Collins, *The Bridgettine Breviary of Syon Abbey* (Henry Bradshaw Society, 96; Worcester,

1969). Collins provides a description of the manuscript on pp. xlii–xliv. It is no. 935 in Frere.

The contents of the manuscript leave no doubt that it was made for the Syon nuns. Fols. 6v–7r are reproduced in de Hamel, p. 92 and fols. 122v–123r in *ibid.*, p. 106.

9 Cambridge, Magdalene Coll., 12 (F.4.12) (de Hamel, no. 13) s.xv

This is a Bridgettine Breviary, followed by a Psalter, which is very similar to **A.8** described immediately above, except that the rubrics are in Latin. The differences between the two appear mainly in the material between the daily Offices and the Psalter (which begins on fol. 150), and the addition of the Hours of the Holy Spirit and the Office of the Dead at the end of the volume. Minor differences are recorded in the footnotes to Collins' edition of **A.8**. See further Collins, pp. xliv–xlv. The manuscript is no. 936 in Frere.

As with **A.8**, the contents of the manuscript leave no doubt that it was made for the Syon nuns.

10 ?Cambridge, Magdalene Coll., 13 (F.4.13) (de Hamel, no. 39) s.xvi[in]

An extensive collection of devotional material in Latin and English preceded by theological excerpts and a few verses in Latin (including Walther 3034) and English (including Brown/ Robbins 1937 and 4129). There is a Calendar (fol. 3) followed by a variety of tables, including tables for finding the new moon, tide-tables for London and other coastal towns, a table of auspicious days for blood-letting, a table of moveable feasts, and other astronomical/astrological tables. The prayers, in Latin and English, begin on fol. 19. Mixed in among them are a commentary on the Lord's Prayer (in Latin), prayers to one's guardian angel (including Brown/Robbins 1051), the *Stabat Mater*, 'devout confessions', various indulgences, popular pseudo-Bernardine prayers and verses (including Walther 17126), the Fifteen Oes of St Bridget (with English rubric), the *Golden Litany* (in Latin, with English rubric), prayers on retiring at night, a Litany, and brief exhortatory texts attributed to John Gerson, Bonaventure, and James of Gruytrode. An original and detailed table of contents appears on fols. 220–2. Much of this is reproduced by M. R. James in his *Descriptive Catalogue of the Manuscripts in the Library of Magdalene College*,

Cambridge (Cambridge, 1909), pp. 24–33. Among the material on the fly-leaves are some medical receipts in English.

This beautifully written manuscript was originally made by or for Jasper Fyloll, a London Dominican, but the book seems to have been at Syon by 1521. (fol. 1v [s.xvi]) *Jasper Fyloll of the Blacke Freers in London oweth this booke. Yf it fortune at any tyme to be reklesly forgoten or loste, he prayeth the fyndar to bryng yt to hym agayn, and he shal haue iijˢ iiijᵈ for his labour and good thankes of the owner and goddis blessyng.* (fly-leaf i [s.xvi¹]) *Elisabeth Crychley off Syon 13 Jan. a<nn>o 1521.* 'Elyzabeth Crucheley' is recorded as a lay-sister of Syon in the 1539 Pension List (Aungier, p. 90), and 'Elizabeth Crowcheley' appears in the Marian Pension List of 1554/5 (Aungier, p. 92). The death of an Isabella Cruchley, *focaria*, is recorded in the *Martyrology* fol. 66v on 5 December 1538, but there is no Elizabeth.

11 Cambridge, Magdalene Coll., 23 (F.4.23) (de Hamel, no. 44) s.xv.

a (fol. 1) Bridgettine Calendar, with *obits* of Henry V, *fundator huius monasterii*, and a number of Syon nuns. **b** (fol. 13) *Comptus Kalendarii*, extracted from Book 8 of the *Rationale divinorum officiorum* of William Durandus (see J. F. von Schulte, *Die Geschichte der Quellen und Literatur des canonischen Rechts von Gratian bis auf die Gegenwart* [Stuttgart, 1875], vol. 2, p. 155). **c** (fol. 23v) Ranulph Higden, *Ars kalendarii*. A treatise *In literam calendarii* is attributed (uncertainly) to Higden by John Bale (*Index Britanniae Scriptorum*, ed. R. L. Poole & M. Bateson [Anecdota Oxoniensia, Mediaeval and Modern Series, 9; Oxford, 1902], p. 336), but no *incipit* is given. Bateson, *Catalogue of the Library of Syon Monastery*, p. 239, suggests that the true author might have been Ralph of Lenham/Lynham, but Ralph's Calendar/*Compotus* was in Anglo-Norman (though it was translated from a Latin original) (see J. C. Russell, *Dictionary of Writers of Thirteenth Century England* [London, 1936; rpt. New York, 1971], pp. 108–9). **d** (fol. 39) Martin of Troppau/Martinus Polonus, *Chronicon pontificum et imperatorum* (Kaeppeli 2973). **e** (fol. 106v) Honorius Augustodunensis, *Imago mundi* (ed. V. I. J. Flint, 'Honorius Augustodunensis Imago Mundi', *Archives d'histoire doctrinale et littéraire du moyen âge* 49 [1982], pp. 7–153 [beginning at p. 49, line 3, and incomplete]). **f** (fol. 111v) [Gervase of Tilbury], *De mundi creatione, dispositione, et ornatione,* which is part of the first *distinctio* of Gervase's *Otia imperialia* (see *Dictionnaire d'histoire et de géographie ecclésiastiques*, vol. 20, fasc. 117–8 [Paris, 1983], cols. 1097–99 for edition and studies). **g** (fol. 117v) [Gervase of Tilbury], *Mappa mundi*, which is part of the second *distinctio* of the same work. **h** (fol. 196) William of Tripoli, *De statu Saracenorum, de Mahometo pseudo-propheta eorum, et de ipsa gente et eorum lege et fide* (see A. S. Atiya, *The Crusade: Historiography and Bibliography* [Bloomington, 1962], p. 63, and *Dictionnaire d'histoire et de géographie ecclésiastiques*, vol. 22, fasc. 129–30 [Paris, 1988], cols. 1033–4 for edition [the page numbers in Prutz are 575–98] and studies). This is followed by the end of the *Mappa mundi* and the end of the chronicle of Martinus Polonus, both of which have become separated from the main texts.

This manuscript is much disarranged, and I suspect that it might be a rebound version of what was once the first part (to fol. 152) of volume K.28 in the brothers' library (see Bateson, *Catalogue*, p. 83). Item **c** may have come from the mis-catalogued (and untraced) volume B.3 (see *ibid.*, p. 239). If this were so, the manuscript would have originally formed part of the brothers' library, but the *obits* of the early Syon nuns would seem to indicate that it was at some time in the possession of the sisters (see de Hamel, pp. 72 and 119 [no. 44]).

12 Cambridge, St John's Coll., 139 (de Hamel, no. 29) s.xv

Processional (with music), written for the sisters of Syon, with contents similar to those in **A.6** (q.v.). The manuscript is no. 926 in Frere.

The contents of the manuscript clearly indicate that it was made for the Syon nuns.

13 Cambridge, Sidney Sussex Coll., Bb.2.14 (printed book)

The Chastysing of Goddes Chyldern, printed by Wynkyn de Worde, Westminster, 1493 (*GW* 6583; *STC* 5065; Duff 85).

On fol. 3 (s.xvi[1]) two names appear: *Edyth Morepath* and *Katheryn Palmer*. Edith Morepath appears in the list of Syon nuns in 1518 (Aungier, p. 81) and died 31 October 1536 (*Martyrology* fol. 61v). She was buried *iuxta gerras* at Syon (*Martyrology* fol. 191v no. 15). Katherine or Catherine Palmer is recorded in the Pension Lists of 1539 and 1554/5 (Aungier, pp. 89, 99) and it was she who, after the suppression of the house, led a group of nuns first to Antwerp and then to Dendermonde in Flanders. When Syon was restored under Mary in 1557, she was appointed abbess (Aungier, p. 97) and died 19 December 1576. Her *obit* in the *Martyrology* fol. 68r reads *Domina Catherina Palmer, 8ª. Abbatissa*, and adds the marginal note in a different hand: *Sepulta apud Augustinenses Macklinie.* Dr Ann Hutchison has informed me that Catherine Palmer also owned a copy of Laurentius Surius's Latin translation of the *opera omnia* of Johann Tauler (printed in Cologne by Johann Quentel in 1548, formerly preserved at Syon Abbey, and now deposited at the University of Exeter), as well as a copy of the 1494 printed edition of Walter Hilton's *Ladder of Perfection* (now Cambridge, U. L., Inc. 3.J.1.2 3545; see **A.43** below). On the fly-leaf of the Tauler volume appears the inscription *vsui sororis Katherine Palmer* and at the top of the title-page *Ad vsum sororis Katherine palmere*. The book cannot have been at Syon before the suppression of the house in 1539 (it was not published until nine years later), but the inscriptions would seem to indicate that it was in the possession of Catherine Palmer during the short period of Syon's restoration in 1557–8. As to the *Ladder of Perfection*, this was given by Catherine Palmer to Anthony Bolney in 1546 (the inscription on the title-page reads *Katehrin Palmer . . . Dedit hunc librum in Ihu Christi dilectione Antonio bolney pia mater Katherina Palmere Anno dni M.D.xlvj*). When it first came into the possession of Catherine Palmer is unknown.

14 Cambridge, Trinity Coll., C.7.12 (printed book)

A Deuout Treatyse Called the Tree & XII. Frutes of the Holy Goost, two parts, the first part printed by Robert Copland and the second by Robert Copland and Michael Fawkes, London, 1534–35 (*STC* 13608). For a full description of this copy, see Vaissier's edition of the work (cited at **A.3**), pp. xxxii–xxxiii.

(fly-leaf iᵛ [s.xvi¹]) *Mar<gare>t Windesor, domina de Syon.* Margaret Windsor, the sister of Lord Andrew Windsor, is listed as prioress of Syon in 1518 and 1539 (Aungier, pp. 81, 89). She is commemorated in the *Martyrology* on 19 December (fol. 68r) as *Sor<or> Margareta Wyndesor, 9ª. priorissa*, but no date is given. She also owned a volume of Boccacio (**A.31**), and the Psalter recorded at **A.33** was made for her.

15 Dublin, Archbishop Marsh's Lib., Z.4.4.3 (de Hamel, no. 45)
s.xv

Psalter, followed by Canticles, Litanies, *Vigilia mortuorum*, meditations on the Virgin (fols. 106–16), collections of quotations from the psalms, and, in a later and inferior hand, a few prayers in Latin of which two have English rubrics. There is no Calendar. According to de Hamel, p. 75, this is 'a straightforward Sarum Psalter acquired second-hand by Syon and never brought into line [with Syon usages].'

(fol. 127 [fol. xvi¹]) *Alys Rade*, and below that in a different hand, *Alys Hastyngs* (written twice). (end paste-down [s.xvi¹]) *Of yowr charyte pray for yowr sester Alys Hastyngs.* Both Alice Rade and Alice Hastings are listed as nuns of Syon in 1518 (Aungier, p. 81), but they do not appear in any later list. An Elizabeth Rade was a nun at the same time (*ibid.*). Alice or Alicia Rade died 28 February 1530; Alicia Hastyngs died 17 January 1527; and Elizabeth Rade died 24 January 1538 (*Matyrology* fols. 28v, 23v, 24r). Their burials are recorded in the *Martyrology* fols. 191r–v.

16 Durham, U.L., Cosin V.v.12 (de Hamel, no. 49) s.xv/xvi

a (fol. 2) John Cressener, *The Sawter of Mercy*, in Latin with English rubrics. The author is described as 'Ser Johan Cressener bacheler of [. . .]', and he composed the work in 1495. The 'Ser' probably indicates a cleric rather than a knight. This appears to be the unique copy of this treatise and it has never been edited. Nothing is known of the author. The *Sawter* is followed by a series of Latin prayers with English rubrics. **b** (fol. 20) Jordan of Quedlinburg (or Jordan of Saxony, O.S.A. [to be distinguished from Jordan of Saxony, O.P.]), *Meditations on the Life and Passion of Jesus Christ*. This is an English version of Jordan's *Meditationes de passione Christi / Articuli lxv de passione Domini cum theorematibus et documentis*, a very popular work which (in Latin) survives in more than a hundred manuscripts and a dozen editions. In the Cosin manuscript, the *Meditations* are in English and the prayers in Latin. I am indebted to Dr A. I. Doyle for providing me with a description of this manuscript.

(fol. 1 [s.xvi]) *Tressham* (her Christian name is erased). Clemence, Clemencia, or Clementia Tresham is listed as a nun at Syon in 1518 (Aungier, p. 81) and 1539 (Aungier,

p. 89). In the Marian Pension List of 1554/5 she appears as 'Clementia Tresham, late religious there' (Aungier, p. 99), and she returned to the house under the Marian restoration in 1557 (Aungier, p. 97). Her death is recorded in the *Martyrology* on 11 September (fol. 55r), but no year is given. Her name also appears, written in the same hand, in **A.17** immediately below.

17 Durham, Dr A. I. Doyle (printed book)

Thomas à Kempis, *Opera Thomae a Campis cognomento Malleoli*, printed by J. B. Ascensius, Paris, 1523. See P. Rouillard, *Bibliographie des impressions et des oeuvres de J. B. Ascensius* (Paris, 1908) 2: 260–1. The volume contains 26 *opera* of Thomas and five *opera addititia*, as follows: *Alphabetum monachi, De imitatione Christi, De sacramento altaris* (= *De imitatione Christi, lib. IV*), *De disciplina claustralium, Dialogus novitiorum, Doctrinale iuvenum, De fideli dispensatore, De vita solitaria, De silentio, De paupertate, humilitate et patientia* (*De tribus tabernaculis*), *De vera compunctione, Hortulus rosarum, Vallis liliorum, Consolatio pauperum et infirmorum, Epitaphium seu enchiridion monachorum, Vita boni monachi, Manuale parvulorum, Hospitale pauperum, Soliloquium animae, Sermones ad novitios, Sermones ad fratres, Epistolae morales, Vita venerandi patris Gerardi Magni, Vita venerabilis sacerdotis Florentii discipuli Gerardi, Vita plurimorum discipulorum eorundem, Canticum de laudibus sacrarum virginum et caelestium spirituum ac virtutum. Opera addititia: De meditatione cordis M. Iohannis Gersonis, Fragmentum de meditatione mortis, Tractatus alter de eadem, Speculum peccatoris, Carmen de illustrium virorum morte.*

(title-page [s.xvi]) *Clemence Tressham*. Lower down, in either a different hand or a different script, is *Yn Syon*. (foot of contents-page [s.xvi]) *Clemens Tressham*. For Clemence Tressham, see **A.16** immediately above. I am indebted to Dr A. I. Doyle for a description of this volume and for a copy of the page of contents.

18 Firle Park, Sussex, Lord Gage (de Hamel, no. 73) s.xv

Psalter, preceded by a Calendar, and followed by Canticles, Athanasian Creed, a Bridgettine Litany (ending with a prayer for the soul *regis Henrici fundatoris nostri*), Hours of the Holy Spirit, Office of the Dead, and various prayers and collects.

Dr. Kathleen L. Scott, to whom I am indebted for a description of this volume, suggests that it was written c. 1450–60.

Evidence from the Calendar and the Litany clearly indicates a Syon provenance, and since some of the prayers contain feminine grammatical forms, there can be no doubt that this magnificent Psalter was once in the keeping of the Syon nuns. There is no inscription of ownership. I am also informed by Dr. Scott that 'the historiated initial on folio 8 of a Crucifix-Trinity is rare, if not unique, among surviving 15th-century English psalters in the *Beatus* rather than *Dixit Dominus* position, and that it may reflect the wishes of the original commissioning party' (personal communication).

19 Glasgow, U.L., Hunterian Mus., 136 (T.6.18) (de Hamel, no. 11) AD 1502

Thomas à Kempis, *Musica ecclesiastica* (L/B/E 526). This is the first (anonymous) English translation of Books 1–3 of Thomas's *De imitatione Christi*.

(fol. i^v [s.xvi^{in}]) *O uos omnes sorores et ffratres presentes et futuri, orate queso pro uenerabili matre nostra Elizabeth Gibbis, huius almi monasterii abbatissa, cuius cura hic liber conscriptus est anno dominice incarnacionis millesimo CCCCC secundo.* (fol. ii) *O uos omnes sorores et ffratres presentes et futuri, orate queso pro uenerabili matre nostra Elizabeth Gibbis, huius almi monasterii abbatissa, necnon pro deuoto ac religioso uiro Dompno Willelmo Darker, in artibus magistro, de domo Bethleem prope Shene ordinis Cartuciensis, qui pro eadem domina abbatissa hunc librum conscripsit anno dominice incarnacionis millesimo CCCCC secundo.* Elizabeth Gibbs was abbess of Syon from 1497 to her death on 30 August 1518 (VCH *Middlesex.* vol. 1, p. 190; *Martyrology* fol. 52v [her parents are commemorated on 1 September (fol. 53r)]). Aungier confused her with her predecessor, Elizabeth Muston, and accordingly attributed to her an abbacy of fifty-seven years! Ker, p. 309, repeats this error, though Muston's death is clearly recorded on fol. 36r of the *Martyrology* on 28 April 1497 (*Domina Elizabeth Muston, 4. abbatissa*). William Darker was a Carthusian of Shene who copied a number of volumes both for his own house and for Syon, including **A.29** and **B.3** (see *The Rewyll of Seynt Sauioure and Other Middle English Brigittine Legislative Texts, Vol. 2: The MSS. Cambridge University Library Ff. 6. 33 and St. John's College Cambridge 11,* ed. J. Hogg [*Salzburger Studien zur Anglistik und Amerikanistik,* Bd. 6; Salzburg, 1978], pp. iii–iv, n. 5). See also Part I of this study, Chapter 3, n. 143.

20 Göttingen, U.L., 4° Theol. Mor. 138/53 Inc. (printed book)
   a *The Chastysing of Goddes Chyldern* (GW 6583; STC 5065; Duff 85), and b *The Tretyse of Love* (STC 24234; Duff 399), both printed by Wynkyn de Worde, Westminster, c. 1493. The *Treatise* is an English translation of a French adaptation of the *Ancrene Riwle*.
   (fol. Ir [Göttingen enumeration], immediately preceding the beginning of the text [s.xvi]) *Thys boke ys myne, S<yster> Awdry Dely, of the gyfte of Syster Mary Nevell. God reward her in heven for yt.* Both Awdry Dely and Mary Nevell are listed as nuns of Syon in 1539 (Aungier, p. 90 ['Audery Dely' and 'Marye Nevell']); both appear in the 1554/5 Marian Pension List (Aungier, p. 99 [with Audery Dely spelled Awdrey Delby]), and both were members of the restored community in 1557 (Aungier, p. 97). The death of 'Etheldreda Dely, Sor<or>" is recorded in the *Martyrology* fol. 35r on 19 April 1579, and that of 'Maria Nevell, Soror', on 17 October 1557 or 1558. The entry on fol. 60r of the *Martyrology* gives 1557; the entry on fol. 192r, which records her burial *prope murum*, reads *Maria Nevel, Sor<or>, Anno domini 1558 17 die [erased] obiit hic in Syon*. This amount of detail is unusual. Mary Nevell's name also appears in **A.40** below. Another Dely—Margaret—is recorded at Syon in 1539 (when she was treasurer) and as a member of the restored community (Aungier, pp. 89, 97). The *Martyrology* fol. 59r commemorates her death on 10 October, but no year is given, and her memorial brass from Isleworth Church is illustrated in Aungier. I am indebted to Dr Helmut Rohlfing of the Niedersächsische Staats- und Universitätsbibliothek Göttingen for providing me with a xeroxed copy of the ownership inscription in this book.

21 ?London, B.L., Add. 24661 s.xv
   a (fol. 2) Richard Rolle, *Emendatio vitae*, preceded by a table of contents (Allen, pp. 230–45; Stegmüller 7314,1; Bloomfield 3191). There is still no critical edition. b (fol. 14) Richard Rolle, *Incendium amoris* (an abridged and heterogeneous version: see Allen, pp. 216–7, 321). For this manuscript, see Deanesly, *Incendium Amoris* (see **A.7e** above), 1–2. c Richard Rolle, *De excellentia contemplationis* (Allen, pp. 320–3), followed by extracts from the *Incendium amoris*. d (fol. 61) *Ps.*-Bernard of Clairvaux, *Sermo de vita et passione Domini* (PL 184: 953–66), appearing here under the title *Sermo beati Bernardi de admirandis beneficiis*

Dei. The true author may have been Eckbert of Schönau (see P. Glorieux, *Pour revaloriser Migne. Tables rectificatives* [Mélanges de science religieuse, 9 (supp.); Lille, 1952], p. 72). **e** (fol. 66v) *Ps.*-Augustine, *De diligendo Deo* (*PL* 40: 847–64). This is followed by some theological excerpts attributed to Bernard and Augustine. **f** (fol. 76) *Ps.*-Augustine, *Meditationes, cap.* 11–30 (*PL* 40: 909–25). **g** (fol. 83v) Three excerpts (*de ratione, de voluntate,* and *de memoria*) from Book I, Part II, Chapters 5 and 6 of the *De exterioris et interioris hominis compositione* of David of Augsburg (*ps.*-Bonaventure) (Bloomfield 5676). Book I Part II of this work regularly circulated as a separate treatise under the title *De profectu religiosorum.*

This is the second of the Grenehalgh-Sewell manuscripts discussed in the introduction to this list of books from Syon (see also **A.7** above). In the left margin of fol. 18v appears the combined monogram, J.G.S., which also appears in **A.43** and which is illustrated in Deanesly, *Incendium Amoris,* p. 82. For a full description of the manuscript, see Sargent, *James Grenehalgh as Textual Critic,* vol. 2, pp. 493–9.

22 London, B.L., Arundel 146 (de Hamel, no. 48) s.xv^{ex}

The Additions to the Rule of Saint Saviour (L/B/E 236). These are the fifty-nine chapters of additions to the modified Augustinian Rule, designed for the sisters of Syon. The manuscript lacks the first and last chapters. London, St Paul's Cathedral, 5 (de Hamel, no. 17) provides the version intended for the brothers. There are three editions of the two sets of *Additions*: (i) Aungier, pp. 249–404; (ii) Veronica R. Hughes, *The Syon Additions to the Rule of St. Saviour* (Liverpool Univ., M.A. Diss., 1952); and (iii) James Hogg, *The Rewyll of Seynt Sauioure, Vol. 3: The Syon Additions for the Brethren and the Boke of Sygnes from the St. Paul's Cathedral Library Ms. (Salzburger Studien zur Anglistik und Amerikanistik,* Bd. 6; Salzburg, 1980) and *The Rewyll of Seynt Sauioure, Vol. 4: The Syon Additions for the Sisters from the British Library MS. Arundel 146 (Salzburger Studien zur Anglistik und Amerikanistik,* Bd. 6; Salzburg, 1980). Of the three, Hogg's editions are the best and by far the most easily available.

There is no reason to think that this manuscript should have been anywhere other than at Syon.

23 London, B.L., Cotton App. xiv (de Hamel, no. 30) s.xv^{ex}

Hours of the Holy Spirit, followed by the Penitential Psalms, Gradual Psalms, a Bridgettine Litany, the Office of the Dead,

Commendatio animarum, and (fol. 124v) an extensive collection of Latin prayers with English rubrics. These begin with
prayers for brothers and sisters who are sick, prayers to be
said when they recover, a litany to be recited if there are
problems, and *Commendatio animarum* if they die. These are
followed by the 'vij obites used to be kepte in the monasteri',
beginning with the *obit* of the founders of Syon (Henry V and
Edward IV and their wives) and continuing with the *obits* of
Thomas Fishbourne (the first Confessor-General), Sir Henry
FitzHugh (who, in 1406, promised land to the Order if they
would found a house in England), and others. The seven *obits*
are printed (with some errors) in Aungier, pp. 528–9. We then
have a blessing to be said before chapter and various other
prayers for special friends, for dry weather, for tempests, for
sailors, for the king and queen, for prisoners, for the pope and
his prelates, for the heathen, ending (fol. 164) with a prayer
for 'alle quicke and dede'. Many of these prayers appear in
other Bridgettine Breviaries, and a number have been printed
in Collins, pp. 147–50 (from **A.8**). The manuscript includes
neither a Calendar nor the Hours of the Virgin.

(fol. 56v [s.xv^{ex}]) *Of your charite praye for the sowlys of John
Edwarde and Margaret hys wyffe and for Elizabethe ther doughter,
professed yn Syon, for whos vse thy<s> boke was made.* The inscription is reproduced in de Hamel, p. 95. Elizabeth Edward or
Edwards is listed as a nun of Syon in 1518 and 1539 (Aungier,
pp. 82, 89), but does not appear in the later lists. Her death is
recorded in the *Martyrology* fol. 59r on 10 October (*Elyzabeth
Edwards, Sor<or>*), but no year is given. An Anna Edwarde
was also a sister at Syon and died on the 20 July of an
unrecorded year (*Martyrology* fol. 47r).

24 London, B.L., Harley 487 (de Hamel, no. 12) s.xv

Psalter, preceded by a Calendar and followed by Canticles,
Athanasian Creed, a Litany, and (fol. 201) Hours of the Holy
Spirit. The Nativity, Canonization and Translation of St Bridget are all classed as *maius duplex*. For the similarities between
this manuscript and **A.41**, see de Hamel, pp. 67–8.

(fol. 218v [s.xvi]) *Suster Elyzabeth Ogull* (s.xvi). Elizabeth
Ogull or Ogle is listed as a nun at Syon in 1518 and 1539
(Aungier, pp. 81, 89 ['Elysabeth Ogle']). She received a pension
in 1554/5 (Aungier, p. 99), but does not appear to have been a
member of the restored community. Her death is recorded in

the *Martyrology* fol. 23r on 15 January (*Elyzabeth Ogle, Soror*), but no year is given.

25 London, B.L., Harley 993 (de Hamel, no. 37) s.xv

a (fol. 1) Walter Hilton, *A Treatise of Eight Chapters* (L/B/E 677). **b** (fol. 24) *A Treatise of Discretion of Spirits* (L/B/E 240 [the first few lines are missing]).

(fly-leaf ii [s.xvi]) *Thys boke is ssuster Anne Colvylle*. (fol. 39v [s.xvi]) *D. Anne Colvilee* at the top of the leaf, and *Anne Colvylle* at the bottom. Anne Colville was a nun of Syon in 1518 (Aungier, p. 81 ['Anna Covyle']), but since she died on 30 October 1531 (*Martyrology* fol. 61v, where her name appears as 'Anna Covell'), she does not appear in any later list. Her name also appears in **A.35**. The colophon on fol. 38 indicates that the book was one of the 'common profit' manuscripts, but this does not relate specifically to Syon (see *Deonise Hid Diuinite*, ed. P. Hodgson [EETS/OS, 231; London, 1955], p. xi).

26 London, B.L., Harley 2387 (de Hamel, no. 52) s.xv

Walter Hilton, *The Ladder of Perfection*, Parts I and II (L/B/E 255).

(fol 130v [s.xv]) *Istum librum legauit domina Margeria Pensax dudum inclusa apud Bysshoppisgate monasterio sancti Saluatoris de Syon iuxta Shene*. Margery Pensax is recorded as being an anchoress at St Botolph's, Bishopsgate, in 1399 and 1413 (see John Stow, *A Survey of London*, with introduction and notes by C. L. Kingsford [Oxford, 1971], vol. 2, p. 397(vi) [note to vol. 1, p. 164, line 15]).

27 London, B.L., IB.55119 (printed book)

Nicholas Love, *The Myrroure of the Blessed Lyf of Ihesu Cryste (Speculum vitae Cristi)* (a translation of *ps.*-Bonaventure, *Meditationes vitae Christi*) (L/B/E 553). This is Caxton's edition, printed at Westminster in 1490 (*GW* 4764; *STC* 3260; Duff 49). The Mirror is followed by *A shorte treatyce of the . . . sacramente of Crystes blessid body* and *A short deuoute prayer to Jhesu Crist & his blessyd body in the sacramente of the aulter*.

(fol. a2 [the first leaf present [s.xvi]) *Susan Purefeye owethe thys booke*. According to S. de Ricci, *A Census of Caxtons* (Oxford, 1909), p. 14 (no. 10,1), 'Early owner: Susan Pureseye [De Ricci has misread lower case f as s]. Was before the Reformation in Sion Nunnery. Found by Maskell in a Catholic Seminary of the West of England. Sold through him in 1864 to the British Museum.' Susan Purferaye appears in the Pension List of 1539, the Marian Pension List of 1554/5 ('Susanna Purfrey'), and was a member of the restored community in 1557 ('Susan Purefey') (Aungier, pp. 89, 99, 97). She died 24 December 1570 (*Martyrology* fol. 68v). The family of Purefoy (and variant spellings) was well known in Leicestershire, and the names of Michael and Anna Purefoy appear in **A.7**, fols. 192r and 193r.

28 London, Lambeth Palace, 535 (de Hamel, no. 35) s.xv^ex

Psalter, preceded by a Dominican Calendar, and followed by Canticles and a Bridgettine Litany.

M. R. James points out that 'the suppliant in a Collect at the end is female', and I follow his suggestion that 'a nun at Syon was very likely the owner' (M. R. James, *A Descriptive Catalogue of the Manuscripts in the Library of Lambeth Palace: The Mediaeval Manuscripts* [Cambridge, 1932], p. 736). The manuscript is not included in Ker and Watson.

29 ?London, Lambeth Palace, 546 (de Hamel, no. 34) s.xv

A collection of prayers and devotional pieces, including (fol. 7v) the Fifteen Sorrows of Our Lady, (fol. 21) *The Sacrament of the Altar* in English attributed (erroneously) to Albert the Great (L/B/E 572), (fol. 29) the *Golden Litany* in English (L/B/E 442, printed from this manuscript by W. Maskell, *Monumenta Ritualia Ecclesiae Anglicanae* [Oxford, 1882²], vol. 3, pp. 263–74), (fol. 52v) prayers to the Virgin (one of these, attributed to Rolle, has been printed [Allen, pp. 343–4 (with edition); L/B/E 616]), (fol. 56) the Office of the Holy Face (with English rubric), and concluding (fol. 57) with a dozen prayers in English and Latin. This last section, fols. 57–77v, appears to be in the hand of William Darker of Shene, who also copied **A.19** and **B.3**. A comprehensive description of the manuscript is provided by James, *Descriptive Catalogue of the Manuscripts in the Library of Lambeth Palace*, pp. 750–2.

Fol. 29 is headed IHS MARIA BIRGITTA, which led James to state that 'I have no doubt the book belonged to a member of Syon Monastery, probably a sister' (p. 751). This is confirmed by the appearance of the name of *Sister EW* (written as a monogram) on fol. 56 and, on the preceding folio, the inscription (s.xv/xvi) *Good syster of your charyte I you pray, remember the scrybeler when that ye may, with an Ave Maria or els thys swete word Ihesu.* The only EW to appear in the lists printed by Aungier is Elizabeth Woodford, a nun of Syon in 1518 (Aungier, p. 81), who died 5 March 1523 and was buried in the abbey church (*Martyrology* fols. 29v, 191r no. 22).

30 ?London, Lambeth Palace, 3600 (formerly Bristol, Baptist Coll., Z.e.37) (de Hamel, no. 33) s.xvi[1]

A collection of prayers and directions for prayer in Latin and English. Many of them are indexed in Hoskins, pp. 383–444. They include prayers to the Virgin, to the Five Wounds, to one's guardian angel, to God the Son, prayers of the Five Sorrows of the Virgin, and prayers to be said on retiring at night. A full description may be found in Ker/*MMBL*, vol. 1, pp. 198–200.

That this manuscript was written in England for a female religious is certain; that she was a nun of Syon is probable (see Ker/*MMBL*, vol. 1, p. 200). Fols. 58v–59r are reproduced in de Hamel, p. 105.

31 New York, Pierpont Morgan, 600 (printed book)

Boccaccio, *De la ruine des nobles hommes et femmes*, printed by Matthias Huss and Johann Schabeler, Lyons, 1483 (*GW* 4433). This is the French translation of the work prepared by Pierre Faivre. The volume is described in the *Catalogue of Manuscripts and Early Printed Books . . . Now Forming Portion of the Library of J. Pierpont Morgan* (London, 1907), vol. 3, pp. 49–50 no. 600 (with facsimiles).

(fol. 1v [s.xvi[1]]) *Cest lyuere partient a moy Henry Parkar.* (fol. 2r) *Cest liure apertient a moy Marguerete Wyndesore*, followed by her monogram. This inscription is reproduced in the *Catalogue of Manuscripts* (cited above), vol. 3, p. 48. (fol. 174v) *Thys boke ys myne, Margaret, yan gevyn by master Parkar.* (recto of last flyleaf) *Mastres Margrett yan.* For Margaret Windsor, see **A.14** and **A.33**. I am indebted to Anna Lou Ashby, Associate Curator of Printed Books at the Pierpont Morgan Library, for providing me with a detailed description of this volume.

32 New York, Public Lib., Spencer Collection, Eng. 1519 (printed book)

Catherine of Siena, *The Orcharde of Syon*, printed by Wynkyn de Worde, London, 1519 (*STC* 4815). The work is an anonymous English translation of Raymond of Capua's Latin version of Catherine's Italian *Dialogo*. It was prepared specifically for the nuns of Syon. The attribution of the English translation to a 'Dom James' has been shown by Phyllis Hodgson to be based on a misreading of the text: see P. Hodgson, '*The Orcherd of Syon* and the English Mystical Tradition', in J. A. Burrow (ed.), *Middle English Literature: British Academy Gollancz Lectures* (Oxford, 1989), p. 77. Hodgson's paper was originally read on 1 July 1964.

(on a blank page at the end of the book [s.xvi[1]]) *This boke perteynyth to syster Elyzabeth Stryckland, professyd in Syon.* Below this is a second inscription which records that Sir Richard Assheton of Middleton, 'executor unto my lady Stryklond decessed', gave the book to his wife on 15 December 1542, which must have been the year of Elyzabeth Stryckland's death. She is listed as a nun of Syon in 1518 and 1539 (Aungier, pp. 81, 89), and her death is recorded in the *Martyrology* fol. 24v on 25 January (the year is not given). De Hamel, p. 112, notes that this volume 'is the first book from Syon which can be demonstrated to have passed into secular hands after the dissolution.'

33 Oakley Park, Earl of Plymouth (de Hamel, no. 74) s.xv[ex]

Psalter, preceded by a Sarum Calendar, and followed by Canticles, Athanasian Creed, a Bridgettine Litany, and various collects. 'Deuoute prayers to be saide to the moste holye sacrament of the Autyr' (in Latin, *inc.* 'Ave sanctissimum corpus domini nostri Ihesu Christi') have been added at the beginning of the volume in a later hand (s.xv/xvi). A brief description of the manuscript may be found in [S. C. Cockerell], *Burlington Fine Arts Club: Exhibition of Illuminated Manuscripts* (London, 1908), p. 76 no. 154.

The Psalter was made specifically for Margaret Windsor (see **A.14** and **A.31**) and seems to have been a gift from her brother, Lord Andrew Windsor. He also left her the very large annuity of £80:6:8 to pray for his soul and the souls of their parents (see Aungier, p. 81, n. 3). The Windsor escutcheon appears at the foot of fol. 15r surrounded by the inscription *Orate pro anima Andree Wyndesore militis.* Two of the historiated initials contain portraits of Margaret Windsor, dressed in the Bridgettine habit and kneeling in prayer. In the second of these (fol. 97v) she is saying her name: *Margareta Wyndesou[r].* The Calendar contains *obits* of John and Maud (or Matilda) Trowell, the parents of John Trowell, the sixth Confessor-General of Syon who died 23 April 1523 (*Martyrology* fol. 35v).

34 Oxford, Bod. Lib., Auct. D.4.7 (S.C. 1961) (de Hamel, no. 25) s.xv[1]

Bridgettine Breviary (with Latin rubrics), beginning with a Sarum Calendar (with Bridgettine additions) and followed (fol. 73) by a Psalter, Canticles, the Hours of the Holy Spirit, and the Office of the Dead. The manuscript is described in Collins, pp. xlv–xlvii, and is no. 133 in Frere.

The manuscript is entitled (fol. 1r) *Ordo seruicii sororum ordinis sancti Saluatoris*, and there is a prayer with feminine grammatical forms on fol. 72r. There are also *obits* of Thomas Fishbourne, the first Confessor-General of Syon (13 September: this seems to be a later addition), and, on 21 May, of Elizabeth Fetyplace: *Obitus Elyzabethe ffetyplace, 155[?6]*. This last was undoubtedly written by Eleanor Fetyplace, Elizabeth's sister, who was one of a group of nine Syon nuns who found refuge with James Yate at Buckland after their expulsion from Syon in November 1539. Eleanor was the aunt of James Yate's daughter, another Elizabeth, whose Breviary and printed Psalter have survived (**A.42**). Elizabeth Fetyplace herself had been a nun at Amesbury (see Aungier, p. 99, n. 2; Collins, p. xlvii). Eleanor reentered Syon at the Marian revival in 1557 (Aungier, p. 97), was expelled again at the final dissolution of the house two years later, and died 15 July 1565 (Collins, p. xlvii; *Martyrology* fol. 46v [*Elienora ffetiplase, Soror*]). We may presume that this volume was her personal Breviary. She also owned a Psalter (**A.4**) and a copy of Richard Whytford's *Pype, or Tonne, of the Lyfe of Perfection* (**A.37**). An Ursula Fetyplace was also a nun of Syon at the time of the surrender, and appears both in the Marian Pension List of 1554/5 and as a member of the restored community in 1557 (Aungier, pp. 99, 97). Her death is recorded in the *Martyrology* fol. 65r on 28 November, but no year is given. The cost of refitting the monastic buildings for reoccupation at the Marian restoration had been borne by Sir Francis Englefield, who had married Catherine Fetyplace, a relative of Eleanor and Ursula (VCH *Middlesex*, vol. 1, p. 190).

35 Oxford, Bod. Lib., Laud misc. 416 (S.C. 1479) (de Hamel, no. 31) AD 1459

a (fol. 1) Peter Idley, *Instructions to His Son* (Book II only) (Brown/Robbins 1540). **b** (fol. 66) *Cursor Mundi* (Brown/Robbins 2153), preceded by the *Calendarium de cursor mundi.* **c** (fol. 182) John Clifton's (unprinted) translation of the *De re militari* of Vegetius. **d** (fol. 227) John Lydgate, *Siege of Thebes* (Brown/Robbins 3928). **e** (fol. 255) John Lydgate and Benet Burgh, *Secrets of Old Philosophers* (Brown/Robbins 935). This is an English metrical paraphrase of the *ps.*-Aristotelian *Secretum secretorum.* **f** (fol. 288) Chaucer, *The Parliament of Fowls* (vv. 1–142 only [two folios]) (Brown/Robbins 3412).

(end pastedown [s.xvi]) *Syster Anne Colvylle,* and below it, *Of your charyte prey for Sustyr Clemens Trys<?>burght.* For Anne Colville, see **A.25** above. Clemencia Thraseborough, like Anne Colville, appears only in the 1518 list of Syon nuns (Aungier, pp. 81, 82). She died 13 March 1536 and was buried *prope murum* in the abbey church (*Martyrology* fols. 30v, 191v no. 16 [*Clementia Tharysbrugh Sor<or>*]). The date of the manuscript is provided by the colophon at the end of the translation of Vegetius (fol. 226v): *Scriptus Rhodo per Johannem Neuton die 25 Octobris 1459.* Rhodes is not the island of Rhodes, but possibly Rhodes in Lancashire (see Watson/*Oxford*, vol. 1 no. 603, and vol. 2 pl. 565 [fol. 210v]). For other suggestions, see de Hamel, pp. 81 and 141 n. 77.

36 ?Oxford, Bod. Lib., Rawlinson C.781 (de Hamel, no. 53) s.xv

Breviary Offices (Bridgettine Use) for the week and feasts (with Latin rubrics), ending with directions for processions similar to those in **A.8** and **A.9** above. Two prayers have been added in a later hand. There is no Calendar, but the manuscript has been much mutilated. A brief description may be found in Collins, pp. xlvii–xlviii, and it is no. 134 in Frere.

The volume is entitled *Ordo seruicii sororum ordinis sancti Saluatoris, traditus et ordinatus ex precepto sanctissime matris Birgitte, immo uerius Ihesu Christi, per magistrum Petrum Olaui, confessorem ipsius beate Birgitte, diuiditur principaliter in septem historias quas sorores dicti ordinis impermutabiliter cantare debent omni septimana per totum annum, exceptis diuersis festiuitatibus inferius annotatis.* For Petrus Olavi (Peter Olafsson), see Collins, pp. xviii–xxx *passim.*

37 Oxford, Bod. Lib., 4° W.2 Th. Seld. (printed book)

Richard Whytford, *The Pype, or Tonne, of the Lyfe of Perfection*, printed by Robert Redman, London, 1532 (*STC* 25421). The work includes a translation of Bernard of Clairvaux's *De prae-cepto et dispensatione* (fols. 112–170v) and is essentially an anti-Lutheran tract. This copy of *The Pype* is reproduced (with all the annotations) by James Hogg, *Richard Whytford's The Pype or Tonne of the Lyfe of Perfection* (Salzburg Studies in English Literature: Elizabethan and Renaissance Studies, 89; Salzburg, 1979), four volumes, of which the first contains an excellent study of Whytford's life (vol. 1, pt. 1) and works (vol. 1, pt. 2, published in 1989).

(end leaf [s.xvi]) *Elynor ffetyplace.* For Eleanor Fetyplace, see **A.34** above.

38 ?Oxford, All Souls Coll., 25 (de Hamel, no. 55) s.xv

Walter Hilton, *The Ladder of Perfection*, Parts I and II (L/B/E 255). A full description of this manuscript may be found in S. J. Ogilvie-Thomson, *Index of Middle English Prose, Handlist VIII* (Cambridge, 1991), p. 2.

(fol. 135 [s.xvi]) *Rose Pachet, professyd in Syon.* Rose Pachet is listed among the nuns of Syon in 1518 and 1539 (Aungier, p. 82 ['Rosa Packett'], 89 ['Rosse Paget']). She received a pension in 1554/5 (Aungier, p. 99 ['Rose Paget']), and was prioress and first searcher in the restored community in 1557 (Aungier, p. 97 ['Rose Pachett']). The duties of the prioress and the searchers are set out in chapter 55 of the *The Additions to the Rule of Saint Saviour*, ed. J. Hogg (see **A.22**), pp. 181–5. Her death is recorded in the *Martyrology* fol. 21v on 4 January (*Rosa Pagett, 10ᵃ. priorissa*), but no year is given.

39 ?Oxford, Jesus Coll., 39 (de Hamel, no. 32) s.xv

Disce mori (in English) (Jolliffe A.6; L/B/E 343). The work derives largely from the *Somme le roi* of Frère Laurent d'Orléans (see BRUISYARD 2), with additional material from Richard Rolle, Walter Hilton, and other English writers. Incorporated in the text at pp. 305–15 is a brief tract on the cleansing of the soul (Jolliffe I.35 [b]). For a full description of the manuscript, see Ogilvie-Thomson (cited at A.38), pp. 38–9.

(fol. iii [s.xvi]) *Dorothe Slyght.* Dorothy Slyghte, Slighte, or Sleight appears in the Pension Lists of 1539 and 1554/5, and as a member of the restored community in 1557 (Aungier, pp.

89, 97, 99). Her death is recorded in the *Martyrology* fol. 29r
on 4 March (*Dorethea Slithe Sor<or>*), but no year is given. Her
name also appears in **A.45** below.

40 Oxford, St John's Coll., 167 (de Hamel, no. 63) s.xv[ex]

Processional (with music), written for the sisters of Syon,
with contents similar to those in **A.6**. The manuscript is no.
525 in Frere.

The manuscript was obviously written for the sisters of
Syon, and at the very beginning of the volume we also find the
names of *Syster Mare Neuel*, *Sister Tomysyn Grove*, and *Brother
James Stock*. For Mary Nevell, see **A.20**. Neither of the other
names appears in any of the lists printed by Aungier, but the
death of *Thomesina Grove, Sorror* (*sic*) on 27 October 1566 is
recorded in the *Martyrology* fol. 61r. Like Anne Dyngue and
Anne Amersham, Mary Nevell and Thomasina Grove may
also have walked together in Syon processions (see **A.6**).

41 Oxford, St John's Coll., 187 (de Hamel, no. 70) s.xv

Hours of the Holy Spirit, followed by the Penitential
Psalms, Gradual Psalms, a Bridgettine Litany, various prayers,
the Office of the Dead, *Commendatio animarum*, hymns, and
further prayers. From fol. 103 the prayers are similar to those
noted in **A.23**. The manuscript includes neither a Calendar nor
the Hours of the Virgin.

Prayers containing feminine grammatical forms occur on
fols. 47r and 104r, and there are three commemorations for
the soul of Henry V, *fundator noster* (fols. 46v, 54v–55r, 85r).
De Hamel, pp. 67–8, draws attention to the close similarity
between this manuscript and **A.24**.

42 Oxford, University Coll., 25 s.xvi[in] and AD 1522 (part manuscript and part printed book) (de Hamel, no. 46)

Psalter (with Calendar), printed by Francis Byrckman, Paris,
1522 (*STC* 16260), preceded (in manuscript) by Hours of the
Holy Spirit and followed (again in manuscript) by Breviary
Offices (Bridgettine Use) for the week and feasts, prayers to
be said by a sister after receiving Extreme Unction, the Litany
of the Sick, and *Commendatio animarum*. The manuscript is
described in Collins, pp. xlviii–xlix.

(fol. 4 [s.xvi]) *This booke perteynethe to me Elyzabeth Yate*.
Elizabeth Yate, the daughter of James Yate (see **A.34**), appears
in the Pension Lists of 1539 and 1554/5, and as a member of

the restored community in 1557 (Aungier, pp. 90, 97, 99), but her name is not recorded in the *Martyrology*. Collins, p. xlviii, suggests that 'the ugly little volume was brought together by or on behalf of Elizabeth for use at Buckland, the home of her father, after the suppression in 1539.'

43 Philadelphia, Rosenbach Foundation, Inc. H491 (printed book)

Walter Hilton, *The Ladder of Perfection (Scala perfectionis)*, printed by Wynkyn de Worde, Westminster, 1494 (*STC* 14042; Duff 203). The Rosenbach copy includes Part III of the work, the *Vita mixta* or 'Medled Lyfe'.

This is the third and last of the Grenehalgh-Sewell volumes discussed in the introduction to this list of books from Syon (see also **A.7**). On fol. (a.iv)[v] is the inscription *This boke belongyth to Dame Jhone Sewelle, Syster in Syon, professed the yere of oure saluacion a thousand and fyve hundreth*. This is followed by Joan Sewell's monogram. Under the monogram, at the foot of the page, is *In die sancti Vitalis martiris XXVIII Aprilis*. The inscription is reproduced in Sargent, *James Grenehalgh as Textual Critic*, vol. 1, p. 173, and (better) in *idem*, 'James Grenehalgh: The Biographical Record', p. 43. The volume was probably given to Sewell by Grenehalgh at the time of her profession. On fol. 135v she has written her name, *Johanna Sewell*, combined it with a monogram, and surrounded it with *Sanctus Saluator, Birgitta, Sanctus Augustinus*, and *Maria*. The folio is reproduced in Deanesly, *Incendium Amoris* (see **A.7e** above), frontispiece, Sargent, *James Grenehalgh as Textual Critic*, vol. 1, p. 203, and *idem*, 'James Grenehalgh: The Biographical Record', p. 49. Elsewhere we find Sewell's monogram, J.S., and the combined monogram, J.G.S. All these annotations are transcribed and discussed by Sargent in *James Grenehalgh as Textual Critic*, vol. 1. pp. 164–212, who also provides a full description of the book in *ibid.*, vol. 2, pp. 536–40.

44 Rotthalmünster, Antiquariat Heribert Tenschert (formerly Lord Mowbray) (de Hamel, no. 56) s.xvi[in]

Psalter, preceded by a Calendar (Bridgettine Use) and followed by Canticles, Athanasian Creed, a Litany, various prayers, Hours of the Holy Spirit, the Office of the Dead (Sarum Use, with some English rubrics), and Bridgettine collects with English rubrics. Additional prayers have been added in a later hand on fols. 179v–82v, some of which are printed in Collins, pp. 147–9.

The volume was originally intended for a brother of Syon (prayers on fol. 208 are in the masculine form), but then passed into the hands of one of the sisters when prayers were adapted into feminine forms and numerous *obits* added to the Calendar. Amongst these are the *obits* of William and Isabel Smyth, and these led Dr de Hamel to the persuasive suggestion that the Psalter belonged to Agnes Smyth, a nun of Syon in 1518 and 1539 (Aungier, pp. 82, 89; de Hamel, p. 94). Her death is recorded in the *Martyrology* fol. 66r on 1 December, but no year is given. Fol. 74r of this Psalter is reproduced in de Hamel, p. 93.

45 Syon Abbey (South Brent), 1 (de Hamel, no. 68) s.xv[ex]

Processional (with music), written for the sisters of Syon, with contents almost identical to those in **A.6** above. A complete reproduction of the manuscript has been published by James Hogg in 'Processionale for the Use of the Sisters of Syon Abbey', *Analecta Cartusiana* 35:11 (*Spiritualität Heute und Gestern*, Bd. 11) (1991), pp. 45–299.

That this processional was written for the Syon nuns is not in doubt, but it also contains the names of two (or perhaps three) Syon nuns. *Dorothe Slyght* (see **A.39**) appears on fol. 1, and *C. Browne* on fol. 129r. The latter is undoubtedly Constancia Browne, who was elected abbess of Syon in 1518 and died 16 July 1520 (VCH *Middlesex*, vol. 1, p. 190; Aungier, pp. 81, 533 [with details of her family]; *Martyrology* fol. 46v [*Domina Constancia Browne, sexta abbatissa*]). Immediately below *C. Browne* is written *My lady Anne*, and de Hamel, p. 86, follows the suggestion of Drs Doyle and Hutchison that the lady in question might have been Anne de la Pole, prioress of Syon, who died in 1501 (see *Miscellaneous Records* **b** below). This cannot, however, be regarded as certain.

46 Syon Abbey (South Brent), 2 (de Hamel, no. 78) s.xv

A Bridgettine Calendar, Hours of the Holy Trinity, *Cursus de eterna sapientia* (cf. **D.2**), Hours of the Holy Spirit, Hours of the Passion, Hours of the Compassion of the Virgin, and a large collection of prayers, commemorations, *memoriae*, and similar material, nearly all in Latin. Included are prayers before and after communion, prayers on Christ's Passion, prayers to the three persons of the Trinity, the Virgin, and a variety of saints, the Fifteen Oes of St Bridget, Latin verses in praise of the Virgin, the Penitential Psalms, Gradual Psalms, various collects, litanies, the Office of the Dead, and the Seven Oes of St Gregory. There are rubrics in both English and French. A full description of the manuscript may be found in Ker/*MMBL*, vol. 4, pp. 336–42.

The contents of the manuscript leave no doubt that it was written for the Syon nuns: see Ker/*MMBL*, vol. 4, p. 342. Prayers in female form appear on fols. 140r and 206v.

47 Syon Abbey (South Brent), 6 (de Hamel, no. 79) s.xv[1]

This volume is essentially a Lectionary, but since the Lessons for the week (for Matins, Lauds, and Compline) are followed by a Litany and the weekly Offices for all Hours, it may fairly be referred to as a Bridgettine Breviary. At the end are the lectionary texts for various major feasts. Titles and marginalia are in English; rubrics are in English and Latin. A brief description of the manuscript may be found in Collins, p. xlviii, and a complete reproduction, presented by James Hogg, in 'Syon Abbey MS. 6—A Medieval Brigittine Lectionary for the Use of the Syon Sisters', *Analecta Cartusiana* 35:10 (*Spiritualität Heute und Gestern*, Bd. 10) (Salzburg, 1990), pp. 27–252. Hogg suggests that 'the compilation probably served the cantor of the week, the hebdomadaria' (p. 28).

The contents of the manuscript leave no doubt that the volume was written for the Syon nuns.

48 Syon Abbey (South Brent), fragments (de Hamel, nos. 81–85) s.xv–xv/xvi.

Bifolia, leaves, and parts of leaves containing fragments of the *Rule of St Saviour* (in English), the Syon *Additions for the Sisters*, a Lectionary, Bridgettine Breviaries, and (probably) a Gradual. See Ker/*MMBL*, vol. 4, pp. 348–9. These fragments are not included in Ker and Watson.

B) *Books belonging either to the Sisters or the Brothers*

1 Cambridge, U.L., Dd.2.33 (de Hamel, no. 51) s.xvi[in]

[David of Augsburg], *The Instruccion of Novices*, an English translation of the *Formula novitiorum/De exterioris et interioris*

hominis compositione of David of Augsburg (Bloomfield 4155).
See P. S. Joliffe, 'Middle English Translations of *De Exterioris
et Interioris Hominis Compositione'*, *Mediaeval Studies* 36 (1974),
pp. 259–77, where this manuscript is discussed.

The volume was 'wrytten by the hand of Thomas Prestius
brother of Syon.' Thomas Prestius is probably the 'Tho. Pre-
cyouse' listed by Aungier, p. 90, among those who received a
pension when the house was suppressed in 1539. He died at
Stanwell five years later (*Martyrology* fol. 57r [erasure]). In all
probability, he was also the translator of the work, but that
is not specifically stated. De Hamel, p. 120, suggests that the
manuscript probably formed part of the men's library, but it
is equally possible that it was written (or translated) for the
sisters. That is certainly the opinion of Dr Jan Rhodes, who
also assumes (too swiftly) that Prestius was the translator: see
J. T. Rhodes, 'Syon Abbey and its Religious Publications in the
Sixteenth Century', *Journal of Ecclesiastical History* 44 (1993),
p. 16.

2 ?Cambridge, U.L., Ff.6.18 s.xvi[in]

Additional lections and services for new festivals (see R. W.
Pfaff, *New Liturgical Feasts in Later Medieval England* [Oxford,
1970], p. 58) beginning with the lections *in tempore paschali*
and including the feasts of the Nativity of St Bridget (the
full services), St David, St Chad, St Erkenwald, St John of
Beverley, the Translation of St Bridget, and the Visitation. The
manuscript is no. 783 in Frere.

The manuscript is probably from Syon, but there is no indication as to whether it belonged to the sisters or the brothers.

3 ?Cambridge, U.L., Ff.6.33 (de Hamel, no. 57) s.xv

a (fol. 1) *Benjamin* (L/B/E 4). This is an abridged, free
translation of Richard of Saint-Victor's *Benjamin minor*. **b** (fol.
21v) *Notable Sayings of Holy Doctors on the Virtue of Holy Prayer*
(Jolliffe M.6). **c** (fol. 26) Two brief commentaries in English on
the Lord's Prayer, and the *Ave* and *Credo* in Latin and English.
These are preceded by brief notes on indulgences proclaimed
by Pope John XXII. **d** (fol. 33v) *The Four Requests of Our Lady
to Her Son*, written for Queen Isabel of France. **e** (fol. 37v)
Treatise on the Nine Virtues (L/B/E 256 [see also *ibid.*, 410 and
847]; Jolliffe I.12 [j]). **f** (fol. 38v) The Bridgettine Rule/*The Rule
of Saint Saviour* in English, edited from this manuscript by

H. S. Waltzer, *An Edition of the Middle-English Translation of the Regula Sancti Salvatoris, Cambridge University Library MS. Ff. vi. 33* (Yale Univ., Ph.D. Diss., 1950). A reproduction of folios 38v–67r of the manuscript may be found in J. Hogg, *The Rewyll of Seynt Sauioure and Other Middle English Brigittine Legislative Texts, Vol. 2: The MSS. Cambridge University Library Ff. 6. 33 and St. John's College Cambridge 11* (*Salzburger Studien zur Anglistik und Amerikanistik*, Bd. 6; Salzburg, 1978), pp. 1–58. **g** (fol. 67v) *The Five Wiles of King Pharaoh* (Jolliffe K.7 [a]). **h** (fol. 88) The Augustinian Rule/*Regula ad servos Dei* (*CPL* 1839b) in the Syon redaction. **i** (fol. 98v) *A Little Short Treatise of the Direction of a Man's Life* (Jolliffe K.4). **j** (fol. 114) A message from Christ to the pope confirming the Rule of St Bridget. This is a brief extract from St Bridget's *Revelations*, IV, 137. **k** (fol. 115) *A Ladder of Four Rungs* (a translation of the *Scala paradisi* of Guigo II of La Chartreuse) (L/B/E 76; Jolliffe M.1 = O.2). **l** (fol. 138) *An Epistle of St Machary* (Jolliffe H.12 [a] = O.22 [a]). This is an English translation of the Latin translation of the first letter attributed to Macarius the Great: see A. Wilmart, 'La lettre spirituelle de l'abbé Macaire', *Revue d'ascétique et de mystique* 1 (1920), pp. 58–83 (with an edition of the Latin text).

This manuscript is in the hand of William Darker, who also copied **A.19** and **A.29**. According to Phyllis Hodgson, *Deonise Hid Diuinite* (EETS/OS, 231; London, 1955), p. xiv, n. §, 'from its contents, this [manuscript] may well have been transcribed for the Bridgettine nuns of Syon.' Hogg, likewise, suggests that it probably 'formed part of the nuns' library' (Hogg, *Rewyll of Seynt Sauioure*, p. iii). I agree with both Hodgson and Hogg, but we cannot be certain that this was the case. De Hamel, p. 120, rightly lists it as belonging to either the men's or the women's library.

4 Cambridge, U.L., Rit. c.351.1 (printed book)

Primer of Sarum Use (*Horae beatae Mariae Virginis ad Usum Sarum pro pueris*), together with a Calendar, printed by Francis Byrckman, Paris, 1514 (*STC* 15918; Hoskins, p. 16 no. 45). An additional quire in the volume contains the 'vij anniversaries to be kept in this monastery of Syon' (cf. **A.23**). *Pace* Ker, p. 185, the Primer is in Latin, not English. It is also misbound and lacks many leaves.

There is no doubt that the manuscript was at Syon, but although a Primer was more likely to be found in the keeping of one of the sisters, this cannot be regarded as certain.

5 Cambridge, Emmanuel Coll., 32.6.49 (printed book)

This volume comprises four separate printed books: **a** Henry VIII, *Libello Huic Regio Haec Insunt. Oratio Joannis Clerk apud Ro. pon. in exhibitione operis regij. Responsio roman. pont. [Leo X]. Bulla ro. pon. ad regiam maiestatem. Responsio eius operis confirmatione. Summa indulgentiarum . . . concessarum. Libellus regius aduersus Martinum Lutherum haeresiarchon. Epistola regia ad illustrissimos Saxoniae duces pie admonitoria,* printed by Richard Pynson, London, 1521 (*STC* 13083). **b** Alphonsus de Villa Sancta, *Problema indulgentiarum, quo Lutheri errata dissoluuntur,* printed by Richard Pynson, London, 1523 (*STC* 24729). **c** Alphonsus de Villa Sancta, *De libero arbitrio adversus Melanchtonem,* printed by Richard Pynson, London, 1523 (*STC* 24728). **d** *Sermones Amici,* printed by Nicholas Kessler, Basel, 1501 (H. M. Adams, *Catalogue of Books Printed on the Continent of Europe, 1501–1600, in Cambridge Libraries* [Cambridge, 1967], vol. 2, p. 205 [S 983]). I am informed by F. H. Stubbings, Honorary Keeper of Rare Books at Emmanuel College, that this last item 'seems to be a sort of commonplace book, alphabetically arranged, on topics of theological interest.' *Amicus* is not the name of the author (who is unknown), but the catchword of the opening entry. I am greatly indebted to Mr Stubbings for providing me with a description of this volume.

The Syon provenance of this book is indicated by a distinctive tab which projects from the beginning of item **d** and which is intended to assist the reader in finding his or her way through the volume. These tabs are described in detail in de Hamel, pp. 103–6 (with illustration). European Latin theological literature of this nature seems to have appealed more to the brothers at Syon than to the sisters, and I suspect that the volume formed part of the brothers' library (though it does not appear in the catalogue). This, however, cannot be regarded as certain.

6 Cambridge, St John's Coll., 11 (de Hamel, no. 24) s.xv[2]

A collection of Bridgettine legislative texts in Latin containing **a** (fol. 1) *Regula sancti Salvatoris.* **b** (fol. 17) *Regula sancti Augustini / Regula ad servos Dei* (*CPL* 1839b). **c** (fol. 25) Form of profession for entering the Bridgettine Order (in Latin and English). **d** (fol. 43) *Quod episcopus diocesanus sit uisitator huius religionis* (= Chapter 23 of the *Regula S. Salvatoris*). **e** (fol. 43v) *Qualiter visitabit episcopus.* **f** (fol. 51) *Ordo* for the consecration of an abbess (in Latin and English). **g** (fol. 59v) *Ordo* for the promotion of a brother (added in a cursive hand). A reduced facsimile of the entire manuscript has been published by James Hogg in *The Rewyll of Seynt Sauioure and Other Middle English Brigittine Legislative Texts, Vol. 2: The MSS. Cambridge University Library Ff. 6. 33 and St. John's College Cambridge 11* (*Salzburger Studien zur Anglistik und Amerikanistik*, Bd. 6; Salzburg, 1978), pp. 59–176. For a description of the manuscript, see *ibid.*, pp. viii–x.

The manuscript is obviously Bridgettine, but there is no clear indication in which library it belonged.

7 ?Edinburgh, U.L., 59 (de Hamel, no. 1) s.xv

Psalter (imperfect), preceded by a Calendar and followed by Canticles and the Athanasian Creed. There is no Litany.

The Calendar rubricates two feasts of St Bridget and the volume is probably from Syon. There is no indication as to whether it belonged to a sister or a brother, though a sister may be more likely (see de Hamel, pp. 111–2).

8 ?London, B.L., Add. 30514 (de Hamel, no. 76) s.xv

Hours of the Virgin, preceded by a Calendar (with Bridgettine entries) and followed (fol. 67) by commemorations of St Bridget and other saints, an *ordo* for visiting the sick, an *officium ad deferendum corpus exanime ad ecclesiam*, the Penitential Psalms, a Litany, the Office of the Dead, and *Commendatio animarum*.

There is little doubt that the volume was written for Syon, but there is no indication as to whether it belonged to a brother or a sister. I agree with Dr de Hamel that the latter is perhaps more likely.

9 London, Private Collection (de Hamel, no. 75) s.xv^ex

A collection of prayers and offices including prayers to the Virgin, requiem offices and commemorations of the dead, the Fifteen Oes of St Bridget, abbreviated offices for the days of the week, abbreviated Hours of the Cross, and a collection of prayers similar to those noted in **A.23** above (including the

Litany and the 'vij obites'), ending with a prayer 'in tyme of discipline'. As with the Cotton manuscript, the rubrics are in English. Of the female saints mentioned in the Litany, only St Anne is placed higher than St Bridget (see fol. 32).

That the volume comes from Syon is obvious, and it is probable, though not certain, that it was the property of one of the sisters.

10 London, Private Collection (de Hamel, no. 72) s.xv

A Book of Hours of Sarum Use, but the original Calendar and Litany have been removed and replaced by a Bridgettine Calendar (containing the *obit* of Thomas Fishbourne) and Bridgettine Litany.

There is no inscription of ownership in this little volume and no clear indication as to whether it belonged to a sister or a brother. I agree with Dr de Hamel that the book probably belonged to one of the sisters, but that cannot be regarded as certain.

11 Manchester, Chetham's Lib., 27907 (Mun.A.3.129) (de Hamel, no. 60) s.xv[2]

A Hymnal (with music), containing *temporale* (followed by two and a half folios of hymns *in dedicatione ecclesiae*), *sanctorale*, and Common of the Saints. The volume contains hymns for the canonization and commemoration of St Bridget (fols. 84–86v, 88v).

The manuscript is English and, apparently, Bridgettine. Ker/*MMBL*, vol. 3, p. 377, suggests that it was 'for the use, presumably, of the brothers of Syon', but we cannot be certain that it belonged to the brothers.

12 Oxford, Brasenose Coll., 16 (de Hamel, no. 43) s.xv

Psalter (with a prologue *inc.* 'Prophecie spiritus') followed by Canticles, Athanasian Creed, the Office of the Dead, Litanies, and various prayers. Appended to the end of the manuscript at fol. 240 is a Calendar which has been taken from some other later manuscript, possibly Franciscan (see Pfaff, *New Liturgical Feasts* [see **B.2**], pp. 127–8, n. 1).

The Psalter is certainly from Syon, but there is no indication as to whether it belonged to the sisters or the brothers (see Pfaff, pp. 127–8).

C) *Books belonging to the Brothers*

The following manuscripts appear to have been in the library or in the keeping of the brothers of Syon and have therefore been excluded from the above lists. Further information will be found in Ker and Watson.

1) *Evidence from the Library Catalogue*

The following manuscripts have been identified in the catalogue of Syon (edited by Mary Bateson, *Catalogue of the Library of Syon Monastery Isleworth* [Cambridge, 1898]), and must therefore have belonged to the brothers:

Cambridge, U.L., Hh.6.8 (de Hamel, no. 58); Cambridge, St John's Coll., 131 (de Hamel, no. 28) and 219 (de Hamel, no. 50); Cambridge, Trinity Coll., 339 (de Hamel, no. 6); Glasgow, U.L., Hunterian 332 (de Hamel, no. 15) and 509; Karlsruhe, Badische Landesbibl., Skt Georgen in Villingen 12 (de Hamel, no. 36); Lincoln, Cathedral, 60 (de Hamel, no. 41) and 244 (de Hamel, no. 23); London, B.L., Add. 5208 (de Hamel, no. 7) and 40006 (de Hamel, no. 2); London, B.L., Harley 42 (de Hamel, no. 16), 612 (de Hamel, no. 38), 632 (de Hamel, no. 3), and 1298 (de Hamel, no. 19); London, Dutch Church (pr. bk.); London, Sion Coll., A.51.2.Aq.5Be (pr. bk.); Oxford, Bod. Lib., Auct. D.3.1 (de Hamel, no. 10); Oxford, Bod. Lib., Barlow 49 (de Hamel, no. 26); Oxford, Bod. Lib., Bodl. 212 (de Hamel, no. 9) and 630 (de Hamel, no. 8); Oxford, Bod. Lib., Lat.th. f.20 (de Hamel, no. 69); Oxford, Brasenose Coll., 15 (de Hamel, no. 42); Oxford, Corpus Christi Coll., 245 (de Hamel, no. 26); Oxford, St John's Coll., A.9.5–7 (pr. bks.); Oxford, Trinity Coll., 53 (de Hamel, no. 5); San Marino, Huntington Lib., HM 35300 (formerly Bury St Edmunds, Cathedral 1) (de Hamel, no. 21); St Peter Port, Guernsey, Mr J. S. Cox (de Hamel, no. 61); Worcester, Cathedral, Sel. B.50.3 (pr. bk.).

2) *Evidence from Inscriptions*

The following manuscripts bear inscriptions indicating that they were in the keeping of particular brothers, written for particular brothers, or intended specifically for the brothers' library. They do not, however, appear in the catalogue or have not yet been identified:

Cambridge, U.L., Add. 4081 (binding and endleaf only); Cambridge, St John's Coll., 109 (de Hamel, no. 27); Cambridge, Trinity Coll., 792 (de Hamel, no. 47) and 1336; Durham, Mr A. I. Doyle (pr. bks. [Pelbartus and B. Senensis]); Ipswich, Central Lib. (pr. bk.); London, B.L., Royal 13 D.viii (see de Hamel, p. 147, n. 7); London, Lambeth Palace, 1486.4 (pr. bk.); Manchester, John Rylands Lib., Eng. 81 (de Hamel, no. 40); Oxford, Bod. Lib., Rawlinson D.403 (de Hamel, no. 54); Oxford, Bodl. Lib., Douce N.300 (pr. bk.); Oxford, Bod. Lib., 8° A.11 Th. (pr. bk.); Oxford, Merton Coll., 76.b.11 and 77.a.20 (both pr. bks.); Stonor Park, Hon. S. Stonor (pr. bk.); Uppsala, U.L., C.159; Xanten, Stiftsbibl., 3970B [Inc.] 241 (pr. bk.).

3) *Evidence from Grammar*

In the following cases, the manuscripts contain prayers in masculine form:

Oxford, Bod. Lib., Bodl. 62 (S.C. 2028) (de Hamel, no. 22) (According to de Hamel, p. 77, this is 'a routine [but nice] London Book of Hours of about 1390 which came into the possession of someone at Syon a hundred years later when additions were made with prayers in the masculine form.' At a later date it was given to the Franciscans of Exeter [see notes to S.C. 2028]); Syon Abbey (South Brent), 4 (de Hamel, no. 77) (prayers in the masculine form occur on p. 111, and I agree with James Hogg that the manuscript was used by one of the Syon priests [J. Hogg, 'The Syon MS. 4', *Analecta Cartusiana* 35:12 [*Spiritualität Heute und Gestern*, Bd. 12] [Salzburg, 1991], p. 49).

4) *Evidence from Content*

The contents of the following manuscripts clearly indicate their place in the brothers' library:

London, B.L., Add. 22285 (de Hamel, no. 66) (the Syon *Martyrology*: see further the introduction to this list of Syon books); London, B.L., Royal 2 A.xiv (de Hamel, no. 18) (see Collins, pp.

l–li, for the evidence that it belonged to the brothers); London, St Paul's Cathedral 5 (de Hamel, no. 17) (the *Additions* for the brothers).

D) *Untraced Books*

The following three manuscripts were sold either by book-sellers or at auction, but their present locations are unknown. **D.1** was certainly made for one of the sisters; **D.2** might possibly have belonged to Catherine Wey or Christina Wayte (but I doubt it); the description of **D.3** provides us with no clue whatever as to the sex of its owner.

1 London, Messrs Maggs, 1935 (de Hamel, no. 67).

A c. 1500 English manuscript (166 folios) described in the catalogue as 'Psalterium Latinum, with Calendar of Brigittine Use . . . The decorations consist of seven full borders contain-ing realistic flowers, insects, and a kneeling Brigittine nun, on coloured backgrounds.' The nun is 'wearing the dress peculiar to the Brigittine Order, and each time appears with a scroll containing the words *Ignare me laudare te virgo sacrata da michi.*' I am indebted to Dr de Hamel for providing me with a copy of Maggs' description of this manuscript. Watson's identification of the volume with **A.4** above is incorrect (see *in loc.*).

The volume was obviously intended for one of the Syon sisters.

2 Sotheby's Sale (Ashburnham Appendix LIV), 1 May 1899, lot 17 (de Hamel, no. 59).

A s.xv English manuscript (107 folios) containing the Office of the Holy Trinity, Hours of the Holy Spirit, 'the seruyce of eternall sapience' (cf. **A.46**), a hymn to St Bridget, and a collection of Latin prayers with English rubrics. There does not appear to have been a Calendar.

(fol. 16) *Of your charite pray for the writer of this seruyce C.W.* C.W. might possibly refer to Catherine Wey or Christina Wayte, both of whom were nuns of Syon in the early sixteenth century (Wey died in 1509 and Wayte in 1516), but I think it more likely that they are the initials of an unknown male scribe. I agree with Dr de Hamel that the volume must be listed under 'men's or women's liturgical use' (de Hamel, no. 59).

3 Sotheby's Sale (J. Meade Falkner), 12–14 December 1932, lot
413 (de Hamel, no. 4).

A s.xv English manuscript (120 folios) containing a Psalter
preceded by a Bridgettine Calendar and followed by Canticles.
The auction catalogue does not mention a Litany.

It is impossible to tell whether this volume belonged to the
sisters or the brothers.

Miscellaneous Records

a In commemorating the founders of Syon and their benefactions to the house, the *Martyrology* fol. 14v records a gift of
rings and books made by John, Duke of Bedford, to the sisters of
Syon, as follows: 'Anno Domini 1426, in die sancte Agathe virginis [5 February] . . . Dux iste [*viz*. Johannes dux Bethfordie, frater
fundatoris nostri] dedit omnibus sororibus prime professionis
anulos quibus profitebantur. Dedit eciam duos pulcros libros
officii sororum et vnam legendam. Et fuit monasterio semper
fauorabilis et benignus. Obiit a<nn>o domini [blank].' John of
Lancaster, the third son of Henry IV, was born in 1389, created
Duke of Bedford in 1414, and died without legitimate issue in
1435. For the strong probability that some fragments of one of
these office books have survived, see the discussion at **A.5**.

b In her will dated 1 April 1495 (probated 27 August 1495),
Cecily, Duchess of York, bequeathed to her 'doughter Anne,
priores of Sion, **1** a boke of Bonaventure and **2** Hilton in the same
in Englishe, and **3** a boke of the Revelacions of Saint Burgitte'
(*Wills from Doctors' Commons: A Selection From the Wills of Eminent
Persons Proved in the Prerogative Court of Canterbury 1495–1695*, ed.
J. G. Nichols & J. Bruce [Camden Society, O.S., 83; London, 1863;
rpt. New York, 1968], p. 3; N. H. Nicholas, *Testamenta Vetusta,
being Illustrations from Wills . . .* [London, 1826], vol. 2, pp. 422–
3). Anne de la Pole was Cecily's granddaughter and the seventh
prioress of Syon (see **A.45** above).

1 The 'boke of Bonaventure' is without question Nicholas
Love's *Mirror of the Blessed Life of Christ*, a translation of the
Meditationes vitae Christi commonly but incorrectly attributed
to Bonaventure (L/B/E 553). **2** 'Hilton', therefore, probably
refers to Walter Hilton's *Mixed Life (Vita mixta)* (L/B/E 147),
a treatise which Love obviously admired and which he rec-
ommends in the *Mirror*. **3** For an edition of a Middle English

translation of the *Revelations of Saint Bridget*, see W. P. Cummings, *The Revelations of Saint Birgitta* (EETS/OS, 178; London, 1929). On pp. xi–xxii Cummings describes seven fifteenth-century manuscripts, of which two contain relatively complete translations. The first printed edition (an anthology) was published by Caxton in 1491.

c The *Martyrology* fol. 71v notes that in 1487 'Dominus Willelmus Hemmynge' gave to Syon a Missal valued at ten marks (£6.13.4), but it is not clear whether it was intended for the sisters or for the brothers.

TARRANT KEYNSTON (Dorset), *Abbey of BVM* (Cistercian Nuns).

1 Dublin, Trinity Coll., 209 (B.5.1) s.xiv

a (fol. 1) *Le livre de Sydrac/Sidrach* (Bossuat 2929–32). **b** (fol. 108) Peter d'Abernon of Peckham, *La lumière as lais* (Bossuat 3585–89, 6657). The manuscript is briefly described in M. Esposito, 'Inventaire des anciens manuscrits français des bibliothèques de Dublin', *Revue des bibliothèques* 24 (1914), pp. 188–9.

(fol. 2 [c. 1400]) *Iste liber constat domine Johanne Kyngeston, abbatisse de Tarent'*. Joan Kingston is probably the Joan who is recorded as abbess of Tarrant in 1402 (VCH *Dorset*, vol. 2, p. 90).

2 Oxford, Bod. Lib., Lyell 23 s.xv

Psalter, preceded by the Office of the Holy Spirit (not the more common Hours of the Holy Spirit) and a Cistercian Calendar with a paschal table and followed by Canticles and the Athanasian Creed. The manuscript originally contained a Litany, but only the collects remain. Certain material has been added at the end, including the Fifteen Oes of St Bridget (fols. 188v–196), a *passio* of St Margaret (fols. 200–213v [a slightly variant version of *BHL* 5305]), and a short Litany for peace.

The association with Tarrant appears from certain *obits* in the Calendar: see A. de la Mare, *Catalogue of the Collection of Medieval Manuscripts Bequeathed to the Bodleian Library Oxford by James P. R. Lyell* (Oxford, 1971), pp. 49–52.

3 Stockholm, Nat. Mus., NMB 2010 (formerly Redlynch, Major J. R. Abbey) s.xiii

Psalter (beginning imperfectly at Ps 2:4), preceded by a Calendar and followed by Canticles, Athanasian Creed, a

Litany, and various collects. The Psalter is decorated with numerous splendid miniatures and is described in Morgan no. 68. Morgan also provides a bibliography of studies on the manuscript up to 1979.

(flyleaf i [s.xiv²]) *Istud psalterium constat Edithe Corf, priorisse; post decessum predicte Edithe reuertatur ad officium cantarie de Tarent'*. In the Calendar (29 May) we find the *obit* of John Corf who is mentioned in various papal and other registers from 1346 to 1382. Edith Corf was prioress of Tarrant sometime in the second half of the fourteenth century, but her precise dates are unknown.

4 Stonyhurst Coll., 9 (HMC 12), fols. 1–3 s.xiii²

Three folios of a Calendar. That these originally preceded a Psalter is clear from the inscription of donation, but the s.xv Psalter at present bound in the manuscript was not the original one. The manuscript is no. 632 in Frere.

(fol. 1 [s.xiii²]) *Hoc est psalterium beate Marie super Tharente de dono domine Leticie de Kaynes. Quicumque istud abstulerit siue defraudare studuerit, anathema sit.* Tarrant Keynston or Kaines was founded by the Kaines (or Kahaynes) family, of which Leticia was a member (VCH *Dorset*, vol. 2, pp. 87–8). Her *obit*, in the same hand as the inscription, appears in the Calendar at 16 January: *Obitus Domine Leticie de Kaynes.*

THETFORD (Norfolk), *Priory of St George* (Benedictine Nuns).

1 ?Alnwick Castle, Duke of Northumberland, 449 s.xiv

Wycliffite translation of the New Testament in the revision traditionally ascribed to John Purvey (L/B/E 119), preceded by a table for finding 'the pistles and gospels that ben rad in the churche after the use of Salisburie.' I regret that I have not been able to obtain a detailed description of this manuscript.

On the inside of the front cover (s.xv/xvi) is the name of *Katherina Methwold, monaca.* A nun of this name is recorded at Thetford in episcopal visitations of 12 November 1492 and 22 June 1514, by which time she was sub-prioress (*Visitations of the Diocese of Norwich, A.D. 1492–1532* [see CAMPSEY 2], pp. 33, 91).

Miscellaneous Records

Margaret Purdans, who bequeathed a copy of the *Doctrine of the Heart* to Bruisyard in 1481 (see BRUISYARD MR 2a) also left 'to the Nunnery of Thetford, an English book of St Bridget' (Harrod, 'Extracts' [see BRUISYARD *MR* 2a], p. 336).

The reference is probably to one of the Middle English translations of or selections from the *Revelations* of St Bridget: see SYON *MR* b.3.

WHERWELL (Hampshire), *Abbey of Holy Cross* (Benedictine Nuns).

1 Cambridge, Fitzwilliam Mus., McClean 45 s.xiii–xiv

Psalter, preceded by a Sarum Calendar (with a few entries in French) and Hours of the Virgin (Sarum Use) and followed by Canticles and a brief Litany.

Wherwell is mentioned in a s.xv inscription on fol. 16v and in an *obit* for 14 March: *Obiit Matild<a> de Littelton, bone memorie, abbatissa de Wherewell.* Matilda or Maud de Littleton was abbess of Wherwell from 1333 to 1340 (VCH *Hampshire and the Isle of Wight* vol. 2, pp. 134–5, 137). There is also a s.xv inscription on the front fly-leaf which reads *Thys is Symon Choppares boke off Oddyam and he that ffyndyd dessyrryng that he will restor yt agayne and he shall haue for the ffynding [excised].* Since the Calendar does not distinguish feasts which were of specific importance to Wherwell, it seems probable that the volume came to the abbey after it had been owned by Simon Choppar.

2 Cambridge, St John's Coll., 68 s.xii

Psalter, preceded by a Calendar and followed by Canticles, a Litany, prayers to the Trinity, the Virgin, saints, one's guardian angel and other angels, Hours of the Virgin (Sarum Use), and the Office of the Dead.

The Psalter was probably written for the abbey of Saint Bertin at Saint Omer and then given by Margaret de Walliers to her daughter Euphemia, abbess of Wherwell from 1226 to 1257. Margaret's *obit* appears in the Calendar at 24 November: *Ob<iit> Margareta de Walliers ma<ter> Eufemie abbatisse.* Euphemia's considerable benefactions to the abbey are recorded in the chartulary of Wherwell (Davis no. 1031) and an English version of the relevant section may be found in VCH *Hampshire and the Isle of Wight*, vol. 2, pp. 132–3.

3 St Petersburg (Leningrad), Publ. Lib., Q.v.I, 62 s.xii

Calendar (twelve folios), followed by verses on the death of Matilda, abbess of Wherwell, and an *epistola consolatoria* by E., prioress of Wherwell. Both the verses and the letter are printed in A. Staerk, *Les manuscrits latins du V*e *au XIII*e *siècle conservés à la Bibliothèque Impériale de Saint-Pétersbourg* (St Petersburg, 1910; rpt. Hildesheim/New York, 1976), vol. 1, p. 275 (MS 112).

The Matilda/Maud mentioned here is not Maud de Littleton (as at no. 1 above), but the long-lived and much loved Maud who was elected abbess of Wherwell in about 1186 and governed the abbey for forty years until her death in 1226 at the age of eighty. She was succeeded by Euphemia, mentioned at no. 2 above, who was undoubtedly the author of the *epistola consolatoria* (VCH *Hampshire and the Isle of Wight*, vol. 2, pp. 132, 137).

4 London, B.L., Add. 27866 s.xiv^{in}

Psalter (with music), preceded by a Calendar and followed by Canticles (with music), Athanasian Creed, a Litany, and the Office of the Dead (with music).

(fol. 131v [s.xv]) *Iste liber constat domine Johanna (sic) Stretford, monasterii Werwellensis sancti cruce (sic)*. Joan Stretford's name is written over the erasure of another name, but nothing is known of her. The original inscription is probably s.xv; Johanna Stretford was obviously added later, but how much later is uncertain.

WILTON (Wiltshire), *Abbey of BVM and St Edith* (Benedictine Nuns).

1 ?London, B.L., Cotton Faustina B.iii, fols. 199–280 s.xv^{in}

a (fol. 199) The Life of St Edith (Brown/Robbins 243), followed by a list of the founders of Wilton priory beginning with Egbert and ending with Henry V. C. Horstmann, *S. Editha sive Chronicon Vilodunense* (Heilbronn, 1883), presents editions of both the Life of St Edith and the appended list. **b** (fol. 265) The Life of St Etheldreda of Ely (Brown/Robbins 3090).

The association of the volume with Wilton is obvious. On fol. 280^v of this manuscript is a brief booklist which *may* be a list of books belonging to the abbey. This cannot, however, be regarded as certain, and for a transcript and discussion the reader must be referred to *English Benedictine Libraries: The Shorter Catalogues*, ed. R. Sharpe *et al.* (*Corpus of British Medieval Library Catalogues*, 4; London, 1995), item B.111.

2 London, Royal Coll. of Physicians, 409 s.xiii

This is the 'Wilton Psalter', of which a full description is provided by E. G. Millar, *Bulletin de la société française de reproductions de manuscrits à peintures* 4 (1914–20), pp. 128–49. The Psalter is preceded by a Calendar and followed by Canticles, Litanies, *Commendatio animarum*, the Office of the Dead, antiphons, and various prayers. On fly-leaf v[rv] there has been added (in a s.xiv English hand) a French commentary on the *Pater noster*. A reproduction of fol. 207 of the Psalter may be found in VCR *Wiltshire*, vol. 2, the plate facing p. 234.

The Litany includes prayers for the abbess of Wilton, and in two prayers which follow the Litany (fol. 206) there is reference to the *congregatio sancte Marie sancteque Edithe*. In 1523 the Psalter was alienated from Wilton and given to a nun of Romsey (see ROMSEY 2).

3 Oxford, Bod. Lib., Rawl. G.23 s.xiii/xiv

Psalter (Dominican), preceded by a Calendar and followed by Canticles, Apostles' Creed, Athanasian Creed, two Litanies, and (fol. 164) Hours of the Virgin.

The second Litany (fol. 171) is a later addition and was composed for a women's house dedicated to St Mary and St Edith, *viz.*, Wilton.

Untraced Books

4 Ker, p. 198, reports an untraced fourteenth-century Processional from Wilton of which a nineteenth-century transcript is now at Solesmes.

WINCHESTER (Hampshire), *Abbey of BVM* (Nunnaminster) (Benedictine Nuns).

1 Cambridge, U.L., Mm.3.13 s.xvi[in]

Ordo (in English) for the consecration of nuns, printed from this manuscript (with numerous inaccuracies) by Maskell, *Monumenta Ritualia Ecclesiae Anglicanae* (see SYON A.29), vol. 3, pp. 331–59. The manuscript is no. 851 in Frere.

(fol. 2 [s.xvi[1]]) *Hic liber attinet ad monasterium monialium sancte Marie in ciuitate Winton' ex dono reuerendi in Christo patris domini Ricardi Fox, eiusdem ciuitatis episcopi et dicti monasterii benefactoris precipui.* Richard Fox was bishop of Winchester from 1501 to 1528 (see STAMFORD 1).

2 ?London, B.L., Cotton Nero A.ii, fols. 3–13 + Cotton Galba
A.xiv s.xi[in]

A book of private devotions, written in a number of hands,
containing a large variety of prayers and collects, the Penitential Psalms, two Litanies (the second is very long), a form
of confession, a form of cursing, various hymns (with music),
and so on. Nero A.ii fols. 3–13 contains a Calendar with tables
followed by other hymns. The Galba manuscript was badly
damaged in the Cotton fire of 1731, but is still, for the most
part, legible. Some of the material in this volume is in Anglo-
Saxon and a description of this, together with an account of
the manuscript, may be found in Ker/*AS*, pp. 198–201 no. 157.
Ker also notes which Latin texts have been edited (p. 200). A
charming description of the Galba manuscript by Edmund
Bishop may be found in his *Liturgica Historica: Papers on the
Liturgy and Religious Life of the Western Church* (Oxford, 1918;
rpt. 1962), pp. 384–91 (first published in the *Downside Review*
for March, 1907). According to Bishop, the manuscript dates
from shortly after 1016 (p. 389).

The appearance of liturgical material relating to St
Machutus and St Swithun suggests that the volume came from
Winchester, and since there are extensive eleventh-century
additions for the use of a female member of a religious house,
Nunnaminster seems most probable.

3 London, B.L., Harley 2965 s.ix

This is a well-known volume of prayers, hymns, and devotional material, written in Latin and Anglo-Saxon, and usually
referred to as the Book of Nunnaminster. It opens with the
accounts of the Passion in Mark, Luke, and John. Included
among the prayers are *orationes* attributed to Gregory the
Great (*PL* 101: 1400–01) and Augustine, a series of forty-three
prayers loosely arranged in the order of the life of Christ (see
W. de Gray Birch, *An Ancient Manuscript of the Eighth or Ninth
Century Formerly Belonging to St Mary's Abbey or Nunnaminster,
Winchester* [Hampshire Record Society; London/Winchester,
1889], pp. 24–5 for a list), and the well-known *Lorica* of Logden
(Laidcenn Mac Baith) (see Birch, pp. 27–8, 120–8 [Appendix
C], and M. Lapidge & R. Sharpe, *A Bibliography of Celtic-Latin
Literature 400–1200* [Dublin, 1985], pp. 80–81 no. 294). Birch's
volume contains a complete edition of the text.

According to Ker/*AS*, pp. 308–9 no. 237, this manuscript probably belonged to Ealhswith, the wife of Alfred the Great, who gave it to the nunnery she founded at Winchester. See also Birch, p. 15. The boundaries of Nunnaminster are recorded on fol. 40v in a passage printed in Birch, p. 46, and reproduced in facsimile in M. B. Parkes, 'A Fragment of an Early-Tenth-Century Anglo-Saxon Manuscript and its Significance', in *idem, Scribes, Scripts and Readers* (London/Rio Grande, 1991) pl. 30b (this study was originally published in *Anglo-Saxon England* 12 [1983], pp. 129–40). For the date of s.ix rather than Ker's s.viii, see J. J. Morrish, *An Examination of Literacy and Learning in England in the Ninth Century* (Oxford University, D. Phil. Diss., 1982), pp. 292–17.

4 ?Oxford, Bod. Lib., Bodl. 451 (S.C. 2401) s.xii^in

a (fol. ii^v) Smaragdus of Saint-Mihiel, *Diadema monachorum* (Bloomfield 2456). **b** (fol. 72) An unprinted anonymous moral tractate in 36 chapters, beginning with *De superbia et fornicatione* (Bloomfield 1452). The chapters are listed on fol. 72. **c** (fol. 95) Fourteen *ps.*-Augustinian sermons as follows: *Sermones (app.)* 75 (*PL* 39: 1889–91), 77 (1895–7), 225 (2160–62), 229 (2166–8), 265 (2237–40), 277–278 (2266–71), 292–295 (2297–2310), Paul the Deacon, *Homilia* 62 (*PL* 95: 1208–10), and two sermons not included in the *PL* collection.

On fol. ii^r is a note in Latin (fifteen lines), written in 1150, referring to *sancta Edburga, sponsa Ihesu Christi*, who was buried at Winchester. At the end of the manuscript the (female) scribe has written: *Salua et incolomis maneat per secula scriptrix*.

5 Romsey, Parish Church s.xv^in

Psalter, preceded by a Calendar and followed by a complete set of Canticles, Athanasian Creed, and a Litany. A full description is provided by F. W. H. Davy in H. G. Liveing, *Records of Romsey Abbey* (Winchester, 1906), pp. 285–302 (with facsimile of fols. 106v–107).

The volume was originally written for Franciscan use in the vicinity of Romsey, but a number of added *obits* indicate that by the beginning of the sixteenth century it was in the possession of the Benedictine nuns at Winchester. For details, see Ker/*MMBL*, vol. 4, pp. 218–9.

WINTNEY (Hampshire), *Priory of BVM* (Cistercian Nuns).

1 London, B.L., Cotton Claudius D.iii s.xiii

a (fol. 3) A fragment of a Latin martyrology. **b** (fol. 3v) Simon of Waverley, Verses (24 lines), edited by Paul Meyer, 'La requête de frère Simon', *Jahrbuch für romanische und englische Literatur* 7 (1866), pp. 45–7. Further on Simon, see J. C. Russell, *Dictionary of Writers of Thirteenth Century England* (New York, 1936; rpt. New York, 1971), p. 156. According to Meyer, p. 46, Simon was 'peu familier' with French! **c** (fol. 3v) A brief inventory, dated 16 October 1420, of the refectory at Wintney. This was a result of the death of Dame Alice Preston, who was in charge of the *frater*. An English translation of the inventory may be found in VCH *Hampshire and the Isle of Wight*, vol. 2, pp. 150–51. The inventory is followed by another fragment of the martyrology. **d** (fol. 6) Bede, *Martyrologium* (*CPL* 2032), preceded (fol. 5) by instructions (in French) on how to use it. **e** (fol. 52) The Wintney version of the *Rule of St Benedict* in Latin and English, edited from this manuscript by A. Schröer, *Der Winteney-Version der Regula S. Benedicti* (Halle, 1888; rev. edn. by M. Gretsch, Tübingen, 1978), pp. 1–147. **f** (fol. 140v) The Wintney Obituary Calendar (s.xiii, with additions to s.xv), printed (with numerous inaccuracies) by Thomas Hearne in *Johannis de Trokelowe Annales Edwardi II*, ed. T. Hearne (Oxford, 1729), pp. 384–93. The Obituary commemorates a number of bishops, abbots, and priors, and eleven prioresses of Wintney. Ker/*AS* omitted this manuscript in error, but provides a brief description on p. xix, n. 2.

APPENDIX:
CARTULARIES AND
RELATED DOCUMENTS

Despite the fact that Neil Ker included only one cartulary from a nunnery (Godstow) in his list of surviving manuscripts from British medieval libraries, there can be little doubt that most of the others would have belonged to their respective houses. The following list is extracted from G. R. C. Davis, *Medieval Cartularies of Great Britain* (London, 1958), and further information, together with references to editions (now sometimes out of date) will be found therein. Thirty-five houses are recorded, but I have not included the Gilbertines.

It may be noted that of the documents listed, three are entirely or partly in English (Bruisyard, Crabhouse, and Godstow), two partly in French (Canonsleigh and Crabhouse), and all the rest in Latin. Sixteen of the documents are either untraced or destroyed.

ACONBURY (Augustinian): Davis nos. 9–10. Davis no. 9 is a s.xiii^{ex} cartulary in Latin; Davis no. 10 is a s.xiii roll of charters in Latin.

ANKERWYKE (Benedictine): Davis no. 13. An untraced fragment of a cartulary.

BLACKBOROUGH (Benedictine): Davis no. 57. A s.xiv^{ex} general cartulary in Latin.

BRUISYARD (Franciscan): Davis no. 82. An untraced cartulary in English.

BUCKLAND MINCHIN (Order of St John of Jerusalem): Davis no. 87. A s.xv general cartulary in Latin.

CAMPSEY (Augustinian): Davis no. 156. A register of s.xvi copies of documents relating to the establishment of a chantry at Campsey in 1390.

CANONSLEIGH (Augustinian): Davis no. 158. A s.xiv general cartulary. The Table of Contents and the titles throughout are in French. See now V. C. M. London, *The Cartulary of*

Canonsleigh Abbey (Harleian MS 3660). A Calendar (Devon and Cornwall Record Society, N.S. 8; Torquay, 1965 [for 1962]).

CARROW (Benedictine): Davis no. 717. An untraced cartulary.

CASTLE HEDINGHAM (Benedictine): Davis no. 217. An untraced cartulary or register.

CHATTERIS (Benedictine): Davis no. 221. A s.xv general cartulary in Latin.

CLERKENWELL (probably Augustinian, but possibly Benedictine): Davis no. 263. A s.xiii general cartulary in Latin.

CRABHOUSE (Augustinian): Davis no. 284. A s.xiii–s.xv^{ex} register containing an account of the foundation of the priory (in French), a terrier and rental (in Latin), and an account of fifteenth-century building work (in English).

DAVINGTON (Benedictine): Davis no. 303. An untraced ledger-book.

DENNEY (Franciscan): Davis nos. 305–306. Davis no. 305 is an untraced transcript of court rolls from 1327 to 1630; Davis no. 306 contains proceedings relating to the appropriation of certain churches.

FLAMSTEAD (Benedictine): Davis no. 405. A brief s.xiii cartulary in Latin.

GODSTOW: see GODSTOW 2 in Part II of this study.

HARROLD (Augustinian): Davis nos. 471–472. Davis no. 471 is a s.xv abstract (in Latin) of charters together with notes of other related documents; for Davis no. 472, see HARROLD 1 in Part II of this study.

HINCHINGBROOKE (Benedictine): Davis no. 490. A destroyed register, burnt in 1830.

KINGTON ST MICHAEL (Benedictine): Davis nos. 514–515. Davis no. 514 is an untraced cartulary; for Davis no. 515, see KINGTON ST MICHAEL 1 in Part II of this study.

LACOCK (Augustinian): Davis nos. 523–524. Two general cartularies, one s.xiii and the other s.xiv^{in}, both in Latin. See now *Lacock Abbey Charters*, ed. K. H. Rogers (Wiltshire Record Society, 34; Devizes, 1979).

LEGBOURNE (Cistercian): Davis no. 547. An untraced cartulary.

LONDON, CLERKENWELL: see CLERKENWELL.

LONDON, HALIWELL (probably Augustinian, but possibly Benedictine): Davis no. 609. An untraced cartulary.

MARHAM (Cistercian): Davis no. 650. A s.xiv general cartulary with later additions, all in Latin. See now J. A. Nichols, *The History and Cartulary of the Cistercian Nuns of Marham Abbey, 1249-1536* (Ohio State University, Ph.D. Diss., 1974).

NORWICH (CARROW): see CARROW.

NUN COTHAM (Cistercian): Davis no. 726. A s.xiii–s.xiv general cartulary in Latin.

NUNEATON (Order of Fontevrault): Davis no. 727. An untraced charter-roll.

NUNKEELING (Benedictine): Davis no. 728. A s.xvi[1] general cartulary in Latin.

ROWNEY (Benedictine): Davis nos. 823A–825. Davis no. 823A is a s.xiv[in] deed-roll; Davis no. 824 refers to a box of three s.xv rolls and other documents containing copies of charters and notes on the priory's possessions; Davis no. 825 is another s.xv roll similar to the three contained in no. 824.

SHAFTESBURY (Benedictine): Davis nos. 885–888. Davis no. 885 is a s.xv[1] cartulary; Davis no. 886 is another cartulary of the same date containing material which complements that in no. 885; Davis no. 887 is an inventory of deeds compiled at the very beginning of s.xvi; Davis no. 888 is an untraced ledger-book. All are in Latin.

STAMFORD (Benedictine): Davis nos. 927–928A. Davis no. 927 is an untraced cartulary; Davis no. 928 is a s.xiii inventory of charters together with a rental, all in Latin; Davis no. 928A is an untraced collection of charters.

STIXWOULD (Cistercian): Davis no. 931. A s.xiii[ex] general cartulary in Latin.

STUDLEY (Benedictine): Davis nos. 940–941. Davis no. 940 is an untraced cartulary; Davis no. 941 is a s.xvi–xvii collection of miscellaneous material which includes a copy of a terrier of Studley.

SWAFFHAM BULBECK (Benedictine): Davis no. 941A. An untraced transcript of the 'Black Book of Swaffham'.

WESTWOOD (Order of Fontevrault, and later Benedictine): Davis no. 1024. A brief s.xiii cartulary in Latin.

WHERWELL (Benedictine): Davis no. 1031. A s.xiv[ex] general cartulary in Latin. The volume also contains (fols. 43–5) a brief history of the abbey to 1261.

WILTON (Benedictine): Davis no. 1035. A s.xiv[in] (?) cartulary containing copies of royal charters in Anglo-Saxon and Latin to 1208.

INDEX I:
INDEX OF WORKS IN ENGLISH

MR = *Miscellaneous Records*

Adam the Carthusian
[*attrib.*]
    A Little Short Treatise (a translation of *De patientia tribulationum*
        attributed to Adam the Carthusian by Bale)   Dartford 7i;
        Kington St Michael 2a
Aesop
    Fables (tr. William Caxton)   Barking (Appendix) 5
Albert the Great
[*attrib.*]
    The Sacrament of the Altar   Syon A.29
Alfonso da Vadaterra
    Prologus in sermonem angelicum de excellentia Virginis Mariae
        Syon A.8a
Aristotle
[*pseud.*]
    Secretum secretorum   Syon A.35e
Augustine of Hippo
    Rule of St Augustine   Dartford 6 (an anonymous commentary
        on the *Rule*); Syon B.3h
[*pseud.*]
    Meditatio   Dartford 71

Benedict of Nursia
    The Rule of Saint Benet (English translation by Richard Fox)
        Stamford 1; Wintney 1e (Latin and English)
Bernard of Clairvaux
    De praecepto et dispensatione   Syon A.37
Birgitta of Sweden
    Revelations   Swine MR; Syon B.3j; Syon *MR* b.3; Thetford
        MR
    Rule of Saint Saviour   Syon A.48, B.3f

Secrets of Old Philosophers (John Lydgate and Benet Burgh) (an
   English metrical paraphrase of the *ps.*-Aristotelian *Secretum
   secretorum*)   Syon A.35e
Siege of Thebes   Amesbury 2a; Syon A.35d

Macarius the Great
[*attrib.*]
   An Epistle of St Machary   Syon B.3L
Misyn, Richard → Rolle, Richard

Nassington, William [of]
   Speculum vitae   Denney 2

Peter of Blois
[*attrib.*]
   The Twelve Profits of Tribulation (a translation of the *De XII
      utilitatibus tribulationis* usually attributed to Peter of Blois,
      but possibly by Hugh of Saint-Cher)   Dartford 7j; Kington
      St Michael 2b
Prestius, Thomas → David of Augsburg
Purvey, John → Bible

Rich, Edmund
   Mirror of Holy Church (excerpts, entitled *A Devout Meditation
      of Richard Hampole*)   Shaftesbury 2h
Richard of Saint-Victor
   Benjamin Minor (an abridged, free translation)   Syon B.3a
Rolle, Richard
   Commentary on the Song of Songs → *Of the Virtue of the Holy
      Name of Jesus*
   Epistle on the Commandment of God   Shaftesbury 2g
   Form of Living   Barking 1d
   The Mending of Life (Richard Misyn's translation of the
      Emendatio vitae)   Dartford 7k
   Of the Virtue of the Holy Name of Jesus (Oleum Effusum)
      Shaftesbury 3b
   Psalter   Hampole *MR*
[*attrib.*]
   Devout Meditation → Rich, Edmund
   Pater noster   Nun Monkton *MR* d (?); Shaftesbury 2e
   Petty Job   Dartford 6b

Prayer to the Virgin   Syon A.29
Prick of Conscience   Arthington *MR*; London (Aldgate) *MR* b.4

Suso, Heinrich
   Treatise of the Seven Points of True Love and Everlasting Wisdom (an English translation of Suso's *Horologium sapientiae*) Ankerwyke 1a, Campsey 2c, Dartford 7d
   See also *Book of the Craft of Dying*

Thomas à Kempis
   Musica ecclesiastica (an anonymous English translation of Books 1-3 of Thomas's *De imitatione Christi*)   Syon A.19

Vegetius
   De re militari (the English translation by John Clifton) Syon A.35c

Whytford, Richard
   The Pipe, or Tun, of the Life of Perfection   Syon A.37

ANONYMOUS WORKS

Additions to the Rule of Saint Saviour, The   Syon A.22, A.48
Ancrene Rule   Canonsleigh 1; Syon A.20b (*The Treatise of Love* is an English translation of a French adaptation of the *Ancrene Rule*)
Arms of Christ, The   Shaftesbury 3d
Ave Maria, English commentary on   Syon B.3c

Bible
   Psalms and Canticles with Anglo-Saxon Gloss   Shaftesbury 7
   Tobit (Wycliffite translation traditionally ascribed to John Purvey)   Barking 5a
   Susanna (Wycliffite translation traditionally ascribed to John Purvey)   Barking 5e
   New Testament (Wycliffite translation traditionally ascribed to John Purvey)   Thetford 1
   Magnificat and *Nunc dimittis* (later Wycliffite versions) Barking 5b

INDEX II:
INDEX OF WORKS IN FRENCH

MR = *Miscellaneous Records*

Adso of Montier-en-Der
  La légende de l'Antéchrist   Barking 15d
Augustin Bongenou → Bongenou, Augustin
Augustine of Hippo
  Rule of St Augustine   Lacock *MR* b
[*pseud.*]
  Les contemplations saint Augustin   Barking 13d
  Les meditations saint Augustin en pensant à Dieu   Barking 13f
  Une oraison de saint Augustin à Dieu (a translation of chapter
    40 of the *ps.*-Augustinian *Meditationes*)   Barking 13e

Bernard of Clairvaux
[*pseud.*]
  Les lamentations saint Bernard   Barking 13a
  Les meditations saint Bernard (a translation of the *ps.*-
    Bernardine *Meditationes piisimae de cognitione humanae
    conditionis*)   Barking 13c
[*attrib.*]
  *Comment saint Bernart reprent et chastie ceulz qui nont compassion
    de la mort Jhesucrist*   Barking 13b
Boccaccio (tr. Pierre Faivre)
  De la ruine des nobles hommes et femmes   Syon A.31
Bongenou, Augustin
  Verses   Barking 13af
Bozon, Nicolas
  Life of St Elizabeth of Hungary   Campsey 5a
  Life of St Paul the Hermit   Campsey 5c
[*attrib.*]
  Life of St Paphnutius   Campsey 5b

Cassian, John → John Cassian

Clémence of Barking
    Life of St Catherine of Alexandria   Campsey 5m
Crestien
    The Gospel of Nichodemus (in verse)   Nuneaton 1c

Giffard, William
    Apocalypse (in verse)   Shaftesbury *MR* b
Gregory the Great
    Regula pastoralis   London (Aldgate) *MR* a.5
    Responsum S. Gregorii secundino incluso rationem de pictoris
        interroganti   Markyate 1
Grosseteste, Robert → Robert Grosseteste
Guernes de Pont-Sainte-Maxence
    Life of St Thomas of Canterbury   Campsey 5d
Guichard de Beaulieu
    Le sermon du siècle   Derby 1g
Guillaume le Clerc
    Bestiaire   Nuneaton 1d
    The Romance of St Mary Magdalen   Campsey 5e
Guillaume de Digulleville/Deguileville → INDEX I

H<enry?> of Sawtrey
    Purgatorium S. Patricii   Shaftesbury 5
Herman de Valenciennes
    L'Assomption de Notre Dame   Derby 1e
    La passion du Christ   Derby 1b
Hugh of Saint-Victor
    Soliloquium de arra animae   Barking 13y

Innocent III
    De miseria humanae conditionis   Barking 13n

John Cassian → *Vitas patrum*
John of Damascus
[*pseud.*]
    L'Histoire de Barlaam et Josaphat   Barking 15c

Laurent d'Orléans
    Somme le roi / Somme des vices et des vertus → INDEX I

Thibaut V, King of Navarre
   Letter to Eudes de Châteauroux concerning the death of Louis
      IX   Barking13w

Urban IV, Pope
   Hours of the Passion (in verse)   Hampole 1a

William the Norman → Guillaume le Clerc
William of Waddington
[*attrib.*]
   Manuel de pechiez   Malling *MR*

ANONYMOUS WORKS

Apocryphal Works → *Cura sanitatis Tiberii*; Nichodemus, Gospel
   of
L'Assomption de Notre Dame → Melito of Sardis *Ps.*
*Aucuns bons enseignemens pour eschiver les pechiez de luxure
   davaric et daccide*   Barking 13p

Bible   Derby 1 (verse paraphrase); Easebourne *MR* a.8; Flixton
   1 (with commentary); London (Aldgate) *MR* a.1
   Apocalypse (in verse)   Nuneaton 1e; Shaftesbury *MR* b (in
      verse)
   See also Psalter
Books: 'a French book'   Denney *MR*

Comment on doit Dieu amer   Barking 13g
Comment on se doit garder contre aucunes temptacions   Barking
   13q
Comment .iiij. pechiez mortales sont segnefiez per iiij bestes sauvages
   Barking 13l
Cura sanitatis Tiberii   Derby 1c

De la age Adam et comment il envoia Seth son filz en paradis terrestre
   Barking 13r
*De la demande que fist la mere saint Jehan et saint Jaque a nostre
   seigneur Jhesucrist*   Barking 13m
Decretals   London (Aldgate) *MR* a.2
Devise de la messe, La   Barking 13s

INDEX III:
INDEX OF WORKS IN LATIN

(Excluding Biblical and Liturgical Material in Latin)

MR = Miscellaneous Records

Abbo of Fleury
 Passio S. Edmundi (excerpts only) Heynings 1f
Alan of Tewkesbury
 Epistolae Nuneaton 2a
 Sermones Nuneaton 2a
Alexander Carpenter
 Destructorium vitiorum Barking (Appendix) 11
Alphonsus de Villa Sancta
 De libero arbitrio adversus Melanchtonem Syon B.5c
 Problema indulgentiarum Syon B.5b
Ambrose of Milan
 De bono mortis Swine A.5
 De mysteriis Swine B.1b
 De officiis ministrorum Swine B.1a
 De sacramentis Swine B.1c
[*pseud.*]
 De lapsu virginis Swine B.1d
Aristotle
 Ethica (Latin translation) Barking (Appendix) 17a
Augustine of Hippo
 De doctrina christiana (excerpt) Barking 4b
 Regula S. Augustini Syon B.6b
[*pseud.*]
 De diligendo Deo Syon A.21e
 Meditationes (*cap.* 11-30) Syon A.21f
 Orationes Augustini (three different prayers) Nuneaton 1g;
  Shaftesbury 4; Winchester 3
 Sermones Dartford 1e (one sermon), Winchester 4c (fourteen
  sermons)

Dionysius the Carthusian
    Commentary on Psalms   Barking (Appendix) 20
    Commentary on the Four Gospels   Barking (Appendix) 21

Eckbert of Schönau → Bernard of Clairvaux *Ps., Sermo de vita et passione Domini*
Erasmus, Desiderius
    Enchiridion militis Christiani   Barking (Appendix) 4
Euphemia, Abbess of Wherwell
    Epistola consolatoria   Wherwell 3

Gerald of Wales
    Expugnatio Hibernica   Nuneaton 2d
    Topographia Hiberniae   Nuneaton 2b
Gervase of Tilbury
    Otia imperialia   Syon A.11f (excerpt from *dist.* I), A.11g (excerpt from *dist.* II)
Glosses   Barking 11a (Song of Songs), 11b (Lamentations); Swine A.12 (Mark)
Goscelin
    Vita S. Ethelburgae   Barking 3a
    Vita S. Edithae   Barking 3d
Gregory the Great
    Responsum S. Gregorii secundino incluso rationem de pictoris interroganti   Markyate 1
[*pseud.*]
    Oratio S. Gregorii   Winchester 3

Haimo of Auxerre (*ps.*-Haimo of Halberstadt)
    Commentary on the Pauline Epistles   Barking (Appendix) 13
Henry VIII
    Libellus adversus Martinum Lutherum haeresiarchon   Syon B.5a
Henry of Ostia
    Summa super titulis Decretalium   Barking (Appendix) 16a
Hildebert of Lavardin
    Vita S. Mariae Aegyptiacae   Barking 3f
Honorius Augustodunensis
    De cognitione verae vitae (attrib. Augustine)   Syon A.7f
    Gemma animae   Heynings 1a

Peter Comestor
  Historia scholastica   Elstow 1a, Swine A.8
  See also Jerome *Ps.*
Peter Lombard
  Sententiarum libri IV   Barking (Appendix) 16b
Peter Tartaret/Tataret
  An unidentified work   Barking (Appendix) 18

Ralph of Lenham/Lynham → Ranulph Higden
Ranulph Higden
  Ars calendarii   Syon A.11c
Ricemarch
  Vita S. Davidis   Barking 3e
Richard Rolle
  Commentary on the Lord's Prayer   Syon A.7d
  Commentary on the Song of Songs   Syon A.7a (three
    sections: *Oleum effusum, Adolescentule, Curremus in odorem*)
  De amore Dei contra amatores mundi   Syon A.7h
  De causa haereticorum et fide Trinitatis   Syon A.7c
  De excellentia contemplationis   Syon A.21c
  De vita activa et contemplativa → *Super mulierem fortem*
  Emendatio vitae   Syon A.21a
  Incendium amoris   Syon A.7e, A.21b, A.21c
  Judica me Deus   Syon A.7b
  Melos amoris/Melum contemplativorum   Syon A.7i
  Oleum effusum → Commentary on the Song of Songs
  Super Mulierem fortem   Syon A.7c
Richard of Saint-Victor
  Allegoriae in Vetus Testamentum   Elstow 1b
Rolle, Richard → Richard Rolle

Smaragdus of Saint-Mihiel
  Diadema monachorum   Winchester 4a
Stephen Langton
[*attrib.*]
  Summa de vitiis et virtutibus   Barking 4e

Tauler, Johann
  Opera   Syon A.13
Thomas à Kempis
  Opera   Syon A.17

Thomas of Verceil/Vercelles
   Paraphrases of the *ps.*-Dionysian *corpus*   Barking (Appendix) 19
Turpin *Ps.*
   Historia Karoli Magni et Rolandi   Polsloe MR (?)

Virgil
   Opera   Barking (Appendix) 1a

William of Auxerre
   Summa aurea super quatuor libros Sententiarum   Barking (Appendix) 17c
William Brito
   Dictionarium/Expositiones vocabulorum bibliae   Lacock 1
William Durandus
   Rationale divinorum officiorum   Barking (Appendix) 14b; Syon A.11b (excerpt from Book VIII only)
William of Paull
   Oculus sacerdotis, Part I   Swine A.6
William of Tripoli
   De statu Saracenorum, de Mahometo pseudo-propheta eorum, et de ipsa gente et eorum lege et fide   Syon A.11h

ANONYMOUS WORKS

Cathalogus sanctorum   Barking (Appendix) 12
Chronicle of English history from Hengist to Egbert   Romsey 1a

De causa boemica   Barking (Appendix) 3
De decem plagis Aegypti   Barking 4b
De modo confitendi   Barking (Appendix) 2a
De patientia infirmitatis   Dartford 7j; Kington St Michael 2b
De peccatore   Barking 1
De sacramento altaris   Barking 4b

Homiliarius → INDEX IV

Inventory of the Wintney *frater*   Wintney 1c

Liber gestorum Karoli, regis Francie   Polsloe MR
List of English kings from Arviragus to Henry VII together with
    their places of burial   Kington St Michael 1a

Mariale → INDEX IV
Mortuary Rolls → INDEX IV

Nicholas of Lyra
    Postillae   Barking (Appendix) 9

Ordines, Miscellaneous (in Latin, English, and French)   Barking
    14; Kington St Michael 1b; Syon A.8a, B.6c, e, f, g; Winch-
    ester 1

Pater noster, Commentary on   Syon A.10
Prayers → INDEX IV

Regula S. Salvatoris   Syon B.6a, d
Rentale (of Dartford)   Dartford 3

Sermones   Barking (Appendix) 10
Sermones Amici   Syon B.5d
Speculum spiritualium (excerpt)   Dartford 1d

Tractatus moralis   Winchester 4b

Verses   Barking 1; Campsey 4a; Canonsleigh 1; Harrold 1; Syon
    A.10, A.46; Wherwell 3
Vision of St John of the Sorrows of the Virgin   Shaftesbury 3a
Vitae sanctorum   Barking 3b, c, g (Hildelitha, Edward the
    Martyr, Ebrulfus); Heynings 1e, f (Rumwold, Edmund
    of Abingdon), Romsey 1b (forty-three surviving *vitae* and
    four lost); Tarrant Keynston 2 (Margaret of Antioch)
Vocabularius iuris utriusque   Barking (Appendix) 7

INDEX IV:
INDEX OF BIBLICAL AND
LITURGICAL WORKS IN LATIN

MR = *Miscellaneous Records*

For the nature and contents of the various books, see C. Wordsworth & H. Littlehales, *The Old Service-Books of the English Church* (London, 1904), cited below as W/L.

Antiphoner (W/L 104–7)   Easebourne *MR* a.3; Redlingfield *MR* a

Bible   Barking 10 (four gospels), 12 (Song and Songs and Lamentations, both with glosses); Barking (Appendix) 2b ('a byble in lattyn'), 15 (canonical epistles, with commentary); Swine A.10 (canonical epistles), A.12 (Mark, with gloss)
See also *Evangeliarium*
Books (unspecified)   Castle Hedingham *MR*; Cheshunt *MR*; Flixton *MR*; Kilburn *MR*; Marham *MR*; Minster in Sheppey *MR*; Redlingfield *MR*; Swine A.7
Breviary (W/L 69–100)   Amesbury 3, 6; Polsloe 1 (printed book [Paris 1519]); Syon A.5, A.8a, A.9, A.34, A.36, A.42, A.47, A.48, *MR* a
See also *Portiforium*

Calendar (W/L 190–3)   Barking 7, 14; Dartford 9; Syon A.10, A.11a; Wherwell 3
See also Psalters
Cathalogus sanctorum   Barking (Appendix) 12
Collectanea (Private collections of prayers and devotional materials)   Barking 9 (Latin and English); Ickleton 1; Syon A.10, A.29, A.30, A.42, A.46, B.9, D.2; Winchester 2
Collect-Book (*Collectarius*) (W/L 123–9)   Easebourne *MR* a.6

Computistical Tables   Barking 7; Campsey 4b; Harrold 1; Littlemore 1; Shaftesbury 5, 7; Syon A.10; Tarrant Keynston 2
Constitutions   Edinburgh 1b
Cursus de eterna sapientia   Syon A.46, D.2

Devotions   London (Aldgate) *MR* b.3

Evangeliarium → Gospel-Book

Fifteen Oes of St Bridget   Barking 9; Godstow 1; London (Aldgate) 4; Malling 1; Syon A.10, A.46, B.9; Tarrant Keynston 2
Fifteen Sorrows of Our Lady   Syon A.29

Golden Litany   Syon A.10, A.29
Gospel-Book (W/L 198–203)   Easebourne *MR* a.10; Edinburgh 1a; Higham *MR*
Grail (*Graduale*) (W/L 203–6)   Redlingfield *MR* a; Syon A.48

Homiliary (W/L 158–9)   Heynings 1d
Hours: Books of Hours were intended for private devotion, and apart from the actual text of the Hours, they invariably contain much additional liturgical and devotional material (see, for example, Amesbury 1). For details, the reader is referred to the individual entries.
    Hours of the Compassion of the Virgin   London (Aldgate) *MR* b.2; Syon A.46
    Hours of the Cross   Amesbury 1; London (Aldgate) *MR* b.1; Syon B.4
    Hours of the Holy Spirit   Barking 9; Godstow 1; Syon A.9, A.18, A.23, A.24, A.34, A.41, A.42, A.44, A.46, D.2
    Hours of the Holy Trinity   Godstow 1; London (Aldgate) *MR* b.2; Syon A.46
    Hours of the Passion   Hampole 1a (Latin and French); Syon A.46
    Hours of St John the Baptist   Amesbury 1; Campsey 3
    Hours of St Mary Magdalene   Campsey 3
    Hours of St Melorus   Amesbury 1
    Hours of the Virgin   Amesbury 1; Dartford 9; Godstow 1; Hampole 1a; Kington St Michael 1f; London (Aldgate) 4;

Malling 1; Shaftesbury 1; Syon B.8, B.10; Wherwell 1, 2; Wilton 3

Hymnal (W/L 117–22)   Amesbury 5; Barking 2; Campsey 3; Syon B.11

Lectionary → *Legenda*

Legenda (W/L 129–36)   Easebourne *MR* a.4; Kilburn *MR*; Kington St Michael *MR*; Syon A.47, A.48, B.2, *MR* a

Mariale   Swine A.2

Martyrology (W/L 145–51)   Easebourne *MR* a.11; Wintney 1a, c, d

Mass-Book → Missal

Mattins-Book → *Legenda*

Missal (W/L 170–94)   Ankerwyke *MR* b; Brewood *MR*; Campsey *MR*; Castle Hedingham *MR*; Cheshunt *MR*; Easebourne *MR* a.1; Heynings *MR*; Kilburn *MR*; Kington St Michael *MR*; Langley *MR*; Marham *MR*; Minster in Sheppey *MR*; Nun Appleton *MR*; Redlingfield *MR* b; Syon *MR* a, c

Mortuary Roll   Castle Hedingham 1; Higham 1

Obituary (W/L 159–64)   Kington St Michael 1e; Wintney 1f

Offices

  Office of the Cross (ascribed to Pope John XXII)   Hampole 1a

  Office of the Dead   Dartford 5 (with psalms, litany, *memoria*, and processional offices)

  Office of the Holy Face   Syon A.29

  Office of the Holy Spirit   Tarrant Keynston 2

  Office of the Holy Trinity   Syon D.2

  Office of the Virgin   Nuneaton 1f; Shaftesbury 1

  Requiem Offices   Syon B.9

Ordinal (W/L 239–47)   Barking 14; St Mary de Pré *MR*

Ordines, Miscellaneous (in Latin, English, and French)   Barking 14; Kington St Michael 1b; Syon A.8a, B.6c, e, f, g; Winchester 1

Portiforium (W/L 69–100)   Burnham *MR*; Easebourne *MR* a.2; Heynings *MR*; London (St Helen's) *MR*; Nun Appleton *MR*; St Mary de Pré *MR*

See also Breviary

Prayers (Latin prayers in non-liturgical manuscripts)   Barking
5f; Shaftesbury 2; Syon A.16a

Primer (W/L 248–54)   Arden *MR*; Easebourne *MR* b.1; Nun
Monkton *MR* e; Syon B.4 (printed book [Paris, 1514])

Processional (W/L 165–9)   Chester 1 (with additional prayers);
Dartford 5; Kilburn *MR*; Syon A.2 (similar to A.6), A.6 (with
a litany, prayers, and other offices), A.12 (with litanies and
other offices), A.36, A.40 (similar to A.6), A.45 (similar to
A.6); Wilton 4

Psalter (W/L 108–16)

The actual text of the Psalter is normally preceded by a Calendar
(often with computistical tables) and followed by canticles,
the Athanasian Creed (sometimes with other creeds, *Gloria*,
and *Pater noster*), a litany (or litanies), the Office of the
Dead, and *commendatio animarum*. After the thirteenth century, when Psalters were used more extensively as books
of private devotion, we also find added prayers, hymns,
memoriae of the saints, and Hours. In the list below, A =
Athanasian Creed, C = Canticles, CA = *commendatio animarum*, H = Hours, K = Kalendar or Calendar, L = litany,
M = *memoriae*, O = Office of the Dead, P = prayers.

Amesbury 5 (with K, C, A); Ankerwyke *MR* a; Broadholme
MR; Bruisyard 1 (with K, C, A, L, P); Buckland Minchin
1 (with K, C, A, O); Campsey 1 (with K, C, A), 3 (with
C, A, O, Hymns, H, P); Carrow 1 (with M, K, C, L, O,
H), 2 (with K, C, L, O, CA), 3 (fragments); Easebourne *MR*
a.5; Edinburgh 2 (printed book [Paris 1552]); Godstow 1
(with C, L, H, Hymns, P, O, CA); Goring 1 (with K, C, L);
Greenfield *MR*; Hampole 1 (with Hymns, H, K, C, L, O, and
other offices); Harrold 1 (with K, C, L, P); Heynings *MR*;
Ickleton 1 (printed book [Paris 1516]; Lacock 2 (with K, C,
A, L, P), *MR* a; Littlemore 1 (with K, C, A, L, P); London
(Aldgate) 5 (with K, C, P, L, H); London (St Helen's) *MR*;
Markyate 1 (with K, C, A, L, P, and other material [q.v.]);
Newcastle-upon-Tyne *MR*; Nun Monkton *MR* a; Romsey 2
= Wilton 2 (q.v.); Shaftesbury 4 (with K, C, A, L, P [Latin
and French]), 5 (with K, C, A, L, P, and other offices), 6
(with K, L, P, A), 8 (with K, C, A, L, O); Syon A.4 (with C,
L, P), A.8b (with K, C, L), A.9 (with K, C, L, H, O), A.15

(with C, L, P), A.18 (with K, C, A, L, H, O, P), A.24 (with K, C, A, L, H), A.28 (with K, C, L); A.33 (with K, C, A, L, P), A.34 (with K, C, H, O), A.42 (printed book [Paris, 1522]), A.44 (with K, C, A, L, P, H, O), B.7 (with K, C, A), B.12 (with C, A, O, L, P, and a later K), D.1 (with C), D.3 (with K, C); Tarrant Keynston 2 (with H, K, C, A, L), 3 (with K, C, A, L, P), 4 (with K); Wherwell 1 (with K, H, C, L), 2 (with K, C, L, P, H, O), 4 (with K, C, A, L, O); Wilton 2 (with K, C, L, CA, O, P), 3 (with K, C, A, L, H); Winchester 5 (with K, C, A, L)

Psalters, Other

Psalter of the Holy Cross (metrical)   Campsey 3
Psalter of the Holy Spirit (metrical)   Campsey 3
Psalter of St Jerome   Barking 9; Hampole 1a; Malling 1
Psalter of the Virgin (*Psalterium beatae Mariae*)   Carrow 1

Seven Oes of St Gregory   Syon A.46

Troper (W/L 206–7)   Easebourne *MR* a.7

INDEX V:
INDEX OF NAMES RELATING
TO INSCRIPTIONS

In the following list, the orthography of the names as they appear in the inscriptions has been retained throughout.

Aelfgyth   Horton 1
Aelfgiva (abbess of Barking)   Barking 10
Agnes (prioress of Castle Hedingham)   Castle Hedingham 1
Alderton, Robert   London (Aldgate) 2
Aldryngton Thomas   Goring 1
Amarson, Anne   Syon A.6, A.40
Amersham → Amarson
Amphelisa (prioress of Higham)   Higham 1
Ashly/Assheley, Elyzabeth   Polsloe 1
Assheton, Richard   Syon A.32
Audley → Awdeley
Awdeley/Awdley, Anne   Shaftesbury 6
Awdeley, Edmund   Shaftesbury 6

Babington → Babyngton
Babyngton, Katerine   Campsey 4
Bacon → Bakon
Baker, John   Kington St Michael 1, *MR*
Bakon, Margery   Bruisyard 2
Bannebury, John de   Burnham *MR*
Barley, Dorothy   Barking 1
Baron, William   Dartford 7
Basset, Adam   Littlemore 1
Bassynburne, Anne   London (Aldgate) 6
Bedford, Duke of   Syon A.5, *MR* a
Bedyngfeld/Bedyngfeild/Bedingfeld, Alice   Redlingfield *MR*
Bedyngfeld/Bedyngfeild/Bedingfeld, Edmund   Redlingfield *MR*

INDEX VI:
INDEX OF INCIPITS

A) ENGLISH

The commaundementes off Almyghty God be rede unto vs to thentent they myght be understand   Dartford 6

When I avy3sed me ryght hertely/How dyverse men even grevously   Dartford 8

B) FRENCH

Al rei de glorie   Derby 1a

Apres ce que Adam nostre premier pere fut gete hors de paradis terrestre   Barking 13r

Cuers en qui Dieu habite doit avoir ces choses. Il doit estre amer en contricion   Barking13k

De nulle viande ne mengust Dieux si voulentiers comme de pechie   Barking 13l

En l'onur de la Trinite   Nuneaton 1c

Entendez envers mei   Derby 1g

Fin amant sont appele cil et celles qui Dieu aiment   Barking 13g

Hier Alixandres faisoit son tresor d'or   Barking 13ab

Il sont .viij. choses qui donnent occasion de cheoir ou pechie de luxure   Barking 13p

Je vois morir, venez avant   Barking 13ac

La sainte escripture dist que Helyas li prophetes averta ou ciel par estourbeillon   Barking13i

261

La vision de Jhesucrist   Nuneaton 1e
La voie par quoy nous devons aler en paradis, cest la voie
     damour   Barking 13h
Les estoilles. Et apres, *Pulcra es et decora*. Et telle la mere comme
     le filz   Barking 13a
Ly livres en quoy nous devons especialement lire sans nul
     entrelaissement   Barking 13a

Maistre, a cest besoing   Derby 1h
Mout par fu   Derby 1b

N'est pas sire de son pais   Barking 13aa
Nous trouvons on viez testament dun roy ot nom nas qui assist
     une cite qui avoit a nom Iabes   Barking 13q

Or reprent ci et chastie saint Bernart ... Dist ilhoms qui es tu
     et quel tuer as tu qui nas compassion de la mort ton
     seigneur?   Barking 13b

Pource que nous sommes mis ou my lien des las de ligier nous
     nous refroidons des de sirs celestielx   Barking 13d

Quant nostre sires Jhesucrist aloit par terre avec ses apos-
     tres   Barking 13m
Quant on sonne la messe si doit on penser que sont li message
     au roy de paradis   Barking13s
Quant .xl. jorz seront passez appres la mort Antecrist   Barking
     15e
Qui bien comence   Nuneaton 1d
Quiconques se veult a droit confesser, il ne doit pas venir
     despourvenement devant son confesseur   Barking 13t

Seignurs ore escutez, ke Deu vous beneie   Derby 1e
Sire Jhesu, ky par toun doux playser   Hampole 1a

C) LATIN

Ave sanctissimum corpus domini nostri Ihesu Christi   Syon
     A.33

Balsamus et munda cera   Barking 1

Cum matutinis sanctae Annae   London (Aldgate) *MR* b.3

Insula ista que nunc Anglia dicitur   Romsey 1a

Narratur in Daniele   Barking 1

Prophecie spiritus   Syon B.12

Robustus iudas horam, nunc eripiens est   Campsey 4b

Scribitur Mathei quinto capitulo   Barking 1
Si sciret homo   Dartford 7j; Kington St Michael 2b

Vidit gloriosissimam Virginem ineffabiliter decoratam
      Shaftesbury 3a

INDEX VII:
INDEX OF MANUSCRIPTS
AND PRINTED BOOKS

Aberdeen, U.L., 134 + Oxford, Bod. Lib., Rawl. C.941   Syon
    A.1
Alnwick Castle, Duke of Northumberland
    449   Thetford 1
    505a   Syon A.2
Ampleforth Abbey, C.V.130 (printed book)   Syon A.3

Baltimore, Walters Art Gallery, 90   Carrow 1
Beeleigh Abbey, Miss C. Foyle   Barking 1
Blackburn, Museum & Art Gallery, 091.21040   Malling 1
Bristol, Baptist College
    Z.c.23   Harrold 1
    Z.d.40   Syon A.6
    Z.e.37   Syon A.30
Brussels, Bibl. Royale, IV.481   Syon A.4

Cambridge, Fitzwilliam Museum
    McClean 45   Wherwell 1
    McClean 123   Nuneaton 1
    2–1957   Shaftesbury 1
Cambridge, University Library
    Dd.2.33   Syon B.1
    Dd.8.2   Kington St Michael 1
    Ee.3.52   Flixton 1
    Ee.6.16   Amesbury 1
    Ff.6.18   Syon B.2
    Ff.6.33   Syon B.3
    Ii.6.40   Shaftesbury 2
    Inc.3.J.1.2 3534 (printed book)   Syon A.13
    Mm.3.13   Winchester 1
    Add. 7220   Campsey 1
    Add. 7634 + London, Private Collection   Syon A.5

490   Dartford 2
Durham, University Library
  Cosin V.iii.16   Syon (introduction) 1
  Cosin V.v.12   Syon A.16
Durham, Dr A. I. Doyle (printed book)   Syon A.17

Edinburgh, Nat. Lib. of Scotland, H8.f17 (printed book)
    Edinburgh 2
Edinburgh, University Library
  59   Syon B.7
  150   Edinburgh 1
Escorial, El, e.ii.1   Horton 1
Exeter University: see Syon Abbey

Firle Park, Sussex, Lord Gage   Syon A.18

Glasgow, U.L., Hunterian Mus., 136   Syon A.19
Göttingen, U.L., 4° Theol. Mor. 138/53 Inc. (printed book)
    Syon A.20

Hildesheim, S. Godehardskirche + Cologne, Schnütgen Mus.,
    M694 (formerly Sürth bei Köln, Dr J. Lückger)   Markyate
    1

Lacock Abbey, Mrs A. D. Burnett-Brown   Lacock 1
Leningrad → St Petersburg
Lincoln, Cathedral Chapter Lib., 199   Heynings 1
London, British Library
  Add. 10596, fols. 25–83   Barking 5
  Add. 11748   Shaftesbury 3
  Add. 18632   Amesbury 2
  Add. 24661   Syon A.21
  Add. 27866   Wherwell 4
  Add. 30514   Syon B.8
  Add. 37790   Syon (introduction)
  Add. 40675   Campsey 3
  Add. 70513 (formerly Loans 29/61; formerly Welbeck Abbey,
    Duke of Portland, I.C.1)   Campsey 5
  Arundel 61   Dartford 3
  Arundel 146   Syon A.22

GENERAL INDEX TO PART I

BIBLIOGRAPHY

The Bibliography is restricted to works cited in Parts I and II of this study.

It does not include editions of texts listed in Part II.

A) Collected Papers

Beyond Their Sex: Learned Women of the European Past, ed. P. H. Labalme (NewYork/London, 1980).

Book Production and Publishing in Britain 1375–1475, ed. J. Griffiths & D. Pearsall (Cambridge, 1989).

De Cella in Seculum: Religious and Secular Life and Devotion in Late Medieval England, ed. M. G. Sargent (Cambridge, 1989).

The English Library Before 1700, ed. F. Wormald & C. E. Wright (London, 1958).

Essays By Divers Hands, being the Transactions of the Royal Society of Literature of the United Kingdom, N.S. 4, ed. E. Gosse (London, 1924).

Latin and Vernacular: Studies in Late-Medieval Texts and Manuscripts, ed. A. J. Minnis (Cambridge, 1989).

Literature and Western Civilization: The Medieval World, ed. D. Daiches & A. K. Thorlby (London, 1973).

Medieval Book Production: Assessing the Evidence, ed. L. L. Brownrigg (Los Altos Hills, 1990).

Medieval Scribes, Manuscripts and Libraries: Essays Presented to N. R. Ker, ed. M. B. Parkes & A. G. Watson (London, 1978).

Medieval Studies Presented to Rose Graham, ed. V. Ruffer & A. J. Taylor (Oxford, 1950).

Monastic Studies II, ed. J. Loades (Bangor, 1991).

N. Orme, *Education and Society in Medieval and Renaissance England* (London, 1989).

M. B. Parkes, *Scribes, Scripts and Readers: Studies in the Communication, Presentation and Dissemination of Medieval Texts* (London/Rio Grande, Ohio, 1991).

Proceedings of the Battle Conference on Anglo-Norman Studies, II, 1979, ed. R. A. Brown (Woodbridge, 1980).

La production du livre universitaire au moyen âge: exemplar et pecia.
    Actes du symposium tenu au Collegio San Bonaventura de
    Grottaferrata en mai 1983, ed. L. J. Bataillon *et al.* (Paris,
    1988).
Sisters and Workers in the Middle Ages, ed. J. M. Bennett *et al.*
    (Chicago/London, 1989).

B) PRIMARY SOURCES

Analecta Hymnica Medii Aevi, ed. C. Blume & G. M. Dreves
    (Leipzig, 1886–1922; rpt. New York, 1961).
O. Bokenham, *Legendys of Hooly Wummen*, ed. M. S. Serjeantson
    (EETS/OS, 206; London, 1938).
The Bridgettine Breviary of Syon Abbey, ed. A. J. Collins (Henry
    Bradshaw Society, 96; Worcester, 1969 [for 1963]).
Chartulary of Cockersand Abbey of the Premonstratensian Order, ed.
    W. Farrer (Chetham Society, N.S. 56; Manchester, 1905).
The Chastising of God's Children, ed. J. Bazire & E. Colledge
    (Oxford, 1957).
The Cloud of Unknowing and The Book of Privy Counselling, ed. P.
    Hodgson (EETS/OS, 218; London, 1944).
A Collection of All the Wills . . . of the Kings and Queens of England,
    ed. J. Nichols (London, 1780; rpt. New York, 1969).
Deonise Hid Diuinite, ed. P. Hodgson (EETS/OS, 231; London,
    1955).
A Deuout Treatyse Called the Tree & the XII. Frutes of the Holy Goost,
    ed. J. J. Vaissier (Groningen, 1960).
The English Register of Godstow Nunnery, near Oxford, ed. A. Clark
    (EETS/OS, 129; London, 1911).
Erasmus, *Collected Works of Erasmus, Vol. 66*, ed. J. W. O'Malley
    (Toronto/Buffalo/London, 1988).
Gervase of Canterbury, *The Historical Works of Gervase of Canter-*
    bury, Vol. 2: The Minor Works, ed. W. Stubbs (Rolls Series,
    73/2; London, 1880).
The Incendium Amoris of Richard Rolle of Hampole, ed. M. Deanesly
    (Manchester, 1915; rpt. Folcroft, 1974).
Letters and Papers, Foreign and Domestic, of the Reign of Henry VIII,
    ed. J. S. Brewer *et al.* (London, 1862–1910).
The Life of Christina of Markyate: A Twelfth Century Recluse, ed. C.
    H. Talbot (Oxford, 1959; rpt. Oxford, 1987).

The Martiloge in Englysshe, tr. R. Whytford, ed. F. Procter & E. S. Dewick (Henry Bradshaw Society, 3; London, 1891).

The Myroure of oure Ladye, ed. J. H. Blunt (EETS/ES, 19; London, 1873; rpt. New York, 1973).

North Country Wills . . . 1383–1558, ed. J. W. Clay (Surtees Society, 116; Durham/London, 1908).

The Ordinale and Customary of the Benedictine Nuns of Barking Abbey, ed. J. B. L. Tolhurst (Henry Bradshaw Society, 65–66; London, 1927–28).

Registra Stephani Gardiner et Johannis Poynet, episcoporum Wintoniensium, ed. H. E. Malden & H. Chitty (Canterbury and York Society, 37; London, 1930).

The Rewyll of Seynt Sauioure and Other Middle English Brigittine Legislative Texts, Vol. 2: The MSS. Cambridge University Library Ff. 6. 33 and St. John's College Cambridge 11, ed. J. Hogg (*Salzburger Studien zur Anglistik und Amerikanistik*, Bd. 6/2; Salzburg, 1978).

The Rewyll of Seynt Sauioure, Vol. 4: The Syon Additions for the Sisters from the British Library Ms. Arundel 146, ed. J. Hogg (*Salzburger Studien zur Anglistik und Amerikanistik*, Bd. 6/4; Salzburg, 1980).

Somerset Medieval Wills (Second Series) 1501–1530, ed. F. W. Weaver (Somerset Record Society 19; London, 1903).

Testamenta Eboracensia: A Selection of Wills from the Registry at York (*Surtees Society* 4, 30, 45, 53, 79, 106; Durham/London, 1836–1902). Vol. 1 was edited by J. Raine; vols. 2–5 by J. Raine, Jr.; and vol. 6 by J. W. Clay.

Testamenta Karleolensia. The Series of Wills from the Prae-Reformation Registers of the Bishops of Carlisle 1353–1386, ed. R. S. Ferguson (Cumberland & Westmorland Antiquarian and Archaeological Society, E.S.9; Kendal/Carlisle/London, 1893).

Valor Ecclesiasticus, temp. Henr. VIII. Auctoritate Regia Institutus (London, 1810–34).

La vie d'Edouard le Confesseur: Poème Anglo-Normand du XIIe siècle, ed. Ö. Södergård (Uppsala, 1948).

Visitations in the Diocese of Lincoln 1517–1531, Vol. 1: Visitations of Rural Deaneries by William Atwater, Bishop of Lincoln, and his Commissaries, 1517–1520, ed. A. H. Thompson (Lincoln Record Society, 33; Hereford, 1940); *Vol. 2: Visitations of*

Rural Deaneries by John Longland, Bishop of Lincoln, . . .
  1517–1531, ed. A. H. Thompson (Lincoln Record Society,
  35; Hereford, 1944); *Vol. 3: Visitations of Religious Houses
  (concluded) by Bishops Atwater and Longland . . . 1517–1531*,
  ed. A. H. Thompson (Lincoln Record Society, 37; Hereford,
  1947).
*Visitations of Religious Houses in the Diocese of Lincoln, Vol. 1:
  Injunctions and Other Documents from the Registers of Richard
  Flemyng and William Gray, Bishops of Lincoln, A.D. 1420–
  1436*, ed. A. H. Thompson (Canterbury and York Society,
  17; London, 1915; rpt. 1969); *Vol. 2: Records of Visitations
  held by William Alnwick, A.D. 1436–1449, Part 1*, ed. A.
  H. Thompson (Canterbury and York Society, 24; London,
  1919; rpt. 1969); *Vol. 3: Records of Visitations held by William
  Alnwick, A.D. 1436–1449, Part 2*, ed. A. H. Thompson
  (Canterbury and York Society, 33; London, 1927; rpt. 1969).
Visitations of the Diocese of Norwich A.D. 1492–1532, ed. A. Jessopp
  (Camden Society, N.S. 43; London, 1888; rpt. New York,
  1965).
Wells Wills, ed. F. W. Weaver (London, 1890).
William of Malmesbury, *De Gestis Regum Anglorum, Vol. 2*, ed.
  W. Stubbs (Rolls Series, 90/2; London, 1889).
*Wills from Doctors' Commons: A Selection From the Wills of Eminent
  Persons Proved in the Prerogative Court of Canterbury 1495–
  1695*, ed. J. G. Nichols & J. Bruce (Camden Society, O.S.,
  83; London, 1863; rpt. New York, 1968).

                              C) OTHER WORKS

H. M. Adams, *Catalogue of Books Printed on the Continent of Europe,
  1501–1600, in Cambridge Libraries* (Cambridge, 1967).
J. W. Adamson, 'The Extent of Literacy in England in the
  Fifteenth and Sixteenth Centuries: Notes and Conjectures',
  The Library, Ser. 4, 10 (1930), pp. 163–93 (reprinted in *idem,
  The Illiterate Anglo-Saxon and Other Essays* [Cambridge,
  1946], pp. 38–61).
H. E. Allen, *Writings Ascribed to Richard Rolle, Hermit of Hampole*
  (New York, 1927; rpt. 1966).
J. Aubrey, ed. J. Britton, *The Natural History of Wiltshire* (London,
  1847; rpt. Newton Abbot, 1969).

G. J. Aungier, *The History and Antiquities of Syon Monastery, the Parish of Isleworth, and the Chapelry of Hounslow* (London, 1840).

A. T. Baker, 'Saints' Lives Written in Anglo-French: Their Historical, Social and Literary Importance', *Essays By Divers Hands, being the Transactions of the Royal Society of Literature of the United Kingdom*, N.S. 4, ed. E. Gosse (London, 1924), pp. 119–56.

J. Bale, ed. R. L. Poole & M. Bateson, *Index Britanniae Scriptorum* (Anecdota Oxoniensia, Mediaeval and Modern Series, 9; Oxford, 1902).

M. Bateson, *Catalogue of the Library of Syon Monastery Isleworth* (Cambridge, 1898).

J. M. W. Bean, 'Plague, Population and Economic Decline in England in the Later Middle Ages', *Economic History Review* Ser. 2, 15 (1962–3), pp. 423–37.

D. N. Bell, *The Libraries of the Cistercians, Gilbertines and Premonstratensians* (Corpus of British Medieval Library Catalogues, 3; London, 1992).

——, 'The Books of Meaux Abbey', *Analecta Cisterciensia* 40 (1984), pp. 25–83.

H. E. Bell, 'The Price of Books in Medieval England', *The Library*, Ser. 4, 17 (1937), pp. 312–32.

S. G. Bell, 'Medieval Women Book Owners: Arbiters of Lay Piety and Ambassadors of Culture', in *Sisters and Workers in the Middle Ages*, ed. J. M. Bennett *et al.* (Chicago/London, 1989), pp. 135–60.

H. S. Bennett, 'The Production and Dissemination of Vernacular Manuscripts in the Fifteenth Century, *The Library*, Ser. 5, 1 (1946–47), pp. 167–78.

——, 'Notes on Two Incunables: *The Abbey of the Holy Ghost* and *A Ryght Profytable Treatyse*', *The Library* Ser. 5, 10 (1955), pp. 120–1.

S. Berger, *La Bible française au moyen âge* (Paris, 1884; rpt. Geneva, 1967).

E. Bishop, *Liturgica Historica: Papers on the Liturgy and Religious Life of the Western Church* (Oxford, 1918; rpt. 1962).

W. H. Blaauw, 'Episcopal Visitations of the Benedictine Nunnery of Easebourne', *Sussex Archaeological Collections* 9 (1857), pp. 1–32.

M. Bloomfield, *et al.*, *Incipits of Latin Works on the Virtues and Vices, 1100–1500 A.D.* (Cambridge, Mass., 1979).

R. Bossuat, *Manuel bibliographique de la littérature française du moyen âge* (Melun, 1951; rpt. Nendeln/Liechtenstein, 1971), with supplements for 1949–53 (with J. Monfrin) (Paris, 1955; rpt. Nendeln/Liechtenstein, 1971), 1954–60 (Paris, 1961), and 1960–80 (Part 1, by F. Vielliard & J. Monfrin) (Paris, 1986).

A. F. C. Bourdillon, *The Order of Minoresses in England* (British Society of Franciscan Studies, 12; Manchester, 1926).

M. T. Brady, 'The Pore Caitif: An Introductory Study', *Traditio* 10 (1954), pp. 529–48.

———, 'Lollard Interpolations and Omissions in Manuscripts of *The Pore Caitif*', in *De Cella in Seculum: Religious and Secular Life and Devotion in Late Medieval England*, ed. M. G. Sargent (Cambridge, 1989), pp. 183–203.

C. Brown, *A Register of Middle English Religious and Didactic Verse* (Oxford, 1916–20).

C. Brown & R. H. Robbins, *The Index of Middle English Verse* (New York, 1943), with supplement by R. H. Robbins & J. L. Cutler (Lexington, 1965).

M. P. Brown, *A Guide to Western Historical Scripts from Antiquity to 1600* (London, 1990).

N. F. Cantor, *Inventing the Middle Ages: The Lives, Works, and Ideas of the Great Medievalists of the Twentieth Century* (New York, 1991).

Catalogue of Manuscripts and Early Printed Books . . . Now Forming Portion of the Library of J. Pierpont Morgan (London, 1907).

Catalogue of the Printed Books and Manuscripts Bequeathed by Francis Douce, Esq., to the Bodleian Library (Oxford, 1840).

S. H. Cavanaugh, *A Study of Books Privately Owned in England: 1300–1450* (University of Pennsylvania, Ph.D. Diss., 1980; University Microfilms International).

R. W. Chambers, *On the Continuity of English Prose from Alfred to More and His School* (London, 1932; rpt. 1950).

C. R. Cheney, 'Harrold Priory: A Twelfth-Century Dispute', *Bedfordshire Historical Record Society* 32 (1952), pp. 1–26, reprinted in *idem*, *Medieval Texts and Studies* (Oxford, 1973), pp. 285–313.

U. Chevalier, *Repertorium Hymnologicum* (Louvain, 1892–1921).

K. Christ, revd. A. Kern, tr. T. M. Otto, *The Handbook of Medieval Library History* (Metuchen/London, 1984).

M. T. Clanchy, *From Memory to Written Record: England 1066–1307* (Oxford, 1993²).

J. W. Clark, *The Care of Books* (Cambridge, 1902²; rpt. London, 1975).

W. G. Clark, 'The Fall of the Wiltshire Monasteries', *The Wiltshire Archaeological and Natural History Magazine* 28 (1894–96), pp. 288–319.

W. G. Clark-Maxwell, 'The Outfit for the Profession of an Austin Canoness at Lacock, Wilts. in the Year 1395, and other Memoranda', *Archaeological Journal* 69 (1912), pp. 117–24.

[S. C. Cockerell], *Burlington Fine Arts Club: Exhibition of Illuminated Manuscripts* (London, 1908).

A. J. Collins (ed.), *The Bridgettine Breviary of Syon Abbey*, (Henry Bradshaw Society, 96; Worcester, 1969 [for 1963]).

H. M. Colvin, *The White Canons in England* (Oxford, 1951).

M. Corbett, 'An East-Midland Revision of the Northern Homily Collection', *Manuscripta* 26 (1982), pp. 100–7.

G. G. Coulton, *Life in the Middle Ages* (New York/Cambridge, 1935 [four vols. in one]).

D. Crane, 'English Translations of the *Imitatio Christi* in the Sixteenth and Seventeenth Centuries', *Recusant History* 13 (1975), pp. 79–100.

J. E. Cussans, *History of Hertfordshire, Vol. 2: Hertford Hundred* (London, 1876; rpt. Menston, 1972).

G. R. C. Davis, *Medieval Cartularies of Great Britain* (London, 1958).

R. J. Dean, 'Elizabeth, Abbess of Schönau, and Roger of Ford', *Modern Philology* 41 (1944), pp. 209–20.

M. Deanesly, *The Lollard Bible and Other Medieval Biblical Versions* (Cambridge, 1920; rpt. 1966).

———, 'Vernacular Books in England in the Fourteenth and Fifteenth Centuries', *Modern Language Review* 15 (1920), pp. 348–58.

——— (ed.), *The Incendium Amoris of Richard Rolle of Hampole*, (Manchester, 1915; rpt. Folcroft, 1974).

A. de la Mare, *Catalogue of the Collection of Medieval Manuscripts Bequeathed to the Bodleian Library Oxford by James P. R. Lyell* (Oxford, 1971).

C. F. R. de Hamel, *Glossed Books of the Bible and the Origins of the Paris Booktrade* (Cambridge, 1984).

———, *Syon Abbey. The Library of the Bridgettine Nuns and Their Peregrinations After the Reformation* (Roxburghe Club, 1991).

———, *Medieval Craftsmen: Scribes and Illuminators* (London, 1992).

J. C. Dickinson, *The Origins of the Austin Canons and Their Introduction into England* (London, 1950).

C. R. Dodwell, F. Wormald, & O. Pächt, *The St Alban's Psalter* (London, 1960).

A. I. Doyle, 'Thomas Betson of Syon Abbey', *The Library*, Ser. 5, 11 (1956), pp. 115–8.

———, 'Books Connected with the Vere Family and Barking Abbey', *Transactions of the Essex Archaeological Society* N.S. 25 (1958), pp. 222–43.

———, 'The Printed Books of the Last Monks of Durham', *The Library*, Ser. 6, 10 (1988), pp. 203–19.

———, 'Publication by Members of the Religious Orders', in *Book Production and Publishing in Britain 1375–1475*, ed. J. Griffiths & D. Pearsall (Cambridge, 1989), pp. 109–23.

———, 'Book Production by the Monastic Orders in England (c. 1375–1530)', in *Medieval Book Production: Assessing the Evidence*, ed. L. L. Brownrigg (Los Altos Hills, 1990), pp. 1–19.

A. I. Doyle & M. B. Parkes, 'The Production of Copies of the *Canterbury Tales* and the *Confessio Amantis* in the Early Fifteenth Century', in *Medieval Scribes, Manuscripts and Libraries: Essays Presented to N. R. Ker*, ed. M. B. Parkes & A. G. Watson (London, 1978), pp. 163–210.

P. Dronke, *Women Writers of the Middle Ages: A Critical Study of Texts from Perpetua (d. 203) to Marguerite Porete (d. 1310)* (Cambridge, 1984).

E. G. Duff, *Fifteenth Century English Books* (Oxford, 1917; rpt. Meisenheim, 1964).

W. Dugdale, ed. J. Caley, H. Ellis, & B. Bandinell, *Monasticon Anglicanum* (London, 1817–30).

R. W. Dunning, 'The Muniments of Syon Abbey: Their Administration and Migration in the Fifteenth and Sixteenth Centuries', *Bulletin of the Institute of Historical Research* 37 (1964), pp. 103–11.

————, 'The Building of Syon Abbey', *Transactions of the Ancient Monuments Society*, N.S. 25 (1981), pp. 16–26.

J. Durkan & A. Ross, *Early Scottish Libraries* (Glasgow, 1961).

C. W. Dutschke, *Guide to Medieval and Renaissance Manuscripts in the Huntington Library* (San Marino, 1989).

M. C. Erler, 'Syon Abbey's Care for Books: Its Sacristan's Account Rolls 1506/7–1535/6', *Scriptorium* 39 (1985), pp. 293–307.

M. Esposito, 'Inventaire des anciens manuscrits français des bibliothèques de Dublin', *Revue des bibliothèques* 24 (1914), pp. 185–98.

W. Everett, 'The Clensyng of Mannes Soule: An Introductory Study', *Southern Quarterly* 13 (1975), pp. 265–79.

L. Febvre & H.-J. Martin, tr. D. Gerard, ed. G. Nowell-Smith & D. Wootton, *The Coming of the Book and the Impact of Printing* (London, 1976).

R. C. Fowler, 'Inventories of Essex Monasteries in 1536', *Transactions of the Essex Archaeological Society* N.S. 9 (1903–06), pp. 280–92, 330–47, 380–400.

J. C. Fox, 'An Anglo-Norman Apocalypse from Shaftesbury Abbey', *Modern Language Review* 8 (1913), pp. 338–51.

W. H. Frere, *Bibliotheca Musico-Liturgica* (London, 1901–32).

J. B. Friedman, 'Books, Owners and Makers in Fifteenth-Century Yorkshire: The Evidence from Some Wills and Extant Manuscripts', in *Latin and Vernacular: Studies in Late-Medieval Texts and Manuscripts*, ed. A. J. Minnis (Cambridge, 1989), pp. 111–27.

T. Fuller, ed. J. S. Brewer, *The Church History of Britain, Vol. 3* (Oxford, 1845).

F. J. Furnivall, 'The Nevile and Southwell Families of Mereworth in Kent, A.D. 1520–1575', in *Notes and Queries*, Ser. 4, 2 (1868), pp. 577–8.

P. Gambier, 'Lending Books in a Mediaeval Nunnery', *Bodleian Quarterly Record* 5 (1927), pp. 188–90.

F. A. Gasquet, *English Monastic Life* (London, 1924⁶).

A. Gibbons, *Early Lincoln Wills. An Abstract of All the Wills and Administrations Recorded in the Episcopal Registers of the Old Diocese of Lincoln, . . . 1280–1547* (Lincoln, 1888).

V. Gillespie, 'Vernacular Books of Religion', in *Book Production and Publishing in Britain 1375–1475*, ed. J. Griffiths & D. Pearsall (Cambridge, 1989), pp. 317–44.

Gesamtkatalog der Wiegendrucke (Leipzig, 1925–38).

P. Glorieux, *Pour revaloriser Migne. Tables rectificatives* (Mélanges de science religieuse, 9 [supp.]; Lille, 1952).

R. Goy, *Die Überlieferung der Werke Hugos von St Viktor* (Stuttgart, 1976).

P. Grosjean, 'Vita S. Roberti Novi Monasterii in Anglia Abbatis', *Analecta Bollandiana* 56 (1938), pp. 334–60.

J. F. Hamburger, 'Art, Enclosure and the *Cura Monialium*: Prolegomena in the Guise of a Postscript', *Gesta* 31 (1992), pp. 108–34.

Hamel, C. F. R. de → De Hamel, C. F. R.

R. Hands, 'Juliana Berners and *The Boke of St. Albans*', *Review of English Studies* N.S. 18 (1967), pp. 373–86.

K. E. Haney, *The Winchester Psalter: An Iconographic Study* (London, 1986).

M. A. Harris, 'Alan of Tewkesbury and His Letters', *Studia Monastica* 18 (1976), pp. 77–108, 299–351.

H. Harrod, 'Extracts from Early Wills in the Norwich Registries', *Norfolk Archaeology* 4 (1855), pp. 317–39.

J. Harthan, *Books of Hours and Their Owners* (London, 1977).

F. Haslewood, 'Will of Sir Walter Quyntyn, of Ipswich', *Proceedings of the Suffolk Institute of Archaeology and Natural History* 7 (1889), pp. 111–2.

——, 'Inventories of Monasteries Suppressed in 1536', *Proceedings of the Suffolk Institute of Archaeology and Natural History* 8 (1894), pp. 83–116.

L. C. Hector, *The Handwriting of English Documents* (London, 1958).

T. Heffernan, 'The Rediscovery of the Bute Manuscript of the *Northern Homily Cycle*', *Scriptorium* 36 (1982), pp. 118–29.

F. C. Hingeston-Randolph, *The Register of Edmund Stafford (A.D. 1395–1419): An Index and Abstract of Its Contents* (London, 1886).

R. Hirsch, *Printing, Selling and Reading* (Wiesbaden, 1967).

Histoire littéraire de la France (Paris, 1865–1949; rpt. Nendeln/ Liechtenstein, 1973–74).

P. Hodgson, '*The Orcherd of Syon* and the English Mystical Tradition', in *Middle English Literature: British Academy Gollancz Lectures*, ed. J. A. Burrow (Oxford, 1989), pp. 71–91.

J. Hogg, *Richard Whytford's The Pype or Tonne of the Lyfe of Perfection, Vol. 1, Pt. 1* (Salzburg Studies in English Literature, 89/1, pt. 1; Salzburg, 1979); *Vol. 1, Pt. 2* (Salzburg Studies in English Literature, 89/1, pt. 2; Salzburg, 1989).

————, 'The Contribution of the Brigittine Order to Late Medieval English Spirituality', in *Analecta Cartusiana* 35 (*Spiritualität Heute und Gestern: Internationaler Kongress vom 4. bis 7. August 1982*, Band 3; Salzburg, 1983), pp. 153–74.

C. J. Holdsworth, *'Another Stage . . . A Different World': Ideas and People Around Exeter in the Twelfth Century* (Exeter, 1979).

W. S. Holdsworth, *A History of English Law, Vol. 2* (London, 1936⁴).

C. Horstmann, *Altenglische Legenden: Neue Folge* (Heilbronn, 1881; rpt. Hildesheim/New York, 1969).

E. Hoskins, *Horae Beatae Mariae Virginis* (London/New York, 1901; rpt. Farnborough, 1969).

K. W. Humphreys, *The Friars' Libraries* (Corpus of British Medieval Library Catalogues, 1; London, 1990).

J. Hutchins, *The History and Antiquities of the County of Dorset* (Westminster, 1861–1870³).

A. M. Hutchison, 'Devotional Reading in the Monastery and in the Late Medieval Household', in *De Cella in Seculum: Religious and Secular Life and Devotion in Late Medieval England*, ed. M. G. Sargent (Cambridge, 1989), pp. 215–27.

In A Great Tradition: Tribute to Dame Laurentia McLachlan, Abbess of Stanbrook, by the Benedictines of Stanbrook (London, 1956).

Index of Middle English Prose, A. S. G. Edwards (general editor) (Cambridge, 1984–).

J. E. Jackson, 'Kington St Michael', *Wiltshire Archaeological and Natural History Magazine* 4 (1858), pp. 36–128.

E. F. Jacob, *The Fifteenth Century 1399–1485* (Oxford, 1961).

M. R. James, *A Descriptive Catalogue of the Second Series of Fifty Manuscripts (nos. 51–100) in the Collection of Henry Yates Thompson* (Cambridge, 1902).

————, *The Ancient Libraries of Canterbury and Dover* (Cambridge, 1903).

————, *A Descriptive Catalogue of the Manuscripts in the Library of Lambeth Palace: The Mediaeval Manuscripts* (Cambridge, 1932).

294 Bibliography

——, 'Manuscripts from Essex Monastic Libraries', *Transactions of the Essex Archaeological Society* N.S. 21 (1937 [for 1933]), pp. 34–46.

J. Janini & J. Serrano, *Manuscritos litúrgicos de la Biblioteca Nacional* (Madrid, 1969).

P. S. Jolliffe, *A Check-List of Middle English Prose Writings of Spiritual Guidance* (Toronto, 1974).

——, 'Middle English Translations of *De Exterioris et Interioris Hominis Compositione*', *Mediaeval Studies* 36 (1974), pp. 259–77.

S. Jónsdóttir, 'Enskt saltarabrot á Íslandi', *Andvari*, 1967, pp. 159–70.

——, 'Heilagur Nikulás í Árnasafni', in *Afmaelisrit Jóns Helgasonar, 30. júní 1969* (Reykjavík, 1969).

——, tr. P. Foote, *Illumination in a Manuscript of Stjórn* (Reykjavík, 1971).

T. Kaeppeli, *Scriptores Ordinis Praedicatorum Medii Aevi* (Rome, 1970–).

L. Karl, 'Notice sur l'unique manuscrit français de la Bibliothèque de duc de Portland à Welbeck', *Revue des langues romanes* 54 (1911), p. 210–29.

C. M. Kaufmann, *Romanesque Manuscripts 1066–1190* (London, 1975).

M. Keen, *English Society in the Later Middle Ages 1348–1500* (London, 1990).

N. R. Ker, *Catalogue of Manuscripts Containing Anglo-Saxon* (Oxford, 1957).

——, *Medieval Libraries of Great Britain* (London, 1964[2]), with supplement to the second edition by A. G. Watson (London, 1987).

——, *Medieval Manuscripts in British Libraries* (Oxford, 1969–92) (the fourth volume was completed by A. J. Piper).

——, 'More Manuscripts from Essex Monastic Libraries', *Transactions of the Essex Archaeological Society* N.S. 23 (1945), pp. 298–310.

M. L. King, *Women of the Renaissance* (Chicago/London, 1991).

M. L. King & A. Rabil, *Her Immaculate Hand. Selected Works By and About the Women Humanists of Quattrocento Italy* (Binghampton, NY, 1983).

C. L. Kingsford, *Prejudice and Promise in Fifteenth Century England* (Oxford, 1925; rpt. London, 1962).

——, 'Additional Material for the History of the Grey Friars, London', in *idem* (ed.), *Collectanea Franciscana, II* (British Society of Franciscan Studies, vol. 10; Manchester, 1922).

D. Knowles, *The Religious Orders in England, Vol. 2* (Cambridge, 1955).

D. Knowles & R. N. Hadcock, *Medieval Religious Houses: England and Wales* (New York, 1972²; rpt. London, 1994).

K. Lambley, *The Teaching and Cultivation of the French Language in England During Tudor and Stuart Times* (Manchester/London, 1920).

A. Långfors, *Les Incipit des poèmes français antérieurs au XVIᵉ siècle* (Paris, 1917; rpt. New York, 1970).

M. Lapidge & R. Sharpe, *A Bibliography of Celtic-Latin Literature 400–1200* (Dublin, 1985).

C. H. Lawrence, *St Edmund of Abingdon: A Study in Hagiography and History* (Oxford, 1960).

M. D. Legge, *Anglo-Norman in the Cloisters: The Influence of the Orders upon Anglo-Norman Literature* (Edinburgh, 1950).

——, *Anglo-Norman Literature and Its Background* (Oxford, 1963; rpt. 1971).

——, 'The French Language and the English Cloister', in *Medieval Studies Presented to Rose Graham*, ed. V. Ruffer & A. J. Taylor (Oxford, 1950), pp. 146–62.

——, 'Anglo-Norman as a Spoken Language', in *Proceedings of the Battle Conference on Anglo-Norman Studies, II, 1979*, ed. R. A. Brown (Woodbridge, 1980), pp. 108–17, 188–90.

R. E. Lewis, N. F. Blake, & A. S. G. Edwards, *Index of Printed Middle English Prose* (NewYork/London, 1985).

H. G. Liveing, *Records of Romsey Abbey* (Winchester, 1906).

R. Lovatt, 'The Library of John Blacman and Contemporary Carthusian Spirituality', *Journal of Ecclesiastical History* 43 (1992), pp. 195–230.

R. J. Lyall, 'Materials: The Paper Revolution', in *Book Production and Publishing in Britain 1375–1475*, ed. J. Griffiths & D. Pearsall (Cambridge, 1989), pp. 11–29.

M. M. Manion, V. F. Vines, & C. F. R. de Hamel, *Medieval and Renaissance Manuscripts in New Zealand Collections* (Melbourne/London/New York, 1989).

P. Meyer, 'Notice du ms. Egerton 2710 du Musée Britannique', *Bulletin de la société des anciens textes français* 15 (1889), pp. 72–97.

————, 'Notice du Ms. Egerton 745 du Musée Britannique, Appendice: Vie en prose de saint Édouard, roi d'Angleterre', *Romania* 40 (1911), pp. 41–69.

R. Midmer, *English Mediaeval Monasteries 1066–1540: A Summary* (Athens, GA, 1979).

E. G. Millar, 'Les manuscrits à peintures des bibliothèques de Londres', *Bulletin de la société française de reproductions de manuscrits à peintures* 4 (1914–20), pp. 83–149.

N. J. Morgan, *Early Gothic Manuscripts (II): 1250–1285* (London, 1988).

J. J. Morrish, *An Examination of Literacy and Learning in England in the Ninth Century* (Oxford University, D. Phil. Diss., 1982).

J. Mountain, 'Nunnery Finances in the Early Fifteenth Century', in *Monastic Studies II*, ed. J. Loades (Bangor, 1991), pp. 263–72.

E. W. B. Nicholson, *Early Bodleian Music. Introduction to the Study of Some of the Oldest Latin Musical Manuscripts in the Bodleian Library* (London, 1913).

G. Oliver, *Monasticon Dioecesis Exoniensis* (Exeter/London, 1846).

N. Orme, *English Schools in the Middle Ages* (London, 1973).

————, *Education in the West of England 1066–1548* (Exeter, 1976).

————, *From Childhood to Chivalry: The Education of the English Kings and Aristocracy 1066–1530* (London/New York, 1984).

————, *Education and Society in Medieval and Renaissance England* (London, 1989) (collected papers).

————, 'The Education of the Courtier', in *Education and Society in Medieval and Renaissance England*, pp. 153–75.

V. H. Paltsits, 'The Petworth Manuscript of *Grace Dieu* or *The Pilgrimage of the Soul*', *Bulletin of the New York Public Library* 32 (1928), pp. 715–721.

W. A. Pantin, *The English Church in the Fourteenth Century* (Cambridge, 1955; rpt. Toronto/Buffalo/London, 1980).

M. B. Parkes, *English Cursive Book Hands 1250–1500* (Oxford, 1969; rpt. Berkeley/Los Angeles/London, 1980).

M. B. Parkes, 'The Literacy of the Laity', in *Literature and Western Civilization: The Medieval World*, ed. D. Daiches & A. K.

Thorlby (London, 1973), pp. 555–77, reprinted in *idem*, *Scribes, Scripts and Readers: Studies in the Communication, Presentation and Dissemination of Medieval Texts* (London/Rio Grande, Ohio, 1991), pp. 275–97.

——, 'A Fragment of an Early-Tenth-Century Anglo-Saxon Manuscript and Its Significance', *Anglo-Saxon England* 12 (1983), pp. 129–40, reprinted in *idem, Scribes, Scripts and Readers*, pp. 171–85.

S. A. C. Penn & C. Dyer, 'Wages and Earnings in Late Medieval England: Evidence from the Enforcement of the Labour Laws', *Economic History Review* 43 (1990), pp. 356–76.

R. W. Pfaff, *New Liturgical Feasts in Later Medieval England* (Oxford, 1970).

H. R. Plomer, 'Books Mentioned in Wills', *Transactions of the Bibliographical Society* 7 (1902–04), pp. 99–121.

A. W. Pollard & G. R. Redgrave, *A Short Title Catalogue of Books Printed in England, Scotland, and Ireland 1475–1640* (London, 1976 [revd. ed.]).

G. Pollard, 'The *pecia* system in the medieval universities', in *Medieval Scribes, Manuscripts and Libraries: Essays presented to N. R. Ker*, ed. M. B. Parkes & A. G. Watson (London, 1978), pp. 145–61.

E. E. Power, *Medieval English Nunneries, c. 1275 to 1535* (Cambridge, 1922; rpt. New York, 1964, 1988).

——, *The Wool Trade in English Medieval History* (Oxford, 1955).

P. Revell, *Fifteenth Century English Prayers and Meditations: A Descriptive List of Manuscripts in the British Library* (New York/London, 1975).

J. T. Rhodes, 'Syon Abbey and its Religious Publications in the Sixteenth Century', *Journal of Ecclesiastical History* 44 (1993), pp. 11–25.

S. de Ricci, *A Census of Caxtons* (Oxford, 1909).

S. de Ricci & W. J. Wilson, *Census of Medieval and Renaissance Manuscripts in the U.S. and Canada* (New York, 1935; rpt. 1961).

F. Römer, *Die Handschriftliche Überlieferung der Werke des heiligen Augustinus, Bd. II: Grossbritannien und Irland* (Vienna, 1972).

J. E. T. Rogers, *A History of Agriculture and Prices in England* (Oxford, 1866–1902; rpt. Liechtenstein, 1963).

J. T. Rosenthal, 'Aristocratic Cultural Patronage and Book Bequests, 1350–1500', *Bulletin of the John Rylands Library* 64 (1981–82), pp. 522–48.

P. Rouillard, *Bibliographie des impressions et des oeuvres de J. B. Ascensius* (Paris, 1908).

J. C. Russell, *Dictionary of Writers of Thirteenth Century England* (London, 1936; rpt. New York, 1971).

P. Saenger, *A Catalogue of the Pre-1500 Western Manuscript Books at the Newberry Library* (Chicago/London, 1989).

M. G. Sargent, *James Grenehalgh as Textual Critic* (Analecta Cartusiana, 85; Salzburg, 1984).

——, 'James Grenehalgh: The Biographical Record', in *Kartäusermystik und -mystiker: Dritter Internationaler Kongress über die Kartäusergeschichte und -spiritualität, Bd. 4* (Analecta Cartusiana, 55; Salzburg, 1982), pp. 20–54.

C. E. Sayle, 'The Mortuary Roll of the Abbess of Lillechurch, Kent', *Proceedings of the Cambridge Antiquarian Society* 10 (1901–04), pp. 383–409.

J. B. Schneyer, *Repertorium der lateinischen Sermones des Mittelalters* (*Beiträge zur Geschichte der Philosophie und Theologie des Mittelalters* XLIII: 1–11; Münster i. W., 1969–90).

W. L. Schramm, 'The Cost of Books in Chaucer's Time', *Modern Language Notes* 48 (1933), pp. 139–45.

R. F. Scott, *Notes from the Records of St John's College, Cambridge. Third Series* (privately printed, 1906–13).

R. R. Sharpe, *Calendar of Wills Proved and Enrolled in the Court of Husting, London* (London, 1890).

J. Sonet, *Répertoire d'Incipit de prières en ancien français* (Geneva, 1956), with supplements by K. V. Sinclair (Hamden, CN, 1979) and P. Rézeau (Paris, 1986).

A. Staerk, *Les manuscrits latins du Ve au XIIIe siècle conservés à la Bibliothèque Impériale de Saint-Pétersbourg* (St Petersburg, 1910; rpt. Hildesheim/New York, 1976).

F. Stegmüller, *Repertorium Biblicum Medii Aevi* (Madrid, 1940–80).

J. Stow, *A Survey of London*, with introduction and notes by C. L. Kingsford (Oxford, 1971).

S. A. Strong, *A Catalogue of Letters and Other Historical Documents Exhibited in the Library at Welbeck* (London, 1903).

H. Suggett, 'The Use of French in England in the Later Middle Ages', *Transactions of the Royal Historical Society*, Ser. 4, 28 (1946), pp. 61–83.

C. H. Talbot, 'The Universities and the Medieval Library', in *The English Library Before 1700*, ed. F. Wormald & C. E. Wright (London, 1958), pp. 66–84.

J. S. P. Tatlock, 'Muriel: The Earliest English Poetess', *Publications of the Modern Language Association of America* 48 (1933), pp. 317–21.

E. M. Thompson, *English Illuminated Manuscripts* (London, 1895).

S. Thompson, *Women Religious: The Founding of English Nunneries after the Norman Conquest* (Oxford, 1991).

R. M. Thomson, *Catalogue of the Manuscripts of Lincoln Cathedral Chapter Library* (Cambridge, 1990).

S. H. Thomson, *The Writings of Robert Grosseteste, Bishop of Lincoln 1235–1253* (Cambridge, 1940; rpt. New York, 1971).

S. L. Thrupp, *The Merchant Class of Medieval London [1300–1500]* (Ann Arbor, 1948; rpt. 1962).

R. Vaughan, *Matthew Paris* (Cambridge, 1958).

J. Vising, *Anglo-Norman Language and Literature* (London/Oxford, 1923).

M. E. C. Walcott, 'Inventories of (I.) St. Mary's Hospital or Maison Dieu, Dover; (II.) The Benedictine Priory of St. Martin New-Work, Dover, for Monks; (III.) The Benedictine Priory of SS. Mary and Sexburga, in the Island of Sheppey, for Nuns', *Archaeologia Cantiana* 7 (1869), pp. 272–306.

———, 'Inventories and Valuations of Religious Houses at the Time of the Dissolution, from the Public Record Office', *Archaeologia* 43 (1871), pp. 201–49.

———, 'Inventory of St Mary's Benedictine Nunnery, at Langley, Co. Leicestershire, 1485', *Transactions of the Leicestershire Architectural and Archaeological Society* 4 (1878), pp. 117–22.

G. Walker, 'Heretical Sects in Pre-Reformation England', *History Today* 43 (1993), pp. 42–8.

H. Walther, *Initia Carminum ac Versuum Medii Aevi Posterioris Latinorum (Carmina Medii Aevi Posterioris Latina* I; Göttingen, 1959–69).

H. L. D. Ward & J. A. Herbert, *Catalogue of Romances in the Department of Manuscripts in the British Museum* (London, 1883–1910; rpt. 1962).

J. C. Ward, *English Noblewomen in the Later Middle Ages* (London/New York, 1992).

A. Watkin, 'Some Manuscripts in the Downside Abbey Library (continued)', *Downside Review* 59 (1941), pp. 75–83.

A. G. Watson, *Catalogue of Dated and Datable Manuscripts c.700–
1600 in the Department of Manuscripts, The British Library*
(London, 1979).

———, *Catalogue of Dated and Datable Manuscripts c.435–1600 in
Oxford Libraries* (Oxford, 1984).

———: see N. R. Ker, *Medieval Libraries of Great Britain.*

R. J. Whitwell, 'An Ordinance for Syon Library, 1482', *English
Historical Review* 25 (1910), pp. 121–3.

R. S. Wieck, *The Book of Hours in Medieval Art and Life* (London,
1988).

A. Wilmart, 'Ève et Goscelin', *Revue Bénédictine* 46 (1934), pp.
414–38, and 50 (1938), pp. 42–83.

K. M. Wilson, *An Encyclopedia of Continental Women Writers*
(Garland Reference Library of the Humanities, 698; New
York/London, 1991).

C. Wordsworth & H. Littlehales, *The Old Service-Books of the
English Church* (London, 1904).

F. Wormald, 'The Monastic Library', in *The English Library Before
1700*, ed. F. Wormald & C. E. Wright (London, 1958), pp.
15–31.

F. Wormald & P. M. Giles, *A Descriptive Catalogue of the Additional Illuminated Manuscripts in the Fitzwilliam Museum*
(Cambridge, 1982).

C. E. Wright, *English Vernacular Hands from the Twelfth to the
Fifteenth Centuries* (Oxford, 1960).

T. Wright & J. O. Halliwell, *Reliquiae Antiquae* (London, 1843;
rpt. New York, 1966).

CISTERCIAN TEXTS

THE WORKS OF
BERNARD OF CLAIRVAUX

Apologia to Abbot William
Five Books on Consideration: Advice to a Pope
Grace and Free Choice
Homilies in Praise of the Blessed Virgin Mary
The Life and Death of Saint Malachy the Irishman
Love without Measure. Extracts from the Writings
    of St Bernard (Paul Dimier)
On Loving God
The Parables of Saint Bernard (Michael Casey)
Sermons for the Summer Season
Sermons on the Song of Songs I - IV
The Steps of Humility and Pride

THE WORKS OF
WILLIAM OF SAINT THIERRY

The Enigma of Faith
Exposition on the Epistle to the Romans
Exposition on the Song of Songs
The Golden Epistle
The Nature of Dignity of Love

THE WORKS OF AELRED OF RIEVAULX

Dialogue on the Soul
The Mirror of Charity
Spiritual Friendship
Treatises I: On Jesus at the Age of Twelve, Rule for
    a Recluse, The Pastoral Prayer
Walter Daniel: The Life of Aelred of Rievaulx

THE WORKS OF JOHN OF FORD

Sermons on the Final Verses of the Songs of Songs I - VII

THE WORKS OF GILBERT OF HOYLAND

Sermons on the Songs of Songs I-III
Treatises, Sermons and Epistles

OTHER EARLY CISTERCIAN WRITERS

The Letters of Adam of Perseigne I
Baldwin of Ford: Spiritual Tractates I - II
Gertrud the Great of Helfta: Spiritual Exercises
Gertrud the Great of Helfta: The Herald of God's
    Loving-Kindness
Guerric of Igny: Liturgical Sermons I - II
Idung of Prüfening: Cistercians and Cluniacs: The
    Case of Cîteaux
Isaac of Stella: Sermons on the Christian Year
The Life of Beatrice of Nazareth
Serlo of Wilton & Serlo of Savigny
Stephen of Lexington: Letters from Ireland
Stephen of Sawley: Treatises

MONASTIC TEXTS

EASTERN CHRISTIAN TRADITION

Besa: The Life of Shenoute
Cyril of Scythopolis: Lives of the Monks of Palestine

Dorotheos of Gaza: Discourses
Evagrius Ponticus:Praktikos and Chapters on Prayer
The Harlots of the Desert (Benedicta Ward)
John Moschos: The Spiritual Meadow
Iosif Volotsky: Monastic Rule
The Lives of the Desert Fathers
The Lives of Simeon Stylites (Robert Doran)
The Luminous Eye (Sebastian Brock)
Mena of Nikiou: Isaac of Alexandra & St Macrobius
Pachomian Koinonia I - III
Paphnutius: A Histories of the Monks of Upper Egypt
The Sayings of the Desert Fathers
Spiritual Direction in the Early Christian East (Irénée
    Hausherr)
Spiritually Edifying Tales of Paul of Monembasia
Symeon the New Theologian: The Theological and
    Practical Treatises & The Three Theological
    Discourses
The Syriac Fathers on Prayer and the Spiritual Life
    (Sebastian Brock)
The Wound of Love: A Carthusian Miscellany

WESTERN CHRISTIAN TRADITION

Anselm of Canterbury: Letters I - III
Bede: Commentary on the Seven Catholic Epistles
Bede: Commentary on the Acts of the Apostles
Bede: Homilies on the Gospels I - II
Gregory the Great: Forty Gospel Homilies
The Meditations of Guigo I, Prior of the Charterhouse
    (A. Gordon Mursell)
Guigo II the Carthusian: Ladder of Monks and
    Twelve Meditations
Handmaids of the Lord: The Lives of Holy Women in
    Late Antiquity and the Early Middle Ages (Joan
    Petersen)
Peter of Celle: Selected Works
The Letters of Armand-Jean de Rancé I - II
The Rule of the Master

CHRISTIAN SPIRITUALITY

Abba: Guides to Wholeness & Holiness East & West
A Cloud of Witnesses: The Development of
    Christian Doctrine (D.N. Bell)
Athirst for God: Spiritual Desire in Bernard of
    Clairvaux's Sermons on the Song of Songs
    (M. Casey)
Cistercian Way (André Louf)
Drinking From the Hidden Fountain (Spidlék)
Eros and Allegory: Medieval Exegesis of the Song of
    Songs (Denys Turner)
Fathers Talking (Aelred Squire)
Friendship and Community (B. McGuire)
From Cloister to Classroom
Herald of Unity: The Life of Maria Gabrielle
    Sagheddu (M. Driscoll)
Life of St Mary Magdalene and of Her Sister
    St Martha (D. Mycoff)
The Name of Jesus (Irénée Hausherr)
No Moment Too Small (Norvene Vest)
Penthos: The Doctrine of Compunction in the
    Christian East (Irénée Hausherr)
Rancé and the Trappist Legacy (A.J. Krailsheimer)
The Roots of the Modern Christian Tradition
Russian Mystics (S. Bolshakoff)
The Spirituality of the Christian East (Tomas Spidlik)
Spirituality of the Medieval West (André Vauchez)
Tuning In To Grace (André Louf)
Wholly Animals: A Book of Beastly Tales (D.N. Bell)

TITLE LISTING

MONASTIC STUDIES

Community & Abbot in the Rule of St Benedict I - II
(Adalbert De Vogüé)
Beatrice of Nazareth in Her Context (Roger De Ganck)
Consider Your Call: A Theology of the Monastic Life
(Daniel Rees et al.)
The Finances of the Cistercian Order in the Fourteenth
Century (Peter King)
Fountains Abbey & Its Benefactors (Joan Wardrop)
A Gathering of Friends: Learning & Spirituality in John
of Forde
The Hermit Monks of Grandmont
(Carole A. Hutchison)
In the Unity of the Holy Spirit (Sighard Kleiner)
Monastic Practices (Charles Cummings)
The Occupation of Celtic Sites in Ireland by the Canons
Regular of St Augustine and the Cistercians
(Geraldine Carville)
Reading Saint Benedict (Adalbert de Vogüé)
The Rule of St Benedict: A Doctrinal and Spiritual
Commentary (Adalbert de Vogüé)
The Rule of St Benedict (Br. Pinocchio)
Towards Unification with God (Beatrice of Nazareth
in Her Context, II)
St Hugh of Lincoln (D.H. Farmer)
Serving God First (Sighard Kleiner)
The Way of Silent Love
With Greater Liberty: A Short History of Christian
Monasticism and Religious Orders
The Wound of Love: A Carthusian Miscellany

CISTERCIAN STUDIES

A Difficult Saint (B. McGuire)
A Second Look at Saint Bernard (J. Leclercq)
Bernard of Clairvaux and the Cistercian Spirit
(Jean Leclercq)
Bernard of Clairvaux: Man, Monk, Mystic
(M. Casey) Tapes and readings
Bernard of Clairvaux: Studies Presented to Dom
Jean Leclercq
Bernardus Magister
Christ the Way: The Christology of Guerric of Igny
(John Morson)
Cistercian Sign Language
The Cistercian Spirit
The Cistercians in Denmark (Brian McGuire)
The Cistercians in Scandinavia (James France)
The Eleventh-century Background of Cîteaux
(Bede K. Lackner)
Image and Likeness: The Augustinian Spirituality
of William of St Thierry (D.N. Bell)
An Index of Authors & Works in Cistercian Libraries in
Great Britain I (D.N. Bell)
An Index of Cistercian Authors and Works in Medieval
Library Catalogues in Great Britain (D.N. Bell)
The Mystical Theology of St Bernard (Etiénne Gilson)
Nicolas Cotheret's Annals of Cîteaux (Louis J. Lekai)
The Spiritual Teachings of St Bernard of Clairvaux
(J.R. Sommerfeldt)
Studiosorum Speculum
William, Abbot of St Thierry
Women and St Bernard of Clairvaux (Jean Leclercq)

MEDIEVAL RELIGIOUS WOMEN

Lillian Thomas Shank and John A. Nichols, editors

Distant Echoes
Peace Weavers
Hidden Springs: Cistercian Monastic Women, 2 Vol.

What Nuns Read: Books & Libraries in Medieval English
Nunneries (D.N. Bell)

STUDIES IN CISTERCIAN ART AND ARCHITECTURE

Meredith Parsons Lillich, editor

Volumes I, II, III, IV now available

THOMAS MERTON

The Climate of Monastic Prayer (T. Merton)
The Legacy of Thomas Merton (P. Hart)
The Message of Thomas Merton (P. Hart)
Thomas Merton: The Monastic Journey
Thomas Merton Monk (P.Hart)
Thomas Merton Monk & Artist (Victor Kramer)
Thomas Merton on St Bernard
Toward an Integrated Humanity (M. Basil
Pennington et al.)

CISTERCIAN LITURGICAL DOCUMENTS SERIES

Chrysogonus Waddell, ocso, editor

Hymn Collection of the Abbey of the Paraclete
Institutiones nostrae: The Paraclete Statutes
Molesme Summer-Season Breviary (4 volumes)
Old French Ordinary and Breviary of the Abbey of
the Paraclete: Text & Commentary (2 vol.)
The Cadouin Breviary (two volumes)
The Twelfth-century Cistercian Psalter
The Twelfth-century Usages of the Cistercian Lay-
brothers
Two Early *Libelli Missarum*

STUDIA PATRISTICA

*Papers of the 1983 Oxford patristics conference
edited by Elizabeth A. Livingstone*

XVIII/1 Historica-Gnostica-Biblica
XVIII/2 Critica-Classica-Ascetica-Liturgica
XVIII/3 Second Century-Clement & Origen-
Cappodician Fathers
XVIII/4 *available from Peeters, Leuven*

Cistercian Publications is a non-profit corporation. Its
publishing program is restricted to monastic texts in
translation and books on the monastic tradition.

*North American customers may order these books
through booksellers or directly from the warehouse:*
Cistercian Publications (Distributor)
St Joseph's Abbey
Spencer, Massachusetts 01562
tel: (508) 885-7011 ❖ fax: (508)-885-4687

*Editorial queries and advance book information
should be directed to the Editorial Offices:*
Cistercian Publications
Institute of Cistercian Studies
Western Michigan University
Kalamazoo, Michigan 49008
tel: (616) 387-8920 ❖ fax: (616)-387-8921

A complete catalogue of texts in translation and studies on early, medieval, and modern monasticism is
available at no cost from Cistercian Publications.